A History of Argentina

A book in the series
Latin America in Translation / En Traducción / Em Tradução
Sponsored by the Duke–University of North Carolina Program
in Latin American Studies

A History of Argentina

From the Spanish Conquest to the Present

Ezequiel Adamovsky

TRANSLATED BY REBECCA WOLPIN

DUKE UNIVERSITY PRESS
Durham and London
2024

© 2024 DUKE UNIVERSITY PRESS
All rights reserved
Printed in the United States of America on acid-free paper ∞
Project Editor: Michael Trudeau
Designed by A. Mattson Gallagher
Typeset in Alegreya by Westchester Publishing Services
Printed and bound by CPI Group (UK) Ltd, Croydon, CR0 4YY
Library of Congress Cataloging-in-Publication Data
Names: Adamovsky, Ezequiel, [date] author. | Wolpin, Rebecca, translator.
Title: A history of Argentina : from the Spanish conquest to the present / Ezequiel Adamovsky ; translated by Rebecca Wolpin.
Other titles: Historia de la Argentina. English | Latin America in translation/en traducción/em tradução.
Description: Durham : Duke University Press, 2024. | Series: Latin America in Translation / En Traducción / Em Tradução | Includes bibliographical references and index.
Identifiers: LCCN 2023015588 (print)
LCCN 2023015589 (ebook)
ISBN 9781478025436 (paperback)
ISBN 9781478020639 (hardcover)
ISBN 9781478027522 (ebook)
Subjects: LCSH: Argentina—History. | BISAC: HISTORY / Latin America / South America
Classification: LCC F2831 .A3313 2024 (print) | LCC F2831 (ebook) | DDC 982—DC23/ENG/20230607
LC record available at https://lccn.loc.gov/2023015588
LC ebook record available at https://lccn.loc.gov/2023015589

Cover art: Xul Solar, *Patriotic Day (Fecha Patria)* (detail), 1925. Watercolor and pen and ink on paper, 28 × 38 cm. Photo © Christie's Images / Bridgeman Images. Original © Xul Solar Museum / Pan Klub Foundation, all rights reserved.

CONTENTS

vii List of Abbreviations

1 ① Violence
   The Conquest and the Colonial Order

37 ② Revolution!
   The End of the Colonial Order, the Wars of Independence, and a Long Period of Discord (1806–1852)

81 ③ The Great Transformation
   The Expansion of the State and the Market in Argentina (1852–1912)

129 ④ Liberal Argentina and Its Constraints
   From Failed Democracy to Peronism (1912–1955)

181 ⑤ The Pendulum
   Dictatorship, the Market, and Popular Power, from Perón's Overthrow to the National Reorganization Process (1955–1983)

228 ⑥ Democracy Devalued
   Between the Promises of Democracy and Neoliberalism, from Alfonsín to Macri (1983–2019)

300 Epilogue
   Argentine History over the Long Term

323 Selected Bibliography
333 Index

ABBREVIATIONS

AFJP	Administradoras de Fondos de Jubilaciones y Pensiones (Retirement and Pension Fund Administrators)
AMIA	Asociación Mutual Israelita Argentina (Argentine Jewish Mutual Aid Association)
ARI	Afirmación para una República Igualitaria (Affirmation for an Egalitarian Republic)
ATE	Asociación de Trabajadores del Estado (Association of Government Employees)
CCC	Corriente Clasista y Combativa (Classist and Combative Current)
CGE	Confederación General Económica (General Economic Confederation)
CGT	Confederación General del Trabajo (General Confederation of Labor)
CGTA	CGT de los Argentinos (CGT of Argentines)
CHA	Comunidad Homosexual Argentina (Argentine Homosexual Community)

CONADEP	Comisión Nacional sobre la Desaparición de Personas (National Commission on the Disappearance of Persons)
CONICET	Consejo Nacional de Investigaciones Científicas y Técnicas (National Council for Scientific and Technical Research)
CTA	Central de Trabajadores de la Argentina (Central Federation of Argentine Workers)
CTERA	Confederación de Trabajadores de la Educación de la República Argentina (Confederation of Education Workers of the Argentine Republic)
CUSC	Comité de Unidad Sindical Clasista (Committee of Class and Union Unity)
ERP	Ejército Revolucionario del Pueblo (People's Revolutionary Army)
FLH	Frente de Liberación Homosexual (Homosexual Liberation Front)
FORA	Federación Obrera Regional Argentina (Argentine Regional Workers' Federation)
FORJA	Fuerza de Orientación Radical de la Joven Argentina (Argentine Radical Youth Force)
FRENAPO	Frente Nacional contra la Pobreza (National Front against Poverty)
FREPASO	Frente País Solidario (Front for a Country in Solidarity)
FTAA	Free Trade Area of the Americas
GAN	Gran Acuerdo Nacional (Great National Agreement)
GATT	General Agreement on Tariffs and Trade
GDP	gross domestic product
GOU	Grupo de Oficiales Unidos *or* Grupo Obra de Unificación (United Officers' Group or Unification Task Force)
IAPI	Instituto Argentino para la Promoción del Intercambio (Argentine Institute for the Promotion of Trade)
IMF	International Monetary Fund
INDEC	Instituto Nacional de Estadística y Censos (National Institute of Statistics and Census of Argentina)

Abbreviations

MAS	Movimiento al Socialismo (Movement for Socialism)
MERCOSUR	Mercado Común del Sur (Southern Common Market)
MMAL	Movimiento de Mujeres Agropecuarias en Lucha (Movement of Agricultural Women in Struggle)
MOCASE	Movimiento Campesino de Santiago del Estero (Campesino Movement of Santiago del Estero)
MTA	Movimiento de Trabajadores Argentinos (Argentine Workers Movement)
MTD	Movimientos de Trabajadores Desocupados (Movements of Unemployed Workers)
NGO	nongovernmental organization
PAN	Partido Autonomista Nacional (National Autonomist Party)
PCR	Partido Comunista Revolucionario (Revolutionary Communist Party)
PDN	Partido Demócrata Nacional (National Democratic Party)
PDP	Partido Demócrata Progresista (Progressive Democratic Party)
PRO	Propuesta Republicana (Republican Proposal)
PRT	Partido Revolucionario de los Trabajadores (Revolutionary Workers' Party)
PSI	Partido Socialista Independiente (Independent Socialist Party)
STP	Secretaría de Trabajo y Previsión (Secretariat of Labor and Social Security)
UCEDE	Unión del Centro Democrático (Union of the Democratic Center)
UCR	Unión Cívica Radical (Radical Civic Union)
UCRI	UCR Intransigente (Intransigent UCR)
UN	United Nations
UNASUR	Union of South American Nations
USA	Unión Sindical Argentina (Argentine Syndicates' Union)
VAT	value-added tax
YPF	Yacimientos Petrolíferos Fiscales (Fiscal Oilfields)

Abbreviations

MAP 0.1. Argentina: provinces and regions.

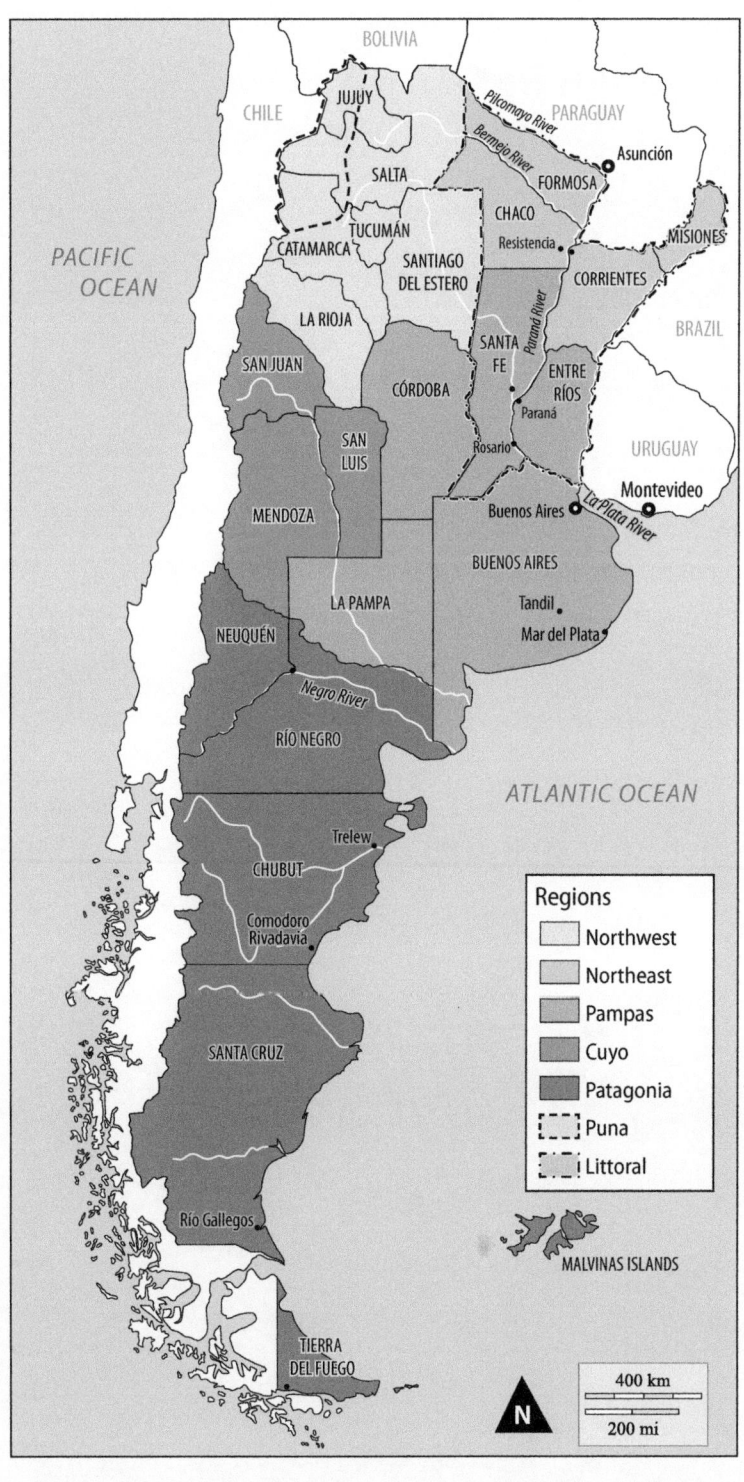

⬤ 1

Violence

The Conquest and the Colonial Order

IN THE BEGINNING, there was violence. Nothing in the territory now known as Argentina indicated that there would be a country here. The dozens of peoples who inhabited these lands before the arrival of the Spaniards lacked ties of any appreciable scale. They were not united by political alliances, a shared language, religion, customs, or even by networks of economic trade that spanned throughout all or most of the territory. The very geography of the region revealed little predisposition toward unity. The dusty heights of the Puna and the ravines of the northwest were like the continuation of an Andean world that extended out from Ecuador. The torrid and impenetrable lowlands of the Gran Chaco were an extension of those that today form part of Paraguay and Bolivia, bordering the Amazon. The fertile grasslands of the Pampas expanded outward without acknowledging the borders of what are now Uruguay and southern Brazil.

The arrival of the Spaniards marked the beginning of a dramatic process of change aimed at adapting the inhabitants to new social hierarchies and connecting them to the transnational economic circuits dominated by Europe. It was the interminable maelstrom of the conquest; it was the way the Spaniards invaded, occupied, and reorganized the territory and its peoples that laid the initial foundations of what, centuries later, would become Argentina. It was the violence of the occupation that would force an arbitrary conformity between men and women of completely different origins on a land that without it might never have harbored a unified nation. Before the Spanish conquest, there was no "Argentina," just as there was no "colonial Argentina." Even after 1810, it was still not clear that there would be a country here separate from the other South American territories. There was no distinctive national identity among the inhabitants of this part of the Spanish territories, whose histories were also intimately tied to the histories of those who lived in what is now Paraguay, Bolivia, and Uruguay.

Of course, the contours and characteristics that the Argentine nation would end up adopting well into the nineteenth century were determined not only by that initial violence (which incidentally persisted over time in different forms and to different degrees) but also by what the inhabitants of these lands did with it, the bonds of cooperation, resistance, and emotional attachment they were able to build out of the relationships forced on them by the conquest. Every step in the country's history can be understood as the effect of that fundamental relationship between power and cooperation, class oppression and resistance, violence and attachment, hierarchy and equality, exclusion and community. It was the inevitable clash between these powerful and intertwined forces that fueled the whirlwind of historical change and chaotically led to what Argentina is today.

But in the beginning, in the brutal act of the conquest, what prevailed was violence.

Before the Invasion

The territory Argentina now occupies was among the last places touched by the expansion of the human race: it saw the arrival of the first *Homo sapiens* only thirteen or fourteen thousand years ago. Small bands of hunter-gatherers entered the region through various routes and began seeking places to settle. By six to eight thousand years ago, they were already well established in several areas, from the Puna in the extreme north to Tierra del Fuego. By this time, they had developed particular ways of life in response to the resources on hand: they were canoeists and shellfish gatherers on the islands and in the channels of the extreme south, guanaco and rhea hunters and seed and root collectors at the base of the Andes in Cuyo and in the Pampas, and fishermen on the banks of the rivers that form the Río de la Plata basin.

In Patagonia, Chaco, the Pampas, and other areas, their organization into small bands or tribes of hunter-gatherers persisted until well after the arrival of the Spaniards. Other regions went through remarkable processes of technological and organizational innovation. Around four thousand years ago, the peoples of Cuyo and the northwest began to domesticate animals and sparked a true revolution when they learned to select and cultivate plants. The practice of agriculture made it possible to produce food surpluses, which in turn enabled population growth and the formation of more complex villages and societies with thousands of members rather than just a few hundred. These societies gave rise to forms of power and social differentiation previously unknown to the more egalitarian hunter-gatherers, though not yet particularly prominent. Around the same time, they also developed pottery, and roughly two thousand years later they were already manufacturing metallic objects and textiles. Their trade networks expanded outward and the circulation of goods connected the Pacific with the Chaco. Roughly one thousand years ago, several of these societies expanded and intensified their political centralization and class divisions.

Toward the end of the fifteenth century, that region was conquered by the Cuzco Incas and incorporated into their powerful empire, which extended south through the mountains to what is now northern Mendoza. Half a century of domination was enough to infuse this area with greater homogeneity, and many Inca customs and organizational practices were adopted. Quechua became a lingua franca throughout the region, connecting more extensive circuits thanks to the extraordinary Inca road system. The power of local chiefs who collaborated with the Incas increased and social inequalities became more pronounced. The conquerors familiarized the subjugated peoples with the custom of mita, which forced them to supply contingents to complete work shifts outside their communities. Rebellions were not uncommon, especially in the valleys of the indomitable Calchaquí people. The empire often responded by relocating the rebels far from their homes, which led to even more blending and homogenization of the population. However, neither the identities nor the particular languages of peoples, such as the Diaguitas, Omaguacas, and others, were completely lost.

MAP 1.1. Aboriginal peoples circa 1500. Adapted from Pablo Yankelevich, *Historia mínima de Argentina*.

Although less dramatic, technical changes and progress were also recorded beyond what is now northwestern Argentina. Peoples of the Amazon expanded across the rivers and brought their agricultural practices with them, most likely toward the end of the pre-Hispanic period. This is the case of the Guaraníes, who reached the Paraná delta, and the Avá warriors, who advanced along the Pilcomayo and Bermejo Rivers to the base of the Andes, from where they frequently attacked the Inca territories. The Comechingones of the Cordoban sierras also practiced small-scale land cultivation. Tehuelches and Pehuenches in Patagonia, Selk'nam and Yámanas in Tierra del Fuego, and Querandíes and other peoples in the Pampas, the northeast, and elsewhere remained essentially hunter-gatherers. However, several of these peoples expanded the scope of their trade, developed pottery making, began hunting with bows and arrows, and produced textiles.

Seen as a whole, the territory of present-day Argentina was a loosely connected mosaic with a wide variety of peoples (see map 1.1). Their origins, cultural patterns, linguistic families, and ways of life were very different. The relationships between them, when they existed, could be either cooperative or hostile. In the Gran Chaco area, several particularly bellicose peoples engaged in wars and rivalries. There, the Avás had subdued the Chanés, keeping them subjugated for centuries, exploiting their labor, and taking Chané women. In contrast, other peoples—such as the Tehuelches or the Huarpes in Cuyo—were noted for their gentleness and hospitality. In any event, it was a heterogeneous world in a constant state of change and upheaval. We have no detailed record of the pre-Hispanic era of these preliterate peoples, but archaeological findings indicate that it was undoubtedly a period rich in innovation, history, and culture.

The Conquest

The arrival of the Spaniards would affect this world in a way that none of its inhabitants could have imagined. For they were not just another people arriving to impose their power, as the Incas had done. The Iberian conquistadors were driven by different impulses.

When Christopher Columbus first arrived in the Americas, Europe was emerging from a long crisis that had begun in the fourteenth century. The feudal structures that had ensured the supremacy of nobles and monarchs during the Middle Ages had reached their limits. Exploiting the peasantry had become more difficult and less profitable; land was running out and they could

Violence: Conquest and the Colonial Order

no longer sustain their ambitions. Large-scale trade conducted in cities and ports now offered the best opportunities for those who sought to rise above the rest. Large-scale merchants, nobles, and monarchs all shared a common interest: to expand trade networks by penetrating into new territories. For the merchants, the enterprise offered the promise of increased profits and perhaps even the potential of being elevated to nobility. For the nobles, it meant more space for feudal estates and consequently greater wealth. For the monarchs, it meant finances that would secure their place in an increasingly fierce competition with rival dignitaries. Even those who had no standing whatsoever but were willing to serve as soldiers could harbor hopes of social advancement in the new lands. Everything was propelled outward, toward conquest. These were the first steps of capitalism as a world system. From this point on, economic interests would play an increasingly important role as the organizing principle of social life, guiding human behavior, forging new links between the various regions of the planet, and defining each individual's place in society. The Americas, a land of plunder and conquest, a source of gold and silver, of raw materials and human labor, would give capitalism its first decisive boost.

The occupation was carried out in the name of the Hispanic monarchy and under the auspices of the Catholic Church. Yet in practice it was essentially a private undertaking. The members of the expeditions that explored the continent were generally not officials sent by the Spanish Crown but rather adventurers backed by capitalists, who provided the costly financing for these incursions in the hopes of future earnings. With the understanding that all conquered territory belonged to them, the monarchs authorized incursions through "capitulations," contracts in which they reserved a share of the profits for themselves and granted the conquistadors rights to land and sometimes to positions or titles of nobility. The conquistadors would gather a few hundred (or sometimes only a few dozen) soldiers with the promise of spoils and arm them, sending them off across a stretch of the new lands. From the leader to the last recruit, everyone was motivated by the desire to reap some sort of reward. In its early stages, the Spaniards mostly engaged in straightforward pillaging.

In South America, they entered by way of the Pacific Ocean, first setting foot in Peru. Paradoxically, the wealthiest and most centralized civilizations turned out to be the easiest to dominate. As Hernán Cortés had done in Mexico, in 1532 it was enough for Francisco Pizarro to overthrow the leadership of the Inca empire in order to gain access to the extensive society it had organized and that, to some degree, was already accustomed to obedience and paying tribute. The Spaniards quickly occupied the most promising lands, and in 1545 they discovered Potosí Mountain, in present-day Bolivia, which would become the most important silver mine in the world and a fabulous source of wealth for the Hispanic monarchs. Potosí's silver proved to be a powerful driver of capitalism: the metal's purchasing power provided a vigorous stimulus to the international trade networks.

After 1545, Spanish expansion through the Americas would slow down because it had to penetrate areas populated by more-fragmented, less-hierarchical societies with less capacity to produce surpluses. This was the case in the territory that Argentina now occupies, which was relatively sparsely populated and devoid of mineral wealth. More than economic attractiveness, the expansion here was driven by political impulses.

Rivalries and scheming soon developed among the conquistadors of Peru. Those who ended up in a subordinate position or who arrived later vied for their share of the spoils. They all sought to win the favor of the Crown and gain land or special rights. But resources were becoming scarce and violent clashes soon followed. In order to avoid losing control, the authorities sought to "clear the land," as they referred to it at the time, encouraging the scheming and disgruntled to try their luck to the south, in territories still unknown to them.

At the same time, the Crown had long been interested in seeking a more convenient entry by way of the Atlantic and sought to protect its dominions from its Portuguese competitor. Thus, conquistadors also attempted to gain a foothold by entering through the Río de la Plata.

Of these two entry points, the most decisive impulse came from the north. The first incursions into what was to become Argentine territory took place starting in 1543: by land, from Upper Peru, and by sea, from Chile. And they were led by some of the soldiers and adventurers who were resentful about not having made their fortunes in Peru. Either self-financed or backed by capitalists, the conquistadors assembled small armies and set out to conquer the area. Inca officials and chiefs familiar with the area helped guide them and identify who was who among the caciques (or indigenous chiefs) of the northwest. Taking advantage of rivalries among the caciques to secure temporary allies, the Spaniards advanced slowly and with difficulty toward the south, looking for riches and indigenous masses to subjugate. Frequent mutinies among the troops, irritated by so much effort for so little gain, made the advances rather chaotic and improvised. Brutal clashes with the natives were common.

Violence: Conquest and the Colonial Order

Nevertheless, during the second half of the sixteenth century, the conquistadors managed to establish thirty settlements, although, due to indigenous attacks and a lack of supplies, only twelve survived. Of these, the first was Santiago del Estero in 1553, followed by Tucumán (1565), Córdoba (1573), Salta (1582), La Rioja (1591), and Jujuy (1593). Entering from Chile, they founded settlements in the Cuyo area: Mendoza (1561), San Juan (1562), and San Luis (1594).

The list ends with the three cities they established in the littoral region, entering by way of the Atlantic. The first voyage up the Río de la Plata—named for the legendary riches it was believed to lead to that nevertheless did not materialize—had taken place in 1516. The first attempt at settlement was in 1527 with a fort in the present-day province of Santa Fe that barely survived for three years. Pedro de Mendoza arrived with a larger expedition in 1536 and succeeded in founding Nuestra Señora del Buen Ayre (the future Buenos Aires), but the settlers were forced to abandon it five years later due to starvation and attacks by the indigenous peoples. Of these initial attempts, the Spaniards only managed to hold on to the fort in Asunción (1537), now the capital of Paraguay, which existed in isolation for years. From there, explorers descended the rivers under the command of Juan de Garay and founded Santa Fe in 1573 and Buenos Aires, for the second time, in 1580. In 1588, Corrientes followed.

Although these settlements were referred to as "cities," they were initially rather precarious hamlets of adobe, sometimes with only two or three dozen inhabitants. Communication between them was difficult and life was very hard. The likelihood of lethal attacks by the natives remained a reality for a long time. Throughout the sixteenth century, the presence of the Spaniards was minimal: by 1570, there were roughly 350 in the entire territory of present-day Argentina. By the end of that century, there were only 250 Europeans in the entire northwestern region; of these, the king had granted around 150 of them the right to collect tribute from as many as 270,000 natives.

Over time, the cities would gradually become established as the seats of civil, military, and religious authorities and of merchants who coordinated the flow of economic activity. They were the center of lettered culture and, much later, of the printed word (there were no printing presses until well into the eighteenth century): islands in a rural ocean inhabited by groups of preliterate peoples with very different customs. Urban spaces thus emerged in the territory of present-day Argentina with quite a different profile from the one they had in Europe and elsewhere. The cities did not grow out of the cultural, political, or economic development of a people but rather out of colonial outposts, footholds of foreign domination, and bastions from which to establish and manage the class, ethnic, and cultural superiority that the Spaniards claimed for themselves.

Colonial Ties and the Encomienda System

Colonial rule was first and foremost a formidable means of extracting tribute from the natives and resources from the land. A new kind of society was built in the Americas that organized work and social differences according to a fundamental distinction: the victors and the vanquished. The forcefulness of the conquest served as a base for a juridical inequality that was justified with ethnic arguments. Differences between people were simplified by classifying them into two large groups. From that moment on, all natives, regardless of whether they were Querandíes, Lules, or Guaraníes, and regardless of whether they had resisted colonization or not, were simply transformed into "Indians" (according to the misleading name Columbus assigned them when he thought he had reached India). Considered inferior and equated with children, they and their descendants became vassals of the king, who gave them as "encomiendas" to a conquistador, meaning the conquistador was granted control over them and their labor. Both the monarchy and the encomendero (the conquistador who had been granted the encomiendas), of course, claimed the right to receive tribute from them.

These bonds also led to an equalization among Spaniards, regardless of their differences at birth. On the Iberian Peninsula, vassals, known as *pecheros* (commoners), were obliged to pay tribute. In contrast, *hidalgos* (from *hijos-de-algo* or "sons-of-something," that is, the nobles) were exempt from payment. This was the fundamental distinction between classes: those at the top did not pay; those at the bottom did. But in the Americas, the Spaniards, even those who had not had the good fortune to be born nobles, were exempt from paying tribute simply because they were not Indians. Those who arrived in the new continent, even if they were poor soldiers, sailors, or artisans, felt they were entitled to preferential treatment. They refused to perform certain types of manual labor—which were now considered "Indian work"—and they aspired to be served by the natives. Since there were so few Spaniards in the area, it was important that there should be no odious legal differences between them. Because of this same demographic weakness, they needed the collaboration of the caciques, who were exempted from paying tribute,

Violence: Conquest and the Colonial Order

granted the honorary title of "Don," and, if they did not yet have the privilege, made hereditary chiefs.

Few conquistadors managed to strike it rich in the relatively poor Argentine territory. Nor did they manage to ennoble themselves: in the entire area occupied by Argentina, the Crown granted only one noble estate, the Marquisate of Tojo (encompassing part of Jujuy and Salta and lands that today belong to Chile and Bolivia).

Every conquistador sought to receive Indians in encomienda from the king, along with the ownership of urban or rural lands. The encomienda consisted of the right to charge the Indians a tribute, which mainly took the form of labor (personal service) in the beginning. In exchange, the encomendero had to protect the king's domains, with military force, if necessary, and instruct the Indians in the Catholic faith. Encomiendas were not granted as property: they were concessions, although in some areas they were often extended to heirs. They could be revoked and reallotted to others.

The encomienda regime was brutal, especially in the early years. While passing through Tucumán and Cuyo on his way to Chile, for example, Francisco de Villagra captured close to six hundred natives and transported them in chains to be used as porters and servants. Many of them died on the way. Sometimes the Indians were divided up in the abstract before expeditions, without knowledge beforehand of what the conquistadors would find. In Paraguay, Córdoba, and Santiago del Estero, an encomienda meant immediate access to the labor of hundreds or even thousands of Indians. But in other regions, such as Santa Fe, it did not result in immediate control, and the encomendero had to subdue a dispersed and reluctant population.

In practice, the encomienda was akin to outright slavery, especially in the early days. The encomendero forced the Indians to work on his lands or properties, in his household service, or in textile mills. He could also rent them to others or send them to the Potosí mines and other Spanish enterprises in Chile or elsewhere.

There were two types of encomiendas. The ones that included established Andean communities repurposed the Inca institution of the mita (originally a form of labor-based tribute) by requiring community members, called *mitayos*, to perform tasks set by the encomendero. The other type of encomienda consisted of uprooted individuals or families, called *yanaconas*, who did not form recognized indigenous communities but instead lived and worked permanently as personal servants on landed property that had been granted to or taken by the encomenderos.

There were initially no regulations on how much tribute was to be collected or in what form; nor was it clear whether women and children had to participate. The number of *mitayos* a community had to contribute and the duration of their service were the subject of negotiations that depended on the relative power or ability of the caciques and of the encomenderos or their stewards. Overexploitation was the norm. In Argentine territory, the most common form of encomienda was through personal service, even after the Crown indicated that it should be collected only in monetary form.

The Spaniards who had not been granted encomiendas also managed to find a way to subject the Indians to menial labor and not just by renting them from encomenderos. During a considerable period of time, they organized what were called *correrías* or *malocas*, rapid incursions into indigenous territory to capture Indians who then became *yanaconas*—although initially they were simply enslaved—or were included in encomiendas. As late as the mid-eighteenth century, colonists in Tucumán were still carrying out manhunts of this type to reduce the indigenous peoples of the Chaco to servitude. The authorities also used to provide Indians "on order" to merchants who were not encomenderos to help with various tasks, particularly transportation. And they were used in the construction of public works.

In addition to its use in mining, the land itself was a valuable resource. Since from a legal standpoint the Crown considered all conquered lands as its own, property access could only be granted as a favor or a concession by the king. Initially, concessions were free (or more accurately, granted in exchange for services), but they soon began to be sold at auctions. In theory, lands belonging to indigenous communities had to be left in their hands so that they could be self-supporting and pay tribute, but the lands were often usurped.

Conquest and Gender

The conquest also established a system of privileges for men, exceeding what they had known in Europe. Indigenous societies were already patriarchal before the arrival of the Spaniards. But the meaning and organization of the patriarchy could vary greatly. Men were in charge, but women occasionally held positions of influence, especially in ritual functions. Exceptional cases have been documented in which they held the position of cacique or commanded men in a war.

An overwhelmingly male enterprise, colonization was based not only on ethnic and class differences but also on gender differences. Privilege

Violence: Conquest and the Colonial Order

manifested in the sexual, reproductive, and labor-related control of indigenous women. Although only the drama of the white captives has remained in collective memory, the Spaniards' *malocas* often focused on the abduction of native women. The nearly total absence of European women during these initial decades meant that indigenous women were used to satisfy the conquistadors. The appropriation and sexual possession of them took many forms: from kidnapping and rape, to forced occasional sex, extended concubinage, and in some cases legal marriage. They formed part of the colonial spoils.

The trade and control of women was also decisive in the relations between the conquistadors and the indigenous peoples. The alliance with the Guaraní men that allowed the Spaniards to survive in Asunción was sealed with an exchange of gifts: European adornments and tools for local young women. Some amassed as many as sixty women, and it was not uncommon for a Spaniard to have ten (something unthinkable in Europe). Used for sexual pleasure, they were also a source of wealth—due to the labor they provided in agriculture and textiles—and of power, because through them alliances were forged with their relatives.

Reproductive control was crucial: once it became clear that a rigid separation between Spaniards and Indians was unfeasible, the numerous mestizos born to these native women provided the conquest with a critical mass of supporters. These "lads of the land," as they were called, were indispensable in the foundation of the first cities. Those of the littoral region were almost exclusively settled by them. Of the seventy-six initial settlers of Santa Fe, only seven were Spaniards, and of the seventy who refounded Buenos Aires, at least fifty were mestizos from Paraguay.

The control of women was also key to the encomienda system. Indigenous women often supplied the labor in their communities that the *mitayos* were no longer able to provide. When the indigenous men were sent to the mines or forced to serve far from the community, locally powerful men—encomenderos, caciques, mestizos, officials—took advantage of the "surplus" of women in various ways, including sexually. This reinforced their power and the alliances between them. In contrast, access to white women was subject to very strict control. Among men of a certain social status, the virginity of marriageable girls was an absolute condition; marriage was indissoluble and the husband had complete power over their shared property and children. Adultery committed by women was severely punished by the law (whereas adultery by men was usually not).

The organization of the colony therefore led to a reordering of the relationships between people at different levels. Class inequality rooted in ethnic divisions merged with gender inequality in a way that placed native women in a particularly notable state of oppression. Thereafter, *mestizaje*, or miscegenation, became evidence of the victory of the Spaniards—and not only because it contributed to dissolving the cohesion of indigenous communities; the mestizos' bodies themselves reproduced the visual mark of the conquest, evidence of the original possession of women by the conquistadors.

Initial Resistance and Demographic Catastrophe

Though few in number, the Spaniards managed to dominate the local population thanks to their ability to forge alliances with certain peoples who supported them in their military ventures. This was also key to the survival of the first cities: they managed to survive in Asunción because their presence was useful to the Guaraní-Carios who lived there, helping them fight their traditional enemies, the Guaycurúes from Chaco. In Santiago del Estero, the Juríes were also allies.

The difference in weaponry was significant: the Spaniards had crossbows, firearms, good swords, shields, armor, fierce mastiffs, and horses. The natives had only spears, bolas, bows and arrows, slingshots, and stones. Even so, the resistance was fierce. Some of the first explorers on Argentine soil died at the hands of the natives: Diego de Rojas, Juan Díaz de Solís, and Juan de Garay, among others. In some cases, an alliance with the Spaniards only materialized after initial resistance failed. This was the case with the Carios in Asunción, who, in any case, resumed their struggle as soon as it became clear, starting in 1555, that their "allies" were dividing them up into encomiendas. There were other revolts and rebellions after that date, including a major one in 1575–79, which ended in brutal repression.

In other areas, local resistance was unyielding, as in the valleys of the Calchaquí people, which saw large-scale uprisings. It was also there that the capacity of the peoples to establish military coalitions against the invader became apparent. The cacique Juan Calchaquí led the first coalition starting in 1560: the allied forces of the Omaguacas, Lules, Ocloyas, and Chichas destroyed Cañete, Córdoba del Calchaquí, and Londres (other cities suffered a similar fate shortly thereafter).

An even broader coalition was organized in 1578 by Viltipoco, an Omaguaca cacique who managed to unite almost all the mountain peoples of the northwest, including the battle-hardened Avás of Chaco. Together they amassed nearly ten thousand warriors ready to carry out surprise attacks on the main cities and destroy them, something they surely would have achieved had they not been betrayed by Indian allies of the conquistadors. The Spaniards caught Viltipoco and halted the rebellion.

Peoples in other areas also resisted. Their success was hindered by the fragmentation and rivalries between caciques as well as their limited capacity to generate sufficient economic surplus to sustain prolonged military efforts. The Spaniards exploited this weakness with lightning attacks on horseback that destroyed crops and left defiant populations on the verge of starvation.

This resistance meant that the Spanish conquest of the territory was uneven. The valleys of the Calchaquí people remained indomitable throughout the sixteenth century. Some groups along the Río Uruguay maintained their independence until the middle of the eighteenth century. Patagonia, the Pampas, and the Chaco were autonomous during the entire colonial period.

The conquest of the Americas unleashed one of the greatest demographic catastrophes in history; nothing spared the population of the territory that is now Argentina from its worst effects. A combination of factors produced a dramatic decline in the number of inhabitants. To begin with, there was the extermination of those who resisted the conquistadors when they arrived. Those who attempted to avoid their domination in later years were also assassinated. Additionally, the introduction of diseases unknown in the New World, such as smallpox and measles, decimated entire communities.

Overexploitation led to a general increase in mortality and likely to a lower birth rate as well. The breakdown of communal production due to the dispossession of land or the use of the workforce for other purposes also played a part in this. Some fled to avoid this fate. The appropriation of women by the Spaniards and the phenomenon of *mestizaje* contributed as well.

The catastrophe cannot be quantified with categorical figures, but the figures we do have point to a sharp decline in population. Estimates suggest there were about half a million Guaraníes at the time of the invasion. After fifty years of contact with the Europeans, only a third or perhaps a quarter of that number remained. In the Tucumán region, the decline appears to have been more severe. From half a million inhabitants when the Spaniards arrived, only 15 percent remained a century later.

The data on Indians working under encomienda are equally revealing. In Santiago del Estero, more than 80,000 were held under encomienda in

1553; thirty years later only 18,000 remained. The decline continued during the seventeenth century. In the region of Tucumán, in 1596 there were 56,500 tributary natives; by 1607 they were reduced to 16,200, and at the beginning of the following century there were barely 2,000.

The Colonial Order

The first explorers often performed the role of civil authorities themselves in the cities they established. After the initial pillaging, a colonial order gradually developed, with laws and institutions controlled by the Spanish monarchy, albeit with decisive local participation. It was not a state as such but rather a network of concurrent civil and religious powers, with overlapping and sometimes competing jurisdictions.

The territory Argentina now occupies was initially included in the Viceroyalty of Peru, a colonial administrative district covering much of Spanish-dominated South America. As the king's representative, the viceroy had broad executive, legislative, and judicial powers. The king also appointed the governors of the most important administrative subdivisions. During certain periods, these positions were available for purchase. This led to flagrant abuses in order to recover investments as well as several scandalous dismissals. Other officials in various positions—chief magistrates, lieutenants, captains, and chief justices—acted as judges in smaller districts. Additionally, several Reales Audiencias (Royal Councils) were established as courts of appeal. The Argentine territory initially answered to the Audiencia of Charcas (present-day Sucre), with the exception of the cities in Cuyo, which answered to the Real Audiencia of Chile. Each city had its cabildo (municipal council), which was in charge of local affairs, including those of the surrounding rural areas. Its authorities were elected by *vecinos* or those males considered "respectable" members of society in terms of class and racial background.

The main function of the colonial administrative apparatus was to manage the vast mechanism for extracting profits from the land and from indigenous labor. Ensuring the flow of trade, collecting taxes, countering contraband, keeping rebellions and indigenous attacks on cities at bay, protecting the circulation of goods along the roads, and defending possessions from rival European nations: these responsibilities all required an administrative apparatus.

Above all, it was important to ensure the flow of metals from Potosí and other mines to the Iberian Peninsula. To this end, the Crown organized

Violence: Conquest and the Colonial Order

a commercial monopoly supervised by its officials called the "fleet and galleon system." In theory, it was quite simple: only a few ports on the Iberian Peninsula were authorized to trade with the Viceroyalty of Peru (and to connect with another few ports in the Americas). The viceroyalty was strictly forbidden from trading with other Spanish territories. Merchants in Lima were granted a local monopoly over the trade of all goods arriving from Europe. Everything was shipped there, and then agents would distribute and sell products in the various communities. The system required, as a counterpart, that as much gold and silver as possible be amassed in Lima and then shipped to the Iberian Peninsula.

If in theory it was simple, in practice it was extremely complicated. The goods arriving in Lima and the metals departing from there were transported along the Pacific Coast in ships that connected Peru with Panama. Once they arrived at the Isthmus of Panama, the goods had to be transported over land from one ocean to the other. After arriving at the Atlantic Coast, they were loaded onto other ships that traveled to the Old World in large formations to guard against pirate attacks. The long and costly journey and the numerous agents and middlemen involved made it a tremendously expensive system. In terms of purchasing power, metals from the Americas lost much of their value.

Therefore, circumventing this monopoly through contraband was an irresistible temptation for merchants in the Americas (except those from Lima, of course) and strongly encouraged by merchants of rival nations who did not want to be excluded from the business.

With direct access to the Atlantic, the port city of Buenos Aires was an ideal place for illegal trade, which for a long time was its main activity. Ships of many different origins unloaded merchandise and enslaved people, which were then sold by merchants in Buenos Aires to the continent's interior. In payment, the foreign merchants received precious metals and certain commodities that they transported back to Europe.

The Crown oscillated between suppressing smuggling and tolerating it, since it was a way of financing the city of Buenos Aires, which it needed to have well equipped as a bastion against the expansionism of the Portuguese and other rivals. To capitalize on this and set some limits on illegal trade, in 1622 an inland Customs Office was established in Córdoba (which certain smugglers nevertheless evaded). Additionally, partial authorizations were granted so that Buenos Aires could trade some goods on a temporary basis. None of these measures succeeded in suppressing the growing amount of contraband in Buenos Aires, which gradually became a hub of international trade.

The Catholic Church and the Missions

The Church contributed to the colonial enterprise in various ways. In fact, civil and religious authority overlapped on the Iberian Peninsula itself, where those in power defined themselves as "Catholic Monarchs."

The imperative to "evangelize the infidels" and save their souls provided ideological legitimacy for the subjugation of the natives. The cross and the sword penetrated side by side. But the clergy also directly intervened in the control and discipline of the Indians. Under the Crown's policy of grouping the natives into settlements known as "reductions," the religious orders had control of the most significant ones. During the first decades of the conquest, very few priests were present. It was only toward the end of the sixteenth century that a greater number of secular clergy and the Franciscan, Jesuit, Mercedarian, and Dominican orders settled in the territory now occupied by Argentina. From then on, the Church played a central role in the new order, although the monarchy had reserved the right to designate bishops in the Americas. This added coherence to the invaders' efforts but did not prevent disagreements and conflicts.

Priests were instrumental in the acculturation of the natives. The indigenous peoples spoke dozens of different languages and had distinct worldviews, although they were generally not familiar with the European sense of responsibility or individual autonomy (their cultures were collectively based), nor did they share their moral criteria. Certainly none of the indigenous peoples of the region shared the European obsession with controlling the virginity of young women. Women could have sexual relations with multiple partners of their own volition or at the request of their fathers or husbands (the offering of women was a common form of hospitality toward strangers). Unions could be stable or exclusive, in accordance with the customs of each people. The Mocovíes, for example, were normally monogamous. In contrast, polygamy was common among the Mapuches and the Guaraníes. Although there are no extensive accounts of these topics, there are mentions of the existence of homosexuality among the Guaraníes and of two-spirit Mapuches. Native religious rituals sometimes involved the consumption of alcoholic beverages or hallucinogens.

The Church played a major role in disrupting these traditions. Wherever it could, the Church prohibited polygamy and reinforced male domination of women's sexuality. Along with the civil authorities, it embarked on an intense persecution of "sorcerers" and the "extirpation of idolatries" through horrendous punishments, including burning people alive. But it was not all a matter of repression: part of the Church's success can be explained by its ability to allow syncretism with a certain number of local beliefs, which survived reformulated as part of Catholic worship. Despite this, the penetration of Christianity among the indigenous peoples was quite superficial for many years, and traditional beliefs and forms of double worship persisted.

The Church was a major economic force and accumulated so much wealth that it was even able to act as a moneylender. The religious orders were among the most powerful agriculture and livestock producers. In a vast territory that spanned parts of present-day Argentina, Uruguay, Brazil, and Paraguay, the Jesuits established their well-known missions, which became veritable political and economic powerhouses.

With a focus on evangelizing the indigenous peoples, the missions were formidable mechanisms of production. The Guaraníes who lived there had certain advantages over those who lived under the despotic command of the encomenderos. They did not have to pay as much in tribute (for a time, they did not need to pay tribute at all) and were not subject to the mita. Each family received a plot of land of its own to cultivate and had to do a share of work on communal mission lands. The Jesuits managed and sold the surplus. The system combined family and collective elements and even relied on some of the customs of the Guaraníes themselves. It made production more efficient and enabled the indigenous peoples to have a better standard of living than in other places. This was reflected in the changing demographics; while the number of Indians under encomienda fell dramatically, the population in the missions increased.

For more than a century and a half, the Jesuits controlled a veritable empire within the Spanish empire. Moreover, the missions had the ability to mobilize the Indians militarily for whatever the authorities required. In 1644, they were granted permission to use firearms, something forbidden to other indigenous peoples. The missions also protected the Guaraníes from the depredations of the *bandeirantes*, bands of itinerant raiders from São Paulo who hunted enslaved people for the sugar plantations in northeastern Brazil. By 1730, 140,000 people lived in roughly thirty Jesuit missions, some of which had as many as 1,500 to 7,000 inhabitants, more than most cities at the time.

The Church also played a central cultural and "moralizing" role in the life of the cities, which were conceived as Catholic communities. Most education—provided in convents, parishes, and a few schools—remained in its hands. It also controlled the University of Córdoba, the only university during the colonial period in what is now Argentine territory. Religion featured prominently in community life. In typically Baroque religious style, great emphasis was placed on the externalization of faith through rituals and theatrical stagings, with music and devotional images. Colorful processions, funerals, and celebrations of saints' days were central to social life at the time and served as occasions for contact between people of different social and economic status (although at the same time, there was a tendency toward ethnic segregation in churches).

The Economy and Labor

The new colonial order also brought about other changes in the local economy. The encomenderos soon began to focus the labor force on the production of saleable goods, especially for the market in Potosí, which by the early seventeenth century had more than a hundred thousand inhabitants and produced nothing of what it consumed. Occasionally they forced indigenous people to regroup in organized villages in order to produce a specific good, such as textiles.

Gradually, regional specializations began to emerge. Throughout the northwest of what is now Argentina, campesino women and children made linen and blankets from cotton and wool. In the sixteenth century, the region of Tucumán was one of the main centers of cotton production on the continent, and the city of Tucumán was known for manufacturing various artisanal goods. Paraguay was a source of yerba maté (the Jesuit missions excelled in this crop), as was Corrientes, which also cultivated tobacco. In the littoral region and in Córdoba, Tucumán, Jujuy, and Salta, mules were bred for Potosí. In the mid-eighteenth century, Salta introduced the sugar industry, while the Cuyo area was a major producer of wine and aguardiente.

Buenos Aires, Santa Fe, and other parts of the littoral region were unique in that in their green grasslands, cows and horses abandoned after the first failed attempts at colonization had multiplied spectacularly. *Vaquerías*, which were mounted expeditions focused on hunting this wild livestock in order to sell it, flourished. Horses were broken in and sold alive. Cattle either had their tendons severed or were stunned with bolas or lassoed at full gallop to be slaughtered on the spot once they had collapsed. After the hide and tallow had been removed, the meat and the rest of the animal were left to rot in the sun. Leather was mainly destined for overseas export. By the early eighteenth century, the *cimarrón* or wild livestock was disappearing and the local economy shifted to breeding mules and cattle. Specialization and a focus on the mining market fueled the flow of goods to Potosí but also between the various zones, which supplied each other with whatever they themselves did not produce.

There were different scales and types of productive operations. The northwest was dominated by haciendas (sizeable estates) with large tracts of land, although there were also small- and medium-sized ranches. Production on the haciendas was diversified—agriculture, livestock, and textiles—and they housed a significant number and wide range of dependents, including day laborers, enslaved people, and tenant farmers. In the littoral region, there were few haciendas of this type. Instead, there were estancias (cattle ranches) specializing in livestock production, where a much smaller number of people worked, both enslaved people and laborers.

In the major urban centers, small- and medium-scale artisanal production flourished, and agricultural production throughout the region helped supply the cities. Of the numerous farmers, some worked the land with their own hands and others used enslaved people or seasonal laborers.

In the Pampas, agriculture was very rudimentary; wooden plows and even hoes made from cow scapulae were used. Additionally, there were still shepherds and a subsistence peasantry, who sometimes incorporated European crops and livestock. It was all very heterogeneous: one could be dependent—like those living on the haciendas—or independent, communal or individual, a tenant farmer or one who owned land.

Santiago del Estero, for example, had an extensive indigenous peasantry with a very precarious agricultural system. Although they were independent, the farm workers and campesinos also generated surpluses for other sectors. Peddlers roamed the countryside offering goods on credit; those who acquired them incurred a debt that they repaid through future production, particularly artisanal. Since the peddlers also took on debt to finance their dealings with large merchants in the cities, the campesino surplus ended up flowing to the latter.

The indigenous peoples located outside the areas controlled by the Spaniards became progressively more involved in economic exchange. The ponchos made by Mapuche women were the most important textile product in regional trade in the eighteenth century. At the end of that century, an extended period of peace on the frontier facilitated the expansion of the trade flow: the indigenous peoples sold textiles and ornaments to the white settlers and bought weapons, yerba maté, alcohol, and other goods. Starting in 1784, at least thirty delegations of indigenous groups from the Pampas arrived in

Buenos Aires, where they were received by the highest authorities and engaged in negotiations with merchants.

Women of all ethnic groups played an important role in production. They worked under encomienda in domestic service, sewing, and textile production. They worked as prostitutes and in numerous other occupations and services. Some managed to become the owners of *pulperías* (trading posts) or small stores, the heads of small farms and estancias, and even leather merchants.

The labor supply was an issue from very early on. As always in the peripheries of capitalism, the forms of labor varied widely, with a high proportion of unfree labor. There was no "backwardness" in this: it was only in the late nineteenth century that free wage labor would become the exclusive practice in Europe, where a variety of servile or semifree labor relations persisted.

The encomienda was initially the dominant system, but it gradually lost economic relevance, displaced by other arrangements and affected by the sharp decline in the indigenous population. By the end of the eighteenth century, it remained significant only in Jujuy and Paraguay. More-or-less-free wage labor was gaining ground. The campesinos and even the indigenous peoples of the Chaco who were not living in "reductions" were often employed on a seasonal basis for the harvests in Salta and Jujuy, returning afterward to their communities.

In areas such as the province of Buenos Aires and other parts of the littoral region, where land and livestock were plentiful and the population density was very low, it was hard to find workers. As a result, wages were relatively high. Despite this, demand for labor occasionally exceeded the supply. In this area, there was a rural population with no fixed occupation that enjoyed freedom of movement, was difficult to control, and found ways to earn a living without being employed by others, or at least not on a permanent basis. In the eighteenth century, they were called gauchos or *gauderios*, and the authorities accused them of rustling livestock and of being "lazy and idle." Laws and coercive measures were introduced in an attempt to force them to work for the estancias. At least initially, the laws were not very effective.

The demographic catastrophe coupled with the scarcity of available labor prompted producers to introduce enslaved people throughout the Americas. Capitalist expansion thus relied on slavery, which provided a labor force often seen as more in keeping with ancient times but which reappears everywhere hand in hand with capitalism.

Captured in Africa or, less frequently, brought over from Brazil, enslaved people played a very important role in the territory of the future Argentina.

Violence: Conquest and the Colonial Order

Between 1580 and 1640, some twenty-five thousand entered through the port of Buenos Aires, most of them bound for Chile, Upper Peru, and the Tucumán region (where they were used in cotton production).

In Buenos Aires itself, where there was no other source of manual labor, they were essential in a range of urban tasks and on small-scale farms and estancias. In many areas, they were used in domestic service. According to one estimate, by 1650 there were already ten thousand Black and ten thousand biracial Black-white enslaved people in the territory of present-day Argentina, and the number continued to grow. Between 1680 and 1777, approximately forty thousand arrived and at least another seventy thousand were added between that year and 1812. Many of those arriving at the port of Buenos Aires were imported as contraband.

The slavery trade was accompanied by unprecedented levels of violence. Africans arrived in Buenos Aires in overcrowded ships, beaten and malnourished, to the point that it was common for a fifth of them to die along the way. In Africa, hunting of enslaved people bled the demography dry and, for three centuries, decimated the population by taking the youngest and the fittest, subjecting them to extreme levels of interethnic brutality. There is no doubt that this resulted in slowing that continent's development, leaving a wake of suffering, the effects of which can still be felt today.

The splendor of European "civilization" had its counterpart in the barbarism it was financed with: the enslavement of the African continent and the reduction to servitude of the Americas. The territory of present-day Argentina (and of the Americas in general) can be said to have played an ambiguous role in the international division of the advantages and disadvantages established by the capitalist system. If on the one hand it suffered the subjugation of its indigenous population and the plundering of its resources for the benefit of Europe, on the other, it—particularly Buenos Aires merchants—reaped the benefits from the enslavement of an entire continent.

The *Sistema de Castas*

The introduction of enslaved people to the Americas added a third category of people, whose legal status differed from both the conquistadors and the Indians.

The initial expectation of the Spaniards was to maintain three perfectly delimited groups. To achieve this, "Indian villages" (*pueblos de indios*) were established, with their own authorities and cabildos, which were expected to coexist with those of the white settlers. This was in contrast to enslaved people, who were not granted any political rights. Most of these villages would eventually disappear, but some survived (in Jujuy and Santiago del Estero, they even lasted up to the period of independence) and were a bastion for the preservation of indigenous traditions.

The civil and religious authorities sought to prevent white settlers from forming relationships with people from the other two groups. But an unstoppable process of *mestizaje* made this idea unfeasible. As a result of contact with local customs, the distance from the Iberian peninsula, and the absence of Spanish women, the moral standards and courtship practices of European men were laxer than in the Old World. In addition to occasionally taking young Black or native women by force, it was very common for Spaniards to have, alongside their "legitimate" families, mestiza, indigenous, or enslaved concubines with whom they fathered children.

White women, especially those of some status in society, had far less latitude for moral transgressions. They could seldom escape male control, unless they chose to live in a convent, which some did. Scrutiny was less intense for those of more modest means, and they sometimes had children by nonwhite men.

Regardless, human bodies copulated and reproduced with complete disregard for the prejudices and regulations of the authorities. Whether as a product of rape, necessity, or love, they gave birth to other humans whose very existence transgressed ethnic boundaries. Initially, the mestizos born to indigenous mothers inherited rights and legal status from their white fathers (slavery, on the other hand, was passed down through the mother's side of the family). In the cities of the littoral region, where a significant majority of the founders were mestizo, they were considered *vecinos*, with the same rights as their white neighbors. This was not the case in other regions, however, and, as the years went by, this initial permissiveness gradually disappeared throughout. Social differences were based on ethnic distinctions; therefore, lineages could not be allowed to mix and lose all importance.

Consequently, in the seventeenth century, the social hierarchy was reorganized through a new, more complex system that combined ethnic criteria with distinctions based on skin color. Known as the *sistema de castas* (caste system), it was consolidated in the eighteenth century with the requirement of a certificate of "purity of blood" in order to gain access to the benefits that came with being white/Spaniard.

Those who did not have "pure" blood were classified into one of the castes. Initially there were five main groups: Black, Indian, *zambo* (a biracial

Violence: Conquest and the Colonial Order

combination of the former), "mulatto," and mestizo (biracial combinations of each of the first with white, respectively). The three biracial combinations were later divided into subtypes, with more specific denominations that indicated the proportion of each race in the mix: *tercerón* ("octoroon"), *cuarterón* ("quadroon"), *mulato prieto*, and many others.

The castes were intended as a system of ethnic hierarchy backed by both legal provisions and informal practices. Those who belonged to a caste could not hold public, military, or ecclesiastical positions. During some periods, they were not allowed to bear arms, walk alone at night, be educated alongside white people, or dress sumptuously. Everyone did have the right to litigate in court. Even enslaved people could bring lawsuits against their enslavers and did so—at times successfully—in cases of extreme abuse, to avoid being separated from their families, or to be allowed to marry. Obviously, the treatment they received from the judges was discriminatory. The caste system was accompanied by a belief in the superiority of "pure blood" and the inferiority of others as well as by a distribution of labor and economic opportunities according to caste divisions, so that those who were in the worst position on the scale of ethnic-racial prestige were also the most economically disadvantaged.

In theory, castes were defined by birth and permanent. However, there was some mobility. Those who were able to ascend socially due to their financial ability, family ties, or political contacts and managed to disguise their origins could pass as Spaniards. They could even obtain an official certificate of "purity of blood" (something only attainable by those who were not very dark-skinned). This was largely defined by the context: it depended on the consensus that the person in question could achieve among their respectable *vecinos*, who had to accept them as a peer. Segregation was more rigid in the cities than in the countryside and on the frontiers, where society was generally more permissive. The mestizo condition could also be reversed through repeated intermixing with Europeans: anyone with less than an eighth of indigenous blood was considered white. Conversely, it was not uncommon for a person of exclusively European origin who was very poor to be called mestizo by extension. Ethnic and class categories overlapped.

The demographic dynamics produced a constantly changing and highly varied population. In 1778, the percentage of people recorded in the census as "Black" was very high in some cities: more than 40 percent in Salta and Córdoba, more than 50 percent in Santiago del Estero and Catamarca, and 64 percent in Tucumán. "Indians" represented a major percentage of the population in these cities as well, reaching 53 percent in La Rioja and 82 percent in Jujuy.

Those considered white/"Spaniards" were a minority, except in Buenos Aires (68 percent), Mendoza (51 percent), and San Luis (53 percent).

There is a possibility that these regional differences were somewhat smaller than these figures suggest. Few of the 1778 censuses included "mestizo" as a category, even though they represented a significant portion of the population, so in some places they were classified as Spanish and in others as indigenous or Black. The high number of "Spaniards" in Buenos Aires likely reflects the fact that it was a more open society with greater social mobility than the societies of the northwest, enabling mestizos who had achieved a certain degree of economic success to be more easily perceived as white.

Given the relative mobility it enabled and the association between skin color and social status, the *sistema de castas* spawned a "pigmentocracy" that would persist even after its abolition during the period of independence. Skin color and other physical traits—such as hair texture—would continue to play a crucial role in defining who was better than whom. Consequently, the local class structure evolved differently from that of modern Europe, where the ruling classes believed themselves to be superior to the workers on the basis of a number of attributes that nevertheless did not include racial superiority. This prejudice resulted in a variety of consequences in the relations between the upper and lower classes in Latin America, including the territory now occupied by the Argentine state. It is one thing to have class differences between people who consider themselves part of the same "we" and share a territory, but the inequality established when one group considers itself racially superior to the rest and occupies that territory, imagining it as a colony, is something quite different.

Interethnic Relations and City Life

Relations between ethnic groups were complex. The *sistema de castas* obviously meant ethnic hierarchy and differentiated rights. Additionally, there were enslaved people and enslavers, encomenderos and those who labored for them. Of those perceived as white, individuals born in the Americas did not enjoy all the prerogatives of those born in Europe. For many indigenous communities, *mestizaje* was a form of ethnocide that accelerated their disappearance—in part because mestizos were often not integrated into the community but also because some Indians sought to pass for mestizos in order to improve their status and thus abandoned their communities. Often mestizos were outsiders: they did not belong entirely to either the indigenous world or the white

Violence: Conquest and the Colonial Order

world. This ambivalence, embodied in their physical appearance, undoubtedly had a particular psychological impact.

The Black population was faced with a range of living conditions. Those who had been brought over as enslaved people had an extremely hard life. They lost their names and were given the surnames of their new enslavers, for whom they were forced to work. It was not uncommon for them to be subjected to corporal punishment or for the women to be raped by their enslavers or the enslavers' relatives. For these reasons, enslaved people made huge efforts to win their freedom. Attempts to escape were not uncommon. Those who were able to save some money tried to buy their freedom, something that more than a few succeeded in doing. There were also cases in which the enslavers ended up freeing certain enslaved people out of genuine affection for them or for the children they had with them, so that they would not pass slavery on to their offspring.

By 1810, more than 20 percent of the Black inhabitants of Buenos Aires were free. However, of the forty-three thousand inhabitants of the city at the time, ten thousand were still enslaved. Free or captive, Africans and their descendants played a key role in society. In the countryside, they carried out all manner of tasks, including that of ranch foreman: sometimes, even while enslaved, they supervised white laborers. A considerable number of the farm workers of Buenos Aires province were Black. In the city, enslaved people occupied a central role in domestic service, while free Black laborers excelled in artisanal production (a few even became enslavers themselves).

Although they came from very diverse peoples and geographic spaces, the Black inhabitants of this territory built a strong sense of identity. In Buenos Aires in the eighteenth century, they formed organizations by "nations" (according to their place of capture in Africa), met in *tambos*, and held dances on Sundays. They also had their own Catholic brotherhoods. Unlike in other regions, they did not live their daily lives segregated from the rest of the popular classes, with whom they worked and socialized. Relationships between poor white men and Black, indigenous, or mestiza women were not uncommon; those between poor white women and men of other origins were less frequent.

The ethnic heterogeneity and complex relationships between people of different social standing were evident in the cities more than anywhere else. After the initial period, the main class consisted of large-scale merchants, landowners, and, depending on the region, other groups that had become wealthy through various activities, such as owners of bodegas, sawmills, slaughterhouses, shipyards, and wagon trains. They were white and generally born in the Americas. This class also included high-ranking officials—mostly Spaniards—and the clergy.

A gradual change had taken place during the seventeenth century. The traditional elites, formed by the "distinguished" families associated with the founders and the first encomenderos, were replaced by families who had arrived later and became wealthy through trade. That was the case in Buenos Aires. In Salta, Jujuy, Córdoba, and Tucumán, the conquistador families maintained their preeminence until the mid-eighteenth century, when they were displaced by merchants, many of them from the Iberian Peninsula or other parts of the Americas. In some cases, it was the "distinguished" families that dominated commerce in their cities, so that conflict and displacement were not always necessary.

Below the main class, other white inhabitants occupied intermediate spaces. The Spaniards who had arrived first easily ascended to the top, but that became increasingly difficult as the colonial order grew more established. Social differences emerged among the Spaniards and, of course, among the white settlers born in the Americas: there were *pulperos*, innkeepers, small-scale merchants, artisans, foremen of haciendas and sawmills, transport owners, and small-scale producers.

In all these categories there were also people from the castes, especially in lower-ranking occupations: they were day laborers; peddlers; water, milk, and bread deliverers; fishermen; slaughterers; butchers; stevedores; and so on. Caste women were often employed as ironers, laundresses, or wet nurses or worked in the slaughterhouses. Enslaved people formed the lowest echelon of the popular classes. At the top were the artisans—shoemakers, tailors, harness makers, silversmiths, tanners, blacksmiths, et cetera—whose trades were the best positioned among those available to ordinary working people.

As in Europe, artisanal work was organized hierarchically, with the master heading the establishment and directing production. He was assisted by one or more salaried journeymen and one or more apprentices, young people whose families placed them in the care of the master to learn the trade and assist him in exchange for lodging, food, and sometimes clothing. The workforce of a craftsman's workshop could also include the artisan's own enslaved people or rented ones.

Among the artisans, there were various ethnic groups, including free Black laborers, whose contributions in cities such as Buenos Aires were significant. In some trades, they sought to organize themselves into guilds, similar to those in Europe, in order to regulate their activities and collectively defend

Violence: Conquest and the Colonial Order

their interests. In Argentine territory, these attempts were generally unsuccessful or weak, in part due to ethnic divisions among the masters.

Toward the end of the colony, within this diversity in conditions, a simpler division became apparent, one that opposed "respectable people" versus "the plebs." This was a dichotomy that did not entirely overlap with skin color. Only white people could be respectable, but the plebs included all the poor, including those of exclusively European origin. The "shameful poor" from the lower class were nevertheless distinguished from the "solemn poor," people from good families who were penniless yet recognized as part of the "respectable" half. Lineage, class, and ethnicity therefore came together in a hierarchy that assigned a place to each.

Each city was governed by its cabildo, which was in charge of the administration of urban life, provisions, justice in the first instance, public celebrations, the allocation of available land, and the maintenance of roads. It also organized militias responsible for defending the city.

Urban life was controlled by those considered "respectable" *vecinos*, who had the right to elect and be elected as representatives in the cabildo and to join the militias. The colonial authorities were not supposed to intervene in the cabildo but sometimes managed to get their candidates elected to the council.

The category of *vecino* did not include everyone who lived in the city but a more restricted group of people. Initially, *vecinos* were the encomenderos and conquistadors. Later, other groups were gradually granted this privilege, such as hacienda owners, merchants, and eventually the heads of propertied families and those of certain economic status. "Purity of blood" was required to be a *vecino*, which excluded the castes. However, mestizos were considered *vecinos* in the foundational stage of some cities and even later if they were able to conceal their origins. The rural population, all women (whether from the countryside or the city), and most urban males were excluded from the category of *vecino* as they belonged to the "inferior classes."

Within this general context, cities began developing regional characteristics. Since there was no indigenous population in Buenos Aires to be subjected to encomienda, manual labor initially fell to the colonists themselves, who were overwhelmingly mestizos. For a long time, there was no great potential for economic accumulation. This combination of regional traits led to a relatively egalitarian tone in social interactions and to a more participatory local politics. Something similar happened in other cities of the littoral region, where the potential to survive by hunting wild livestock resulted in a population of low means but haughty and jealous of its independence. The cities of the northwest were different in this sense. The elites there were able to set themselves apart based on clearer and more pronounced class and ethnic differences, and the prevailing tone was more hierarchical and feudal.

Rebellions and Social Tensions

The colonial order persisted for two and a half centuries, although not without tensions. The indigenous peoples continued to resist in various ways.

In the valleys of the Calchaquí people, there was a second wave of rebellions between 1630 and 1643, with a major uprising led by the cacique Chalemín and supported by several indigenous groups in the region (others, such as the Pulares and the Famatinas, joined the Spanish side).

A third wave broke out between the mid-1650s and the 1660s, led by a Spaniard, Pedro Bohorques, who was proclaimed an "Inca" monarch by the rebellious Indians. The repression was severe. The defeated peoples were deported to geographically distant places. The last to surrender, the Quilmes, were relocated to a territory in the south of the province of Buenos Aires that today bears their name.

In 1781, there were uprisings in Salta and Jujuy, coinciding with the great rebellions of Túpac Amaru II in Peru and Túpac Katari in what is now Bolivia. The revolt in Jujuy was led by José Quiroga, a mestizo raised in a Jesuit reduction. His message had a strong indigenist and anti-colonial tone. Now that there was an "Inca king" in the north, he announced that from that point on "only the Indians will govern," since "the poor want to defend themselves from the tyranny of the Spaniards." His followers were a heterogeneous group and included mestizos, Indians, and "criollos" (a term referring to people of European descent born in the Americas, although it also tended to suggest some degree of *mestizaje*). They attempted to march on the city of Jujuy but were driven back. They gained support in other parts of the viceroyalty and generated considerable concern among the upper classes everywhere. The repression was very harsh. In Jujuy, the authorities killed around ninety Wichis after the rebellion, including women and children (in Upper Peru, it was worse: around six thousand rebels were killed in La Paz out of a total population of twenty thousand).

Beyond (or between) the major uprisings, resistance also took place on a smaller scale. The indigenous peoples learned to use Spanish colonial law to their advantage and to litigate with the authorities in attempts to legally

Violence: Conquest and the Colonial Order

defend their lands against further dispossession. They were occasionally successful.

The indigenous peoples who remained independent were also active. The Pampas and Patagonia underwent an intense transformation as a result of the influence of the Araucanians, who lived in what is now Chile. The peoples on this side of the Andes acquired some of their customs, and Mapudungun became the lingua franca. By adopting the Spanish horse, which they became experts in handling, they gained more mobility. New groups, such as the Ranqueles, were formed through the fusion of other preexisting groups. No political unity was established among the various factions, but their ties did intensify.

By the eighteenth century, the main leaders of the Patagonian indigenous peoples were generally mestizos. They spoke Spanish, traded intensely with the Europeans, established diplomatic agreements with them, and maintained settlements or camps where fugitives and white captives were kept.

Malones, lightning raids on colonial settlements or haciendas to steal animals, became a regular occurrence. Although *malones* were primarily an economic enterprise, they were also used as a political tool to resolve disputes and define dominance between chiefs, to force negotiations with the white settlers, and as a punishment when an agreement was not honored. The captives abducted in *malones* were often used for this purpose.

From the mid-eighteenth century, the renewed threat of the indigenous peoples led the Buenos Aires authorities to establish a system of forts and military outposts along the frontier. In later years, a policy was developed that aimed to transform these forts into agricultural settlements. In the Buenos Aires countryside, Chascomús, Rojas, Areco, and Salto were established this way, although they were initially more focused on livestock than agriculture. Not long after, a similar policy was introduced in Córdoba, San Luis, Mendoza, Salta, and Entre Ríos, also affected by indigenous incursions. These new settlements, together with a policy of forging alliances and treaties with the indigenous peoples, gave the Christians peace of mind for a prolonged period.

The frontier with the "savage" Indian was not a precise or definitive boundary. On the contrary, it was a porous zone of contact and of commercial, cultural, and political exchanges. This broad swath of land was also inhabited by a population that lived beyond the reach of the law: Christians who had run into trouble, fugitive enslaved people, Indians who had escaped from the encomiendas, and enterprising cattle ranchers who settled there through private agreements with the caciques.

Although to a much lesser extent, the frontier with the indomitable Chaco people also permitted contact and exchanges. During the seventeenth century, they harassed the inhabitants of the settlements in the northwest as well as in Paraguay. In the eighteenth century, they caused great difficulties in Santa Fe. Like their Patagonian counterparts, they managed to maintain their independence until long after the end of the colony.

Enslaved people, on the other hand, had no opportunity for such open or massive resistance, although there were some scattered and limited mutinies. In any case, as we will see in the next chapter, there were some hints of unrest toward the end of the eighteenth century, and in 1803 there were several major episodes of enslaved people escaping in Montevideo, apparently with the intention of founding a free community, or *quilombo*, in the country's north.

The mestizo and white people born in the Americas also expressed their discontent in various ways. From very early on, the privileges enjoyed by the Spaniards generated some minor tensions, and as early as 1573 they were the cause of an uprising in Santa Fe. In the eighteenth century, there were some larger-scale movements. In Paraguay, there was a series of rebellions by *comuneros* (commoners) in which mestizos, campesinos, and soldiers staged riots against the authorities. These became quite intense between 1720 and 1735 and led to the death of the new governor in 1733 at the hands of the rebels, who then appointed their own leader.

In Corrientes, there were several rebellions, including a mutiny in 1732 against the highest local authorities, a repercussion of the Paraguayan rebellion. In 1764, inhabitants staged their own *comunero* uprising against the lieutenant governor, with broad plebeian participation.

In Traslasierra, Córdoba, there was an uprising in 1774 on behalf of the "commons" against the authorities of the cabildo in which both the affluent and the mestizo peasants participated. They demanded they not be governed by a European. Conscription for military service on the frontier also caused uprisings, such as those of 1752 in Catamarca and La Rioja.

The urban masses were a constant source of fear for the wealthy classes. Public celebrations and festivities—Carnival, bullfights, even religious festivities—were sometimes the occasion for popular unruliness and the transgression of norms and hierarchies and were therefore carefully supervised by the authorities.

Violence: Conquest and the Colonial Order

The Rise of Buenos Aires and the Bourbon Reforms

The colonial order emerged along with the initial core of the world capitalist economy as it expanded outward from its European birthplace. Given this relationship, the territory of present-day Argentina was highly dependent on the fluctuations of international trade.

The seventeenth century was a period of general crisis due to the depletion of the Potosí mining industry, the scarcity of indigenous labor, and the decline of European trade. Complications in the trade flow had a particularly strong impact on Buenos Aires. The decline of Potosí, the problems in Spain, and the hostilities and thieving that the Dutch carried out on the Iberian ships in the Atlantic had immediate repercussions and a negative effect on the economy of Buenos Aires.

Dependence on international trade increased decisively from the mid-eighteenth century onward. In England, the Industrial Revolution triggered technical and organizational changes that boosted the expansion of capitalism. It developed the factory system, which significantly lowered the cost of manufacturing production, and alongside it a network of banks and trading companies that supported the production and circulation of goods. These developments prompted England (and later other European powers) to look for markets to sell its products and source the raw materials needed to supply its smoky factories.

Within this context, the Iberian trade monopoly became intolerable. The ascendant England, allied with Portugal, exerted considerable pressure and finally gained access to Spanish American markets (a pressure it would redouble after losing its own North American colonies in 1776). In an attempt to stem the inexorable rise of the British, Spain allied itself with France and participated in the Seven Years' War (1756–63), a contest between imperial powers. Unluckily, it ended up on the losing side, making its position in the Americas more vulnerable, particularly in the Río de la Plata region, where the Portuguese were exerting pressure from the north.

In order to avoid losing control of the area, the Spanish Crown made a decision that would have tremendous consequences. For several decades, a new dynasty of kings, the Bourbons, had been trying to revitalize the economy of their dominions and strengthen their power in the Americas. A series of benefits for the mining industry in Potosí succeeded in reactivating production, which improved the Crown's revenues and brought greater prosperity to the entire region. The greatest reformist impulse occurred during the reign of

Charles III (1759–88), who made a significant effort to set up a centralized and more efficient state apparatus. He sought to establish a cadre of officials in the colonies who could break the resistance of local elites, protective of their interests. To this end, he abolished the sale of positions and consolidated the ranks of career officials from Spain.

But it was the response he gave to the challenge of the Portuguese and the British on the Río de la Plata that was the most important. In 1776, he sent a large expedition led by Pedro de Cevallos in order to assert Spain's military presence. To give him greater authority on the ground, Cevallos was granted the powers of viceroy. This was supposed to be provisional but ended up being definitive. The Viceroyalty of the Río de la Plata was thus created, independent from that of Peru, with jurisdiction over the present-day territories of Argentina, Paraguay, Uruguay, and Bolivia. The provinces of Cuyo, which until then had formed part of the Captaincy General of Chile, were integrated into the new jurisdiction. The riches of Potosí would be administered by the new viceroyalty in order to help support it.

This territorial reorganization confirmed Buenos Aires' ascendancy and gave it a significant boost. It became the capital city of the viceroyalty and the seat of a Real Audiencia as well as a consulate charged with regulating commerce. Two years later, its importance grew decisively, when the Free Trade Regulation of 1778 allowed it to trade freely with other territories of the Crown and to legally import enslaved people and Spanish goods. This commercial freedom meant the end of Lima's monopoly on trade. Merchants in Buenos Aires began to dominate the export of silver, which continued to represent the bulk of all exports, but they also controlled trade with the interior, including Upper Peru.

Customs revenue grew exponentially. Buenos Aires went from exporting 150,000 hides a year in 1778 to shipping 1.4 million in 1783. Its population expanded exponentially from twenty-two thousand inhabitants in 1770 to nearly forty thousand in 1800, making it the largest city in the viceroyalty and a central consumer market in its own right.

These changes generated a regional imbalance that would prove to be long-lasting. The hub of colonial economic life shifted from the Pacific to the Atlantic. Before the viceroyalty was created, the Government of Tucumán was the economic and demographic center of the territory that would become Argentina, and Potosí was its driving force. By 1778, 58 percent of the population lived in the northwest, and Córdoba still had more inhabitants than Buenos Aires. The littoral was a comparatively underdeveloped area at the time.

Violence: Conquest and the Colonial Order

Buenos Aires' explosive demographic growth and the new economic focus on the Atlantic led to changes. Associated with the export of leather and, to a lesser extent, salted meat, the littoral region (Buenos Aires, Corrientes, Entre Ríos, Santa Fe, the southeast of Córdoba, and the Banda Oriental) became as much a driving force of the economy as Potosí. The northwest entered a stage of relative decline due, among other things, to the effects of free trade, which had an impact on some of its products. For example, manufacturers of wine and aguardiente from San Juan and those of aguardiente from Catamarca were unable to compete with alcoholic beverages imported from Europe and experienced a definitive decline.

Therefore, the international division of labor, which had previously focused colonial life on the production of metals, now functioned in a way that encouraged the dissolution of incipient internal economic ties, generated regional imbalances, and oriented production other than mining to foreign markets. By the end of the eighteenth century, of the Spanish colonies in the Americas, the territory of the Río de la Plata was the fourth-largest exporter to Europe, following the regions with their centers in Mexico, Peru, and Cuba, and it was expanding dramatically. However, at the same time, the region's peripheral and subordinate position and its internal imbalances were also being reinforced.

The Atlantic orientation of the new viceroyalty positioned the merchants of Buenos Aires as the main class, which would also lead to consequences in the future. The Buenos Aires bourgeoisie, white and born in the New World, had flourished in commerce and had strong ties to contraband smuggling. It had grown wealthy through the trafficking of enslaved people and trade with various regions of the world. Without access to mines or haciendas, it was an almost entirely mercantile group. Their entrepreneurial spirit was strong, they had already managed to secure their own ships (some of them overseas), and they had links to other merchants in distant parts of the world. However, their relationship with the production of goods was weak, if not nonexistent. Toward the end of the colonial period, they had tried manufacturing salted meat to sell to seamen and for the slavery plantations of the Antilles, but it was still a fundamentally merchant bourgeoisie (their interest in the countryside and livestock farming would not develop until the following century). Their capital was already significant but still modest in comparison with the elites of other regions. A successful merchant in Buenos Aires could amass as much as a third of the wealth of his Cuban counterpart and a fifth of that of a Mexican. Due to its focus on trade and its position as a port city, the Buenos Aires bourgeoisie tended to value free trade and to reject any type of monopoly. The liberalization ushered in by the Bourbon reforms was certainly welcome. It was, however, a freedom that applied almost exclusively to trade with Spain and its territories. Restrictions on trade with other nations remained in place (and, along with them, smuggling).

The Bourbon reforms brought about other significant changes that affected social relations. In an effort to centralize power and exert more control, the Crown imposed limits on the activities of the religious orders. Those who suffered the most were the Jesuits, who were unexpectedly expelled from the Americas in 1767. The powerful empire they commanded through their missions in the northeast rapidly collapsed; the smaller-scale missions they operated in other areas also shut down. The king's untimely measure generated considerable discontent and several acts of resistance in the Guaraní area, Córdoba, and Buenos Aires. Despite this, the communities that the Jesuits had organized were soon dismantled. The towns saw their populations fall dramatically; their inhabitants were left to work as cattle ranchers or in cities. The lands and animals under their control passed into the hands of private individuals.

Under the same logic of centralizing power, the Crown stipulated that all the officials appointed from that point on must be Spaniards and that those born in the Americas, now displaced, were only to hold minor positions. The local elites saw their dominance undermined, which they naturally disliked. Under the new colonial structure, the cabildo of Buenos Aires had less power. The elites in Buenos Aires still managed to form alliances with the new officials, either through shared business ventures or by connecting them with their marriageable daughters. They were thus able to mitigate the loss of power these reforms entailed. But the elites of other cities did not have that possibility.

Below the elites, those born in the Americas of lesser rank also felt displaced by the Spaniards, who in Buenos Aires and other regions held privileged positions in the artisan trades, small-scale commerce, and other activities. The Bourbon reforms also reorganized the tax system, introducing several unwelcome changes, such as an increase in the tobacco tax. The Spaniards, or "Goths," as they were referred to pejoratively, thus earned themselves the antipathy of the American-born population in those years.

Around the same time, at the initiative of the local elites rather than the king, a series of legal measures was introduced to improve the supply of manual labor. A requirement was implemented obligating the independent

Violence: Conquest and the Colonial Order

rural population to carry *papeletas de conchabo*, documents signed by their employers to prove that they were not "vagrants." The requirement was imposed between 1772 and 1791 in the northwest and in Córdoba and for the first time in Buenos Aires in 1804, although prior to this there had been other forms of similar pressure.

The free population was therefore forced to seek employment. Those who did not have a job would be pressed into military service or moved to the frontier to inhabit forts and new towns. At the same time, the reorientation toward cattle ranching in the wake of the definitive extinction of the *cimarrón* livestock gave the land a value it had not previously had, which in the long term was also detrimental to the independent population of the countryside.

In general, the late eighteenth century was a time of intensified pressure to secure social hierarchies, class differentiations, and control over the lower classes. New legislation strengthened the power that fathers had over their children's marital decisions, to avoid undesirable unions (especially those that crossed caste barriers).

The Church also pushed to reform popular practices and habits. As a result, limitations were placed on the celebration of Carnival, for instance. The elites began to encourage supposedly more "enlightened," intimate, and austere ways of expressing faith, far removed from the more intense and public forms that were prevalent among the popular classes.

The period of the Bourbon reforms thus added new tensions to existing ones in the colonial order. The white, American-born population had more motives for discontent with the Spaniards, and the lower classes with the upper classes. However, until the early nineteenth century, neither the figure of the king nor the colonial order, sustained without a need for the presence of European armies in the territory, were strongly questioned.

This apparent calm would soon be shaken by a violent storm that would disturb the very foundations of the edifice the Spaniards had constructed.

2

Revolution!

The End of the Colonial Order, the Wars of Independence, and a Long Period of Discord (1806–1852)

IN THE LATE EIGHTEENTH CENTURY, a wave of revolutions shook Europe and America, ushering in a period of unrest and profound change that would last for decades. Several British colonies in North America declared their independence from England in 1776. France had its great revolution in 1789, and in the years after, other European countries followed suit. The North American example was important for the French, whose actions in turn inspired the enslaved people in their colony of Santo Domingo (now Haiti) to stage their own revolution in 1791, culminating in the Declaration of Independence in 1804. It was a precursor in Latin America and the first with anti-racist content.

By 1810, almost all of Spanish America found itself immersed in revolutions in which the examples and ideas of the preceding ones also resonated.

There were other local rebellions as well in various parts of Europe and in Brazil.

Each revolution had its own motives, but they all shared some relatively new ideas. Each in its own way raised the issue of self-government and the right of the people to choose the best way to organize society. Notions of equality among men were raised (some even proposed equality for women) and privileges of birth were questioned, although not everyone agreed regarding the extent to which this should be pursued. The idea that there were inalienable human rights that no sovereign could infringe upon also began to take root. In many cases, there were discussions of the matter of popular sovereignty and how to extend it to eliminate the power of kings and nobles, if necessary. The connection between politics and religion—especially the idea that the sovereignty of monarchs was divine in origin—was deeply questioned.

Travelers and sailors brought these new ideas and the news of the revolutionary uprisings to the shores of the Río de la Plata, where they became entwined with the already well-established tradition of local resistance. By that time, the Bourbon reforms had encouraged the circulation of rationalist ideas and the expansion of education, at least for the children of the wealthy classes, for whom a few schools had been created. In 1779, Buenos Aires acquired its first printing press (the only one in the territory of present-day Argentina during the rest of the colonial period; it arrived from Córdoba, where it had barely been used), which fueled a modest circulation of printed publications. At the behest of Manuel Belgrano, in 1801 the viceroyalty's first newspaper, the *Telégrafo Mercantil*, was printed, dedicating space to some of the intellectual novelties of the period. Belgrano was the son of a wealthy local merchant and had been introduced to these new ideas between 1786 and 1793 while studying law in Spain. They included economic liberalism, which would accompany him for the rest of his life, but also more radical ideas, such as those of Jean-Jacques Rousseau and the Abbé Raynal.

As the new century dawned, another inquisitive young man of lesser means, Mariano Moreno, was strongly attracted to the more incendiary ideas of the French, which he discovered in a private library while studying law in Chuquisaca. But the revolutionary influences also came from below, far from the world of the small minority of scholars. In 1794, during a peak of intensity in the events in Haiti, there were several reports that Porteño enslaved people were more unruly than usual, and a circulating pamphlet that was sympathetic to the Haitians caused a great deal of fear among the wealthy classes.

A judicial investigation was launched and the arrival of enslaved people from the French colonies was forbidden as a precaution.

The British Invasions

The conditions that set the stage for the revolution in the Río de la Plata region were also fueled by the loss of legitimacy of the colonial authorities and the experiences of popular organization resulting from an unexpected event in Buenos Aires: the British invasions.

By the late eighteenth century, the affirmation of British imperial dominance had begun to cause difficulties in the Río de la Plata. First there was a naval blockade on European ports, which abruptly cut off trade with Spain. Then, in 1806 and 1807, the British invaded the viceroyalty's capital twice, considering it an excellent beachhead from where to assert their dominance over the region.

In the first incident, a fleet of fifteen hundred men managed to seize Buenos Aires with little difficulty. Viceroy Rafael de Sobremonte not only failed to organize an effective defense but fled to Córdoba, while the rest of the colonial officials—the consulate, the audiencia, and the bishopric—quickly accepted the invaders' authority. Despite this defection, resistance soon broke out in rural areas and the city, with significant participation from the popular sectors (including women, such as the famous Manuela Pedraza from Tucumán, who fought hand-to-hand against the invaders). Santiago de Liniers, a French official working for the Spanish Crown, organized a brigade of soldiers and militiamen that marched on the capital city from the Banda Oriental del Uruguay and finally succeeded in liberating it.

The British attempted to invade yet again in 1807, this time with more than eight thousand men, and once again it was not the colonial authorities but the urban resistance coordinated by the cabildo that succeeded in repelling them. The fighting in the streets of Buenos Aires was fierce and left about two thousand casualties on each side. Those who were not involved in combat on the ground threw everything they could from their terraces to injure the invaders. Once again, the plebeian sectors played a leading role. Even a group of enslaved people armed with knives was allowed to participate in the struggle.

The ineffectiveness displayed by the colonial authorities triggered unprecedented political changes. Once the invaders were defeated in 1806, a crowd of several thousand gathered for a *cabildo abierto* (open town meeting) and demanded the viceroy hand over military command to Liniers, the hero of the reconquest. Sobremonte refused and took refuge in Montevideo. Liniers effectively took on the proposed position and immediately set about organizing voluntary militias, which involved 30 percent of the city's adult males. They ended up playing a crucial role in defending the city during the second British attempt, after which the cabildo decided to dismiss Sobremonte from his position. The Crown later officialized the situation and appointed Liniers as the new viceroy.

However, the fact that the population had defied the colonial hierarchy, ousted the king's representative, and established new authorities on its own was nevertheless undeniable. And more importantly, the city had organized massive militias consisting of not only "respectable" members of society (*vecinos*) but also the castes, with special corps of Indian, *pardo* (mulatto), and *moreno* (Black) men. They received a salary that was somewhat higher than what people of the subaltern class could earn in other jobs. Expenses were covered by contributions from the wealthier sectors. Additionally, the militiamen had been given the right to choose their commanding officers.

The emergency had thus interfered with the political, social, military, and racial hierarchies underpinning colonial life. The military mobilization of those at the bottom, the political weight that the militias and their leaders had acquired, the discrediting of the colonial system, and the atmosphere of popular debate triggered by the British invasions contributed to the emergence of a new political and social order. Although the king's authority was not called into question at this point, the invasions nevertheless set the tone and prepared some of the organizational resources that fostered the revolution that was to follow.

The Revolutionary Wave in Spain

The colony's abrupt end can only be understood within the context of the rebellions and wars that took place on Spanish soil after 1808 and shook the Iberian monarchy. By then, Napoleon Bonaparte, using military force, was taking some of the reforms that had driven the French Revolution beyond France's borders. In 1808, his troops occupied Spain, fueling a resistance movement against the invaders that merged with existing discontent with King Charles IV. A popular uprising forced the king to abdicate in favor of his son Ferdinand VII, who was associated with the rebels. Quick to react, Napoleon took advantage of the confusion and invited both to a meeting on the other side of the border with France, in theory to solve their disagreements. However, once there, he forced them both to abdicate in his favor, after which he appointed his brother Joseph Bonaparte as the new king of Spain. Charles and Ferdinand were held in captivity.

Napoleon's actions sparked an unprecedented political crisis followed by a war of liberation that lasted six years. Several Spanish cities rebelled and proclaimed their loyalty to Ferdinand VII. But since the king was absent, they decided to establish juntas of representatives who would govern in his name until he returned. In September 1808, they convened a Central Junta that had to move from one location to another (including Seville) under threat of the Napoleonic armies. In January 1809, the Junta declared that the territories in the Americas were not "colonies" but part of the Spanish monarchy, and the peoples of the new continent were therefore invited to elect representatives and send them to Spain. However, in early 1810, cornered, the Junta dissolved itself and handed over power to a Council of Regency of only five people, which sought refuge in Cádiz, a city besieged by the French. For those who supported the Junta, the council lacked legitimacy: juntas could at least claim they reflected the will of the cities, but it was hard to imagine that these five people had the credentials to govern on behalf of everyone.

Out of extreme weakness, the Council of Regency was forced to summon representatives from across the peninsula to establish General Courts. The elected representatives, once assembled, declared themselves a Constituent Assembly, and in 1812 they promulgated Spain's first constitution, which was liberal in orientation. The new charter opted for constitutional monarchy as the form of government. It established that sovereignty no longer belonged to the king but to "the nation" and that a parliament elected by indirect universal male suffrage would henceforth limit the power of the monarchy. The colonies were considered part of the nation, although they would be severely underrepresented in their seats in parliament. Under these conditions, they were invited to elect and send their representatives. Some of the American territories did so, but the experience was short-lived.

Restored to the throne by Napoleon, who was in steady decline, Ferdinand VII returned to Spain in March 1814 determined to put an end to the movement supporting the Junta, or at least its most progressive sectors. The Constitution of Cádiz and the parliament were suppressed. Reinstated as king, Ferdinand VII reigned in an absolutist manner until his death in 1833, and he pursued several initiatives to crush the revolutionary movement in the Americas. However, the nearly constant political instability he faced on the peninsula itself severely limited those efforts.

Revolution! The End of the Colonial Order

Each of the changes in the situation in Spain had direct repercussions on the American territories, either generating new opportunities or threatening uncertainties that affected the course of the revolution.

The Revolution in Buenos Aires

In July 1808, the ships arriving in Buenos Aires brought news, all at the same time, of the uprisings in Spain, the abdication of Charles IV, and the capture of Ferdinand VII. Shocked, the city's authorities swore allegiance to Ferdinand, but on the opposite shore of the Río de la Plata something happened that hinted at the troubles to come: Montevideo formed a junta that, following the example of those on the peninsula, declared itself in custody of the rights of the imprisoned king. It thus placed itself on equal footing with the other juntas, which in practice meant that it withdrew from the authority of Buenos Aires and Viceroy Liniers. This opened a Pandora's box that would not be closed for decades: without the king's legitimacy to clarify the question, no one knew for certain who had the right to rule over whom.

Buenos Aires soon became a hotbed of political intrigue. To ensure local loyalty, emissaries arrived from all the disputing parties, from those sent by Napoleon to those of the ambitious Infanta Carlota de Borbón, wife of the Prince Regent of Portugal (who had taken refuge in Brazil at the time). The latter, as the sister of Fernando VII, offered to act as the guardian of dynastic legitimacy. Notable *vecinos*, especially those from Spain, took advantage of the situation to attack Liniers, who had never been to their liking, arguing that in view of these events, they did not want to be governed by a "French viceroy." In early 1809, they demanded his resignation in the name of a junta validated by the cabildo. But the viceroy managed to thwart the attempt with the support of the militias.

His satisfaction was short-lived, however, because in February of that year the Central Junta appointed Baltasar Hidalgo de Cisneros as the new viceroy. He was well received in Montevideo (which dissolved its junta) and reluctantly in Buenos Aires, where fondness for the hero of the battle against the British persisted. The invitation to send representatives to Spain sparked an unprecedented electoral process in which the *vecinos* participated through their cabildos in cities such as La Rioja, Corrientes, Montevideo, and Santa Fe. Buenos Aires, in contrast, took its time. In any event, the elected representatives never got the opportunity to participate in the courts.

That same year, a new dynamic began to emerge that would help shape the future: the possibility that this virtual acephalia would lead to avenues of popular participation that would ultimately turn against the local elites. In July 1809, a *cabildo abierto* in the Upper Peruvian city of La Paz formed a junta that, like the one in Montevideo the previous year, declared it would not obey any authority other than that of the king. In this case, however, it was headed by a mestizo who was rejected by the city's elite. Lima and Buenos Aires sent troops to put an end to this situation.

The colonial authorities had even more serious problems when the Council of Regency replaced the junta in early 1810. Some cities in the Americas—Montevideo, Lima, Mexico City—accepted the council, but in others a renewed movement in support of the junta broke out, replacing the colonial officials, albeit still in the name of Ferdinand VII. This was the case in Caracas, Buenos Aires, Bogotá, Santiago de Chile, and Quito.

The news that the Central Junta had been dissolved reached Buenos Aires on May 18 and had a direct impact on Cisneros's power. The *vecinos* began to turn against him. They demanded a *cabildo abierto*, which was held on May 22 and determined that a junta would be elected to replace him. Two days later, Cisneros made a last-ditch attempt to remain in power, proposing a junta that included himself as president. The option was rejected under pressure from the militias and on May 25, as a crowd waited outside the cabildo, a junta was formed and took over the government. Its nine members most certainly belonged to the "respectable" classes, but those who had gained influence through the militia or through journalism played a prominent role as well. From the beginning, the junta was divided into two tendencies: a moderate one, headed by President Cornelio Saavedra and supported by the militias, and a more radical one, epitomized by the secretary, Mariano Moreno, and supported by the educated elite. Other members included Manuel Belgrano and Juan José Castelli. Later it would be known as the Primera Junta de Gobierno Patrio (First Patriotic Government Junta).

Those involved soon identified what had just taken place as a "revolution," the Revolución de Mayo (May Revolution). However, at the time, the question of independence was not discussed, let alone the elimination of the figure of the king. Like the other juntas, the one in Buenos Aires had taken power in the name of Ferdinand, according to an ancient principle that stated that if for any reason the monarch was absent, sovereignty reverted to the pueblo. *Pueblo*, in Spanish, means both "town" and "people," and at that time it had a different

Revolution! The End of the Colonial Order

meaning than it does today. It did not refer to the population as a whole but to the city—to each city—as a corporation with its own institutions and as a body of *vecinos*. If the king was absent, then sovereignty should revert to the pueblos. However, in colonial territory it was not clear how this principle was applied because the pueblos were part of intendencies with governors and head cities that ruled over them, and these, in turn, were administratively dependent on the capital. So, which of them would regain sovereignty? Only the head cities? Any city that had a cabildo? If the answer were "any of them," that would mean that the hierarchy between cities was abolished and no city could claim jurisdiction over another.

Immediately, the Porteño Junta defended the status of capital city that the monarchs had granted Buenos Aires and declared itself the authority over the entire viceroyalty, inviting the other cities to send representatives to join it. There would be a single junta, and in theory it would represent everyone. In reality, however, having founded it, the Porteños enjoyed the advantage of hosting it and benefited from the numerous tactics employed to ensure its continuity. In the years that followed, the revolution carried out intense military confrontations against royalist troops and sought to clarify questions of hierarchy among the cities.

The War against the Royalists

Like all revolutions, the May Revolution had to stage an armed defense against counterrevolutionary efforts that sought to dampen its zeal. This included thwarting occasional conspiracies, such as the one organized by Martín de Álzaga in Buenos Aires in 1812, which was punished with the execution of thirty-three Spaniards before an enthusiastic crowd. However, unlike other regions, Buenos Aires and indeed most of the viceroyalty did not have to endure a war against royalist troops in its own territory, since their presence was limited to the area that spanned from Tucumán to the north and the Banda Oriental del Uruguay, the two weakest points of the revolution. It was there that the battle played out between those who sought to promote and those who sought to prevent the autonomy of the Río de la Plata.

Contrary to what is often assumed, it was not a confrontation between *americanos*, or those born in the Americas, and the Spaniards. Although the former were predominant among the supporters of the revolution, there were many on both sides. Spain barely participated in the wars of independence in the early years: most of the officers of the royalist armies that descended from Peru were born in the Americas and so were the overwhelming majority of the militiamen they commanded. Only after 1813 did reinforcements begin to arrive from Spain, which nevertheless did not change the fact that most royalist troops were still American born. Indeed, it was not so much a war of national liberation against a foreign army as a civil war between *americanos* who wished to maintain the colonial order and *americanos* who wished to change it. What was at stake was not only whether the territory belonged to Spain but also the continuity of a social order that benefited a sector of those born in the Americas.

As soon as the revolutionary process began, Porteños had to confront a royalist stronghold that was dangerously close to home. In early 1811, the governor of Montevideo, already a vocal opponent of Buenos Aires, was designated by the Council of Regency as the new viceroy of the Río de la Plata (he was, of course, not acknowledged on the other side of the river). Montevideo was predominantly conservative. However, that same year, José Artigas, a captain of rural militias, took charge of a spontaneous mobilization in the countryside and began organizing a patriot army that he placed at the disposal of the junta in Buenos Aires. He then led an uprising of the towns in the countryside of the Banda Oriental del Uruguay that threatened Montevideo's royalist stronghold. He even managed to lay siege to the city but had to abandon it in 1814 due to disagreements with the Porteño government, which finally occupied it that same year with its own troops.

In the north, matters were much more complicated. Tucumán, Jujuy, Salta, and Upper Peru were involved in a long war, with advances and retreats that lasted until 1824. The proximity of Lima—the main royalist stronghold in South America—and the importance of Potosí's silver mines, which no one was willing to lose, meant that the battle was fierce.

When the revolution began, the Upper Peruvian elites were hesitant. Buenos Aires quickly sent an army led by Juan José Castelli, a supporter of Moreno. Arriving in what is now Bolivia, Castelli ordered the leaders of the opposition to be executed and, to the dismay of the local elites, appealed to the support of the indigenous people, promising an end to all tributes and complete equality between them and the white settlers. In a speech heavy with symbolism that he delivered before the ruins of Tiahuanaco, he spoke of "equal rights of citizenship" for the Indians. It was possibly the most radical moment of the revolution and one that truly revealed its egalitarian potential.

Castelli's move prompted the local "respectable" classes to come out in strong opposition to Buenos Aires, and the military aid sent from Lima caused the revolution to lose Upper Peru for a time. The patriot army was forced to retreat to the south. By then under the command of Manuel Belgrano, appointed to replace Castelli, it was involved in one of the most dramatic episodes of the conflict. While retreating, on Belgrano's orders the soldiers destroyed the food supply in Jujuy to complicate the enemy's advance. They also forced the inhabitants of the city to abandon it and march south (in what later became known as the Jujuy Exodus). Disobeying orders from Buenos Aires, the Army of the North stationed itself in Tucumán and engaged in battle. In September 1812, it pushed the royalist forces into a retreat and in 1813 defeated them again in Salta, which allowed the revolutionaries to attempt to recover Upper Peru for a second time. This prospect was thwarted when they were defeated and forced to withdraw to Tucumán. Salta fell into royalist hands again in 1814. A rebellion of indigenous peoples and mestizos in Cuzco that same year allowed the revolutionaries some relief but not for long. The Army of the North had to withdraw. From Jujuy to the north, the resistance continued as guerrilla warfare. In Salta it was led by Martín Miguel de Güemes and in Upper Peru by Manuel Padilla and Juana Azurduy, among others. In 1817 and again in 1820, the royalist troops would occupy Jujuy and Salta.

By 1816, the situation was desperate. The viceroy of Peru had managed to defeat the revolution in his viceroyalty, and his military power could be felt to the south. Reinstated to the throne, Ferdinand VII had dispatched a large military expedition that defeated the independence movements in Venezuela and New Granada. The revolution remained standing only in the Río de la Plata region. Its leadership was divided and was having a hard time securing its northern frontier. By then, the command of the revolutionary armies had been handed over to José de San Martín, who devised a completely new strategy. It was clear that they would not succeed in breaking the royalist stronghold in Peru by advancing by land, as they had been attempting to do. It seemed it might be more viable to assemble a large army to cross the Andes into Chile through Mendoza, defeat the royalists there, and join forces with the Chilean rebels in order to attack Lima together by sea.

The son of a colonial official, San Martín had received his military training in Spain. The revolution broke out while he was there, and he immediately embraced its cause. After visiting London, where he connected with other pro-independence leaders, he had returned to Buenos Aires in 1812. As the head of a secret society he personally organized, the Lautaro Lodge, he soon became an influential figure in Porteño politics. In 1814, he succeeded in securing the position of intendant of Cuyo and settled in Mendoza, where he spent three years assembling a professional army. In January 1817, commanding more than five thousand soldiers, he crossed the Andes to defeat the royalist forces in Chile. Once that was complete, he prepared a fleet of ships and finally, in 1820, landed in Peru. The viceroy mounted a poor resistance, weakened by the unrest in Spain and the desertion of a portion of his troops, who defected to the revolutionary side. Having taken Lima, in 1821 San Martín declared Peru's independence (Lima's elites complied with the decision for fear of popular uprisings). Instability in the area persisted for some time.

Following their famous meeting in Guayaquil on July 26, 1822, San Martín left Simón Bolívar, another liberator whose army had been advancing from the north, with the task of quashing the last holdouts of royalism. Bolívar's triumph in the Battle of Ayacucho in late 1824 effectively put an end to the wars of independence. The revolution had triumphed.

The Revolution from Within

While this extraordinary military effort was taking place, the revolution was blindly searching for answers to unprecedented problems. On what basis could the legitimacy of power be claimed, now that there was no king? How could the issue of territorial organization and the hierarchy among the cities be resolved? If each of the pueblos once again had their own sovereignty, how would they find common ground to wield it in a unified manner? Should a constitution be drawn up? And in that case, who would choose the representatives required to do it and how many did each city have the right to send? And in the event that it were to be defined, what would be the best form of government: a republic? a monarchy?

Faced with these dilemmas, the revolution engaged in a chaotic process of political experimentation. Its first decade saw a frenzied succession of different forms of government, assemblies, legislative codes and constitutional drafts, and all manner of ideas on how to organize what would inevitably be a new society. Proposals and interests rarely coincided, making for turbulent times. While a new legality was being invented, it was often brute force that imposed its law.

Once the Primera Junta was established in Buenos Aires, several cities recognized its authority, some with enthusiasm, others hesitantly. They included Tucumán, Santa Fe, Corrientes, San Luis, Santiago del Estero, Catamarca, San Juan, the government of Misiones, and, after some initial complications, Mendoza. Opinions in Entre Ríos were divided, while other cities refused. In addition to Montevideo, this was the case in Córdoba, whose authorities, led by the former viceroy Liniers, supported the Council of Regency. The Porteños were categorical: they immediately sent an expedition of fifteen hundred soldiers that forced the cabildo to recognize the junta. The rebels were mercilessly shot, Liniers included. Salta was also subdued by force. Troops were sent to Asunción to establish order, but in this case they were defeated, in what became the first step toward Paraguay's autonomy. In addition to the rebellions against the capital city, some of the smaller cities sought to break away from control of the head cities of the intendency, as was the case with Jujuy, Tarija, Tucumán, and Mendoza. The territory's hierarchy was tottering.

These tensions were transferred to the junta in Buenos Aires as the representatives arrived from the interior. In December 1810, there was a debate on whether they should be integrated into an expanded junta or become a constituent congress. The second option, which Mariano Moreno and the more radical tendency supported, implied an acceleration of the revolution because it meant not only safeguarding the sovereignty of the king but also changing the legal order. However, the more conservative position, defended by Saavedra and the representatives from the interior, triumphed, and on December 18 the Junta Grande was formed.

Defeated, Moreno set off on a diplomatic mission to Europe to rally support; he would die at sea before reaching his destination. In April of the following year, using the pressure of a popular demonstration, Saavedra succeeded in getting the junta to expel the members who had supported Moreno and restore military authority to him, which at Moreno's request had been transferred to the entire junta.

Tensions between the capital and the other cities were quick to resurface. In September 1811, disregarding the junta's authority, a *cabildo abierto* in Buenos Aires designated a triumvirate, formed by Feliciano Chiclana, Manuel de Sarratea, and Juan José Paso, with the intention of consolidating power over the entire territory. It was not clear what powers the Junta Grande would then have. The representatives accepted the fait accompli by enacting a regulation that stated that the legislative power was reserved for the junta and the triumvirate was recognized as the executive power. Nevertheless, in November the triumvirate ordered the dissolution of the junta. The provinces were left without any representation in the government. This caused tensions to increase.

When in 1812 the new Spanish Constitution was enacted in Cádiz, it left little room for half measures. A decision had to be made whether to recognize it and send representatives or, conversely, venture into the territory of open sedition. Much of Spanish America embraced the new constitution, but Buenos Aires decided to reject it. By then the Lautaro Lodge, backed by Moreno's supporters, was already pushing the government toward independence. In contrast with the situation in 1810, the idea of independence was now openly debated. By means of a popular rally—a method that had by then become common practice—the lodge and its allies succeeded in bringing about the fall of the First Triumvirate. It was replaced by the Second Triumvirate, formed by Juan José Paso, Nicolás Rodríguez Peña, and Antonio Álvarez Jonte, which in January 1813 summoned a constituent congress with the idea of declaring independence and providing the country with its own constitution.

Once the representatives of each city had gathered in what was called the "Assembly of the Year XIII," they decided to swear an oath as representatives not of their respective cities but of the whole nation (just as the representatives had done during the French Revolution and in the Cortes of Cádiz). This was a complete novelty because it also referred to a nation that nobody quite knew the details of yet. Attentive to the shifting tides in Spain, where Ferdinand VII had just returned to power, and to the fact that the prospects of the revolution in the rest of Spanish America were looking rather bleak, in the end the Assembly neither declared independence nor drafted a constitution. Instead, it took a series of measures that proved to be a powerful boost to the revolution—among them, the *libertad de vientres* (free birth) law, which stipulated that the children of enslaved people would be freed; the freedom of the press; the end of indigenous "personal service" and of mita (the tribute had been abolished a short time before); and the suppression of titles of nobility. This alone critically weakened the old colonial order. Additionally, to make the executive branch more efficient, in 1814 it decided to put an end to the tripartite governments and replace them with a single person under the title of "supreme director."

Artigas and the League of Free Peoples

Discussions in the Assembly had been heated, particularly on the point of territorial organization. One group favored a centralized government with sole and undivided sovereignty over the entire territory, while the other, which dubbed itself "federalist," sought a system in which the provinces retained their sovereignty, at least in part. Among the latter there were different proposals, not always clearly defined. Some envisioned a confederal organization, with the provinces retaining sovereignty and a very limited central power (in charge of foreign relations and little more than that). Others had more of a federal model in mind, with a strong central government that nevertheless left the provinces with broad autonomy. The Assembly was strongly dominated by the Porteño centralist groups and the issue was not settled.

The problem of territorial hierarchies became evident in the bitter disagreement between José Artigas, a caudillo or popular military leader from the Banda Oriental del Uruguay, and the government of Buenos Aires. Artigas had expressed a willingness to join the Assembly, but under the condition that he could send a greater number of representatives and that the future constitution would be confederal. He wanted the Banda Oriental del Uruguay to keep its autonomy and did not want Buenos Aires to be the capital. The authorities in Buenos Aires found his demands unacceptable, rejected the representatives he sent, and declared him a traitor. Artigas, in turn, broke off relations.

In Uruguay and Entre Ríos, Artiguism had been emerging as a popular and egalitarian movement with a rural base, much to the chagrin of the "respectable" classes. It was decidedly republican in nature and fostered the political participation of the gauchos and Indians. In 1815, during his brief government in Montevideo, Artigas proclaimed that "the wretched will be the most privileged" and declared that the "free blacks, the *zambos* of this class, Indians, poor criollos" should receive lands expropriated from the "bad Europeans and worse Americans." The local elites feared him and breathed a sigh of relief when the Portuguese, tacitly supported by the supreme director in Buenos Aires, invaded the Banda Oriental in 1816 and removed him from power.

Perhaps the greatest challenge Artigas launched was the Liga de los Pueblos Libres (League of Free Peoples), which in 1814, following the rift with Buenos Aires, organized a bloc of regional support that eventually included the Banda Oriental, Entre Ríos, Corrientes, Misiones, Santa Fe, and briefly Córdoba. This bloc did not at all respond to the authority of Buenos Aires, which led the Porteños to seek to defeat it by military means. During Carlos de Alvear's brief tenure as supreme director, centralism acquired dictatorial tones as well. The discontent that this caused in all sectors culminated in a military uprising in 1815 accompanied by riots in Buenos Aires that led to the fall of Alvear and the dissolution of the Assembly itself. Once again, the power vacuum was filled by the Buenos Aires cabildo, which appointed the next director. Meanwhile, autonomism spread throughout the interior.

Independence at Last

The supreme director who replaced Alvear, Ignacio Álvarez Thomas, was faced with the need to continue the arduous task of establishing legitimacy for the central government. As a bargaining chip for the dissolution of the Assembly in 1815, the provinces were invited to a new constituent congress. The selection of representatives would be done through popular elections, which meant a further broadening of political participation and one more step away from the exclusive control of the *vecinos*.

The congress was convened in Tucumán in 1816 and on July 9 made its most important decision: to proclaim independence. However, it was not "Argentina" that became independent. That nation did not yet exist and the congress was not even a reflection of the territory it would have in the future. Rather, the declaration was made in the name of the United Provinces of South America, and its signatories included several representatives of places that today form part of Bolivia. Those involved in the decision were not at all clear that Upper Peru, the Banda Oriental, and Paraguay would not form part of this new country (in fact, this would not become clear for some time).

The population of most of the present-day territory of Argentina did not participate in the congress. The entire region up to the very north of Patagonia—including what are now the provinces of La Pampa, Neuquén, a large part of Buenos Aires, and the south of Mendoza, San Luis, and Córdoba—was still the autonomous territories of the indigenous peoples (see map 2.1). The same was true for the Chaco, which extended to the present-day provinces of Formosa; the north of Santa Fe; and vast parts of Salta and Santiago del Estero. This whole area was much more extensive than that of the provinces gathered in Tucumán. Furthermore, the provinces in Artigas's league, which occupied a territory almost as extensive as that of the signatories (in fact, it could have formed a separate nation, as the Oriental Republic of Uruguay later did), did not send representatives either.

The United Provinces of South America was, for the moment, an alliance of provinces that had decided to proclaim their independence from Spain and were trying to build a political community. In doing so, cannons would be fired not only against the royalists but also between the provinces themselves. Until 1819, Buenos Aires would continue to launch devastating military attacks against some of the provinces that adhered to the league, especially Santa Fe.

The Congress of Tucumán could not agree on another central issue: the form of government. Some representatives supported republican ideas, while

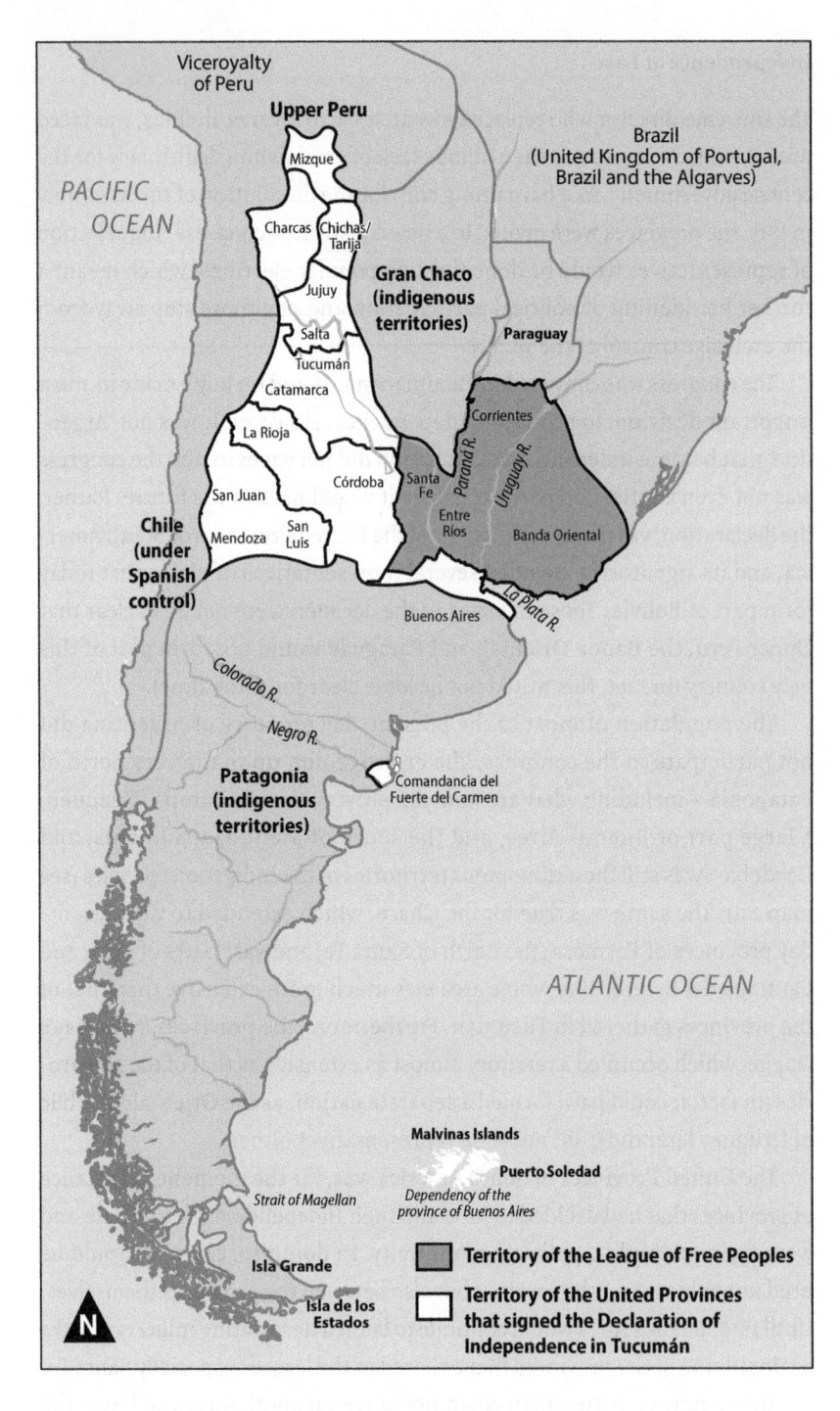

MAP 2.1. The Viceroyalty of the Río de la Plata in 1816.

others believed that the new country should be a constitutional monarchy. Of course, the problem was to find a candidate for king who had the legitimacy for such a position. Options were sought among the reigning European houses, but no viable figure was found. Belgrano suggested enthroning a descendant of the Inca emperors, but his proposal was rejected. And then there was the issue of territorial organization.

In 1817, the Congress moved to Buenos Aires to continue its sessions there, and in 1819, it drafted the first constitution, strongly centralist in orientation. It did not resolve the question of the form of government, but it did establish that, whatever form it took, it would be based on the separation of powers and would have a representative system. As the demands for autonomy from the provinces of the interior continued to go unheeded, several provinces rejected it.

The central power was finally dissolved when the supreme director ordered the army to return from Chile and attack the Artiguists. As San Martín refused to fire on his compatriots, Buenos Aires was left without any real authority, and in this context, the caudillos Estanislao López and Francisco Ramírez, strongmen of Santa Fe and Entre Ríos, respectively, took advantage of the situation to attack the city. In the Battle of Cepeda in 1820, the Porteño forces were defeated and the victors forced the authorities to sign the Treaty of Pilar, which established the free navigation of the rivers (to avoid the checkpoint at the port of Buenos Aires) and stipulated that the future organization of the country would be federalist.

After this disaster, the Porteño cabildo once again took over the government in Buenos Aires and, pressured by the victors, dissolved the position of supreme director and the Congress. The central government had been completely eliminated. This acephalous situation also extended to within Buenos Aires. The cabildo created a Junta of Representatives, which would henceforth be in charge of appointing the governor. But the struggle of several factions competing for power led to a dizzying succession of appointed and deposed governors and juntas that were repeatedly elected and dissolved. This is known as the "anarchy of the year XX."

Despite its victory, the League of Free Peoples also collapsed. In January 1820, Artigas attempted to drive the Portuguese from his homeland, but his efforts were thwarted. Not long after, once the Porteños were defeated, his ally Francisco Ramírez turned his troops against Artigas and defeated him as well. Artigas was forced to flee to Paraguay, where he spent the rest of his days. Ramírez died at the hands of his former ally López. By 1821, the league had completely disappeared.

The fragmentation of the former viceroyalty peaked in 1820, a turbulent year. Buenos Aires found itself alone: it was no longer the capital of anything and the provinces were acting autonomously (for a brief period, Tucumán and Entre Ríos even declared themselves independent republics). The Banda Oriental, occupied by the Portuguese, was annexed to the Portuguese Empire in 1821. Upper Peru finally declared its definitive separation from the United Provinces in 1825, when it proclaimed itself an independent republic. And although it would not do the same until 1842, Paraguay had already been functioning autonomously for years.

Ironically, San Martín, who had insisted more than anyone else on proclaiming independence, since he did not want to advance on Chile at the head of a group of rebels but rather in the name of a new country, found himself arriving in Lima representing a power that no longer existed. Aware of the complications of leading an army that did not know to which authorities it responded, he told his officers they were free to choose their commander. His men, however, refused to be led by another, arguing that San Martín's authority came from the people and not from the official who had appointed him. This was a clear reflection of the political changes brought about by the revolution.

The Leading Role of the Subaltern Sectors

The progressive radicalization of the revolution was undoubtedly fueled by the leading role that the lower classes played in it. The war effort, in particular, required the leaders to summon an increasing number of commoners, which in turn created new avenues for social advancement and political participation.

After the May Revolution, the Juntistas ordered gazettes and proclamations be read aloud in the meeting places of each city so that they could reach the illiterate majority. Hundreds of copies of the 1816 Declaration of Independence were printed in Quechua and Aymara (in addition to Spanish) as a way of inspiring enthusiasm among the indigenous peoples. Other proclamations were translated into Guaraní. Moreover, popular demonstrations began to be used from very early on as a way of intervening in the struggles between factions of the leadership. An appeal was made to the lower classes; they were both called to action and feared.

In Buenos Aires, starting with the British invasions, the involvement of the popular classes was crucial. Crowds vociferating in front of the cabildo became a regular feature of the revolutionary landscape. And although initially these crowds mainly consisted of *vecinos*, they were soon joined by the lower classes. In the demonstration that Saavedra, president of the Junta Grande, instigated to settle accounts with Moreno's supporters on April 5 and 6, 1811, the core group was plebeian. The more than fifteen hundred people who gathered—an enormity for the time—included the militias (among them, those of the *pardos* and *morenos*) as well as people from the countryside. They went to support Saavedra but at the same time protested the revolution's moderate nature, which in their view had put very little pressure on the Spanish. In their hatred of the Spaniards, there was already a more general feeling of hostility toward "the bosses." It was both social and political in nature: those who supported the opposing political view, even if they had been born in the Americas, were referred to as "Goths" or "Galicians." The demonstrators also presented themselves as *el pueblo* (the people), thus expanding the meaning the word had had up to that point in a more democratic and modern direction. *Pueblo* referred not only to *vecinos* with their urban corporations but to all free men.

There were other important popular demonstrations in the years that followed, such as the one that led to the fall of the triumvirate in October 1812 and the fall of Alvear in 1815. The protest in 1820 against reintroducing the position of supreme director was especially strong and plebeian, which terrified the "respectable" classes. The repression required the involvement of the rural militias and resulted in more than three hundred fatalities. In all these demonstrations, there were intermediate players, political organizers who were known as "tribunes of the plebs," who acquired great importance. Several were militia leaders or *pulperos* (owners of *pulperías* or trading posts).

The rural lower classes also gained new prominence. It was especially noticeable in the popular and egalitarian movement of Artiguism, which was supported by armed bands of gauchos and small-scale producers. In Entre Ríos and the Banda Oriental, the word *montoneras* was used for the first time to describe these irregular forces that fought *en montón* (en masse). It was they who provided the movement with its egalitarian tone, embodied in its famous slogan: "Naides más que naides" (Ain't nobody better'n nobody).

Likewise, in Salta, the mobilization of peasants of diverse ethnic origins led to the radicalization of political life, especially when small landowners, tenant farmers, and farm laborers began to rise to the rank of officers.

Perhaps in an attempt to counter the insult thrown at them by the royalists who called them "gauchos," these groups reclaimed the term, seldom used in the north at the time, and transformed it into a name and an identity that unified them. They were patriotic gauchos. Güemes, leader of the resistance in Salta, made it official when he created his famous División de Gauchos de Línea Infernales (Division of Infernal Gauchos of the Line). For their services, Güemes's gauchos were awarded a number of important concessions, such as the right to stop paying rent or providing services to landowners, and were given "military privileges" that granted them certain powers, such as the right to slaughter cattle belonging to landowners without asking permission and without fear of punishment. It was for reasons like this that the Salta elites detested the gauchos and their protector, Güemes, whom they tried to oust several times from his position as provincial governor. In 1821, they did manage to briefly overthrow him, but the decisive action of his gauchos restored him to his position. However, he did not last long there: he was killed that same year during a surprise raid by the royalists.

The indigenous peoples participated actively on both sides in the wars of independence (in some cases, they also armed self-defense forces to protect themselves from both sides). The caciques contributed thousands of soldiers to Lima's royalist armies. There is nothing strange about this: from the point of view of the indigenous peoples, it was not at all obvious that life would be better if they were governed directly by the local elites, who would oppress them without the mediation of the king's officials. In fact, hostilities against the indigenous peoples would intensify during the period of independence. Some of the achievements of the revolution, such as equality before the law, paradoxically brought new threats to the survival of indigenous communities because they led to the disintegration of the *pueblos de indios* (Indian villages) and the end of communal land rights. The abolition of the tribute certainly benefited them, but in places like Jujuy it was reintroduced under another name (*contribución indigenal*), and as late as the 1840s forms of "personal service" persisted.

Despite this, many indigenous communities fought on the side of the patriots. Their help was decisive in some battles. Güemes's troops included many indigenous people. A good number from Puna joined, and in Upper Peru they were legion (the legend of an "Inca Castelli" who would bring them freedom persisted there for years). In the valleys of the Calchaquí people, on the other hand, there was little or no support for the revolution.

Toward the east, involvement was very intense, especially as part of Artiguism. Several Guaraní communities with their caciques in the lead joined the movement, adding their demands for equality before the law and certain gestures of hostility toward the white elites. The most well-known leader was Andresito Guacurarí, who became a commander and played a central role in Artiguism. In August 1818, he and his troops occupied the city of Corrientes, where the elites were trying to restore their loyalty to Buenos Aires. During his time there, he forced some *vecinos* to clean the public square themselves and their wives to dance with the troops: an unspeakable humiliation exacted as compensation for their traditional disdain. He also rescued indigenous children who were held captive in the homes of wealthy families and forced to perform menial labor. Guacurarí attempted to unify the former Jesuit province under his control but was defeated by the Portuguese and taken prisoner in 1819. Other Guaraní leaders continued to accompany the Artiguist movement until the end.

The revolutionary tide also prompted actions by the indigenous peoples who were still in autonomous territories. In the Chaco, they took advantage of the fact that the white settlers were busy fighting among themselves and advanced toward the south. In 1815, they seized lands in the north of Santa Fe, and the following year they caused difficulties in Córdoba. In Santa Fe, the authorities managed to contain them through agreements to deliver clothes and money. Further south, relations continued to be relatively peaceful, and the Pehuenches negotiated with San Martín, granting free passage through their territory in exchange for the army purchasing cattle and other goods from them. To the north of Buenos Aires, on the other hand, indigenous actions were more confrontational, especially because the Artiguists and Porteños encouraged the caciques, in particular the Ranqueles, to get involved on one side or the other.

For their part, Black *americanos* were intensely involved in the revolution, which they strongly supported. It was an enslaved person who denounced his enslaver, Martín de Álzaga, as the leader of the conspiracy thwarted in 1812. As they had earlier in Buenos Aires, militias of *pardos* (mulattos) and free Black soldiers were organized in 1811 in places such as Córdoba and Salta. Enslaved people also participated that year. In the Banda Oriental for the first time, they were offered their freedom in exchange for joining the military effort. Many accepted this option enthusiastically. In the north, Güemes did something similar, and in other places the patriot authorities forced owners to deliver quotas of enslaved people for the armies, who were given the promise of freedom after a minimum of five years of service. Black soldiers were crucial in San Martín's liberating army: of the more than 5,200 soldiers he managed to assemble to cross over to Chile, 1,550 were former enslaved people (not counting other free Black soldiers who participated). San Martín considered them his best infantrymen, and several rose to the rank of officer.

In order not to antagonize owners, the revolution made very slow advances against slavery. In 1812, trafficking was prohibited, and in 1813 the *libertad de vientres* (free birth) law was proclaimed, but at the same time it was determined that children born to enslaved people had to remain in their enslavers' homes and serve them until they reached adulthood. Not content with that, to circumvent the law some white people sent their enslaved people to give birth in Brazil or directly registered the babies as enslaved people, which the mothers resisted through lawsuits. The abolition of slavery would not come about until the 1853 Constitution (except in Buenos Aires, where the government delayed it until 1860).

Beyond the slow pace with respect to legal changes, the position of *morenos* or Black people in society changed during the course of the revolutionary process; they pushed the limits toward greater radicalism, driven by promises of liberty and equality. A good example is that of the illiterate *pardo* Francisco Benítez, who became one of the leaders of Artiguism and commanded troops, much to the dread of the elites in the east. He was among those who pushed for Artigas to adopt the policy of land distribution among "the wretched," which became a distinctive characteristic of the latter.

Black inhabitants occasionally crossed the line of what was tolerated, as in Mendoza in 1812 when roughly thirty enslaved people planned an uprising. The two ringleaders—Joaquín Fretes, a free Black man who could read, and an illiterate enslaved person named Bernardo—rallied the others with the rumor that the revolution had abolished slavery but local authorities were hiding it. Bernardo was later reported saying that the Black people from Mendoza should imitate those in Haiti and kill the white people to gain their freedom. The authorities reacted with the full force of the law. In January 1819, a mutiny of the Porteño militia led to riots, nightly meetings in Black neighborhoods, and open expressions of racial tension. Fear prompted white neighbors to arm themselves, and the mutiny was suppressed militarily. A short time later, these tensions resurfaced in Salta. In a surge of anger following Güemes's death, people looted to the cry of "Death to the *cariblancos* [white-faced]!," a slogan that did not necessarily express a Black identity but did reflect racial antagonism.

The revolution produced few changes in the legal status of women, who continued to be excluded from political life and the right to vote in elections.

However, women did participate in the struggles of the time. In Buenos Aires, the salons and social gatherings organized by women of the "respectable" classes, such as those led by Mariquita Sánchez, were a key site of sociability among revolutionaries and a place for debates that occasionally enabled women to take the floor. Among women of the lower class, some gained a prominent place during the war. The Army of the North had several female combatants, including María Remedios del Valle, an Afro-Argentine who earned the rank of captain for her military merits. Juana Azurduy, who was from a mestizo family, accompanied by other female warriors played a central role in the guerrillas of Upper Peru and rose to the rank of lieutenant colonel. Macacha Güemes also actively collaborated in the enterprises of her brother Martín Miguel.

Irreversible Changes

The revolution generated immediate social, political, cultural, and economic changes. Because of the ideals it brought into play and the participation of the plebeian sectors, a rapid process of democratization ensued. The lower classes (at least those who were free and male) gained access to rights they did not previously have, such as the right to participate in the *cabildos abiertos* and in the general elections. For rural peasants, who had never had any political influence or channels of participation, it was an absolute novelty. Whether by voting or by mobilizing in the streets or in the militias, the plebs gained an indispensable place in politics that they would never again lose.

The hostility toward the Spanish monarchs and "bosses," combined with the value that egalitarianism and popular sovereignty had acquired, made republicanism an inevitable choice. As in all of Spanish America, the republic would make its way in a world that was still inclined toward monarchy. Of course, it would also have its own "bosses." But these changes helped ensure that they were a new type of leader. The old elites—the colonial bureaucracies—were quickly replaced with a political class that drew heavily from the wealthier sectors, but not always and not necessarily. In a period marked by a long war and upheavals of all kinds, this new leadership also emerged from the ranks of those who were noted for their military skills and their ability to mobilize broad support, including from the popular classes. It was a strictly political (or political-military) leadership that occasionally confronted the wealthy elites to demand funds and contributions that they were reluctant to give.

Revolution! The End of the Colonial Order

Along with all these changes, the "sacred dogma of equality," as Moreno described it (or the federalist "Ain't nobody better'n nobody"), became a highly valued ambition. It was in these years that equality before the law was established and, with it, the end of the *casta* system. Of course, discrimination continued on a daily basis, and there was no lack of state violence against nonwhites, but there was no longer any official ethnic hierarchy or racial segregation backed by specific laws, like those that would persist in countries such as the United States for another century and a half.

The language of the revolution permeated throughout in those years, creating a common vocabulary that accompanied and gave meaning to an experience that at the same time unified. *Liberty*, *equality*, *independence*, and *federation* were some of the new key words. *Pueblo* was another, with that expansive use that was sliding toward its modern sense: the political subject consisting of all free males. That subject, however, was not yet the *pueblo argentino*, or "Argentine people." Everyone claimed to fight for their "homeland," but during that period, as in colonial times, the word still referred to one's birthplace. You could be Cordoban, Tucumano, Mendocino, or Porteño but not yet "Argentine." At the same time, it was a politicized "homeland" that went beyond one's birthplace: it was tied to the nation formed by all those born in the Americas who were fighting the royalists. There was a "we" in the revolution.

From very early on, this revolutionary political community invented ceremonies, celebrations, and emblems to strengthen its cohesion. From 1811 onward, the Fiestas Mayas (May Festivities) were celebrated with great enthusiasm by the people every May 25 (later, the Fiestas Julias were added to mark the anniversary of the declaration of independence in July). In 1812, for the first time, General Manuel Belgrano raised a blue-and-white flag to distinguish his troops, possibly based on the colors of the house of Bourbon. The following year, the Assembly of the Year XIII established the use of the emblem that has become the national coat of arms, with a design copied from one used by the Jacobins in France, and commissioned a "patriotic march" that would later become the National Anthem.

In short, the experience of the revolution and the war had connected people from worlds that were not previously connected: poor white people, Black people, and indigenous people mixed with officials from the "respectable" classes, united in their common opposition to the royalists. Undoubtedly, that initial "we," that first political community, would play a fundamental role in the later emergence of an "Argentine we"—despite the fact that internal divisions were already evident at the time, such as the strong anti-Porteñism that surfaced in the provinces (a correlate of the obstinate Porteñism of the Porteños).

The revolution produced significant cultural changes as well. In 1810, the only printing press in the region ended up in the hands of the patriots, who put it to feverish use. The printed word began to circulate profusely for the first time in the Río de la Plata region. In fact, there was more circulation of printed matter there at the time than in any other region in Latin America. Political leaders, seeking to reach the lower classes, expressly instructed that materials be read aloud to the illiterate, who were the overwhelming majority. Ordinary people participated in print culture, read or had the gazettes read to them, and used them to justify their demands or to define their loyalties. It was the first encounter between the printed letter and the oral world of the popular classes. This encounter would have many consequences in the future, but to begin with, it gave birth to a surprising cultural manifestation in the Río de la Plata area. It was called "gaucho poetry" and was the first literary expression with a distinctively local tone.

Its first known creator was Bartolomé Hidalgo. A Montevidean of modest origins and the son of Porteños, he formed part of the Artiguist movement. In his writings, there was always a gaucho speaking in verse in the first-person singular to present his views on current affairs through *cielitos* (a form of popular dance music at the time) or in dialogue with another character. Hidalgo published his poems in print, but they were written in an oral style using the rural speech typical of the Río de la Plata region, with its distorted versions of standard Castilian Spanish. In other words, his works were narrated by a gaucho in a plebeian style, addressing an audience that was also of the popular classes. It was quite a strong position to take: it meant defending the local and the plebeian and challenging the authority of the colonizers' language. Moreover, Hidalgo's characters supposedly channeled the voice of the people: the first gaucho poems he produced reflected enthusiasm for the revolution, while the last, from the early 1820s, revealed frustration and disenchantment with its unfulfilled promises.

Although Hidalgo and other lesser-known poets were part of the lettered world, they combined the knowledge they gleaned from their education with the oral traditions of the *payadores* (bards) and the songs sung by the poor countrymen who fought against the royalists. The gaucho genre therefore emerged at a crossroads between the "cultured" world, which descended in search of popular support, and the voices of the people that made themselves heard within the revolutionary climate. The voice of the people and the defense of a figure such as the previously despised gaucho thus filtered into the birth of a national literature, with the mediation of educated writers. There is every indication that these features are what enabled gaucho poetry to reach an audience of modest means, who listened to it read by others in *pulperías*, staging posts, and markets, and sometimes even memorized it. There was nothing comparable at the time in Latin America. This literature with local color appeared in the Río de la Plata region before it did elsewhere and well before anything like a national "cultured" literature existed. What is remarkable is that it did so entwined with the plebeian voice and politics. This would have profound consequences in the subsequent development of Argentine culture.

Finally, there were the economic changes, which were dramatic. The loss of Upper Peru meant nothing less than the complete disintegration of an economy that, up to that point, had been centered on Potosí's silver mines. Silver accounted for 80 percent of Buenos Aires' exports until 1810. Salta and Jujuy had been almost entirely focused on producing for the Potosí market, which was also an important destination for the rest of the country's production. All of that suddenly disappeared.

The war also had a devastating effect for several other reasons: it required that productive workers be sent to the front lines, it imposed extraordinary levies and taxes on merchants, and it decimated livestock (especially in the northwest and the littoral provinces).

As often happens in wars, the destruction of wealth had a paradoxically positive effect on its distribution. Merchants, landowners, and cattle ranchers, forced to finance the war effort, suffered heavy losses. The popular classes provided the most valuable contribution as cannon fodder. But those who did not lose their lives had access to military salaries, while the scarcity of labor kept wages high. The independence period thus saw a decrease in inequality and a somewhat more egalitarian distribution of wealth, accompanied by greater political openness and the relative democratization of social relations.

At the same time, these economic changes led to increased inequality between regions. Without Potosí, the Buenos Aires customs office became the main source of resources and stimulating free trade became a financial necessity. This naturally reinforced the shift toward the Atlantic that the economy had already witnessed in late colonial times. And of course, this benefited the Porteños more than the inhabitants of the interior. During this period, the population of Buenos Aires grew, while that of the rest of the country stagnated (or declined, in the case of Santa Fe). The provincial governments, for their part, would become increasingly dependent on the Buenos Aires treasury.

In addition, the shift toward the Atlantic and the war with the Spanish consolidated Great Britain's position as the new commercial hub. Britain established itself as a supplier of manufactured goods and, before long, as a consumer of the main export as well, which at the time was still leather. British merchants and diplomats gained considerable influence during this period, which weak local governments had little chance of circumventing. Cotton cloth and other goods from Britain became important in Buenos Aires, although they had not yet undermined the artisanal products of the interior, still protected by the cost of transport. In any case, the new reality would soon generate tensions among the Porteño elites, proponents of free trade, and their counterparts in the provinces. Therefore, while the ties with the international market created new economic possibilities for the region, they also generated a harmful influx that deepened regional imbalances, social differences, and political disagreements.

Seeking Order in the Midst of Fragmentation

Fearing popular unrest and tired of the war, pro-independence leaders sought to bring a close to the revolutionary phase as soon as possible. Enthusiasm for the end of Spanish tutelage was tempered by the fear of plebeian political activism. Indeed, the statute promulgated by the triumvirate in 1811 proclaimed the need to impose "the rule of law" in order to control "popular impulsiveness." Viewed in this light, it appears that it was not a matter of legislation *by* or *for* the people: confronting each other as if they were enemies, on one side was the law and, on the other, the presence of "the popular." At the same time, the civil and military authorities had also become used to resorting to insubordination when they did not agree with the decisions of leadership. The colonial order had collapsed and there was an urgent need to establish a new one in its place. The Congress of Tucumán in 1816 declared "the end of the Revolution, the beginning of order." Yet the year 1820 marked the failure of all attempts to generate order. The collapse of authority left a fragmented territory, devoid of shared institutions, with commercial ties that were not very solid, barely connected by the memory of having once formed part of the same viceroyalty. There was also an incipient sense of belonging that remained after having fought a triumphant revolution. But for the moment, it was embodied in an armed and rebellious population that it would be very hard to regain control of.

Since it had proven impossible at the central level, order first began to take hold at the provincial level. After 1820, each province became self-administered and attempted to establish its own legal, fiscal, and political order. They all chose representative and republican systems, but at this stage their outcomes were very different. Entre Ríos suffered acute and chronic instability. In contrast, neighboring Corrientes was a model of order. The majority alternated between these two extremes, and there was no shortage of factional confrontations. In general, the centralization that had not been achieved on an overall scale nevertheless progressed internally. After 1820, all the provinces abolished the cabildos in their cities and replaced them with legislatures representing the entire territory; rural space took on greater importance at the expense of urban space.

The 1820s and subsequent decades were dominated by powerful provincial caudillos. Their power was based on their ability to establish personal loyalties, a closeness to the people, and military skills. Many of them had headed militias, and most came from the wealthy classes (although there were also some of plebeian origin). The great majority supported the federalist cause, but there were also some with centralist ideas. José Félix Aldao in Mendoza, Juan Felipe Ibarra in Santiago del Estero, Facundo Quiroga in La Rioja, Juan Bautista Bustos in Córdoba, Alejandro Heredia in Tucumán, Estanislao López in Santa Fe, and Juan Manuel de Rosas in Buenos Aires would play leading roles in the years that followed. Although some of them had considerable personal power, it did not necessarily come at the expense of law and institutions: on the contrary, the caudillos themselves helped forge institutional structures in a land that still lacked them. And although they defended provincial autonomies, they never abandoned the hope of achieving some type of formal interprovincial order. Convening a constituent congress was still an option, and the provinces insisted that Buenos Aires should not reap all the benefits of international trade simply because it had the good fortune of being a port. For the caudillos of the littoral region, the free navigation of the rivers was a persistent demand.

Within this context, Buenos Aires was in a unique situation. With customs under their control, the local elites focused on developing the province, momentarily ignoring the problems of the other regions. A so-called Partido del Orden (Party of Order), liberal in orientation, united the leadership that had the most support from the upper classes and came to power. One of the most prominent leaders within its ranks was Bernardino Rivadavia, who promoted a series of deep reforms that laid the foundations for a state apparatus and an economy focused on livestock exports. Through a law passed under Rivadavia in 1822, the state offered long-term leases to enormous tracts of land at very low prices, contributing to the strengthening of a class of powerful landowners, which from that point on would have an undeniable influence. Policies were also implemented to attract immigrant settlers but with little success. From this period on, the Porteño upper class focused mainly on cattle ranching to export hides and to a lesser extent on production in *saladeros* (meat-salting plants), activities in which Buenos Aires replaced a ruined littoral region. These factors all generated a greater interest in land ownership, which gradually ceased to be a cheap and abundant resource.

In 1822, at the government's initiative, a consortium of local and British merchants created the first bank in Latin America, the Banco de Descuentos de Buenos Aires, which printed its own paper money to replace Peruvian silver as the circulating currency (in those years, London bills of exchange were also used for commercial transactions, a reflection of the importance that Britain had acquired).

In 1824, the province signed its first loan with the London firm Baring Brothers in order to finance infrastructure works on the port. The loan was taken during negotiations with the British Empire to recognize the independence of the United Provinces, which was crucial considering the Spanish threat to reconquer the region. Shortly thereafter, London would grant recognition in exchange for a free-trade agreement in its favor. The loan turned out to be ruinous: the works announced were never carried out and the interest accumulated, generating a debt eight times greater than the funds received, which would take the country eighty years to finish paying. The Partido del Orden formed an alliance between liberal politicians, the commercial and ranching sectors, and imperialist financial and geopolitical interests that would prove to be long-lasting.

At the political level, the reforms were even more profound. The cabildo, which had played a leading role up to that point, was abolished in 1821; the new legislature no longer had any other institution overshadowing it. Due to a ruling issued that same year, its members would be chosen through elections: half of them would be elected by the city—which gave weight to the insubordinate urban plebs—but the other half would come from the countryside, where the major landowners had the greatest influence. Thus balanced, the legislators, among other things, were in charge of electing the governor. Due to a law passed in 1821, all free men could vote in the elections without restrictions based on skin color or social position (although they had to be landowners to run for office). It was the first law of its kind in Latin America and was implemented at a time when elections in much of Europe did not exist at all or were still reserved for property owners. This reflected the important position the lower classes had gained in politics. Simultaneously with Buenos Aires, Corrientes also granted broad civil rights, and in subsequent years the remaining provinces (except for Córdoba and Tucumán) would follow suit.

It would be inaccurate, however, to claim that it was a democratically inspired law or the sign of an unwavering commitment to the popular will. Not long before, in 1817, the Congress of Tucumán had established that the vote would exclude the poorest, and new steps were taken in the same direction in 1826. "Democracy" was a term that the elites at the time used in a negative sense to refer to popular assemblies, the practice of public debates in the streets, and collective action typical of the lower classes. Although risky, having them vote for politicians and delegating certain decisions to them was a way of deactivating this "democratic threat." Moreover, there were many ways to control voters: voting was neither individual nor secret, and justices of the peace and commissaries often led large groups of people to the polling stations to express their preferences in public, recorded by head count.

Along with the political changes, there was a whole series of legal, financial, and ecclesiastical reforms. Among other things, freedom of worship was ensured, public education was encouraged, and, in 1821, the University of Buenos Aires was founded. Rivadavia also established a series of regulations aimed at disciplining the populace. Military reforms reduced the importance of the militias and reoriented them to the defense of the frontiers.

The Partido del Orden's ability to win elections would soon be challenged by the creation of an opposition group, headed by Manuel Dorrego, which began gaining popular support. In order to seduce the electorate, Dorrego dressed as the lower classes did, took up some of their demands, and criticized foreigners and the upper classes, which resonated strongly with the Porteño plebs. In contrast, Rivadavia's group was perceived as having a close relationship with the wealthy classes. The ultimate displacement of the Partido del Orden would come during a new attempt to achieve national unity, something the British had demanded in order to grant the desired recognition. The government of Buenos Aires summoned the provinces to a new constituent congress held in Buenos Aires in late 1824. Among other things, this congress established the position of president of the nation and in early 1826 chose the person who would have the honor of being the first, none other than Rivadavia. Inevitably, the question of the relationship between the central power and the provinces resurfaced. It was not only the Porteño representatives, who held sway from the outset, that supported the idea of a liberal and centralist system; it was also supported by several representatives from the interior, who saw it as a way to curb the power of their local caudillos. During the congress, it was evident that there were already two parties, the Unitarians and the Federalists, destined to face off in bitter confrontations. Both had supporters in the interior as well as in Buenos Aires.

However, the tensions did not end there. In 1825, the congress decided to accept representatives of the Banda Oriental, sparking an unavoidable war with Brazil, which saw it as its own territory. The war, which lasted until 1827, generated discontent in various sectors. Additionally, Rivadavia began to encounter resistance from the upper classes of his province (and incidentally the lower classes as well) when he supported the idea of nationalizing the city of Buenos Aires, which would mean that the Porteños would lose control of customs. Finally, there was the question of political rights. The Unitarians proposed that the poorest should not have the right to vote, something the Federalists strongly opposed. The constitution was finally approved in December 1826; it established the representative, republican, and unitary form of government and adopted the Republic of Argentina as its new name, replacing the United Provinces of South America. It was the first time that Argentina was used as a designation for the entire country. From the Latin *argentum* (silver), "Argentine" had originally been used to refer only to the population adjacent to the Río de la Plata. The fact that it was now extended to the entire country was indicative of the influence that the Porteños had in the congress.

Not surprisingly, there was growing discontent in the provinces. Since 1825, Riojan caudillo Facundo Quiroga had become the focal point of a realignment of loyalties in the interior, dissatisfied with Rivadavia and his centralism. These included Cuyo, Córdoba, Santiago del Estero, and of course La Rioja, and Quiroga sought to expand this outward to the littoral region. Due in part to his influence, the provinces gradually withdrew support from the new president and almost all ended up rejecting the draft of the constitution, which was never enacted. At the same time, in 1827, Dorrego, backed by the Federal Party, won the election in Buenos Aires and became the new governor, thus displacing the Partido del Orden. The coup de grâce for Rivadavia was the inept way in which his envoy negotiated peace with Brazil. The terms they agreed to represented an utter humiliation for Argentina, which in mid-1827 led to the resignation of the short-lived president. With this, the position of president was eliminated, along with the congress. As in 1820, all central power collapsed and the provinces were left to their own devices. It would be the last attempt at unity until 1853.

After the collapse, a peace agreement was signed with Brazil in 1828 under the terms proposed by the British Empire, which demanded that the Banda Oriental be an independent country. Two years later, the Banda Oriental enacted its first constitution and adopted the name Estado Oriental del Uruguay (Eastern State of Uruguay).

The Rise of Rosas and the Federal Pact

Displaced from the government, the Porteño Unitarians took advantage of the return of the army that had been fighting in Brazil to retake power through a coup d'état. With the support of that party's leaders, on December 1, 1828, a military mobilization dissolved the legislature and General Juan Lavalle illegally proclaimed himself the new governor. Dorrego was imprisoned and then executed a few days later by order of the de facto governor and at the instigation of the Unitarians, who were wary of the support he enjoyed among the popular classes. The assassination caused a commotion throughout the country: up to that point, politics had been relatively free of this type of violence, at least at the level of the top leadership.

Unexpectedly, the popular indignation triggered by the execution brought the rural lower classes, a previously inconspicuous actor in the province of Buenos Aires, onto the scene. An unprecedented spontaneous uprising of farm workers, shepherds, and laborers, along with indigenous peoples, galvanized the Buenos Aires countryside. They fought mainly in *montoneras* (informal rebel armies), guerrilla warfare style, and managed to corner Lavalle's army. It was the first major rural uprising and completely redefined the terms of Buenos Aires politics. The rebels claimed commander Juan Manuel de Rosas as their leader and the only heir to Dorrego's popularity. Retreating, Lavalle agreed to step down. After a brief interim, in December 1829 the legislature almost unanimously elected Rosas as the new governor, granting him emergency powers to bring the unstable situation under control (something that previous governments had also been granted, albeit for a limited time). He was hailed as the Restorer of Laws.

Rosas was a powerful estanciero (ranch owner), but he enjoyed popularity thanks to the close relationship he had established with the rural lower classes through his position as campaign commander. Additionally, he was well acquainted with the indigenous peoples of the area and spoke the Pampa language. Catapulted to the position of governor, he also cultivated the sympathy of the urban plebs and the favor of the livestock exporters, whose economic prosperity he favored. With support from these sectors, he would become the strongman of Buenos Aires politics for the next twenty years, the first period of anything resembling stability since the May Revolution.

After the failure of Lavalle's coup, the Unitarians lost all ground in Buenos Aires, though not in the rest of the country. Another veteran of the war with Brazil, General José María Paz, managed to gain a stronghold in Córdoba in 1829 and, from there, challenged the federalist coalition headed by Facundo Quiroga. Paz, a brilliant military strategist, successfully repelled the attacks of the Riojan caudillo that year and the following one. Through alliances and the conviction of his troops, Paz managed to assemble a Unitarian Liga del Interior (League of the Interior) that soon controlled Mendoza, Catamarca, Santiago del Estero, and even San Juan and La Rioja. It briefly looked as if Quiroga were in decline. However, in response to this situation, in January 1831 Rosas and the littoral provinces signed a Federal Pact that established a series of joint obligations and made a commitment to undertaking national organization as soon as possible. Agreement in hand, they launched an attack on Paz. From their perspective, there would be neither stability nor organization as long as Unitarianism survived. The country was thus divided into two leagues, Unitarian and Federalist, each determined to eliminate the other.

With the backing of the littoral region, Quiroga recovered part of the territory he had lost. By a stroke of luck, in 1831 the allies managed to take Paz prisoner without having defeated him. Without its leader, the Unitarian league collapsed. The federalists thus achieved a national hegemony centered on three figures: Quiroga, Rosas, and Estanislao López from Santa Fe. One by one, other provinces joined the Federal Pact and national order seemed within reach. However, Rosas always found some excuse to refuse to honor his commitment to convene a constituent assembly, something his colleagues kept demanding. With the control of customs and the management of foreign relations delegated to him by the provinces, he was in no hurry to submit to a constitution.

The two caudillos who could compete with Rosas soon disappeared from the political scene. In February 1835, Facundo Quiroga was ambushed and assassinated in Barranca Yaco, Córdoba. The crime shook the entire interprovincial balance of power and ended up favoring Rosas. Alejandro Heredia, governor of Tucumán, tried to organize a new northern alliance, but he was assassinated in 1838. That same year López also died, in his case of natural causes. With all potential obstacles removed, Rosas began controlling the national scene informally from his base in Buenos Aires, intervening in the affairs of the other provinces in numerous ways, from weaving ties of personal loyalty to threats, intrigues, and even military force, if necessary. From that point on, he enjoyed the powers of a national ruler but without the burdens or constraints of a legal framework.

The Federal Pact thus became the cornerstone of a de facto confederation that functioned until 1853 without a constitution or central institutions. It should be noted, however, that not all of Rosas's achievements were based on his political and military maneuvers. By late 1835, the Porteño caudillo had passed the Customs Law, which clearly reflected the interests of the Buenos Aires cattle-ranching sectors but also imposed import tariffs that protected certain products from some provinces as well as Porteño artisans. The interprovincial balance he achieved was also the result of a nascent compromise between free trade and protectionism.

This precarious order came, however, at a terrible cost. The quarrel between Unitarians and Federalists unleashed a civil war that would have long-lasting effects. Local politics became extremely factional and intolerant. Both parties developed a whole series of ideas, expressions, and epithets to demonize the other and deny each other legitimacy. The press and Unitarian proclamations described the Federalists as ferocious "hordes of savages" who were "thirsty for human blood." Adopting terms the Europeans used to justify their colonial domination of Asia and Africa, in the 1830s the Unitarians introduced the idea that they were fighting for "civilization," while their adversaries represented "barbarism" and should therefore be crushed without hesitation. The Federalists were no different: for them the Unitarians were "savages," "impious," and "unclean." Both sides were constantly shouting "Death to . . ." at the other. And it was not just a matter of words. The conflict took the war to areas that had not seen it during the independence period, such as Catamarca, La Rioja, Córdoba, and Cuyo. After Dorrego's execution, political violence became perpetual and took on horrifying tones, with forms of extreme cruelty on the battlefields, including hacking enemies to death, slitting their throats, and even skinning them alive. Both sides excelled in such atrocities. Even once the war between the Unitarians and Federalists ended, international conflicts and later challenges to Rosas's power prolonged the warfare almost continuously until 1847. The hatred professed by his enemies even led them to support military incursions by European governments with clear imperialist objectives just to see Rosas overthrown.

The Rosas Governments

The Unitarian league was not the only challenge Rosas had to overcome in order to assert his power. His years in government were marked by conflicts and major disagreements, both at home and abroad.

When Rosas finished his first term as governor, the legislature offered him a second one but without the emergency powers he had enjoyed during the first. This is because within federalism itself there was strong resistance to the concentration of power the caudillo desired. Faced with this scenario, Rosas preferred to reject the offer and focus instead on strengthening his power outside of office. In 1832, he promoted and personally led the so-called Expedition to the Desert, an extensive military campaign into indigenous territories aimed at ensuring the security of the borderlands, something of great interest to the estancieros, who supported the enterprise with funding. The offensive was a combination of military threat and peaceful negotiation with the frontier population and was highly successful. Rosas managed to secure an important stretch of productive land for the white settlers and gained great prestige for himself.

During his absence from the city, however, things were not as simple as he had hoped. His successor turned out to be less compliant than anticipated, and a group of Federalists organized a faction opposing Rosas that gained strength in the legislature. Rosas once again appealed to popular mobilization. While he was still away on his campaign, his supporters founded the Sociedad Popular (Popular Society), an organization led by his wife, Encarnación Ezcurra. The new association was dedicated to intimidating Rosas's opponents in the legislature and beyond, especially through its armed wing, the famous Mazorca, a clandestine force linked to the police that would later sow terror among his opponents. (While this was taking place, in January 1833 Great Britain took advantage of the situation to occupy the Malvinas Islands, without the government of Buenos Aires able to do anything but present a diplomatic protest.)

The legislature again offered the governorship to Rosas, who again rejected it unless he was granted emergency powers, which most federal representatives

Revolution! The End of the Colonial Order

refused to do. Their commitment to the separation of powers finally faltered with the news of Facundo Quiroga's assassination. Fearing another tragic period of chaos and civil war, the legislature proposed that Rosas assume "the sum of public power." He was offered a five-year term during which he would have not only executive but also legislative and even judicial powers. Rosas accepted (this offer-rejection sequence would become a sort of ritual in the years to come) but decided to ratify his designation with another unprecedented political event: he immediately organized a plebiscite in which nine thousand voters—an impressive number for the time—declared themselves in favor of his appointment. His legitimacy was established in the streets and at the ballot box as much as through the institutions.

That was the beginning of the authoritarian tendency that Rosas's governments would acquire. While it is true that he was always legally appointed to his post—elections for the legislature continued to be held, along with frequent plebiscites to reaffirm his popularity—at the same time, election after election he succeeded in introducing loyal representatives into the legislature until it was drained of any real power. Rosas also kept a close eye on the appointment of judges and their rulings. The press was subjected to strict controls, and at the same time an important official propaganda machine was set in motion. Opponents were persecuted and many were forced to go into exile in Entre Ríos or Montevideo. Public life became strongly factional. The general public was compelled to display visual signs of their allegiance, such as the *divisa punzó*, a red ribbon worn as a symbol of loyalty to the Federal Party. "Long live the Holy Federation! Death to the savage Unitarians!" was a slogan of mandatory repetition, even after the disappearance of the Unitarian league.

Given these characteristics, Rosas's regime was not an archaic-style personal dictatorship but rather a modern republican authoritarian regime. It shared the styles and values of the republican politics of the time and was based on popular legitimacy expressed through elections and embodied in institutions. Of course, these were persistently manipulated. But there is no question that he enjoyed an actively mobilized popularity. Additionally, the corruptibility of the vote, the partisan takeover of institutions, the interventions in other provinces, and the limitations on the press did not prove to be exclusive to his government but rather were an enduring feature of Argentine politics.

The worst moments of authoritarianism were those in which Rosas had to face real threats, the most serious of which occurred between 1837 and 1842. The first of these challenges was a war against the Peruvian–Bolivian Confederation over the city of Tarija. This was followed in 1838 by the blockade of Buenos Aires' port by a French fleet. France demanded that it too be given the commercial status of "most favored nation" that had been granted to Great Britain in 1825. But the conflict became enmeshed with domestic politics and party struggles in Uruguay, since the Unitarian opposition in Montevideo sought to take advantage of the context and promote an alliance between the French, the Uruguayan Partido Colorado, and other parties in Argentina to overthrow Rosas, who in turn supported the Uruguayan Partido Blanco from across the Río de la Plata.

An initial attack led in 1839 by the governor of Corrientes was quickly defeated. That same year Juan Lavalle, exiled at the time in Montevideo, received financing from the French for a new offensive and advanced on Buenos Aires with an army. When he realized that his troops were not arousing the popular sympathy he had expected, he retreated, fearing he would lose the battle. At the same time, there was an attempted rebellion in the province's south, where groups of landowners had armed a militia of laborers and were determined to rise up against Rosas. The Libres del Sur (Freemen of the South), as they called themselves, were easily defeated by the frontier militia with the help of indigenous groups. Rosas concluded this first series of challenges by negotiating an agreement with France to lift the blockade in exchange for giving French residents the same privileges as the British.

During those years in Buenos Aires, there was a group of young intellectuals who did not pose a threat as significant as those that Rosas had defeated but who did provide powerful and enduring narratives and arguments against him. From the early 1830s, they had begun to coalesce around Esteban Echeverría, who had returned from a five-year sojourn in Paris with forward-looking ideas. They were known as the New Generation or the Generation of 1837 and included figures such as Vicente Fidel López, Juan Bautista Alberdi, and Juan María Gutiérrez. Other young people joined this initial nucleus, including Bartolomé Mitre and Domingo Faustino Sarmiento. Influenced by European Romanticism, they were noted for their attacks on Rosas, although initially they had been very critical of Rivadavia's government as well, which they accused of attempting to copy the policies of European liberalism without the slightest attention to local realities.

The group combined admiration for progressive and democratic European ideas with a marked skepticism regarding the capacity of the criollo lower classes to live up to them. They declared themselves democratic but at the same time called for the suppression or limitation of universal suffrage, since for them the lower classes were not yet ready to exercise full citizenship. In

Revolution! The End of the Colonial Order

their opinion, prematurely allowing the lower classes the right to vote in 1821 had ended up destroying the Unitarians and had paved the way for Rosas's tyranny. The New Generation believed in the need for intellectual tutelage over political life and the "sovereignty of Reason," which was none other than the government of the most capable. In addition to promoting European ideas, they campaigned to Europeanize local customs on all fronts, for instance, through the magazine *La Moda* edited by Alberdi. By 1838, they operated as a clandestine political agitation group, for which many would end up in exile.

In partnership with longtime Unitarians, the young men of the New Generation participated in a new challenge to Rosas's regime. In 1840, the Northern League was formed, uniting the governments of Tucumán, Salta, Jujuy, Catamarca, and La Rioja against Rosas, but Rosas launched a military campaign against them in 1841 and 1842, putting an end to their vagaries. Also in 1840, the tireless General Paz tried to march again on the littoral region, but by 1842 Rosas had managed not only to gain control of the area but also to make a decisive advance on Uruguayan politics in support of his ally, Manuel Oribe. By 1842, the confederation was firmly in Rosas's hands and would remain so for the following ten years.

In the turbulent period before the calm, between 1840 and 1842, the Mazorca unleashed a veritable wave of terror in Buenos Aires. At least forty people had their throats slit in their homes during the first year and at least as many in the last. Many more were beaten or tortured. It is not clear if Rosas himself gave the orders or if the organization acted autonomously, but the government certainly did nothing to impede it. Once calm was achieved in 1842, the Mazorca's activities ceased and from that moment on tranquility reigned. Some exiles were able to return and Buenos Aires resumed its intense social life.

Nevertheless, Rosas had one more challenge to overcome. In April 1845, allied British and French fleets initiated a new naval blockade of Buenos Aires to limit Rosas's interference in Uruguay and ensure the free navigation of the rivers up to Paraguay. In November, the Porteño troops vigorously fought the Battle of Vuelta de Obligado to prevent the invading ships from going up the Paraná River, but they ultimately lost. This victory for the foreigners, however, did not yield the desired results. The coastal populations along the river received the European traders with anything but sympathy. There were more than a few attacks that, along with the difficult navigation of the river, made trade uneconomical. As a result, Rosas was able to negotiate peace on terms that were not entirely unfavorable. France and Great Britain agreed to lift the blockade in 1848 with a promise from Rosas that he would not annex Uruguay but with the acceptance, on their part, that the navigation of the rivers was exclusively a local matter. Rosas emerged from the situation without appearing defeated and with the prestige of having put up a fight against powerful countries.

The years that followed were unusually calm. The country was pacified and in federal hands. The confederation functioned as a national order, even without having any central institutions. Not that everyone supported the Buenos Aires governor: opposition to Rosas was still strong in the interior. But for the moment the opposition had lost its ability to act. If the succession of conflicts in which Rosas had emerged victorious had demonstrated anything, it was the military superiority of the Buenos Aires armies, which in turn came from the province's incomparably superior economic resources. This was to have a decisive influence in the years to come.

The establishment of order fostered significant growth in the economy. Under the aegis of Rosas, Buenos Aires intensified its orientation toward the livestock industry. His efforts to push back the Indian frontier and his replacement of the long-term leases promoted by Rivadavia with the large-scale privatization of fiscal lands led to an increase in the creation of large estancias, counterbalanced by land donation policies that benefited shepherds and farm laborers of modest means (by the late 1830s, half of the families living in the Buenos Aires countryside had their own holdings). In Rosas's last years in power, livestock farming also turned toward sheep breeding for wool export. This was a very prosperous period for Buenos Aires, and it was finally during these years that livestock exports managed to compensate for the deficit that the loss of Upper Peru had generated.

The peace under Rosas also allowed the economy of other provinces to recover. In the mid-1820s, economic trade with Chile and Peru was reestablished, which created opportunities for areas such as Salta and Mendoza. From the 1840s, Entre Ríos and Corrientes and, to a lesser extent, Santa Fe recovered their prosperity, always in conjunction with livestock farming. Tucumán found a market for its artisanal products in the littoral region. However, there were no major changes in the modes of production, which remained similar to those of colonial times. Although the use of forced labor declined, it was not an abrupt decline: to alleviate the lack of manpower, in 1831 Rosas reopened the indirect slavery trade for two years; additionally, enslaved people who had been purchased in Brazil as minors during the war with that country were put to work as *libertos* (freedmen), who in this region lived in a condition of semislavery until they reached adulthood. Some forms of non-free indigenous labor also persisted. Haciendas and estancias were still organized in the traditional way and continued to coexist with a varied universe of small- and medium-sized producers and, in several areas, with subsistence farming as well. The popular classes (primarily through the labor of women) continued producing textiles and selling them to merchants. Their handmade wool fabrics and indigenous ponchos were still marketed even in Buenos Aires, where cotton ponchos manufactured in Manchester were already widely available.

The focus on livestock exports continued to exacerbate the imbalance between the littoral region and the northwest. During this period, the former surpassed the latter in terms of population, largely due to the internal migration of lower-class families seeking better opportunities and, to a lesser extent, to an influx of European immigrants. The mobile and multiethnic nature of the littoral population accentuated the more open and egalitarian features of its society compared to the more traditional and hierarchical society of the northwest.

The Popular Classes, Politics, and Culture during the Rosas Era

The pursuit of order led to greater pressure from the elites on the popular classes. In Buenos Aires and the littoral region, more controls were placed on so-called vagrants: the requirement to circulate with a *papeleta de conchabo* (proof of employment) was extended even further and the justices of the peace—who were not career officials but "notable" *vecinos*—were given greater powers. Internal migrants (who tended to be mestizos or *pardos*) were the most adversely affected by this; having the fewest ties, they were the most vulnerable. At the same time, a stronger state apparatus was able to exert greater control over property: access to land was by formal contract of sale and there was less leeway for occupation without legal title or for slaughtering other people's livestock. Even so, the effects of these disciplining efforts were limited. Manpower remained scarce, which kept wages at relatively high levels. In fact, during Rosas's era there was a significant increase in purchasing power. There is every indication that the living conditions of the poorest improved (in part due to public policies but also because the export of leather resulted in abundant meat at a low price in the local market). During these years, the trend continued toward greater equity in income distribution and of the wealth the revolution had produced—and along with it, the independence and haughtiness of the laborers that so irritated the landowners. Porteño artisans were impacted by the introduction of imported goods, but the 1835 Customs Law provided some protections for them as well.

In the rest of the provinces, on the other hand, the situation was different: life for the general population did not improve, wealth remained in the hands of the privileged groups, and efforts at disciplining the population were more successful. In Salta and Jujuy, for example, Güemes's death was followed by a veritable revenge of the upper classes, which gradually eliminated the concessions that the gauchos had won at the time of independence. Nevertheless, open expressions of popular resistance, mutinies of soldiers, desertion from the armies, and widespread forms of banditry persisted everywhere. Regardless of how much the provincial governments had been strengthened, there was still an archipelago of frontier zones where those in trouble with the law could take refuge.

For the indigenous peoples, the situation did not bring about any obvious improvements. The end of the *pueblos de indios* and ethnic authorities, along with increased pressure for property, often resulted in the loss of their communal lands. In the northeast, the end of the Artiguist experience meant a decline in the political power that the Guaraníes had gained. The white settlers advanced on them in military offensives that occasionally ended in massacres. The zone of the former missions was razed to the ground and many villages were abandoned.

For the indigenous peoples who remained autonomous, these were also turbulent times. In the Chaco, they took advantage of the disputes among the white settlers and managed to retake land and livestock from them. In the 1830s, the Mocovíes besieged the Santa Fe frontier until a peace agreement was brokered with them. The entire Patagonian region right up to the border with Córdoba was the scene of various conflicts between Mapuche, Tehuelche, and Ranquel factions, and between them and the white settlers, whose advances on the land were met with *malones* or raids, some of them devastating. Rosas's campaign and his proposal of dialogue and negotiations was a turning point. Several of the most important caciques, such as Catriel and Cachul, became allies and helped consolidate peaceful trade. They came to depend on the livestock and goods that the Buenos Aires government gave them and participated in political life by supporting the Federalists whenever necessary. Other groups, in contrast, maintained their autonomy and negotiated their occasional collaboration with the government, such as those under Calfucurá, the powerful cacique of the Pampas. Still others remained hostile, such as the Ranqueles of Yanquetruz. Mendoza and Buenos Aires launched a joint military campaign against them in 1833 (in which allied Indians also fought), resulting finally in pacification.

Meanwhile, Afro-Porteños gained an unprecedented prominence in public life during these years. From the 1820s onward, they founded their own "African societies" based on their respective origins in Africa in order to provide mutual aid and organize social events. Gathering for dances and festivities, they developed their own cultural expressions, such as *candombe*, which combined music, dance, and religious rituals. In Rosas's time, they were intensely involved in politics. The governor protected them and won their support. He attended some of their celebrations along with his family, and in 1838 he allowed them to participate with their drums in the Fiestas Mayas and in Carnival, which the "respectable" classes found appalling. It is even possible that the Black servants working for the families of the opposition acted as a network of informants at the service of the government.

The political position of the popular classes was changing rather ambivalently. There is no doubt that they were subjected to greater pressures from the elites and lost a certain amount of the autonomy, radicalism, and spontaneity that had characterized their participation during the revolution. But it is no less true that, at least in Buenos Aires and other areas, they maintained the ability to influence public policies through their participation in the Federal Party. The confrontation between the Unitarians and the Federalists reflected for the first time within a party system the dispute between the two visions of how to organize the country, as well as the class differences. The leaders of both parties clearly belonged to the wealthy sectors, and it would be unfair to say that the Unitarians completely lacked support from the lower classes, which they did have to some degree. Nevertheless, the Federalists cultivated a closeness to the plebeian and the rural spaces that their adversaries, identified from early on with urban interests and the "respectable" classes, did not manage to achieve. Dorrego, for example, warned his followers against the "aristocracy of money" and defended the popular vote when the Unitarians tried to restrict it. The Federalists also consistently sought to associate themselves with the "homeland" and denounced the Unitarians for their ties to foreign interests (which were quite evident in the case of Rivadavia, among others). Beyond the popular contempt for the "gringos," as the Europeans were known, there was an acknowledged distaste for the privileges they enjoyed—

such as being exempt from conscription and able to instead devote themselves to prospering in their private businesses—and for their ties to "bosses" and "dandies." The Federal Party connected well with these ideas, even in their more indirect manifestations, such as the defense of Catholicism (which was widely practiced by the lower classes) in the face of the Rivadavian policy of decreeing freedom of worship to accommodate foreigners, especially British Anglican merchants. And the inevitable association of Unitarianism with Porteño interests resonated strongly with the poor of the interior. The Unitarians unwittingly contributed to the recognition of their adversaries as allies of the plebeian world when they accused them of having the dregs of society as their base of support, as they did in response to Rosas's gestures toward the Afro-Porteños.

In order for federalism to take advantage of popular support—as it did—it had to channel plebeian aspirations, at least to some degree. Federalist caudillos, in those years, did not encourage the radicalization of the lower classes as Artigas or Güemes had done, but they did offer a channel for popular participation and addressed some of their demands. What the popular classes lost in autonomy was perhaps the cost they paid for the order that, in the end, they too craved after years of a grueling revolution. The case of Rosas is very illustrative in this sense: he came to power thanks to a spontaneous popular uprising, and from there he set out to channel the energy of this popular unrest toward the Federal Party. With the elimination of the Unitarians and dissidents, popular participation declined and the previously unruly Buenos Aires became calm. Rosas thus had a disciplining influence on the lower classes, a "merit" that even his worst detractors recognized. But the cost of this deactivation was paid in concessions embodied in some of the policies he was forced to adopt and in a federalist identity among the lower classes that would have repercussions for years after his downfall.

The tension embodied in this compromise was most evident when it came to culture. Rosista gazetteers capitalized greatly on gaucho poetry to mobilize support and excoriate their enemies, thereby reinforcing the legitimacy of the figure of the proud gaucho as the bearer of the truths of the Argentine people (and of plebeian speech as the way to express them). In the gazettes that Luis Pérez published in the 1830s, for example, in addition to supporting Rosas and attacking the Unitarians, the gaucho characters claimed to represent popular interests and opposed their voices to those of the city "doctors," ridiculing them. In Pérez's publications, Black voices were also given room to express their opinions, reflected in their own unique way of speaking. Thus, the plebeian voice, insubordinate and critical of the lettered classes—and obviously filtered through Pérez's pen—took center stage.

From that point on, the centrality of the plebeian voice was unavoidable. When the young writers of the Generation of 1837 set out to create a "cultured" national literature, they attempted to revive the figure of the gaucho, endowing it with romantic overtones distanced from politics. Given the overwhelming success of Pérez's gazettes, the Unitarians sought to emulate him and had their own gaucho writers—such as Hilario Ascasubi—who penned gaucho characters but depicted them as friends of the elite, doctors, and foreigners. They were much less successful. Whether they used gaucho poetry or not, the enemies of federalism encountered serious difficulties grappling with the ubiquity and legitimacy that plebeian speech had gained. When Esteban Echeverría wrote "El matadero" (The Slaughterhouse), arguably the first Argentine short story, he used it to demonize the lower classes, describing them as brutal, foul mouthed, and homicidal. For better or worse, as a mark of legitimacy or a threatening presence, the plebeian world and its tirades had taken center stage in the nascent national literature, much as they had in political life.

Finally, it should be noted that in this battle of words and printed texts that accompanied the confrontation between parties, even women had a voice, both real and fictional. In Pérez's gazettes, poor criollo women and Black women played a prominent role, discussing politics as much as men did. Furthermore, between 1830 and 1831 the Imprenta del Estado (State Printing House) in Buenos Aires published the first Argentine newspaper aimed at a female audience, featuring a defense of women's rights. It was called *La Aljaba* (The quiver) and was edited by Petrona Rosende.

3

The Great Transformation

The Expansion of the State and the Market in Argentina (1852–1912)

JUST WHEN Juan Manuel de Rosas appeared to have achieved undisputed power as the de facto ruler of the country, an unexpected coalition suddenly removed him from the scene. His supremacy had begun to irritate other federalist leaders; his interference was also upsetting to some in Uruguay and Brazil, where they did not take kindly to his efforts to regain influence over Paraguay. Justo José de Urquiza, the governor of Entre Ríos and, until then, one of Rosas's allies, launched the first challenge. His armies set out with support from Montevideo, the Empire of Brazil, Corrientes, and eventually Santa Fe. In the Battle of Caseros on February 3, 1852, Urquiza's army quickly defeated the Porteño forces. Rosas escaped and, with assistance from the British chargé d'affaires, sailed off into exile in Britain, where he lived out the rest of his days.

Plunged into confusion and devoid of authorities, the city of Buenos Aires witnessed a wave of looting that was only contained following the execution of at least two hundred people. Urquiza also contributed to the violence by shooting several officers of the enemy forces and hanging dozens of soldiers in the trees near Rosas's residence, to make the cost of disobedience clear. A short time later, the new authorities in Buenos Aires carried out yet more executions, this time of former members of the Mazorca. Urquiza became the new leader of the Federal Party and remained so until his death. The new hegemony had begun drenched in blood.

Urquiza quickly called for a constituent congress. But the initiative was complicated by a breakaway group that emerged, not coincidentally, in Buenos Aires. With the return of the exiles and the reconversion of several of those who had, until then, been Rosas's officials, a new political group formed rapidly. It was galvanized by the distrust they felt toward Urquiza, whose plans they saw as a threat to the autonomy of Buenos Aires. From early on, Valentín Alsina, a former Unitarian from Rivadavia's group, and Bartolomé Mitre, one of the young men of the New Generation, stood out in this new Partido de la Libertad (Freedom Party), as it quickly came to be known. Although they no longer believed in the possibility of a Unitarian system, they defined themselves as liberals and saw themselves as carrying on with Rivadavia's work. Due to their traumatic experience of Rosas's regime and the popularity that federalism continued to hold, it was a liberalism with a strong distrust of the lower classes and of popular sovereignty.

The opposition to Urquiza won the provincial legislative elections and a heated debate ensued: a decision had to be made as to whether to participate in the constituent assembly. This situation revealed the extent of the tension between the traditional meaning of the word *homeland* and the new one that was emerging. Vicente Fidel López, a politician who formed part of the New Generation, argued in favor of participating, declaring: "I love the people of Buenos Aires, where I was born, as much as anyone but I will raise my voice to declare that my homeland is the Argentine Republic and not Buenos Aires!" His vehemence was in vain. In September 1852, the legislature voted to reject the constituent assembly. Valentín Alsina became governor and Mitre the minister of internal affairs.

Things were not easy for the Porteño leaders. A rural uprising with broad popular support surrounded the city, demanding that the province join its "sister provinces" in their meeting to create a constitution, and Urquiza organized a naval blockade of the port. The city once again took advantage of the power of its incomparable finances and was able to resist for six months. In the meantime, it bribed enemy officers and soldiers until the threat was dispelled. The rural troops, discouraged by the lack of payment for their services, accepted the money offered by the Porteños and went home. A decisive victory was achieved when the commander of Urquiza's squadron deserted in exchange for five thousand ounces of gold paid by the Porteños, finally putting an end to the blockade.

While Buenos Aires was busy resisting the siege, the representatives of the remaining provinces had met in Santa Fe and, with remarkable speed, had agreed on the text of the new constitution, which was enacted on May 25, 1853. Thirteen provinces formally began the process of national organization without Buenos Aires. In the elections in November of that year, Urquiza became president of the nation and the city of Paraná was declared the provisional seat of government. In a highly symbolic gesture during a speech, Urquiza tore off the *divisa punzó* (a sign of loyalty to the Federal Party) and announced that from that point on the antagonisms between the Unitarians and Federalists were over. The ministers he chose were indeed from different parties. The Chamber of Deputies and the Senate were constituted in the same elections (the judiciary would take much longer to set up). Without access to revenues from the Buenos Aires Customs, Urquiza had very limited funds for the implementation of the state apparatus, which severely hampered progress. He made up for this lack of resources by borrowing abroad at very high rates. Nevertheless, he did make some progress with respect to institutional organization, and the one-time caudillo from Entre Ríos managed to pass the presidential sash on to his successor, Santiago Derqui from Córdoba. It was a peaceful transfer of power, a major turning point in Argentine politics.

Separated from the other provinces, Buenos Aires also claimed to represent Argentina and moved forward with the consolidation of its institutions. The nation, from its inception, was institutionally divided. Relations between the two sides were very tense. Buenos Aires encouraged the formation of like-minded liberal groups in the provinces, while at the same time Urquiza's government backed groups that sought to unseat the Buenos Aires liberals. The troops on both sides finally confronted each other in 1859 in the Battle of Cepeda, with a resounding victory for Urquiza. Buenos Aires was forced to sign a peace treaty in which it committed to joining the confederation. The agreement was endorsed in the meeting between President Derqui and Mitre, the new governor of Buenos Aires, at Urquiza's palace in Entre Ríos.

However, the disagreements resurfaced. In several provinces, the fighting between federalists and liberals was fierce. In San Juan, for instance, two federalist governors were assassinated at the behest of the liberals, and a liberal governor suffered the same fate shortly thereafter. Paraná and Buenos Aires each accused the other of being behind these crimes. Hostilities increased and, on September 17, 1861, both sides clashed again in the Battle of Pavón. The confederate armies prevailed once again, but then inexplicably, in the middle of the battle, Urquiza ordered his troops to retreat and withdrew all his support from Derqui. As a result, the Porteños claimed victory and the confederation collapsed. Mitre was, in effect, the new head of state and Buenos Aires emerged as an undisputed power.

The reason for Urquiza's defection was never clear, but in the years that followed he demonstrated a constant willingness to negotiate agreements with the liberals, to the displeasure of some of his followers who suspected he had betrayed federalism. Meanwhile, Mitre left him in peace in Entre Ríos, contrary to the demands of some of his allies, such as future president Domingo Faustino Sarmiento, who insisted, unsuccessfully, that Urquiza be taken to the gallows.

How Should the Nation Be Organized?

The task of organizing the nation was left to the Porteño elites. As to how to go about this, in the most general terms they had no major disagreements with those who had gathered in Santa Fe at Urquiza's behest to draft the constitution. Beyond their competition for power, they did share the same ideological framework. The Porteño leaders were called "liberals," but in truth, liberal ideas were also dominant among their rivals. Both sides agreed that popular sovereignty should be limited in various ways so as not to endanger the preeminence of the wealthy classes and that it had to be channeled through representatives in an institutional system that included a separation of powers. They also agreed on the need to reserve a series of rights for individuals that were beyond the reach of the will of the people, starting with the right to property. Additionally, they held the common belief that economic growth had to be promoted by granting ample liberties and opportunities to private initiatives. Inspired by Adam Smith, Juan Bautista Alberdi—at the service of the confederation and as an intellectual rival of the Porteño liberals—even spoke out in favor of "selfishness," since by enriching themselves, individuals were at the same time working toward the country's greatness. They also shared the opinion that there should be railroads and foreign investments and that immigration and education should be encouraged.

In fact, the constitution sanctioned in 1853 under the auspices of the federalists was based on these principles and was inspired by the United States Constitution, a model of liberal republicanism. The text affirmed the individual as the sole subject of rights: neither communities, nor nature, nor past or future generations were recognized as having rights, only individuals. It ensured equality before the law (slavery was finally abolished) and preserved a series of liberties and broad civil rights, such as the rights to trade, to move freely through the territory, to associate, to publish ideas, and of course to own property. The constitution did not differentiate between Argentines and foreigners and in fact gave the state the mandate to promote "European immigration." It granted religious freedom (except in the case of the indigenous peoples, who would not be equal before the law, at least on this point, since the constitution mandated they be encouraged to convert to Catholicism).

These liberties were defined in the liberal manner as "negative liberties," and any impediment that might block them was removed, but the text disregarded the economic, ethnic, and gender constraints that might enable some to take advantage of them and not others. Similarly, it established a whole series of checks and balances to prevent rulers from potentially exercising power in a despotic manner and encroaching on individual rights. However, it did not provide any similar protections against the potential of the wealthy or market performance to have negative effects on the actual liberties of other social sectors or on the collective future.

The constitution outlined two clearly differentiated domains: the public and the private. The "private actions of individuals" were questions in which the state should not interfere. Issues such as class relations or relationships between men and women remained in the private domain; they were not regarded as matters for political discussion, much less for legislation. As for political rights, nothing was specified—it was understood that all adult males would continue voting as before—but it warned that the people could not govern themselves except through representatives. All gatherings of individuals claiming to be the voice of the people and petitioning on their behalf were forbidden.

With respect to the organization of the state, the constitution established a federal system in which the provinces retained certain powers, although not the power to establish internal customs, mint their own currency, or restrict the navigation of rivers. At the same time, it established a strong executive branch that could intervene in exceptional situations. The president would not be elected through the direct vote of citizens but indirectly through representatives assembled in an "electoral college."

The legislative branch would consist of two chambers, with a Chamber of Deputies for the entire nation and a Senate representing the interests of each province (with senators appointed by their respective legislatures). The logic of opting for a bicameral system was not only to balance out the power of each province but also to reserve a series of powers for a more elitist body, such as the Senate, thus "safeguarding" them from the will of the majority (the electoral college had the same purpose). Senators, for example, controlled the appointments of certain crucial positions, such as judges and the military, and could block laws proposed by representatives.

Finally, the judiciary would be headed by a Supreme Court appointed by the executive branch with the Senate's consent. Judges, including those of the lower courts, would hold their positions for life. The rationale behind these regulations was that the judiciary should not be beholden to the government in power but that it should also be kept beyond the reach of voters, who would not be able to influence its decisions in any way.

In short, it was a "counter-majoritarian" system—as the specialists call it—for the separation and balance of powers, designed not only to channel the will of the people but also to impose very precise limitations on it. Within this system, ordinary people were given no say whatsoever; nor were women.

Sarmiento and Alberdi

Although there was overall agreement on these very general terms, the differences began just below the surface. In the practical application of these principles and the manner of conceiving the task of national organization, there were a number of discrepancies, not only between the two parties but also among the liberals themselves. In fact, national organization was preceded by an intense intellectual debate that provided many of the ideas guiding the process. There was a range of positions, but two young members of the New Generation stood out for their contributions: Domingo Faustino Sarmiento and Juan Bautista Alberdi, considered the founding fathers of the Argentine liberal tradition. Both were very skeptical regarding the capabilities of the criollo population and, as a result, believed in the need for a profound reshaping of the customs of this population as a precondition for what was then called "progress."

In 1845, Sarmiento had published *Facundo o civilización y barbarie en las pampas argentinas* (*Facundo: or, Civilization and Barbarism*), destined to become the most influential book in Argentine history. In it, he offered a detailed narrative of the country's difficulties and potential ways of overcoming them. For Sarmiento, the disputes of that time were not mere confrontations between parties but a dramatic struggle between two historical tendencies. It was about "civilization" (which the Unitarians embodied despite their errors) seeking to make its way in a territory still dominated by "barbarism" (represented by the Federalists). It was an antinomy that the Unitarians had already introduced in the previous decade, borrowed from the vocabulary used by the Europeans to justify their colonialist expansion. This confrontation between parties reflected deep social and cultural realities. "Civilization" came from the educated classes in the cities, especially Buenos Aires, which represented an enclave of European culture and customs, the bearers of progress. "Barbarism" was strong in rural areas, especially in the country's interior and among the lower-class biracial criollo settlers, who formed the ranks of the *montoneras*, or informal rebel armies. In short, it was not a battle between two parties but between two different and opposing countries. Progress meant eradicating the forces of "barbarism" at their roots, a way of conceiving their mission at the time that naturally encouraged intolerance toward political adversaries and the lower classes, at least as they appeared at that time.

Alberdi fully coincided with this disdain toward the criollo population. In 1852, he wrote *Bases y puntos de partida para la organización política de la República Argentina* (Bases and starting points for the political organization of the Argentine Republic), which served as the basis for the constitution drafted the following year. In it he explained that more than writing good laws, it was a question of reshaping the nature of the population. It was a matter of "replacing our present Argentine family with another equally Argentine family, but one more capable of freedom, wealth, and progress." To this end, populating the country with immigrants of the "Anglo-Saxon race" who were industrious, skilled in commerce, and well suited to freedom was indispensable. Through their seed and their example, they would modify the ethnic and cultural profile of the country's inhabitants until they were worthy of republican life.

There were, however, interesting nuanced differences between Sarmiento and Alberdi. Alberdi was confident that immigration and economic growth would slowly transform the population, which would be educated "through things," that is, through work and through the example of their neighbors' prosperity. While that process was taking place, it was better to restrict the political rights of the lower classes and leave the government in the hands of the elites. An imperfect and limited "possible republic" should be erected first; the time for a "true republic," more open and participatory, would come later. The task required patience and efforts to avoid violating traditions, which could generate political backlash and end up aborting the mission.

Sarmiento, of a more anxious disposition, was not willing to wait for such things. He agreed on the need to attract immigrants but argued that the state should also intervene more actively in order to immediately lay the foundations for "progress." He called for the federalists and the *montoneras* to be quashed without hesitation. However, with respect to the supposed incapacity of the local population, he was confident it could be remedied with an intense public education policy that established primary schools in every corner of the country. He had tremendous confidence in the "civilizing" role of culture and science. In the schools he envisioned, education was to be comprehensive, equal for men and women of all social classes. His thinking, in this respect, was ahead of its time. He also proposed there be land policies aimed at forming a broad class of independent farmers. For him, as for all liberals at the time, property ownership was conducive to autonomous and rational behavior, indispensable to republican life. Finally, he was confident that political participation, especially at the municipal level, would also be a formidable education for citizenship.

Compared to Alberdi, Sarmiento seemed more willing to open up the political game relatively early, more concerned with facilitating access to property, and more interested in the massive dissemination of knowledge. The downside of this apparent democratism was that it presupposed an emphatic intervention from above that would shatter any resistance. The pedagogical capacity of the elites and their benevolent disposition toward the lower classes depended on the latter consenting to be obedient pupils and quickly learning to behave in a "civilized" manner. In the mission that Sarmiento envisioned for urban culture and the lettered elite—to take the rural, lower-class, and mestizo world by storm and obligate it to refashion itself according to the European model—there was still something of the spirit of the colonial conquest. Alberdi's ideas were more explicitly elitist, but the greater patience he called for may have meant less violence in the short term.

In the end, national organization followed neither Sarmiento's nor Alberdi's proposals, although it did take elements from both. The advance of capitalism, pressures from the international market, and the interests of the local cattle-ranching bourgeoisie ended up shaping the new nation as much as or more than the initiatives of the political-intellectual elites. Massive immigration soon arrived, spontaneously rather than as a result of state policies; it brought people from southern and eastern Europe rather than the desired Anglo-Saxons. Sarmiento would never live to see the realization of his desired land division among medium-sized landowners, but he did see the implementation of his ideas on public education. Openness toward the increased political participation of the lower classes would still have to wait for many decades. In fact, the opposite took place, with a greater monopoly of decision-making in the hands of a restricted elite, to a degree that ended up scandalizing even Alberdi himself.

Led by the liberal Buenos Aires elites and their counterparts in the interior, national organization was accompanied by intense state violence directed at the federalists, indigenous peoples, and the lower classes in general. The federal system that was finally implemented was as close as possible to the centralism that the Unitarians had advocated.

The Construction of a National State and Market

The rights enshrined by the national constitution and those that each province drafted in line with their guiding principles revitalized political life. If not in all districts, in at least some there were factions that organized to compete for power. The press flourished in several cities and became an unavoidable part of political life, shaping public opinion and promoting candidacies. Revolutions, violence, and the call to form armed "popular assemblies" remained frequent, although they were slowly being displaced by institutional politics.

In Buenos Aires, and later in several other areas, "political clubs" emerged with neighborhood leaders that served as channels of communication between the top political leadership and voters. Voting was not an individual and secret act, as it is today, but rather a collective and public event in which the groups participating were mobilized by clientelistic and other means. Those who controlled the state apparatus always had an advantage since they could use its resources to their own benefit. But elections were often competitive and the outcome was not always known in advance. Few turned out to vote (at times only a quarter of those who were eligible), but those who did tended to belong to all walks of life, including the lower classes. The federalists had disappeared from Buenos Aires, but they remained very strong in the country's interior.

After his victory in the Battle of Pavón, Governor Mitre had the freedom to use his military power throughout the country in order to bring it more in line with his policies. He moved quickly and imposed liberal governments in all provinces, despite the fact that the liberals were in the minority. The federalists were displaced throughout the country (except for Entre Ríos, where Urquiza was left in peace).

Mitre's forces faced a serious challenge when they reached La Rioja, province of Ángel Vicente Peñaloza, better known as "Chacho," one of the most prestigious caudillos in the history of federalism. Adored by the lower classes of the region, Peñaloza was one of the federalists who had rebelled against Rosas in his last years and had later served Urquiza, who had promoted him to the rank of general in the national army. Outraged by the affronts of the Porteños and with the authority of his military rank, he formed a sizeable *montonera* and set out to retake the governments of the neighboring provinces for the federalists. He was followed by farm workers, laborers, muleteers, and artisans, for the most part poor "gauchos," many of indigenous or African descent.

The national government did its best to paint the *montoneras* as bands of outlaws, but during this period they were generally formed based on provincial militias and sometimes laid claim to that status; they tended to maintain a military-type hierarchical structure. The combatants who enlisted did so for a combination of reasons: expectations of economic benefits (such as receiving clothes or eating beef) or social advancement (the potential to become officers); because they felt that the movement defended the poor or their ethnic origins; or simply because they identified with the federalists and felt that the liberals were nothing more than the old Unitarians in a new guise, which in some places was quite true. Defeated several times by the Porteño army, Peñaloza's forces retreated to the plains and the mountains and attacked again. Finally, in May 1862, Chacho agreed to sign a peace treaty with Mitre: he accepted the authority of the latter in exchange for control over the pacification of La Rioja.

After subordinating the provinces, Mitre organized elections under the tutelage of the liberal authorities he had installed throughout the country, who of course secured him a victory. He took office in October 1862, thus marking the beginning of the first presidency of a truly unified country under the aegis of Buenos Aires. Once in power, he set about building a state, which in turn was a precondition for another of the crucial changes of what was then called "progress": the establishment of a national market governed by capitalist norms, which would offer suitable terrain for the activities of local and foreign capital.

The task was certainly a Herculean one. Mitre had already accomplished a fundamental achievement: a strong national leadership. But much more was needed. To begin with, it was important to ensure that the state had a monopoly over the use of force and control of the territory. This involved building a truly national army (which did not yet exist) and, more importantly, disarming the rebellious provincial militias and putting an end to the practice of *montonera* uprisings. There was also a need to curb the ability of the indigenous peoples to maintain their autonomy. Boundaries had to be set outwardly as well. Since independence, it had been common for governments throughout the region to interfere in each other's affairs, not only by sheltering exiles but often by financing or supporting their armed incursions, which obviously challenged the state's monopoly on force. But these boundaries also had to be marked in a literal sense, since it had yet to be established where the borders with the neighboring countries would be drawn. And this was not a question of minutiae: it involved vast territories (all of Patagonia, for instance, over which Chile and Argentina both laid claim).

Following this, there was a vast range of public institutions and departments responsible for various aspects of state affairs, from ministries to schools and post offices, with their respective civil servants, that had to be set up. Unified criminal, civil, and trade laws and codes had to be drafted and a judiciary had to be established. A financial system was also needed to cover all these expenses, which meant negotiating an integrated tax system with the provinces. This last was further complicated by the fact that there was still no national currency—the various regions used precious metals, their own banknotes, or those of neighboring countries. A unified system was therefore vital. In order to achieve this, a national bank, which did not yet exist either, was needed to control currency issuance. And finally, in order for private capital to take advantage of the country's resources, the state had to embark on an intense policy of investment in basic infrastructure, especially a network of railroads.

By 1886, following the governments of Mitre and his immediate successors—Domingo Faustino Sarmiento, Nicolás Avellaneda, and Julio Argentino Roca—the essential aspects of this complex construction were in place. The institutional foundation of the nation was not built from scratch or by combining the bricks and mortar contributed by the various provinces but rather out of what the Porteños already had at the time. Especially in the first phase led by Mitre, it was an expansion of the Porteño institutions into the rest of the country. This was most evident in the case of the national army that the president formally constituted in 1864, whose officers and troops were essentially those of the Buenos Aires National Guard he had just used to occupy the country's interior.

The same applied to the Code of Commerce: the one in force in Buenos Aires was simply declared to be of national scope (the Civil and Penal Codes, however, were drafted from scratch). The management of Customs and the growing revenues it provided made solving the financial issue easier for Mitre than it had been for Urquiza, who had included an initial agreement to share the revenues with the provinces. On the other hand, Mitre's proposal to transform the Bank of Buenos Aires into a national entity issuing a single currency was not successful. In 1872, progress was made in establishing a National Bank, but it failed soon after. Due to the financial instability of the period, this aspect would be the last to be resolved. The creation of a unified currency would have to wait until 1881, with the establishment of the Peso Moneda Nacional. And it wasn't until 1891, when the Banco de la Nación Argentina was created, that there was a national bank.

During these years, the state also actively intervened to expand and solidify the market and trade relations throughout the territory. It did so not only by abolishing internal Customs Offices and creating the order, laws, and institutions necessary for it to function but also by intervening directly in the economy.

Through a series of military campaigns against the indigenous peoples, the state acquired millions of hectares of productive land in Buenos Aires, Córdoba, and Santa Fe, which were quickly privatized. By 1903, more than 32 million hectares had been delivered as property. Due to the way this was done and the characteristics of the property market, the vast majority ended up concentrated in the hands of large-scale landowners. The state also promoted the creation of rural colonies of medium-sized producers, although they only had a significant impact in Santa Fe and Entre Ríos.

Policies to attract foreign capital and state investments in port and railway infrastructure were crucial. The first railway line in the country, the Ferrocarril Oeste, was built in 1857, a mere 6.2 miles between the Buenos Aires city center and Flores. It was financed through public funding but managed by local businessmen until 1862, when it was taken over directly by the state. Most of the rest of the railroad network developed after that date was in the hands of British investors, but the state signed contracts with them, ensuring a minimum earnings level (if not achieved, the Public Treasury topped them up, which happened on several occasions) and other benefits, including the free cession of hundreds of thousands of hectares of land. By 1874, there were already 828 miles of railroads that crossed the most fertile areas of the Humid Pampas and reached Córdoba and Tucumán. By 1890, they totaled 5,840 miles and radially connected nearly the entire country with the Buenos Aires port. The less profitable branch lines were built and managed directly by the national or provincial governments. By the early twentieth century, Argentina had the most extensive railroad network of Latin America and one of the largest in the world.

Communications also took a quantum leap thanks to the installation of 3,000 miles of telegraphic lines during Sarmiento's presidency. In 1870, Argentina was connected to the first transoceanic cable, bringing it into closer contact with the rest of the world.

Investments in infrastructure were not only aimed at economic growth; they also helped consolidate political unity. In effect, the state managed to break down the resistance of the provincial elites not only through force but also by co-opting them through alliances paid for in public works that benefited the districts and the leaders who accepted them.

Finally, national organization was accompanied by new modes of state intervention with respect to the population. As a result of the terrible yellow fever epidemic that struck Buenos Aires in 1871, the state began to develop more active policies in the areas of public health and urban improvement. And two years earlier, it had begun census taking to provide basic information on the population in order to better govern it, as was the practice in Europe.

More importantly, starting in the 1860s, the country implemented a vigorous policy aimed at expanding the public education system, the first of its kind in Latin America (and comparable only to that of Uruguay). Mitre founded secondary schools in several provinces. During Sarmiento's presidency, the emphasis was on primary school education: roughly eight hundred schools were established throughout the country and the number of children attending them tripled. Roca continued on this path, and in 1884 his government passed Law 1420, establishing free, secular, and compulsory education for children ages six to fourteen. During his presidency, it was also decided that the state would be in charge of the population's civil records (births, deaths, and marriages) and that civil marriages should precede religious marriage ceremonies, which were made voluntary. These measures led to a bitter conflict with the Church that culminated in cutting off diplomatic

The Great Transformation

relations with the Vatican, which were interrupted until 1900. Although the state would continue to support Roman Catholic worship because it was mandated by the constitution, these decisions fatally shattered the colonial notion that society was first and foremost a community of Catholics.

From Internal War to the Paraguayan War

The expansion of the national state and the market throughout the territory was accompanied by familiar forms of violence, along with other new ones of unprecedented tenor and magnitude. Mitre had managed to impose his dominance throughout the country, but the federalists soon reorganized, once again under Chacho Peñaloza. Dissatisfied with the unfulfilled promises of Mitre's pact, the Riojan spoke out, making proclamations in which he presented himself as a defender of the liberties and constitutional rights violated by the tyranny of the Porteños. Several federalist caudillos responded to the call, and in 1863, with their base in La Rioja, their forces advanced on Catamarca, San Luis, Mendoza, and San Juan. They expected Urquiza's support, but he remained silent. Mitre declared that it was not a political movement but gangs of delinquents, and he sent troops to suppress them accordingly. Sarmiento, who insisted on the need to quash them without hesitation, was put in command of the forces sent to Cuyo and La Rioja. In his capacity as commander, he dictated a state of siege and a series of blatantly unconstitutional measures to put an end to his adversaries.

After several clashes, Peñaloza suffered a decisive defeat in Córdoba and was captured while escaping toward La Rioja. The officer in charge of the captors murdered him in cold blood and then cut off his head, which was nailed to a pike and exhibited in the village square as a lesson. The crime generated a countrywide wave of indignation. Nevertheless, Sarmiento welcomed the assassin as a hero in San Juan and praised his act, including the exhibition of the head. Extreme brutality was necessary, in his opinion, to put an end to the uprisings of "the rabble." Mitre expressed his reservations over the act, but the assassin was not punished.

Two years later, the long-standing partisan quarrels would unexpectedly lead to a tremendous international conflict: the Paraguayan War. The dispute was sparked by the habit the nascent governments still had of intervening in each other's affairs. As they had done since independence, the Buenos Aires liberals continued to interfere in Uruguayan politics. Starting in 1863, they gave military support to their allies in the Partido Colorado in their attempt to overthrow the government of the Partido Blanco, a traditional ally of the Argentine federalists. Brazil, whose imperial court was dominated by liberals at the time, backed the Colorados, who ended up imposing a new government by force of arms.

In light of this situation, Francisco Solano López, president of Paraguay, decided to intervene to help the Blancos and hinder Brazilian aspirations. He requested Mitre's authorization for his army to pass through on its way to Rio Grande do Sul. Mitre refused, so in March 1865 López also declared war on Argentina and his troops occupied Corrientes (where they were received with expressions of support by a population that distrusted Brazil and regarded the Paraguayans with sympathy).

López speculated that this move would arouse support from the head of the Argentine federalists, but Urquiza once again preferred to maintain his alliance with the Porteño liberals. It was in this context that Mitre signed the Triple Alliance, an agreement with Uruguay and Brazil against Paraguay, and sent the Argentine army to wage war against López. Everyone expected a brief conflict, but the determination of the Paraguayans to defend their territory— even the women and children fought—extended the conflict for five years.

The Paraguayan War was the longest and bloodiest war in South America and one of the worst conflicts globally in the nineteenth century. It claimed 300,000 lives, mostly Paraguayans. For Paraguay it was a disaster of lasting consequences: the country lost 60 percent of its population, particularly men of working age, and was left in total ruin. At the end of the war, Brazil and Argentina established their new borders in a way that stripped the defeated country of 40 percent of its previous territory. The victors also imposed free trade and the free navigation of the rivers, forcing Paraguay to abandon the protectionist policies it had maintained up to that point.

Argentina withdrew its troops in 1868; it took the Brazilian emperor two more years to defeat the Paraguayans, during which horrifying war crimes were committed. By that time, thousands of Argentine soldiers had lost their lives on the front lines or from diseases associated with battle. They fought in harsh conditions, underfed and underdressed. Britain had financially supported the allies with loans that left Argentina with a very substantial foreign debt.

While the conflict lasted, Mitre governed under a state of siege, which he took advantage of to shut down several of the newspapers that were critical of him. He waged war in the name of "civilization" against the "barbarism" that in this case was a foreign threat, although the Paraguayan War should be considered a central episode in the process of building the Argentine state. It served to put an end to the possibility of direct intervention by other countries in internal politics. It was also crucial in resolving the question of the geographical boundaries in the northeast, which were now clearly drawn. Most importantly, the war served to strengthen the national army, which until then had been small, poorly disciplined, and poorly armed. By the end of the conflict, it had grown in size and in funds and had acquired Remington repeating rifles and cannons that would render it unbeatable against the provincial militias. The experience of war also served to strengthen the camaraderie among the officers and to establish among the troops a sense of identification with the state. From that moment on, the army would become an institution with its own political weight.

Alberdi, a fierce critic of the war, bluntly denounced its purpose as being domestic policy rather than foreign. The problem was not Paraguay but settling "the long-standing civil war" that Buenos Aires had with the provinces. And it was not only about politics: Mitre himself acknowledged that the conflict was also connected to the task of strengthening market dominance over the territory, during a speech in which he pointed out that in Paraguay "the Argentine Republic [had triumphed] in its political capacity as a nation" but also in "the great principles of free trade" that had been imposed on the vanquished. The soldiers had been true "apostles of free trade."

Mitre's project triumphed in part thanks to the war. But, paradoxically, that victory cost him the hegemony he had held over Buenos Aires politics up to that point, and which he would never recover. A short time earlier, the Partido de la Libertad had split into two: the "nationalists" who were loyal to Mitre and the "autonomists" led by Adolfo Alsina (the son of former Buenos Aires governor Valentín Alsina). The criticism leveled against the president for the costly military adventure on which he had led the country gave new impetus to his Partido Autonomista (Autonomist Party) rivals, who set out to establish ties with groups from other provinces in order to win the presidency. The opportunity came with the 1868 elections, held in the middle of the war. In the electoral college, Mitre's designated successor was defeated by a motley alliance that members of the military had played a significant role in assembling. Their candidate was a consensus figure who was not a clear member of any of the groups backing the alliance: Domingo Faustino Sarmiento, who at that time was distanced from Mitre after having served in his government. Sarmiento's victory, like that of his predecessor, was achieved through interventions in the provinces that ensured control over the electoral college.

State Consolidation and the Decline of Federalism

The Paraguayan War generated considerable anxiety among the federalists, who saw the Paraguayans as allies in the struggle against the liberals (destroying this solidarity was precisely one of the tasks that the centralized state had set out to achieve). In addition, forced conscription for the battle's front lines sparked significant resistance among the popular classes, including riots and mass desertions.

In several provinces, the federalists became the voice of this discontent. At the time, federalism maintained its identification with the lower classes and with anti-Porteño sentiments, which were powerful in the interior. On top of this, there was an incipient Americanism that contrasted with Mitre's indifference toward the first efforts on the continent to strengthen Hispano-American unity in the face of imperialist aggressions.

The *montoneras* reappeared in La Rioja, led by caudillo Aurelio Zalazar, who was eventually defeated and executed. Mendoza was the scene of the 1866 "Revolution of the Colorados," which led to another series of federal mobilizations that occurred following the arrival of Felipe Varela, one of Chacho's former lieutenants who seized the opportunity to return from exile in Chile. The federal rebellion spread throughout Cuyo, La Rioja, and Catamarca. In his proclamations, Varela declared himself against the "tyranny" and centralism of Buenos Aires and claimed to be an Americanist and a defender of the constitutional principles that had been violated. After several tough battles—including the famous Battle of Pozo de Vargas in April 1867—he was defeated and managed to flee to Bolivia. The following year, there was still the occasional *montonera* in the area, but they were soon eliminated. The liberals made decisive progress in their control of the region.

The last gasp of federalism occurred soon after, on the other side of the country, in Entre Ríos. To the despair of many of his followers, Urquiza had left the Paraguayans and Uruguay's Blancos to their fate. Not only did he not oppose the war, but he profited from it as a supplier to the army. During these years, he also reconciled with the new president and invited him to his home, a visit that Sarmiento took great pains to present to the public as the ultimate victory of the liberals. Many were finally convinced that Urquiza had betrayed federalism.

In April 1870, a federalist uprising led by Ricardo López Jordán—a caudillo who had until then been very close to the head of the party—culminated in Urquiza's assassination. López Jordán was chosen as the new governor of

Entre Ríos, a challenge that Sarmiento responded to by immediately dispatching military forces under his command. The caudillo managed to resist for months, resorting to guerrilla warfare tactics, but was finally defeated and forced to flee to Brazil. In 1873, López Jordán returned to Entre Ríos with his troops, but after several months he was defeated (he would try once more, in vain, in 1875).

After quashing the rebellion, Sarmiento strengthened his control over the region and dismantled what was left of federalism there as well. This effectively marked the demise of the powerful political force that had dominated Argentina's political scene for decades. From that moment on, it no longer had any relevant presence, although it did remain for a long time in popular memory. The exploits of figures such as Chacho or López Jordán would be passed on by word of mouth and became part of oral folklore for many years to come. Chacho's story was even reproduced in popular cheap pamphlets that were printed for decades.

The federalist rebellions were not the last challenge the state faced on the path to consolidating its authority. When Sarmiento became president, it was clear that Mitre's star was on the wane. The 1874 elections appeared to confirm this when Mitre's rival, Nicolás Avellaneda from Tucumán, won the presidency. His triumph was due to an amalgam of support similar to what Sarmiento had enjoyed, including Alsina's autonomists, who gave him a clear majority in the electoral college. Mitre proclaimed that he had been defeated through fraud, and in September 1874 he took up arms. The forces he was able to mobilize were quite similar to the *montoneras* he had personally opposed: most were soldiers from the provincial militias as well as a group of the cacique Catriel's lancers. Ironically, he was rebelling against the national state that he, more than anyone else, had helped establish. The new president had to face this challenge as soon as he took office, and he did so without great difficulty: the national army decisively demonstrated its superiority on the battlefield. Although equally seditious from the perspective of state legality, Mitre did not receive the treatment he himself had inflicted on his adversaries in the past: shortly after the defeat, he and his supporters were amnestied and were able to return to political life unhindered.

Mitre's was not the only irony in this story. The last provincial rebellion the state had to face was none other than that of Buenos Aires, the province that had most strongly pushed for a centralization with which it was now not entirely satisfied. Relations between Buenos Aires and the nation were plagued by a thorny issue, the resolution of which had been postponed. The constitution established the city as the country's capital, but that required the provincial legislature to accept the loss of its most valuable district, which it had not done yet.

When Mitre took office, he came up with a stopgap solution: the city was declared a temporary residence for the national authorities, which in fact meant that they were "invited" to share the same space with the governor of Buenos Aires, who maintained his jurisdiction over the urban area. Relations between the two dignitaries had not been easy and grew more strained during the elections for Avellaneda's successor. The alliance that had brought Avellaneda to power had formed what would soon be known as the Partido Autonomista Nacional (National Autonomist Party, or PAN) and was preparing to elect another Tucumán native, Julio Argentino Roca, as the new president. He was supported by a veritable "League of Governors" that had managed to counterbalance the influence of Buenos Aires. But his candidacy was strongly opposed by Carlos Tejedor, governor of Buenos Aires, who once again resorted to armed rebellion.

In late 1879, Tejedor began to organize a military force, calling on ordinary citizens to join him (his call was enthusiastically received by a segment of the popular classes, including Afro-Argentines, who armed themselves to defend the dignity of Buenos Aires, which they felt had been undermined). President Avellaneda found himself forced to transfer his government to the town of Belgrano in view of the threat. The national army and local forces—with about ten thousand combatants each—finally engaged in battle on June 20 and 21, 1880. The fighting was bloody, especially on the outskirts of the city, but the national army was once again victorious.

The defeat of Buenos Aires enabled rapid progress on the pending issues of state centralization. After Roca took office, Congress passed a law prohibiting the provinces from forming any kind of armed corps. This ruling marked the end of the long tradition of militias dating back to colonial times: from that point on, the only troops in the territory were those of the national army.

Congress passed another law stipulating that the federal capital was to be the city of Buenos Aires, whose boundaries were soon expanded to include the surrounding towns, such as Belgrano and Flores. The Buenos Aires legislature was forced to accept the deal, and the province of Buenos Aires was left without a capital (a short time later, its governors would move their residence to the city of La Plata, built especially for that purpose). With the federalists out of the picture and Tejedor's defeat, the most decisive period of the process of national organization was over. Progeny of Buenos Aires, the state had been forced to defeat it in order to finally assert itself.

Roca adopted the slogan "Peace and Administration" for his government and, indeed, from that moment on, interprovincial confrontations ceased. The new party that had led him to the presidency, PAN, would dominate national politics for the next three decades. During this period, voting lost its significance. Previous elections had not been clean and transparent—far from it—but at least they had tended to be competitive. They were won or lost according to the ability of each candidate to mobilize support (which in turn gave the plebs the potential to obtain advantages in exchange for their votes). Now controlled by PAN's well-oiled electoral machine, the results were no longer a surprise to anyone. In addition to fraud, the national executive branch took advantage of its power to dictate federal interventions in the provinces: from Mitre's inauguration until 1900, three dozen were decreed (almost all the provinces experienced multiple interventions). For its adversaries and for posterity, the elite that managed the country's future after 1880 was a true "oligarchy."

The consolidation of the state in the hands of liberal leadership led to one of the least pluralistic and most politically closed periods in Argentine history. Its control of the electoral mechanism neutralized its political competitors and reduced the bargaining power of the plebs. The end of the Federal Party and of the potential for rebelling in *montoneras* removed all influence from the rural lower classes. During these years, Argentine politics lost one of its distinctive features: the central role that plebeian participation had played. It would only recover that element in the new century, when the workers' movement took shape and there were finally clean elections.

The "Conquest of the Desert," the Occupation of the Chaco, and Territorial Consolidation

State consolidation also ended the long history of coexistence with independent indigenous societies. Rosas had managed to secure vast tracts of land for the white settlers through a system of negotiations with "friendly" indigenous peoples. That system had collapsed after his downfall, resulting in an upsurge of violence on the frontier. The powerful cacique Calfucurá, previously inclined to peaceful negotiation, organized a large confederation of tribes. Together they carried out *malones* (raids) of unprecedented proportions and succeeded in expanding their territory, pushing back the frontier at the expense of the white settlers.

During the 1860s and 1870s, the nascent state continued the policy of treaties with caciques, to whom they gave a variety of goods and occasionally paid military posts. In those years, some of them began to proclaim themselves Argentine citizens. But that did not signify an end to the conflicts. In 1875, Manuel Namuncurá, Calfucurá's son and successor, organized a major invasion of the province of Buenos Aires. It was possibly the largest *malón* in history, and he made off with a significant amount of livestock and numerous captives.

While this was taking place, international demand for the livestock products of the Pampas grew, as did interest in securing and expanding the available land, which was increasingly valuable. The elites of the time were instilled with the ideas that the Europeans had promoted to justify the colonization of Asia and Africa. They considered the local indigenous peoples to be "primitive," racially inferior, and destined to be swept away by the tide of "civilization." They had chosen to imagine the lands they occupied as pure "desert," although this was not true in any sense of the word.

From 1876 onward, the state steadily and relentlessly advanced on the indigenous peoples, although the strategies varied. During Avellaneda's presidency, his minister of defense, Adolfo Alsina, pursued a policy of gradual occupation of the territory by digging 230 miles of defensive ditches and establishing a series of forts. His idea was to slowly assimilate the indigenous peoples, trusting that they would voluntarily convert to "civilized" customs when they realized their superiority. The plan was fairly successful, but Alsina died in 1877, and his successor, Julio Argentino Roca, had very different ideas. From Roca's perspective, the Indians had to be immediately subdued by military force and the entire territory was to be occupied.

In 1879, Roca initiated what he called the "Conquest of the Desert," an immense incursion of six thousand soldiers who advanced in several columns simultaneously and quickly took control of all territory north of the Río Negro. Subsequent expeditions pushed further south and secured control of the whole of Patagonia. In 1885, Valentín Saygüeque, the last resisting cacique in Neuquén, surrendered. It was the end of indigenous autonomy in the extensive Pampean-Patagonian territory.

According to official data, the 1879 campaign resulted in the death of 1,313 Indian lancers, in addition to many others who were murdered in the persecutions or who died of hunger or in the smallpox epidemic that accompanied the incursion. Additionally, 1,271 warriors were taken prisoner, along with 10,539 other "riffraff" Indians (women, children, the elderly). The young girls and children were distributed among wealthy families for domestic service, obviously without their consent. Another part of the "riffraff" and the adult males were locked up in concentration camps, such as the one in Valcheta surrounded by barbed wire, where they were kept on the verge of starvation.

In the years immediately following, an estimated fifteen thousand to seventeen thousand indigenous people were victims of massive deportations, sent to serve as laborers in the sugar cane harvest in the northwest, in the wine industry in Cuyo, in the navy and the army, and in domestic service. Despite the constitution's guarantees of individual rights, they ended up reduced to servitude. An unknown number died during relocation or due to harsh working conditions. In a few cases, there were policies that aimed to create reservations or missions under state or ecclesiastical tutelage. A few communities were able to have their lands recognized by the state and managed to survive. A worse fate befell the Selk'nam in the distant Tierra del Fuego, where gold prospectors and estancieros hunted them like animals until they disappeared.

What happened in the extensive Chaco region was similar. There too, although to a lesser extent, there had been a history of ties to white society (the Wichis, for example, traveled to Salta and Jujuy to perform seasonal work in the sugar mills) interspersed with confrontations, such as the Toba attack on Salta in 1862, which resulted in numerous deaths.

The state advanced steadily northward following Sarmiento's decision to create the Government of Chaco in 1872. One after another, military campaigns were carried out in a space that was conceptualized as a "desert," even though it was a dense forest. Bringing "civilization" to this area was once again part of the justification. In 1878, the city of Resistencia was founded, and by 1884 the state already controlled the area, although it would take another three decades and several more military campaigns to finally pacify it. In 1904 and again in 1917, the Mocoví and Toba peoples carried out armed attacks. Massacres by the armed forces continued in the area until the 1940s. Just as in the south, the defeated warriors were sent to work in lumber mills or imprisoned on Martín García Island. Despite everything, many communities managed to survive.

In its relationship with the indigenous peoples, the nascent Argentine state resembled the Spanish conquest. Just as in that era, it set out to occupy land and break up communities, and it used the indigenous peoples as a servile labor force. It also pressured them to give up their cultural patterns. In the territories of the northwest that had been occupied the longest, the long-standing tradition of resistance continued: after 1850, the indigenous conflicts in Jujuy became more radical and there were episodes of armed struggle. However, two decades later, silence dominated there as well.

During these years, as a result of the incursions into indigenous territory, the Paraguayan War, and diplomatic achievements, the territory controlled by the Argentine state practically doubled. In 1876, Brazil and Argentina had established the borders of Paraguay, so there was no dispute over the territory that would eventually be occupied in the Chaco. Chilean claims over Patagonia were settled soon after. In 1881, after a series of incidents, both governments signed a treaty recognizing that territory as part of Argentina and splitting the island of Tierra del Fuego in two. By this point, the country's borders were quite similar to those of the present day (see map 3.1). It was then time to discuss how to administer these new territories, which, unlike the provinces, lacked preexisting institutions. In 1884, it was decided by law that they should be "national territories" administered directly by the executive branch. Their inhabitants would not have a right to citizenship: they would not be entitled to vote for president, governor, or Congressional representatives. According to the debates of the time, there were still very few white settlers in those areas, and the recently conquered Indians did not have sufficient intellectual capacity to participate in political life (at least not until they were "civilized"), so they were therefore incorporated into the nation as "non-citizen nationals." The national territories were to remain deprived of political rights until the 1950s, when they finally became provinces (except for Tierra del Fuego, which had to wait until 1990).

The Agro-Export Model

The expansion of the state and the market added new impetus to the economic growth that had begun under Rosas. Within a few years, the Pampas region became one of the main exporters of agricultural and livestock products in the world. Europe was intensifying its Industrial Revolution and, in addition to raw materials for its factories, it began to demand supplies of

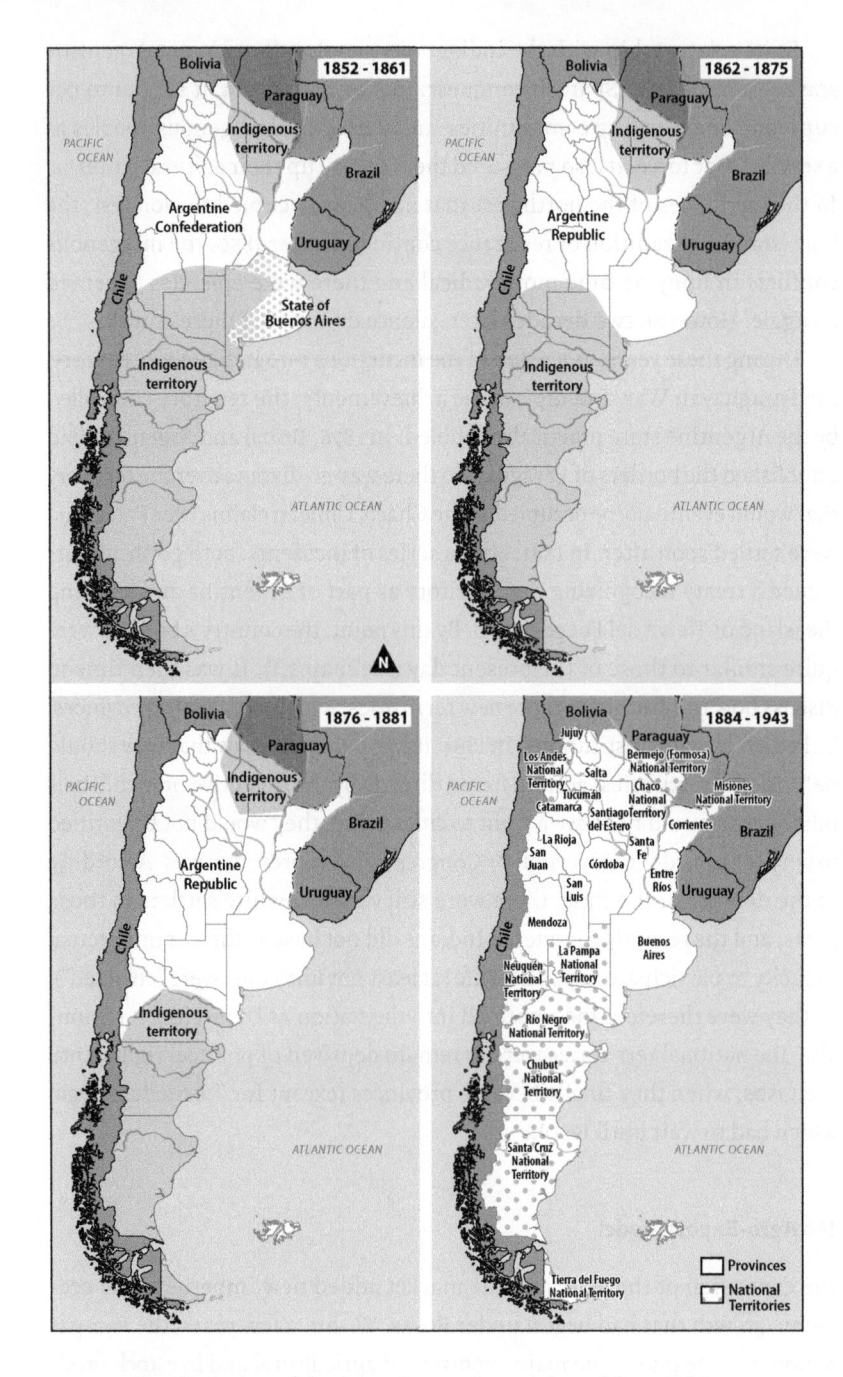

MAP 3.1. The formation of the Argentine territory. Adapted from Pablo Yankelevich, *Historia mínima de Argentina*.

foodstuffs for a population that no longer produced enough. The introduction of faster and larger steamships made it possible to ship provisions in bulk at low cost.

The boom began after 1850 with sheep farming. Wool was sold mainly to France, the United States, and Belgium, and by the 1870s it had surpassed salted meat and hides in the export market. Thanks to the lands expropriated from the Indians, the cattle stock overall expanded dramatically, and in the following decade, when the export of live cattle began, the sector made a comeback. But the greatest growth came with the invention of machines that produced artificial cold, making it possible to ship frozen meat and, by early the next century, chilled meat, especially to Great Britain, Belgium, and France. With heavy investments in meat-packing plants, Britain dominated local production by the early twentieth century, before being displaced by North American capital.

The cattle boom was accompanied by unprecedented agricultural development, facilitated by the railroad and a massive influx of immigrants that alleviated the chronic labor shortage. In 1874, Argentina was still importing wheat, but by 1880 it had achieved self-sufficiency, thanks to the contributions of the agricultural colonies of Santa Fe, Entre Ríos, and Córdoba. Twenty years later, the countryside of Buenos Aires province joined them, and the country became a major world supplier of grains. In the first years of the twentieth century, wheat shipments grew exponentially, and flax and corn were also added. By 1910, these crops accounted for 60 percent of exports, and Argentina had become the world's third-largest supplier of grain.

Foreign trade was in the hands of four companies linked to foreign capital, which were also the ones that provided credit to farmers (they managed prices and rates to their maximum benefit and obtained enormous profits). This agricultural expansion was possible thanks in part to the extraordinary fertility of the local grasslands, which were also very easy to cultivate since they were completely flat and free of trees and stones. The introduction of machines imported from Canada and the United States, replacing the traditional plowing and mowing methods, also contributed. Meat and grains (along with flax) became the country's main exports.

The success of both was in large part due to the fact that the estancieros discovered they could combine agriculture and cattle ranching on the same farm to the benefit of both. They kept the livestock on one part of the estancia and leased another to a farmer—usually an immigrant—who, along with his family, would plant crops in rotation in order to replenish the soil's nutrients:

TABLE 3.1. Main variables of the economy, 1881–1916

Years	Population (in thousands)	Product (1900 = 100)	Exports (millions of pounds)	Imports (millions of pounds)	Railroads (miles)
1881	2,565	21.86	11.6	11.1	1,517
1885	2,880	44.70	16.8	18.4	2,821
1890	3,377	58.59	20.2	28.4	5,750
1895	3,956	82.69	24.0	19.0	8,837
1900	4,607	100.00	31.0	22.6	10,418
1905	5,289	164.30	64.6	41.0	12,229
1910	6,586	197.43	74.5	70.4	17,220
1916	7,885	201.02	99.4	59.8	21,458

Source: Fernando Rocchi, "El péndulo de la riqueza."

flax one year, wheat the next, and alfalfa the third, which the estanciero used as fodder. After three years, the tenants would restart the cycle on another lot. In this way, without having to pay wages, the landowner managed to generate plots of land that were capable of feeding cattle much more quickly than if the pastures were left to naturally renew themselves.

This model meant that those responsible for the explosive growth in agriculture were farmers who did not have access to land ownership. In 1914, only half of the farms nationwide were worked by their owners. With the exception of some parts of Santa Fe and Córdoba where European agricultural colonies were established, the ratio was even worse in the Humid Pampas, where large latifundios or estates dominated (although there were still properties of all sizes).

The growth of the economy was truly remarkable and was at one of the highest rates in the world (see table 3.1). Argentina, which only a hundred years earlier had been a marginal territory of the Spanish Empire, had become a major player in the international market. From 1885 to 1930, the country oscillated between seventh and fourteenth place in the ranking of nations with the highest gross domestic product (GDP) per capita in the world. This fact gave rise to an enduring myth: that Argentina was a rich and developed country comparable to Canada or the United States at that time but then entered a long period of decline that would render it an underdeveloped nation. The decline, according to this view, was due to twentieth-century state interventionism.

However, the idea that Argentina was rich and developed is a mirage. Its growth at that time had feet of clay: it was the result of an extraordinary situation of high international demand harnessed by a region that had an enormous expanse of fertile and unoccupied land, a labor force that was seemingly inexhaustible thanks to immigration, and an influx of British capital attracted to the opportunity. Compared to the truly wealthy countries of the time, Argentina was an anomaly: it had a high GDP per capita but not because its economy had a solid and sustainable base. And the high GDP was not accompanied by another key factor that was present in countries such as Canada or the United States: high cultural capital, fundamental for economic development. The skills of the population, as measured in terms of education, were very low and did not grow at the rate they did in wealthy countries. Despite considerable efforts by the state, the country was not educating its population at the same rate as the growth of its economy (especially in terms of secondary and postsecondary education).

In addition, the agro-export model had other issues that would eventually prove decisive. One of the most notable was that of regional imbalances. The extraordinary growth in the Pampas was not replicated in the rest of the country. Some areas also increased their production but at a much slower pace. Salta exported animals to Bolivia, and Cuyo to Chile. By 1880, Mendoza and San Juan began to specialize in wine production, while Tucumán focused on sugar production, both for the domestic market. Other regional economies managed to market some products locally but on a much smaller scale. And some provinces, such as La Rioja or Catamarca, were decidedly marginalized from the economic boom and subsisted thanks to the funds they received from the nation.

So successful was the primary commodity export economy that few members of the elite felt the need to question the place Argentina was occupying in the international division of labor. Some did propose industrialist policies, but their voices were weak and they failed in changing the general trend. Still, demand from the larger cities did foster a modest increase in industry, especially after the Customs Act of 1876 imposed tariffs on some imports. The measure did not have protectionist aims—it was taken only to improve the state's finances—but it did partially reverse the completely pro-free-trade policies that had been implemented since Rosas's downfall.

During these years, there was a change in the organization and type of manufacturing establishments. In the 1860s, almost all production was still carried out in small workshops that usually combined manufacturing with repairs and retailing. They typically employed a small group of skilled craftsmen and were only barely mechanized. In general, they were owned by a master craftsman who worked alongside the rest. In the mid-nineteenth century, there were only a handful of large establishments in Buenos Aires: *saladeros* (meat-salting plants) and tanneries, a brewery, a mechanical sawmill, a foundry, and several steam mills.

Although small- and medium-sized workshops remained predominant, by the end of the 1880s, the city was already populated by mechanically powered factories with smoking chimneys owned by businessmen that employed thousands of salaried workers. By the turn of the century, some large companies—such as meat-packing plants, sugar mills, and textile and shoe factories—began to introduce Taylorism, a method that divided the production process into an assembly line with repetitive tasks carried out by different types of workers and timed by supervisors. The aim was to increase productivity and to weaken the organizational capacity of the workers, who became a more heterogeneous and less qualified workforce (and therefore more easily replaceable).

Between 1880 and 1914, these changes led to a fifteen-fold increase in the value of manufacturing production, and Argentina became the Latin American country in which it held the most significance. By then manufacturing already represented a quarter of the total product and supplied three-quarters of local demand, especially for the simplest manufactured goods, such as food products, furniture, clothing, and vehicles (more complex industries would still have to wait). Once again, this development had a very strong regional bias. The lower cost of railroad transportation now strongly affected artisanal production in the country's interior. In particular, there was a dramatic decrease in the number of textile workshops, unable to compete with imported products. As a result, due to the influence of both the state and the international market, Buenos Aires and the Pampas acquired a much greater importance than they had previously had, exacerbating the country's regional imbalance. The flip side to the growth of production in that region was the destruction of production in other regions.

Political and Environmental Impacts

The major transformation that took place during these years also brought about a drastic change in the way society related to the environment. The intensification of capitalism meant that an increasing number of goods were marketable commodities. Nature became an open terrain for uncontrolled depredation and a dumping ground for the waste and pollution that the new activities generated. In just a few years, the effects were incomparably more damaging than those caused by human economic activities in all the preceding centuries.

One of the first was massive deforestation. Starting in the 1860s, millions of ties were required for railroad tracks and millions of posts for fences and corrals in the Humid Pampas, the vineyards of Cuyo, and elsewhere. New steam engines and constant construction called for more wood. Indiscriminate logging was used to supply this heavy demand. Santiago del Estero was the first and most deeply affected area. The magnificent quebracho forests in the province's western region were ravaged until what had been a dense forest was transformed into a desert. Between 1906 and 1915 alone, 20.7 million railroad ties were harvested, resulting in the loss of three-quarters of what was left of the province's forests. It was a disaster for the lives of Santiago del Estero's inhabitants, especially those of the popular classes. Campesinos and herders, who depended on the preservation of a delicate balance between forest use and intensive cattle ranching, found themselves left without options. Thousands of them were forced to immigrate to other provinces.

It was in these years that the famous company La Forestal was established with British capital, plundering the forests of northern Santa Fe, Chaco, and Formosa to produce tannin, with similar consequences. It had made its debut after shady dealings with the state in the late nineteenth century, when it was allowed to acquire 12 percent of Santa Fe's surface area for a derisory price. La Forestal managed to amass more than 2 million hectares and became the world's leading supplier of tannin. Well into the twentieth century, after having exhausted the quebracho forests, the company pulled out of the country, leaving behind a wasteland. Catamarca and La Rioja also suffered similar processes of rapid deforestation.

Urban spaces sustained environmental destruction during this period as well. In Buenos Aires, it was evident from early on. By the early nineteenth century, waste from *saladeros*, tanneries, and candle factories had already given the Riachuelo the nauseating odor it still has to this day. The problem grew worse toward the end of the century with the installation of industrial dye works, metallurgical factories, and meat-packing plants. The contamination spread to other rivers and was followed by air pollution, due to industry and, later on, automotive transportation.

In short, during these years, a truly capitalist relationship with the environment was established in Argentina: one that allowed for the private appropriation of natural resources that belong to everyone—either directly by marketing them or indirectly by not paying any cost for their degradation—and passed on the worst consequences to the low-income sectors. The agro-export model left its mark in different ways on two types of spaces: in the Humid Pampas, land resources were protected through crop rotation to ensure sustainable production, whereas other regions were turned into "sacrifice zones" open to the indiscriminate exploitation of resources. Since then, this pattern has only intensified.

The agro-export model also made the country's economy highly dependent on economies to the north. Revenues were tied to the export of a few products, so that any change in relative prices had an immediate impact. And in the long run, the terms of trade would become detrimental: the value of manufactured goods tended to increase more than that of primary goods.

Argentina also depended on foreign investments, two-thirds of which came from Britain during those years. This economic boom increased the state's revenue, but its expenditures grew at a faster rate. As the public coffers were financed mainly by import taxes (those applied to exports remained very low), the state opted to take out international loans, which were mainly supplied by London financiers. By 1890, Argentina was the main destination for British investments. The country established a truly neocolonial relationship with the United Kingdom in which it played the role of an informal economic colony. A short time later, with heavy investments initially in meat-packing plants and then in other industries, Britain and eventually the United States began to capture a significant share of the profits of the still modest developments in manufacturing and transfer them abroad. Due to the liberal bias of the ruling elites, the state did not develop instruments to protect national autonomy or to regulate market functioning during these years.

The economy's vulnerability became apparent in two serious crises that hit the country. The first was in 1873. The previous decade's growth had generated a feeling of prosperity that had pushed everyone—the state and the private sector—to increase expenditures and overuse credit. The trade balance

TABLE 3.2. National budgets and public debt, 1881–1914 (in thousands of pesos gold)

Year	Revenues	Expenses	Public debt	Debt service	% debt over budget
1881	21,345	28,381	107,075	8,766	45.2
1885	26,581	40,515	113,381	10,312	32.5
1890	29,143	38,145	355,762	12,958	38.6
1895	38,226	48,505	401,863	15,469	43.5
1900	64,858	68,580	447,191	26,886	41.5
1905	90,423	141,470	384,437	30,945	34.9
1910	133,094	180,947	452,790	28,518	24.3
1914	110,029	194,371	545,023	37,116	18.7

Source: Fernando Rocchi, "El péndulo de la riqueza."

became negative due to the increase in imports, and a crisis was triggered when access to international credit was cut off. In 1873, this resulted in numerous bankruptcies and adjustment policies in order to meet commitments to foreign creditors, which by then were already absorbing 45 percent of public spending. The livestock sector succeeded in pressuring the government not to increase export taxes, so the solution was, instead, to raise the rates applied to some imports.

A similar situation led to the crisis of 1890. State expenditures had increased once again due to the investment in railroads and the burden of foreign debt. An alarm was sounded after several years of negative trade balance, which was covered with more loans. Confidence in the repayment capacity soon faltered and access to credit was again cut off. President Miguel Juárez Celman tried to overcome the situation with a new fiscal adjustment and a reduction in the salaries of public employees, but the crisis still hit and with it came a drop in production, increased unemployment, and the devaluation of the currency (which ended up favoring the export sectors) (see table 3.2).

This crisis was also political. It culminated in an uprising similar to those that had occurred in the past and heralded more to come in the future. Economic difficulties, political closure, and the prevailing venality—it was possibly the most corrupt period of all time—gradually united various discontented groups. On September 1, 1889, supporters of Mitre, excluded Porteño autonomists, disgruntled Catholics, and indignant youth created the Unión Cívica de la Juventud, which later became the Unión Cívica (Civic Union), where leaders such as Mitre and Leandro N. Alem gained prominence. They demanded political openness and an end to the corruption of the "oligarchy of upstarts" in the government. On July 26 of the following year, the Revolution of 1890 broke out after supporters of the Unión Cívica had advocated for it, gathering some two thousand combatants. Confrontations with the army's troops lasted four days, until the rebels surrendered. The exact death toll is unknown, but estimates place it at three hundred. Juárez Celman won in military terms, but the uprising cost him his position, and soon after he was forced to leave the government in the hands of Vice President Carlos Pellegrini. Following their defeat, the "civics," as they were known, became more popular. After a split due to Mitre's defection, in 1891 they reorganized under the name Unión Cívica Radical (Radical Civic Union, or UCR). In the years that followed, they would spearhead an intense struggle for clean elections, including two more armed uprisings. The first was in 1893, with its epicenter in the provinces of Buenos Aires (where Hipólito Yrigoyen was a prominent organizer), San Luis, and Santa Fe, where settlers in European agricultural colonies, particularly the Swiss, played an active role. The second, also quelled by the government, was in 1905, with major incidents in the capital city and in the provinces of Buenos Aires, Córdoba, Santa Fe, and Mendoza.

Changes in Society

The political elites and those who wielded the economic power had their disagreements but were nonetheless closely connected in those years. In addition to having privileged access to the ears of officials, the landowning classes organized their own entities to exert pressure and set the public agenda. The Buenos Aires Stock Exchange, founded in 1854, was joined in 1866 by the Argentine Rural Society, whose influence grew during the Roca government. In 1875, the Industrial Club was created, forerunner of the Argentine Industrial Union established twelve years later. Commerce, the countryside, and industry all had their advocates. The workers, as yet, did not.

Organized along sectoral lines, with privileged access to a state controlled by an oligarchy, the upper classes enjoyed their moment of greatest splendor starting in 1880. The country was theirs and the profits they reaped were truly extraordinary. The city of Buenos Aires still bears the hallmarks of that

opulence. The mansions and palaces they built in Barrio Norte and Plaza San Martín contrasted with the infinitely more modest dwellings "respectable" families had lived in until the mid-nineteenth century.

The provincialism and simplicity of the upper classes of the past gave way to a veritable "high society" characterized by cosmopolitan habits, sumptuous consumption, and refined tastes. Their social life, lavish weddings, splendid parties and outings, and exclusive clubs would soon be featured in the magazines of the time for the greater visibility of the rest of the population. Porteño high society consisted of families of three different origins, which clearly reflected the changes brought about by the consolidation of the state and the market. On the one hand, there were patrician families from the colonial era who had prospered in the livestock business, such as the Anchorena and Alvear families, who by 1900 owned 635,000 and 102,800 hectares of land, respectively. Second, there were foreign families who had arrived in the nineteenth century; they had not always been wealthy to begin with, but had risen quickly in society (such as the Bullrich, Wilde, and Luro families). They were joined by a third group, consisting of elite families from the interior who had moved to Buenos Aires to become part of the political establishment (such as the Paz, Ibarguren, and Avellaneda families). United by marriage ties and a common sociability, they were the sector that most profited from the recently organized nation.

For the rest of society, life was less glamorous. During these years, Argentina underwent a very deep and chaotic process of change that drastically altered social life. To begin with, there was a spectacular demographic surge. In just forty-five years, between 1869 and 1914, the country's population grew by more than 300 percent: from just under 1.8 million to more than 8 million. This increase was mainly concentrated in the cities, and the country experienced a rapid process of urbanization. In 1869, more than two-thirds of the inhabitants still lived in the countryside. By the turn of the century, half were already living in cities, and this proportion would continue to rise. The cities that expanded the most were by far those in the region of the Pampas, especially Buenos Aires (which grew from 300,000 inhabitants in 1880 to more than 1.5 million in 1914) and Rosario. By 1910, Argentina was one of the most urbanized countries in the world but also had one of the most centralized populations: more than a quarter lived in the capital city and the surrounding areas, in what was already one of the most populated urban areas on the planet.

The city of Buenos Aires witnessed the proliferation of high-rise buildings and the introduction of streetcars for public transportation, among other

The Great Transformation

improvements. In 1913, it inaugurated its subway, the first in the entire southern hemisphere and one of the few in the world at the time.

This growth was largely a consequence of the great influx of immigrants. Between 1881 and 1914, more than 4 million people arrived at the port of Buenos Aires, most of them young men. They were attracted by the high wages compared to those in their countries of origin and by the opportunities available to those who knew how to take advantage of them. Only one out of three returned to their homeland. Seventy-five percent were of Spanish or Italian origin; the rest were British, German, French, Jews from Eastern Europe, Syrian-Lebanese, and other nationalities (including those from neighboring countries). There were even small contingents of Japanese, Boers from South Africa, and Africans from Cape Verde.

Argentina received the greatest proportion of immigrants in the world relative to its local population: by 1914, almost a third of its inhabitants had been born abroad. In this case, too, regional inequalities were notable. That year, nearly half of the inhabitants of Buenos Aires and Santa Fe were immigrants. They also accounted for significant proportions in Mendoza and in some sparsely populated areas, such as La Pampa and Santa Cruz. In areas such as Córdoba and Entre Ríos, they were slightly less, between 12 and 20 percent, and barely 2 percent in other less favored areas, such as Catamarca and La Rioja. The impact was even more remarkable if one considers the children of immigrants, who are listed as native born in the censuses. In 1869, almost half of the population of the city of Buenos Aires was foreign (four out of every five adult males). This means that of the half who in 1914 were listed as native born, a huge proportion of their parents (either one or both) had been born abroad, and they had therefore been at least partially socialized in the culture of their parents. A similar situation applies to the province of Santa Fe. More than immigration, it was a true demographic shift.

Therefore, in addition to imbalances in terms of economy, ecology, population, and urbanization, there was a marked ethnic difference between, on the one hand, the inhabitants of Buenos Aires and what would eventually be known as the "Pampa gringa," and, on the other, those of areas that remained more clearly criollo.

Increased urbanization brought with it a change in economic activities and types of occupations. A growing percentage of the population turned to activities or jobs related to manufacturing, transportation, commerce, construction, and the service industry. The middle sectors and salaried manual workers grew at a faster rate than the general demographic increase. Tens of thousands of small- and medium-sized industries were established throughout the country—woodworking shops, bakeries, tailor shops, smithies, and so on—and the number of commercial establishments multiplied, especially small stores and businesses run by their owners. The best opportunities in commerce and industry tended to be in the hands of immigrants (more than 80 percent of factory owners in 1895 were foreigners, for instance).

Toward the end of the century, Buenos Aires witnessed the birth of a true consumer society, with the proliferation of establishments of all kinds, including large and sophisticated stores such as A la Ciudad de Londres, Gath y Chaves, and, in 1913, a branch of the famous British firm Harrods. Manufacturers and businesses began running colorful advertising campaigns to encourage consumption.

The new commercial, banking, railroad, and manufacturing establishments, as well as the state apparatus, required an increasing number of white-collar employees, civil servants, teachers, and, to a lesser extent, university graduates. In this case, ethnic origins were more varied, with a predominance of criollos among the teachers and civil servants, immigrants working behind the counters, and a mix of both among the professionals, depending on the occupation. There was also a demand for more manual laborers in all areas. By 1870, in Buenos Aires and in other cities, a true working class had begun to emerge and expand, consisting of both foreign-born gringos and criollos (as late as 1947, 20 percent of urban workers were foreigners).

The changes in the countryside were no less significant. In the Pampas, the new agricultural operations were run by small-scale farmers, most of them of immigrant origin. Thousands of them soon inhabited vast tracts of land that had previously been sparsely populated or uninhabited, such as the countryside in the west and south of the province of Buenos Aires. In Santa Fe, Entre Ríos, and Córdoba, there were agricultural colonies of Italians, Swiss, Germans, and Russian Jews, among others. Misiones and other areas of the littoral received thousands of European agricultural colonists—especially Volga Germans, Russians, and Poles—who cultivated crops such as yerba maté and tea. Sometime later, a similar phenomenon occurred in Chaco and Formosa with cotton, although in this case the Europeans coexisted with Paraguayan, criollo, and eventually indigenous producers. Among the rural laborers, the panorama was more varied. A large number of *golondrinas* (migrant workers), both gringos and criollos, seasonally flocked to the Pampas to work in harvesting. The same was true for sheep shearing there and in Patagonia. They joined the farm workers who were permanent inhabitants. The vineyards in Cuyo, the sugar harvest in the northwest, and the lumber mills in the Chaco and in northern Santa Fe almost always employed criollo or indigenous workers.

Viewed as a whole, immigrants tended to occupy the positions offered by the growing middle sectors, while criollos were often relegated to the worst jobs. As is often the case, it was generally the most ambitious who had left their communities to undertake the uncertain adventure of migration. On average, the recent arrivals had a higher level of schooling and more technical skills than the criollos. They also benefited from the preconceptions that many employers held about the criollo population as well as the fact that they frequently did not have children or the elderly in their care. More than a few of the newcomers managed to climb the social ladder, some of them very quickly, and soon they were occupying prominent positions not only in the economy but also in intellectual circles. Their presence was felt in cultural and political life. Starting in the late 1850s, they began to establish ethnically based associations, by country or region of origin, to provide mutual assistance and defend the interests of each particular group. By 1914 there were already 460 Italian and 250 Spanish organizations, along with those of myriad other communities, and dozens of newspapers were published in a wide variety of languages.

For criollos of modest means, times were tough. Those in the Buenos Aires countryside, for instance, saw their situation worsen considerably. The Rural Code approved in 1865 represented an advance in the imposition of property rights to the detriment of the poorest, for whom it became illegal to hunt animals or gather firewood on private land. The increase in the value of property made it less accessible. Additionally, starting in the 1870s, the custom of fencing off fields became more widespread. At the same time, there were stricter controls on the circulation of laborers, and the requirement they carry a *papeleta de conchabo* (proof of employment) became more stringent. This was aimed at forcing them into regular paid employment. The justices of the peace had greater powers at their disposal to enforce the law and punish the paisanos by sending them to serve in the military. The end of what had been the Indian frontier left deserters with nowhere to escape. To make matters worse, the massive influx of immigrants slowed the rising wages. And since the newcomers often got the best jobs, were exempt from military service, and received state support to get settled, the criollos felt left behind, and there were several xenophobic reactions. These were generally mild, except for a few specific episodes: the worst was the massacre of thirty-seven foreigners in Tandil in 1872 at the hands of a group of poor gauchos, apparently encouraged by a medicine man who had announced the coming of the Last Judgment and called on them to do away with the Masons and the gringos, whom he accused of being the cause of their countrymen's misfortunes. In the rural areas of the rest of the country, the condition of the criollos was no better; in the northwest, the laws against "vagrancy" to help recruit labor remained in effect, and there were also expressions of xenophobia.

Despite the tensions, integration of the newcomers and the criollo population was relatively smooth overall, especially considering the magnitude of the influx of immigrants. In the medium term, Argentina did not see the same type of cultural and spatial segregation between different foreign communities that occurred in other countries. Among the urban popular classes in particular, workplaces, social spaces—cafés, "dance academies," Carnival—and even courtship customs brought together people of the most diverse origins. Integration, however, was far from perfect. Even as there was xenophobia among the criollo population, the gringos also had their prejudices. Evidence of marriage patterns indicates that Europeans preferred to marry other Europeans or their direct descendants (even if they were not from the same country) rather than criollos. The fact that they were economically better off reinforced the existing negative stereotypes against the criollo population, which portrayed them as unsuited to progress. During these years, inequality in Argentina continued to be racialized and skin color remained a determining factor in one's future. The racial prejudices that Europeans brought with them from their respective countries may even have helped exacerbate it.

Immigration and the growth of the middle sectors added to the complexity of urban life. The line separating "respectable people" from the plebs was no longer clear. In the disorderly, overcrowded cities of the Pampas in the late nineteenth century, it was no longer evident who was who. The Porteño upper classes were themselves discomfited by the pressure of the "upstarts" and "nouveau riche," and there were expressions of xenophobia toward the newcomers. In some places, the change went even deeper. In Cuyo, for example, the booming wine industry passed mostly into the hands of "gringo" winemakers, who became the new local elite.

Growth and Inequality

The growth of the economy and the middle sectors and the prosperity achieved by many immigrants have led some scholars to claim that in these years Argentine society became essentially more egalitarian, "modern," and inclusive. However, upon analysis, the evidence does not support this optimistic view. There is no doubt that growth brought much more wealth to the country. The increased cash flow swelled the public coffers and allowed for major infrastructure works. Healthcare services and education were made accessible to more people, and there is objective data showing greater social well-being, such as increased literacy and a drop in the mortality rate. However, the material advantages and improved welfare did not benefit everyone equally, nor did they reach all social groups. Of course, there was nothing "modern" or egalitarian about the reduction of subjugated indigenous peoples to servitude. And the relative closure of politics as well as the deep regional and ethnic inequalities, which worsened during these years, have been outlined above. However, there were also countervailing trends among the inhabitants of the regions that reaped the most benefits.

The new economic opportunities made social ascent a possibility for many, although this ascent was generally limited in scope. On the other hand, more dramatic social ascent became less frequent. In fact, it was much more common for a person who did not belong to the upper class to join it before 1880 than after that date, when high society very clearly closed its ranks. At the same time, the economic growth was accompanied by an intensification of income inequality between the rich and the poor. Estimates indicate that by the mid-nineteenth century in the Pampas the incomes of the wealthiest were as much as 68 times higher than those of the poorest. By 1910, this gap had widened tremendously to a differential of 933.

The growth of the middle sectors also overlapped with a different trend: the loss of autonomy of the popular classes. According to the 1869 census, more than half of the middle sectors were self-employed, meaning they were neither wage earners nor dependent on an employer, and they generally owned their own means of production. The rest were wage earners and domestic service workers. However, in later years, opportunities for freelance work diminished dramatically, while almost all workers were pushed to become wage earners. The same can be said about the growth of the middle sectors: the occupational categories that increased the most were neither professionals nor small business owners but white-collar employees.

In short, during these years, a society in which almost two-thirds of the population had at least relatively independent occupations was replaced by one in which the vast majority had become wage earners and were dependent on an employer. This drive toward wage labor marked a change that cannot be described as a shift toward greater egalitarianism. On the contrary, it increased dependence on employers and resulted in a loss of the control of workers over their own work.

Lastly, there was no improvement in equality in gender relations either. Although it is true that during this period several pioneering women forged a path into exclusively male spheres (high-society families produced a handful of distinguished women writers, and universities witnessed the first women graduates by 1885, albeit still very few), during the nineteenth century the general tendency was toward the increased subordination of women to men. Both laws and customs brought new and deeper forms of patriarchal control. In this regard, Sarmiento held unusual ideas for the time: he believed in women's rights and capabilities; he proposed equal schooling for women and men; and he collaborated with Juana Manso, a strong and independent woman, the first to hold a position of relevance within the civil service.

However, this did not prevent the Civil Code of 1869 (during Sarmiento's presidency) from establishing the legal incapacity of married women: they were not allowed to educate themselves; engage in trade activities; or initiate a lawsuit without the authorization of their husbands, who even became the administrators of any assets women may have acquired before marriage. This represented a greater degree of subordination than what women had previously been subjected to. This change was related to others in the economic domain. Echoing what was happening in Europe, in a world increasingly governed by business, competition, and money, there was growing uncertainty among men regarding their social positions and a heightened fear of losing them. In this context, the domestic space served for them as the oasis of peace they needed to withstand the struggles and conflicts that characterized public life. Family life became much more subject to the unchallenged authority of the father. "Morality" (especially that of women) became the object of increased scrutiny, which reached a truly obsessive level. As was also the case in Europe, the flip side of this sexual repression—obviously more pronounced among the middle and upper sectors than the popular classes—was the tremendous boom in prostitution, which became a daily outlet for men and a forced fate for thousands of young women of modest means.

Gender inequality was further reinforced through the process of salarization. Women played a crucial role in providing labor for the expansion of capitalism, both directly and indirectly. The domestic tasks that almost all of them performed—raising children, feeding and clothing their husbands—were fundamental to the reproduction and maintenance of the labor force.

All this essential work went unpaid. Employers benefited from it because they could pay much lower wages than would have been required if there had been no women working for free in these households. But women also contributed more directly through mass employment. Those who were employed in this way were doubly exploited: not only did their domestic tasks go unpaid, but their salaries were significantly lower than those of their male counterparts. By 1895, 15.7 percent of the total industrial labor force nationwide (including manual laborers and employees) consisted of women, mostly criollo, who worked mainly in large factories. In the workplace, they were subjected to exploitation and sexual harassment.

Indeed, societies before and after 1860 were truly incomparable in many respects. More than a question of one society evolving into another, metaphorically speaking it was as if an entirely new edifice had suddenly been erected on top of the previous society, profoundly deconstructing it. Some components from the previous structure were adapted and used, while others were cast aside or hidden from view. Considering these changes as a whole, the idea of "modernization" with its implicit positive bias is hardly appropriate. Instead, what happened during these years should be described as an intensification of capitalism that led not to an essentially egalitarian society but rather to a profound restructuring in the forms of inequality and oppression. At this stage, it did not lead to a balanced or homogeneous nation but to a disorderly aggregate of dissimilar human groups scattered across a territory with deep economic, ecological, class, ethnic, and gender divisions.

The Birth of the Workers' Movement

Despite the political closure and the vast heterogeneity within their ranks, the popular classes were finding new ways to organize and rebuild their capacity to resist. This process was led by the most highly qualified urban workers. It was they who began to adopt forms of organization and resistance that had already proven effective in Europe and of which many immigrants had firsthand experience. The criollos, however, did not need the foreigners in order to embrace the ideas of the international workers' movement, which began circulating even before the great wave of immigration, evident in the pages of the Afro-Porteño newspaper *El Proletario*, for instance, which appeared in 1858.

The first trade union was born, like many others, from a mutual society. Porteño typographers had founded it in 1857, and in 1877 it became the Unión Tipográfica (Typographical Union), the first union in Argentina. Although there had previously been labor demands and work stoppages on estancias, in slaughterhouses and *saladeros*, and at ports in various cities throughout the littoral region (in 1877, for instance, water carriers in Rosario held a strike that lasted several days), the first organized by a permanent organization took place in Buenos Aires in 1878. It was carried out by the Typographical Union, which by that time was already linked to the International Workers' Association (better known as the First International). Starting early in the next decade, the example spread and trade unions were quickly established among railroad workers, bakers, shipyard workers, blacksmiths, cigar makers, and many others, in Buenos Aires as well as in Córdoba and Rosario. The crisis of 1890 unleashed a significant strike movement. Starting in 1896, there were strikes involving entire industries, and the first general strike of national scope took place in 1902.

Around the same time, workers managed to organize themselves into federations. Although there had been previous attempts, the first workers' federation to achieve some degree of stability was the Federación Obrera Argentina (Argentine Workers' Federation), founded in 1901. It was renamed the Federación Obrera Regional Argentina (Argentine Regional Workers' Federation, or FORA) three years later to emphasize the movement's international affiliation. Internationalism was a fundamental value for the workers at that time. In the events they organized, it was common for there to be speeches in several different languages, and the same happened with the trade union press.

The most frequent workers' demands were for better wages, an eight-hour workday, and an end to the repressive measures of the state. As living conditions were extremely harsh, solidarity grew and the struggles extended beyond purely labor demands. In 1907, for instance, in the overcrowded *conventillos* (tenement houses) of Buenos Aires, there was an unprecedented "tenants' strike" against rent hikes in which 120,000 people participated, with women playing a central role.

The state responded mainly with repression. The Residence Law (1902) and the Social Defense Law (1904) were used to deport, imprison, and deprive union activists of basic civil rights, while the police were sent to brutally quash all street demonstrations. During the May Day protest in 1909, as often happened, the police fired on the crowd for no reason, leaving 5 dead and 105 wounded. During the burial of the victims and at a subsequent event, the police again fired on the workers, resulting in more deaths. Nevertheless, the intensity of the strike forced the government to make concessions, and it finally ended after a veritable "Red Week," as it has been known since. As the workers' unrest did not cease, the celebrations of the country's first centennial had to be held under a state of siege.

Although socialist ideas predominated in the early years, it was anarchism that had the greatest influence. The first anarchist group began operating in Buenos Aires in the late 1870s. Argentina would soon have one of the most powerful anarchist movements in the world, with participation from both immigrants and criollos alike. It had a hegemonic influence within the workers' movement and reached its peak in 1910. The anarchists were neither a political party nor a unified group but rather a loose and decentralized federative movement, consisting of groups that sometimes held divergent positions. They saw politics and the state as inventions of the ruling class that served no purpose other than to ensure oppression. On the other hand, they were committed to self-emancipation through education, direct action, and autonomous union organization. They aimed to overthrow the state and the capitalists in one fell swoop in order to lay the foundations for a society of free and equal producers. A minority of the groups used terrorist methods, such as attacks on individuals or buildings that were emblematic within the world of the powerful.

Around the turn of the century, a socialist movement also took shape, in which French, Italian, and especially German political émigrés played a leading role. Unlike the anarchists, they believed that the path forward lay in organizing themselves into a centralized party, capable of bringing workers' representatives to Congress and pushing for greater democratization and reforms that would gradually lead to a socialist society. Accepting the rules of the political game, they were largely opposed to measures such as the revolutionary general strike, which they considered counterproductive.

The Socialist Party was formed in 1895 under the leadership of Dr. Juan Bautista Justo, who imbued it with a moderate spirit. Affiliated with the Socialist International, its electoral victories were quick to follow. It was the most important socialist party in Latin America, and in 1904 it became the first on the continent to have a representative in Congress (Alfredo Palacios, elected for the neighborhood of La Boca). Within the trade union movement, the socialists also had some influence. They initially cooperated with the anarchists but soon competed to organize their own workers' federation. Thus, while FORA remained in the hands of the anarchists, in 1903 the Socialist Party promoted a Unión General de Trabajadores (General Workers' Union).

A third current steadily gained greater weight within the workers' movement, especially after 1910. It was known then as "revolutionary syndicalism" and later simply as "syndicalism." Like the anarchists, the syndicalists rejected the participation of workers in high politics and believed in class independence. Unlike the anarchists, however, they prioritized the unity of the movement more than anything else and therefore tended to avoid any adherence to political doctrines that might cause divisionism. They were especially concerned with consolidating union structures and promoting coordinated and well-planned actions (unlike many anarchists, who believed in "spontaneism"). Although they initially rejected any contact with the state, the syndicalists would later become more flexible in their approach and accustomed to negotiating for improvements and specific reforms.

Women participated in the movement from very early on. In Buenos Aires as early as 1888, domestic workers went on strike against the requirement of carrying proof of employment, and by the turn of the century, female workers in some unions constituted a significant proportion of the striking masses. There was no shortage of prominent female activists, although very rarely did they hold leadership positions in the unions, an area that to this day remains one of the most monopolized by men.

Lettered Culture, Popular Culture, and National Identity

From early on, the state sought to impose national and cultural homogeneity on this heterogeneous mass of people with their broad range of ideas and sentiments—from memories of federalism or the feeling of having been discriminated against ethnically to revolutionary ideas and doctrines. An essential part of this plan was the vigorous intervention carried out through education. Rates of illiteracy fell from 77 percent in 1869 to 35 percent in 1914 (and would continue to fall), although once again regional inequalities were noticeable: in 1914, illiteracy was estimated at 20 percent in the city of Buenos Aires, more than 40–50 percent in most of the provinces, and more than 65 percent in Jujuy and Santiago del Estero. In any case, by the turn of the century a majority of the population was literate. Through schooling, the popular classes received notions of industriousness, morality, and civics in line with the social and political life that the elites sought to construct. Publications were also disseminated through schools: they were no longer the single pages and political gazettes in the gaucho style of yesteryear but rather brand-new textbooks.

Additionally, other publications were reaching wider audiences. Starting in 1870, the press gradually began changing its content and mission. It no longer aimed only to intervene in politics but broadened its interests to include news of all kinds, from international affairs to social life, and began to include feuilletons or serialized narratives, which won a broader readership. General-interest magazines also appeared, and books on a variety of subjects were published. A small group of writers, at that time only from the wealthy classes, began to make a literary career for themselves, including Paul Groussac, Miguel Cané, and Lucio Victorio Mansilla. The numerous popular libraries that Sarmiento helped establish ensured that his works and those of others were available throughout the country.

Closer to the end of the century, a true intellectual field flourished, driven by the ideas of positivism and faith in science and progress. Its general tone was optimistic, although it did hold a critical view of the evils of "modern life," the risks of mass politics, and the obstacles to progress in Latin American countries (generally analyzed as racially based failures). Prominent figures included Juan Agustín García, Agustín Álvarez, José María Ramos Mejía, Carlos Octavio Bunge, and José Ingenieros.

School culture and lettered culture in general instilled nationalist sentiments. In schools, there was no lack of symbols, stories, and patriotic rituals that encouraged pride in being Argentines. The same was true for military service, compulsory for young men starting in 1901.

Bartolomé Mitre, considered the father of Argentine historiography, wrote the first narrative of national history, obviously from a perspective favorable to his party. *Historia de Belgrano y de la independencia argentina* (History of Belgrano and of Argentine independence), published in 1858–59, attributed a key role to Buenos Aires in achieving independence and national progress. The city's bourgeoisie and politicians, the commerce and the spirit of free trade that permeated it, had been crucial in the ultimate triumph of liberty and civilization. On the other hand, rural spaces and the country's interior appeared as sites of narrow localism, backwardness, and a turbulent democracy that would only find a conduit thanks to the impulse of the Porteños. The federal caudillos were described in strongly negative terms or simply ignored. As Mitre saw it, a central ingredient in the success of Argentines on their path toward emancipation and progress had been the predominance of the "European race" among the Río de la Plata population, which set it apart from other less-advanced Latin American nations. Through Mitre's book, which was widely distributed, and others that complemented it (such as Sarmiento's *Facundo*), several generations learned to imagine a national history and to feel Argentine.

It is often said that the nationalism inculcated by the liberal elites was "civic" rather than "ethnic" or "cultural," as it would be in the following century. That is, it called on people of all origins to identify with the laws and the state but without advocating any strong notion of some homogeneous "national being" having this or that specific trait. However, this is inaccurate. Implicitly, liberal nationalism did presuppose a "distinctively Argentine" ethnicity and culture: that of European origin.

The idea that Argentina was distinctively white and European was reinforced at the turn of the century through the spread of the "melting pot" myth, which claimed that all ethnic groups inhabiting the country, old and new, had already merged and generated a homogeneous "Argentine race." The concept of the melting pot may sound inclusive, but it hid an implicit ethnic-racial hierarchy: it argued that all "races" had merged into one, but at the same time claimed that this fusion had resulted in a new, white-European race. The presence of mestizos, Black people, and indigenous people was minimized, and the assertion was made that their contributions, both biological and cultural, had disappeared, swept away by the great wave of immigration. As José Ingenieros, who was born in Italy, said in 1915, the time of the predominantly mestizo "gaucho Argentina" was over: modern Argentina was already of the "white race."

Both the overt racism of Sarmiento's generation and the more veiled racism of Ingenieros's generation had profound effects on the way society perceived itself and on how each group presented itself publicly. Speeches condemning everything that was not European were accompanied by a deliberate effort to make the presence of nonwhites invisible. It was soon decreed that there were practically no remaining Black Argentines and that the Indians were on the verge of extinction. Both statements were false, but the population census of 1895 determined that there was no point in counting "inhabitants who are not of the white race" because they were practically nonexistent. Thus, they disappeared from the statistics. Schools taught that Indian and Black Argentines were vestiges of the remote past. Visual culture, from fine arts to magazine illustrations, reproduced images of Argentine bodies that invariably had light complexions and European features.

Inhabitants whose bodies and histories did not correspond to this ideal were pressured to conceal these marks, and many (though not all) did so. The Pampean-Patagonian indigenous peoples and those from other places tried to pass as "criollos" and in many cases refrained from teaching their languages and culture to their children. The Afro-Porteño community—which in 1880 was numerous, with its own newspapers and associations and a strong public presence—suddenly became invisible. Leaders within the Afro-Porteño community themselves debated the best way to integrate into the nation. Some argued that they should do so as a minority with a distinct and specific culture, which was not white but was nevertheless part of the Argentine people and should be respected as such. It was a risky position because it involved openly challenging the idea of the European nation that the elites had been advocating while at the same time taking on the stigmas of being associated with the "barbarism" of Africa.

In the end, it was the opposite stance that prevailed: to play it safe, leave aside any kind of distinction, and integrate themselves on an individual basis, taking advantage of the fact that the law ensured the same rights to all. Thus, the Afro-Porteño newspapers encouraged their readers to change their behavior; forget the rituals and dress of their ancestors; put aside their rhythms, dances, and instruments; and embrace, instead, those of European origin. The idea was to blend in with the rest of the population. It was better to go unnoticed. The pressure worked: although some did protest (and privately, almost surreptitiously, preserved religious and cultural practices of African origins for decades), the Afro-Porteños became invisible. Similar processes took place in other parts of the country.

The messages, images, and narratives that the elites imparted through lettered culture and the school system were indeed powerful and forged lasting identities. Yet popular culture still managed to come up with its own content, which at times was at odds with government content and challenged its assumptions. Just as the elites proposed narratives, values, and emblems to define what was Argentine, the popular classes also participated by contributing their own, albeit in a more fragmentary and less systematic way. One of the best examples of this was in the surprising rise of *criollista* literature for popular consumption.

The phenomenon began with the resounding success of *El gaucho Martín Fierro* (*The Gaucho Martin Fierro*), published in 1872 by José Hernández, one of several federalists seeking a way to reintegrate themselves into the Buenos Aires political scene, which had become hostile to them. In a fit of enthusiasm he was to regret, Hernández had supported López Jordán's rebellion, which rendered him an outcast. In a period of dismay when he was certain that his journalistic career was over and he should forget about his political aspirations, Hernández wrote *Martín Fierro*, conceived as a denunciation of Sarmiento's government and his abandonment of the rural population. His own distress in that fateful context had allowed him to observe the country from the point of view of its most disadvantaged classes and to compose a heartbreaking lament from that perspective. Following in the tradition of gaucho poetry, he told the story of a meek gaucho who was subjected to all sorts of injustices by the state until he became a deserter and an outlaw. In the account, Fierro defends himself, knife in hand, from the police forces that come looking for him and ends up abandoning "civilized" society to take refuge among the Indians, where he feels more at ease. Through the desperation and loneliness of its main character, its nostalgia, and the hopelessness of its ultimate outcome, Hernández's poem launched a harsh critique that challenged the optimism of the elites. Seen from the eyes of a poor criollo, the "progress" the elites proposed did not appear as such.

Printed as a cheap pamphlet, *El gaucho Martín Fierro* became a surprising best seller. At a time when a "literary" text could be considered successful if a few hundred copies were printed, tens of thousands circulated in the countryside, where the paisanos read it (or had it read to them) with great delight, memorized it, passed it on orally, and made it their own.

This triggered a chain reaction in which Argentina was inundated with gaucho-themed publications aimed at a mass audience, starting with *Juan Moreira*, published by Eduardo Gutiérrez in 1879–80, which also won the hearts of the urban public.

Over the following decades, the public was entertained by dozens of stories of gauchos who rebelled against the state, longed for lost liberties, protested because they had been neglected in the face of the gringos, and complained that "progress" only benefited the estancieros or the city dwellers. Gringos and criollos alike consumed these stories: in a time of oligarchic political closure, both groups identified with a rebellious figure who fought against an unjust state. The criollo circus adapted these gaucho dramas to the stage and took them all over the country. Later they were also performed in the theater (and eventually in films).

The gaucho outlaw was thus transformed into a folk hero and an inescapable emblem of Argentine identity. Ironically, due to the cultural pressure exerted by the mass public, the project of the elites to "de-plebeianize" and culturally Europeanize the country resulted in a plebeian and rebellious criollo becoming a national icon. Worse still, *criollista* literature also implicitly questioned the idea of a white Argentina since its main characters were often described as brown-skinned paisanos who interacted with Black criollos. The same can be said for Mitre's narrative of history, since at times the defense of the rebellious gaucho was extended to the paisanos who had fought in the last *montoneras* and even to "gaucho" caudillos such as Chacho Peñaloza. Therefore, just as José Ingenieros was decreeing the end of "gaucho Argentina" and the advent of a modern nation, Argentina's popular classes were imagining themselves as gaucho and insubordinate. There were even anarchists who became enthralled with the gaucho image because it could so easily be transformed into an oppressed hero fighting against the state, something that suited their propaganda pamphlets perfectly.

Around the same time, the popular classes of the Río de la Plata made another decisive contribution that in its own way also undermined the cultural messages proposed by the elites: tango. Both the music and the dance emerged in the early 1880s. Its roots were clearly plebeian: influenced by African and criollo rhythms, tango emerged in the poor outskirts of Buenos Aires and was danced in brothels and other unsavory spaces. Its lyrics—which combined the gaucho style of speech, the *lunfardo* (slang) of the urban plebs, and the *cocoliche* (blend of Spanish and Italian) of the newcomers—tended to glorify the plebeian world and look down on the upper classes with mockery or contempt. The dance's indecency, the roguery of its early lyrics, and its identification with the *compadritos orilleros* (swaggerers from the city's outskirts) caused it to be immediately rejected by the elite (although this did not prevent it from captivating some upper-class youth who frequented the brothels). By the turn of the century, it had already spread to several working-class neighborhoods and could be found in cafés and dance halls downtown. When, in the early 1910s, a veritable "tangomania" broke out in Europe, tango experienced a triumphant revival in Argentina and was gradually accepted in more "respectable" social circles. Like the figure of the gaucho, it would also become a national emblem, even though it was a poor fit for the visions of the "decent," industrious, white, and European country that schools were promoting.

The nation therefore reached its centennial with not only a heterogeneous mass of inhabitants from different countries but also conflicting images of the Argentine collective "we," its history, its style of speech, and the physical traits that best represented it. Furthermore, the UCR had not ceased its armed rebellions, which represented a challenge along with the emerging multiethnic and cosmopolitan workers' movement of increasingly radical ideas. The liberal elites had managed to monopolize the state apparatus but had failed to achieve political or cultural hegemony.

4

Liberal Argentina and Its Constraints

From Failed Democracy to Peronism (1912–1955)

ON THE SURFACE, the liberal agro-exporting Argentina that the elites had organized appeared to be solid, giving rise to optimistic forecasts. However, it would soon become clear that this structure, cobbled together in haste, would not stand the test of time.

Given the growing challenge of the workers' movement, the Unión Cívica Radical (UCR)—which was engaged in an all-out assault on the regime—and a population that was increasingly beyond their control, part of the governing elite recognized that it was time to make some changes. There was a need to open up the political game a little so that those outside the game would accept its rules, albeit not so much as to risk losing power. The reformist sectors saw the young Roque Sáenz Peña as a candidate to succeed Carlos Pellegrini, but his chances were blocked through a skillful maneuver by the hard-line Roquista wing, which nominated Peña's father, forcing the son to withdraw from the race. Luis Sáenz Peña thus became the new president. Once in office, he did manage to incorporate one of the leaders of the UCR, Aristóbulo del Valle, into his government as a minister. But the Revolution of 1893 put an end to this rapprochement and hastened the fall of the president; once again the government was in the hands of a vice president, José Evaristo Uriburu.

In 1898, Julio Argentino Roca was elected president for the second time and conceded a modest electoral reform, although it was not enough to satisfy the Radicals (as the members of the UCR were known). The deaths of Leandro Alem and del Valle had left the leadership of the Radical Party to Hipólito Yrigoyen, and under his guidance it adopted an intransigent abstentionism. In 1905, shortly after Roca's successor, Manuel Quintana, took office, the UCR once again took up arms with a large-scale insurrection that, though defeated, clearly demonstrated that this situation of political closure was not sustainable. In the years that followed, the UCR would experience remarkable growth. Organized as a full-fledged party, with occasional conventions where leaders elected party authorities and candidates, it expanded its network of committees throughout the country. Despite the fact that in terms of social standing its leadership still strongly resembled the ruling oligarchy, it began to attract lower social sectors, both criollos and people of immigrant origin.

The task of finding a political solution to the situation was left to Vice President José Figueroa Alcorta, who took over the presidency due to Quintana's health problems. Overcoming the reluctance of the more hard-line sectors that responded to Roca's command, Alcorta managed to clear the way so that the reformists finally succeeded in electing Roque Sáenz Peña as president in the 1910 elections. Two years later, a law bearing the new president's name was passed, the first to guarantee fair elections.

The Sáenz Peña Law was certainly a risky maneuver. Argentina was one of the very few countries in Latin America whose laws did not exclude the poor from voting. In all the others, with the exception of Uruguay and Mexico, if you did not own property or were not literate, you were not entitled to citizenship. The same was true in many parts of the world; even in Great Britain, qualified voting was in force until 1918. Some members of the elite—including Roca—regretted not having such a provision, which would have allowed for clean yet exclusive elections, as Juan Bautista Alberdi had recommended in his time. But that was never a real option in Argentina, where contempt for the popular vote had been forced to settle for informal mechanisms of exclusion, such as fraud. Sáenz Peña was convinced that the ruling elite could muster a majority without such methods. The law he proposed established that the military census be used as the basis for voter registration—a guarantee that the latter would not be manipulated—and ensured that voting would be secret as well as mandatory. After intense debate, it was decided that foreigners could not vote, which meant that a considerable portion of the working classes would be excluded, as well as the inhabitants of the national territories. Women's rights were not considered (at the time, there were only two countries in the world where they could vote). The elite never imagined they could lose under these conditions.

The first time the new law was applied was in the 1912 elections in Santa Fe. After some hesitation, the UCR decided to end its abstention, and, to the surprise of many, it won. It did not do so well in other districts in elections held a short time later, but the triumph in Santa Fe was enough to raise the alarm. There were proposals for amendments to the Sáenz Peña Law, but none of them proved possible, and when the 1916 presidential elections came around, the law was still in effect. By then, the successful precedent had generated a wave of enthusiasm for the UCR, which became a mass party, the only one of national scope. The Partido Autonomista Nacional (PAN), in power at the time, had functioned more as an agreement between provincial parties and this time opted to support the candidacy of Lisandro de la Torre, the founder of the Santa Fe Liga del Sur (League of the South). In order to promote de la Torre as a candidate, a party with national ambitions was formed: the Partido Demócrata Progresista (Progressive Democratic Party, or PDP), eventually recognized as the country's main party of liberal-reformist ideas. A very small minority of the traditional political actors decided not to accompany this strategy. Led by key figures in the province of Buenos Aires who, since 1908, had referred to themselves as the Partido Conservador (Conservative Party), they went to the elections without announcing their support for de la Torre.

Despite the fact that these were the first clean presidential elections, popular participation was quite modest: only half of the eligible voters turned out to vote (in fact, in the main districts less than 10 percent of the population voted). The vote count in the electoral college was a surprise. By a slim margin, the UCR had more voters than de la Torre and the Buenos Aires dissidents combined. The traditional elite retained control of many provinces (in some, they had succeeded in committing fraud in spite of the new law) but had been unable to prevent Yrigoyen from being elected as the new president. It was a very hard and unexpected blow for them. The heirs of the oligarchy would never again come to power by democratic means. The people had turned their backs on those who considered themselves the creators of Argentina, those who had organized the state and set a thriving economy in motion. Their 1916 defeat produced a considerable political shift, which would distance them from liberalism's culturally more progressive path to place them instead on a more conservative course. They had not trusted democracy or the masses before, but their previous distrust had at least allowed them to risk politically opening up and supporting a democrat like de la Torre. From this point on, their distrust of the ballot box would turn into a resentful animosity that would push them toward cruder forms of authoritarianism.

The First Radical Government

Yrigoyen became president in 1916 amid a public fanfare rarely seen in the streets of Buenos Aires. In the years that followed, he constructed an intense relationship with his supporters, based on a very unusual type of leadership. During his term in office, portraits, medals, and objects with his image were distributed everywhere to strengthen his popularity. He almost never spoke in public; he preferred to hold personal meetings at the government house with those who requested them. As the more traditional politicians commented in shock, its rooms filled with people of all kinds—including the least "respectable"—who awaited their moment with the president to ask him for help. Additionally, the neighborhood committees of the UCR's extensive network provided local residents with material benefits (such as meat or "Radical" bread at low prices), helped them with paperwork, facilitated access to state positions, and offered cultural activities and entertainment. It was the first mass political movement.

Under Yrigoyen's leadership, the UCR had made clean elections and the complete implementation of constitutional guarantees its only program. It had come to power criticizing "the oligarchy" for the fraudulent way it had handled political life, but it had no fundamental criticisms regarding the orientation of the economy or the very unequal social order it had generated. There would be no significant changes in the agro-export model during Yrigoyen's government. His relationship with the cattle-ranching bourgeoisie showed no sign of strain; in fact, several of his ministers belonged to the Rural Society.

The dynamics of democracy, however, did present some deeper challenges at the provincial level. After 1916, several Radicals were elected as governors or mayors. Some of them proposed substantive changes that contrasted with

Yrigoyen's moderation. In Rosario, Ricardo Caballero presented himself with great success as a defender of the working class and of the "dispossessed criollo masses," in opposition to the "selfishness" of the "unlimited expansion of the right to property." In his speeches, he combined his defense of the workers with references to Argentine history that were full of nostalgia for the gauchos. Around the same time, Lencinism in Mendoza and Cantonism in San Juan, both emerging from the UCR, won the governorships of their provinces, from where they introduced some of the most advanced social rights in Argentina at that time (including women's suffrage, granted in San Juan in 1927). In Jujuy, another Radical maverick, Miguel Tanco, made his mark by presenting himself as a "defender of the proletariat and enemy of company bosses" while vindicating the campesinos and the oppressed indigenous peoples. Without being on the left—at least not according to the standard definition of the term—all these politicians echoed the class-conscious sentiments that existed among vast portions of the popular classes in order to win their admiration and their vote. As a consequence, the local upper classes waged war on them; Federico Cantoni, for example, survived six assassination attempts.

But even Yrigoyen's moderation did not free him from the animosity of the now displaced elite—in reality, partially displaced. The institutional design envisaged in the constitution was intended to establish limits on popular sovereignty by placing mechanisms of power beyond the reach of the majority vote. The first democratic experience clearly demonstrated the consequences of that vision. Yrigoyen became president, but the UCR held a minority in Congress; he eventually obtained a majority in the Chamber of Deputies but always had the Senate in opposition to him. From there, the liberal-conservatives were able to systematically block his initiatives. For its part, the UCR saw itself as the embodiment of the nation and therefore did not recognize any legitimacy in its opponents.

For all these reasons, Yrigoyen's relationship with the legislative branch was stormy. He never ventured outside the law, but he did show contempt for Congress. In order to broaden his power base and dismantle the mechanism of fraud, which was still in place in several provinces, he ordered numerous federal interventions by decree, most of them to displace opposition governments (including those of some "wayward" Radicals moving away from the fold). He also used the distribution of state jobs and other clientelistic measures to attract voters and intermediate-level leaders.

The liberal-conservative opposition—which had never displayed a very solid republicanism—denounced Yrigoyen for disrespecting the institutions and violating legal procedures. With growing insistence, they branded him an authoritarian leader, and more than a few compared him to Juan Manuel de Rosas, associating him with the "barbarism" of the earlier federalists. Class bias also played a role in their distaste for the UCR government, particularly toward the children of immigrants, who were beginning to gain access to positions of authority in the state, and toward the voting masses in general who had turned their backs on them. A strong anti-plebeian reaction emerged in these years: a conservative newspaper criticized Radicalism by calling it a movement for the "manumission of the Negroes" that had come to establish a "Negroid mentality" in the country.

These beliefs helped galvanize an opposition front that united not only conservative politicians and those of the Progressive Democratic Party but also a group of "anti-personalist" Radical leaders, who found common ground criticizing Yrigoyen's supposedly authoritarian style. This front also found common ground with the socialists and some of the "fractious" Radicals from the Buenos Aires province that the leader of the UCR had disavowed.

The Demands of Society and the Workers' Movement

During these years, the gains of the workers' movement and the wave of democratization gave birth to new social demands. In the 1910s, a series of conflicts broke out in the countryside, led by small-scale farmers. In 1912, they organized an extensive strike movement, with its epicenter in Santa Fe, that became known as the "Grito de Alcorta" (Cry of Alcorta). They went on to found the Federación Agraria Argentina (Argentine Agrarian Federation), the main association that would represent this sector for years to come, and demanded changes in the system of land ownership and tenure, accessible loans, and reductions in leasing fees. The strike ended with several of its leaders assassinated and a few modest achievements. The Argentine Agrarian Federation resumed strikes between 1919 and 1921. This time it encountered a slightly more receptive atmosphere and managed to get a leasing law passed. In later years, it would abandon this type of action, as a significant proportion of the farmers gradually became landowners.

Around the same time, a powerful student movement also emerged. Although there had been precedents at the University of Buenos Aires, the spark was ignited at the University of Córdoba in June 1918. The students demanded the democratization of university life, improvements in academic quality, more flexibility in study conditions, and a renewal of the teaching staff. Treated with some benevolence by the government, through their struggle they managed to achieve several of the features that helped shape Argentine universities and still exist in the present day: co-government, academic freedom, and voluntary class attendance. The University Reform—as it was known—also expressed a desire for unity with the workers and had a continental projection. It inspired young people throughout Latin America.

Women also became more active in defending their rights. Starting in the late nineteenth century, anarchists had produced specific publications, such as *La voz de la mujer* (Woman's voice, 1896), in which they addressed the oppression they experienced in domestic life and introduced disruptive issues, such as "free love" and birth control. As the anarchists were not concerned with anything related to state politics, they expressed no interest in proposing women's right to vote, a demand that the socialists and freethinkers, on the other hand, did push for. From the centennial period onward, these last groups fostered several women's organizations and trade union events, and in 1918 helped create the Unión Feminista Nacional (National Feminist Union), through which Alicia Moreau and others carried out an intense struggle for the right to vote. Julieta Lanteri was also a prominent figure on this front and went on to create the Partido Feminista Nacional (National Feminist Party). Other initiatives of this type flourished in the 1920s and 1930s.

As part of this agitation, in 1919 a Radical representative brought a proposal for women's suffrage before Congress for the first time, although it was not passed (in 1932, it would be passed in the Chamber of Deputies but defeated in the Senate). On the other hand, in 1926, at the initiative of the socialists, Congress did pass a law putting an end to the civic inferiority of women. From that moment on, they were no longer required to ask their husbands for authorization to study, do business, or initiate lawsuits, and men lost the right to administer their wives' property (parental authority, on the other hand, remained exclusively male). Practices at the time reflected these modest advances. Vigilance over the morality of young women continued to be strict, but toward the end of the 1910s, in line with what was happening in the rest of the world, attitudes relaxed slightly. Fashion enabled the use of short skirts and bobbed hair, and "respectable" women were able to enter the job market as secretaries or saleswomen without any stain on their morality (factory workers, on the other hand, were still subjected to the commonly held belief that their activity conspired against the decency and "gentleness" proper to a lady).

Yrigoyen's presidency marked a change in how the state dealt with the workers' movement. Previous governments had already understood that mere repression was not enough, and in 1907 President Alcorta had created the Departamento Nacional del Trabajo (National Labor Department), which was tasked with gathering information, particularly on anything related to workers, and seeking contacts among them. The aim was to address a few of their sectoral demands to keep them from converging into a unified revolutionary movement. The Yrigoyen government took this approach one step further and began to mediate in some conflicts with management; it occasionally backed solutions favorable to the workers (which in turn strengthened the shift toward unions, more inclined to interact with the state, and weakened the anarchists). A few labor laws were passed during these years, although resistance from management and the weak capacity of the state to enforce them meant that their actual effects were modest.

None of this brought an end to the repression. On the contrary, the most terrible episodes occurred during Yrigoyen's term in office. In January 1919, a police massacre in response to a metalworkers' strike unleashed a spontaneous insurrection in Buenos Aires, with repercussions in other cities. While the Federación Obrera Regional Argentina (FORA) declared a general strike, there were demonstrations in several neighborhoods; the workers assaulted police stations and armories and erected barricades. For a week, the state lost control of the situation, despite having militarized the city with more than thirty-two thousand troops, assisted by brigades of young people from wealthy families, soon known as the Patriotic League. Led by Manuel Carlés, a Radical who had close ties with the conservatives, the league took charge of setting fire to union premises and attacking workers. It was the first extreme right-wing organization to operate in the country. Leading newspapers collaborated with the repression by spreading stories about a Russian "Soviet" plot behind the riots. Perhaps due to this paranoia, the Jewish community, which was associated with the Russian communists, was also the victim of attacks. The general strike ended after a week, leaving an estimated seven hundred dead.

This "Tragic Week" was not an isolated event. Labor unrest had been on the rise since 1917, partly because wages had fallen behind in the previous years but also because of the wave of enthusiasm that the Russian Revolution had unleashed throughout the world. Its peak in Argentina was in 1919, a year in which ties of solidarity also spread to other sectors. Teachers in Mendoza, for instance, held a strike, which was unprecedented for their union; theater actors, small-scale farmers, switchboard operators, and workers in commerce and banks in numerous cities also rallied; high school students went on strike and marched through the streets waving red flags. Even the police went on strike in Rosario in 1918–19.

The conflict also extended to rural areas. Challenging the despotic power wielded by La Forestal, which subjected them to brutal exploitation, lumberjacks and quebracho workers had succeeded in declaring their first strike in 1919. The company responded with black lists and persecutions that led to new measures and further violence from management. In January 1921, a large strike spread throughout the territory occupied by the company. Police forces, at La Forestal's service, unleashed a campaign of terror, burning down the workers' ranches and embarking on a veritable manhunt for those who escaped through the bush. The death toll is unknown, but it was most certainly high.

In Santa Cruz, there were also epic struggles that ended in even more terrible massacres. The area was dominated by huge estancias dedicated to wool production, many in the hands of the British and the Germans. By 1920, the Río Gallegos Workers' Federation, led by anarchists, had succeeded in broadening membership to include many of the ranch hands, and that same year began a strike movement.

Landowners, organized in the Rural Society and the Patriotic League with support from the British Embassy, demanded the government send troops to crack down on workers. Yrigoyen responded with an intermediate solution: he sent the army but with an order to carry out mediation, which resulted in some concessions to the workers. Management failed to fulfill its part of the deal, and by early November 1921 all of southern Santa Cruz was paralyzed. The press in Buenos Aires, sympathetic to management, then raised the specter of a "Chilean invasion" in Patagonia and spread false stories about crimes committed by laborers on estancias. The pressure on Yrigoyen continued until he decided to send in the army again, which this time acted ruthlessly. Many of the striking workers were captured and summarily shot (the fact that the national constitution prohibited the death penalty for political causes was of no assistance to them). There is no way of knowing how many met this fate; decades later a researcher was able to document 283 cases, but there were undoubtedly many more (the anarchist press estimated no fewer than 1,500). None of those involved in the shootings were ever tried—in fact, quite the contrary. The government promoted the officer in charge of the expedition and the UCR blocked the creation of an investigative commission in Congress.

Liberal Argentina and Its Constraints

Yrigoyen's Succession and the End of the First Democratic Experience (1922–1930)

Having completed his term in office, Yrigoyen designated Marcelo Torcuato de Alvear as his successor, and the latter was elected president in the 1922 elections. A member of one of the wealthiest cattle-ranching families in the country, he had a solid relationship with his mentor and was a proven Radical. However, the cabinet he appointed when he took office made it clear that he would follow his own path. Alvear was moving closer to the "antipersonalists" critical of Yrigoyen. By 1924, both factions of the UCR were in open confrontation.

Apart from certain questions of style and a more harmonious relationship with the opposition, Alvear's government did not introduce any major innovations. The economic model remained the same, and there were no relevant changes in rural production, except for an increase in corn and, in peripheral regions, the expansion of cotton, peanuts, yerba maté, and sugar cane crops, as well as fruit growing in Río Negro.

In 1923, Alvear managed to pass a law to protect small- and medium-scale stockbreeders, who had been harmed by the actions of the large-scale winterers. Closely associated with the meat-packing plants, the latter had forced down the prices paid for fattening animals. Alvear's law aimed to reverse the situation, but the meat-packing plants, most of them American, halted all purchases and forced the government to suspend the law's application. It was a clear demonstration of the weakness of the state with respect to market forces.

There was, however, one important novelty: the beginning of oil development. The first oil fields had been discovered in Comodoro Rivadavia in 1907, and soon after, large American companies had arrived to exploit them. Toward the end of his presidency, Yrigoyen had created a state-owned company, Yacimientos Petrolíferos Fiscales (Fiscal Oilfields, or YPF), which, during Alvear's presidency, would give a strong boost to this activity. Moreover, in 1923, Alvear raised tariffs on imports, fostering the growth of the industry to some extent.

The relationship with the workers' movement continued to oscillate between mediation and repression. But those who were subjected to the worst state violence were the indigenous peoples of the Chaco. In 1924, the government tried to promote cotton cultivation there, involving the Tobas and other groups. In order to force them to take jobs as laborers, they were prohibited from traveling to the sugar mills in the northwest, as they had done for decades in search of better wages. To protest this measure, in May of that year indigenous peoples from various parts of the Chaco gathered in the Napalpí reserve and, echoing the struggles of the workers' movement, decided to declare a "general strike": the laborers refused to work and the campesinos stopped planting cash crops. On July 19, while they were performing a ritual, 130 policemen opened fire on them from a distance without any warning. By the time the carnage was over, some two hundred Indians were dead. The incident was covered up this time as well and the perpetrators remained in total impunity.

Meanwhile, in Buenos Aires the confrontation between Radical factions continued. The anti-personalists hoped to somehow block Yrigoyen's candidacy for a new term, but the 1928 elections approached without that possibility materializing, so they decided to run their own candidates. In the electoral campaign, Yrigoyen accused them of "colluding" with the conservative oligarchy and proposed the nationalization of oil, a message that garnered broad support. The vote count yielded an overwhelming victory: he triumphed with close to 60 percent of the vote. Without controlling the state apparatus, he won in almost all districts and swept the province of Buenos Aires. The election also saw a record turnout: 80 percent of registered voters participated, much higher than the poor showing in 1916. The Argentine people were getting used to the ballot box. On the other hand, the elites were not: for some time, certain sectors had been courting the military, and the defeat in 1928 only reaffirmed their conviction that they had no choice but to seek alternative methods to return to power.

Yrigoyen's second term resembled the first, although tensions intensified. His oil nationalization project was blocked by the senators. The Radical leader responded as before, intensifying efforts to broaden his support through the distribution of jobs and federal interventions. One of these interventions was in Mendoza and resulted in the assassination of Carlos W. Lencinas, for which the opposition blamed the government.

These political problems were compounded in 1929 by economic difficulties. In October, a sharp drop in the New York stock market triggered the Great Depression, the worst world crisis to hit capitalism. Its effects were quickly felt in Argentina, which experienced a decline in exports, inflation, layoffs, and wage reductions. These crises, in turn, had an impact on the 1930 legislative elections, in which the government fared quite poorly. There were calls for Yrigoyen's immediate dismissal.

Finally, on September 6, a poorly organized military coup with only a few mobilized troops managed to seize power. This was not a decision of the army as a whole (many commanders actually sympathized with Yrigoyen). However, the reality is that there were few reactions in defense of democracy. The deposed leader was imprisoned on Martín García Island; a mob looted and set fire to his house. The coup d'état was supported by the employers' associations, nearly all the press, and almost all opposition parties. The Supreme Court—whose judges mostly dated back to the oligarchic era—gave legal cover to the new government with a new doctrine that was to set a precedent: it considered it a "de facto government" that had to be recognized.

This marked the end of the country's first experience with democracy, which had lasted barely fourteen years. The 1930 coup inaugurated a new period, characterized by the liberal-conservative restoration but also by the veto power of the military. From that moment on, for decades, the breakdown of the constitutional order was to be Argentina's fate. Nearly seven decades would pass before another democratic period of the same length could be completed.

Coup d'État and Fraud: The Liberal-Conservatives Return to Power

The coup d'état had been carried out in the name of the institutions sullied by Yrigoyen, but there was little agreement among those involved on what to do next. Those furthest to the right proposed a root and branch reform, replacing democracy with a system of corporative representation like the one fascism was attempting in Italy. Other groups preferred to continue with the liberal order mandated by the constitution and quickly reinstate a civilian government, returning to earlier fraudulent practices if necessary. Initially, the first group prevailed, represented by the new de facto president, General José Félix Uriburu, the scion of an aristocratic family from Salta. His brief tenure was marked by repression. Several Radical leaders were persecuted with poorly substantiated accusations of corruption, and the workers' movement was subjected to deportations and violence of all kinds, including the execution of anarchists Severino Di Giovanni and Paulino Scarfó. During this period, the use of the *picana eléctrica* (electric prod), a method of torture invented in Argentina, became widespread among the police.

Opposition within the ranks of those who had supported the coup blocked the corporatist path that Uriburu was advocating, forcing him to call an election in the province of Buenos Aires. The election was held in 1931 and the UCR won. The government reacted by annulling it. This failed attempt ended the de facto president's career and benefited instead that of his rival, General Agustín Pedro Justo. Justo had more solid political contacts: he had been Alvear's minister and had the support of the liberal-conservatives—who in 1931 regrouped as the Partido Demócrata Nacional (National Democratic Party, or PDN)—as well as the Church, more than a few anti-personalists, and the Partido Socialista Independiente (Independent Socialist Party, or PSI), a group that had split off from the Socialist Party. Most importantly, Justo had the solid backing of the army. With this coalition supporting him, he called a general election and in 1932 became the nation's president.

Of course, the elections were rigged. With Yrigoyen in prison (and then dead in 1933), Alvear had become the undisputed leader of the UCR. However, when his candidacy was prohibited, the party returned to its old method of abstention (it also resumed armed uprisings during this period, with four between 1931 and 1933, all of them quelled). As a result, Justo only had to compete against the coalition formed by the Socialist Party and the Progressive Democratic Party. Additionally, fraud was committed in several districts; in the case of the province of Buenos Aires, it was flagrant and led to the governorship of Manuel Fresco, a nationalist with ideas bordering on fascism. (According to his memorable expression, it was "patriotic fraud.") Nevertheless, Justo's triumph was not overly comfortable. His vice president was Julio Argentino Roca Jr., clearly a symbol that this was a restoration.

It would be inaccurate, however, to view Justo's administration as a mere repetition of the oligarchic governments or to describe it as "conservative" in the strict sense of the word. The political alliance known as the Concordancia that backed Justo's government included, in key positions, figures from the PSI, such as Antonio de Tomaso, who was the son of workers, and Federico Pinedo, who came from an oligarchic background but had been active within socialism. Their contribution was crucial in the implementation of a series of innovative economic reforms, which are discussed in the next section.

What did resemble the oligarchic era was the official favor granted to British interests and the corruption, which in the 1930s reached colossal proportions. The most resounding case was that of the Roca-Runciman treaty, signed with the United Kingdom in 1933. The agreement was aimed at defusing the British threat to interrupt purchases of Argentine meat. To this end, the government accepted very onerous conditions that obligated the country to give the British preferential treatment in Customs, to export primarily from foreign meat-packing plants, to ship the meat on British ships, and to use all the pounds received to purchase British goods or pay the debt incurred with that country. In addition, British service companies were to be given special treatment—all this in exchange for maintaining the purchase of meat at its previous levels. The treaty gave rise to a heated debate in Congress, followed by an investigation headed by Senator Lisandro de la Torre. Evidence showed that the meat-packing plants that benefited from the treaty did not pay their taxes, concealed information, and benefited certain cattle ranchers in particular with purchases at preferential prices, including the minister of agriculture, Luis Duhau. The collusion between the ruling elite, the cattle ranchers, and British imperialism became more apparent than ever. While the debate was taking place on the Senate floor, a thug with ties to the government shot at de la Torre with the intention of killing him. The bullet did not hit him but rather his Senate colleague and protégé, Enzo Bordabehere. (Distressed by this, de la Torre killed himself in 1939.)

That was the most notorious scandal, but it was not the only one. In 1935, Congress also passed a law granting the British a monopoly over all urban transportation in Buenos Aires for fifty-six years. Through bribes, British capital obtained similar advantages for the provision of electricity. Due to corruption, subordination to foreign interests, and the return of fraud, the 1930s would be remembered as the "Infamous Decade."

In the 1938 elections, which again involved notable fraud, the antipersonalist Radical Roberto Marcelino Ortiz was elected to the presidency. He came to power as Justo's ally but shortly after taking office demonstrated greater autonomy than anticipated and began negotiations with Alvear to reach an agreement for restoring democracy. In 1940, however, due to health problems, he had to leave the government in the hands of his vice president, the conservative Ramón Castillo, who preferred to continue with the status quo. In fact, starting in December of the following year, he governed under a state of siege.

The Global Crisis and Changes in the Economy

Responding more to transnational than local forces, the Concordancia government made decisive changes in the economy and expanded the state's capacity to regulate it. Between the outbreak of World War I in 1914 and the end of World War II in 1945, the global capitalist order underwent a crisis of seismic proportions. The wars and the stock market crash of 1929 brought with them an unprecedented destruction of wealth and disrupted trade circuits and the international division of labor. Currencies ceased to be convertible into gold, and the most industrialized countries moved away from free trade to protect their economies. Great Britain, having come to dominate much of the world, fell into decline and was replaced by the United States as the new hegemonic power. Capitalism and the liberal order were challenged everywhere. Within a few decades, following the 1917 Russian Revolution, nearly a third of the world's population shifted to living under communist regimes. Far-right illiberal movements came to power in several countries—among them the Nazis in Germany and the fascists in Italy—and seduced significant portions of the population in others. Politics, economics, ideas: everything underwent a profound transformation.

The upheaval unsettled Argentina. With the agro-export model, the country seemed to have found its place in the world. The relationship with Britain was a dependent one, but it did ensure a certain degree of complementarity: the British consumed the goods that the country produced and provided manufactured goods and capital that the Argentines needed.

The rise of the United States upset this balance. Starting at the turn of the century, the Americans implemented aggressive policies to displace Great Britain: in Argentina they invested in meat-packing plants and public utilities, two areas previously dominated by the British. They also established their own manufacturing plants. Additionally, cars progressively replaced railroads in transporting people and goods. Automotive imports increased, along with radios, phonographs, agricultural machinery, and machinery for local industries, all from the United States. The problem was that, unlike Great Britain, the United States did not need Argentine grain and was quite well supplied with its own meat. There was no possibility of complementarity. What had been a simple two-way relationship then became a complicated triangle in which Argentina sold to some but bought an increasing amount from others. The trade surplus with European partners was used to finance the deficit balance with the United States, which was bound to irritate the former. And when currencies ceased to be convertible, exports did not provide the dollars needed to import.

The new three-way relationship required more sophisticated economic policies than those Argentina had implemented since oligarchic times. Ensuring the availability of foreign currency was increasingly complicated. Moreover, by the time the centennial arrived, the areas suited for agriculture in the pampean region were fully occupied: one of the resources on which the previous prosperity had been based—the abundance of land—was depleted. Another factor, the availability of immigrant labor, suffered sudden ups and downs due to the wars. And the supply of a third factor, capital, was at risk not only because of international financial instability but also because the profits that foreign companies sent abroad exceeded their investments (in addition to the servicing of the heavy foreign debt).

World War I had taken an initial economic toll on the country, but it was not serious enough to trigger major changes. However, the severe crisis that followed the onset of the Great Depression made it clear that the agro-export model was exhausted. The drop in the prices of agricultural products, widespread protectionism in the more developed countries, and the interruption of capital inflows required a fundamental transformation.

Starting in 1931, and more clearly after Federico Pinedo became minister of finance two years later, a series of profound reforms decisively changed the profile of the Argentine economy. Tariff policies became markedly protectionist and this, coupled with the scarcity of foreign currency to pay for imports, acted as a formidable stimulus to industrial development. Following the Keynesian ideas the core countries were applying, the state took an active role in economic regulation and investment. To begin with, it imposed an exchange control for the first time, through which it centralized and administered the sale of foreign currency. It did this to prioritize specific uses, but it also reaped significant benefits that, along with the income tax approved in 1931, swelled the public coffers. Among other things, these funds made it possible to finance a vigorous road construction program undertaken by the Dirección Nacional de Vialidad (National Department of Roads and Highways) created in 1932.

The state also equipped itself with new instruments for intervention. After the convertibility of the peso was abandoned, the Central Bank was created in 1935. It was essentially an entity controlled by private bankers—mostly foreigners—and only supervised by public officials, who would control monetary policy from that point on. National Boards to regulate the trade of various products were also established to protect producers from price fluctuations and keep their revenues as high as possible. The first was the Junta Nacional de Granos (National Grain Board), followed by those overseeing meat, cotton, wine, yerba maté, milk, and so on. The grain board, for example, bought large quantities at a good price and then sold them to private exporters, so that farmers would not be forced to sell them during peak supply; the wine board bought excess grapes in order to destroy them and keep prices high. In short, it was a question of ensuring good profits for the producers, a statism that the businessmen applauded. What did not change, however, was the pro-British orientation of economic policy and diplomacy. In the face of worldwide protectionism, it was a question of "buying from those who buy from us," as several voices in the government and among the cattle-ranching bourgeoisie demanded.

Thanks in part to this set of measures, the economy grew at very high rates in the 1930s. This was especially true of industry, which had attracted new players, but also of those who had made their fortunes in agriculture and livestock farming and diversified their investments, and of course foreign companies—especially from the United States—that sought to avoid high customs duties by producing within the country. The value of industrial production during these years exceeded that of agricultural and livestock production, and the proportion of people employed in the sector grew at the expense of those employed in rural occupations. By the end of the decade, Argentina was already exporting industrial products to neighboring countries.

The beginning of World War II once again put a strain on the local economy. As a way out of the predicament, in 1940 Pinedo proposed a bold new reactivation program: the state would invest heavily in infrastructure and housing and would provide decisive support for strengthening the country's manufacturing capacity. But the plan did not pass the test in the Chamber of Deputies, where the UCR blocked any initiative presented by the government, in protest against the fraud it had committed.

The growth in manufacturing during these years helped boost the economy while at the same time adding to its imbalances. The nascent industrial sector emerged as a result of import substitution: manufacturers aimed to produce what the end consumer demanded and what was now costly to import. It was therefore a light industry that still depended on other imports—machinery, metals, and basic inputs—that were not produced locally. Born out of customs protections, it had little incentive to be efficient or to lower costs, and its revenues relied more on favorable exchange-rate policies and the continuity of the protections. As a result, in the medium term it had difficulties exporting; its main destination was the domestic market, which meant that it used foreign currency to import required inputs but did not generate it.

Furthermore, industrial development was concentrated in Buenos Aires and the surrounding area and, to a lesser extent, in the littoral region, which exacerbated regional imbalances. By 1938, 73.9 percent of the country's manufacturing production was in the Buenos Aires area, which was therefore home to the bulk of the workers. In contrast, starting in 1914 the number of industrial establishments located in the northwest provinces and the number of people employed in them decreased dramatically. This tendency reinforced the process of urbanization and the growth of the city of Buenos Aires, which in the early 1940s would reach a population of 3 million inhabitants, a figure that has remained steady ever since. In addition to this, there was the explosive growth of the Greater Buenos Aires, the metropolitan area surrounding the city. Both areas attracted a highly significant influx of internal criollo migrants, who left the countryside to mix with the workers of immigrant origin in the working-class neighborhoods and the *villas miseria* (shantytowns), which grew in number and size over the course of the decade.

The Discussion of Ideas

The decades following the centennial were one of the richest periods in terms of culture and the discussion of ideas. The relative monochrome of the oligarchic period gave way to a proliferation of multiple ideological and aesthetic positions. Liberalism lost its former centrality and was subjected to profound questioning.

During these years, literacy continued to expand and, with it, lettered culture. Books, libraries, magazines, and lectures became more commonplace in the lives of a broader spectrum of people. The literary scene became much more democratic: "serious" writers were no longer only from the wealthy classes, which led to other perspectives and topics. Jorge Luis Borges, Leopoldo Marechal, Victoria Ocampo, and Roberto Arlt were among those who became prominent in the 1930s. Among the intellectuals, there was a reaction against positivism and a renewed interest in discussing, in somewhat more pessimistic tones, national identity and the problems faced by this country that the oligarchy had constructed. Raúl Scalabrini Ortiz, Eduardo Mallea, and Ezequiel Martínez Estrada wrote memorable essays on the topic. In line with what was happening with aesthetic avant-garde movements worldwide, the 1920s and 1930s also witnessed intense innovation in the visual arts and music.

Leftist culture was experiencing one of its most brilliant moments. During the first decades of the century, trade unions and socialist and anarchist groups feverishly published newspapers and pamphlets and were tireless organizers of cultural and propagandistic events. They were later joined by the Communist Party, founded in 1918 by a group of activists dissatisfied with the moderate tone of the Socialist Party and eager to explore the revolutionary path that the Russians had just taken. Their tirades against capitalism and the bourgeoisie, their militant atheism, their commitment to greater gender equality, their faith in reason and science, and their values of solidarity, internationalism, and egalitarianism had a profound impact on a good portion of the population. Emerging among workers, leftist culture also gained ground among the middle sectors and later gained legitimacy in the intellectual field. The broad consensus achieved in the mid-1930s, worldwide as well as in Argentina, on the need to form a common democratic front against fascism even gave fresh impetus to the communists in intellectual discussion. Because of the emotional impact it had from 1936 onward and the subsequent arrival of thousands of Republican emigrants, the Spanish Civil War also contributed to opening up a significant space for progressive and left-wing ideas. The same was true for the substantial antifascist movement organized shortly thereafter, which converged in the Acción Argentina (Argentine Action) coalition in 1940. Within this context, several progressive and left-wing intellectuals, publishing houses, and magazines gained respectability and prominence.

The anti-imperialist stance became increasingly significant. The aggressive expansionism of the United States in Latin America, evident since 1898, had already generated an initial rejection. During World War I, Yrigoyen upheld Argentina's position of neutrality, and his diplomacy challenged American expansionism on several occasions. Anarchists and socialists also rejected it, and anti-imperialism formed part of the core ideas held by students during University Reform. In the 1920s, intellectuals such as Manuel Ugarte and José Ingenieros participated in initiatives in favor of Latin American unity against Yankee imperialism, a concern that remained very present in later years. The plundering of the Argentine economy by foreign companies also sparked criticism. This was the main focus of the Radical intellectuals of the Fuerza de Orientación Radical de la Joven Argentina (Argentine Radical Youth Force, or FORJA), created in 1935 as a dissident group in opposition to the UCR leadership, in which Arturo Jauretche and Gabriel del Mazo, among others, were prominent.

Toward the opposite end of the spectrum, starting in the late 1920s, various right-wing, antidemocratic, and antiliberal positions gained prevalence. Nationalism was a common denominator for them all. As discussed in chapter 3, the liberal elites who organized the state also encouraged patriotism in public rituals and in schools. Concerned by the workers' unrest and revolutionary ideas, during the centennial period they intensified this message, which became quite aggressive, even xenophobic. At the time, certain intellectuals associated with the ruling elites, such as Ricardo Rojas from Santiago del Estero, began to insist on the need to consolidate nationalism not only by instilling in children a love for the flag and national heroes but also by inviting them to identify with old criollo customs, rural folklore, and the figure of the gaucho. This meant adding new cultural content to what it meant to "be Argentine," distinct from what the state had been advocating up to that point.

In principle, there did not appear to be anything necessarily antiliberal or antidemocratic in these proposals. However, around the same time, certain intellectuals began combining this nationalism anchored in the criollo with more clearly antiliberal content. In 1913, Leopoldo Lugones from Córdoba proposed that the gaucho and *Martín Fierro* become the cornerstone of a nationalist discourse that he later connected to the military and authoritarian order (and finally to fascism). The Patriotic League had a similar stance starting in 1919, and by the late 1920s there was already a whole intellectual movement that, taking up the ideas of European authoritarian thinkers, challenged liberal individualism and democracy in the name of a strong nation, which in turn required firm traditions and an ironclad political order. The newspaper *La Nueva República* (The new republic), founded in 1927 by brothers Rodolfo and Julio Irazusta, was its guiding light. By then they had already gained influence in the army, especially among those who saw Uriburu as their mentor.

Over the following decade, extreme right-wing nationalism developed many other intellectual initiatives and sprang into action through a myriad of antiworker paramilitary organizations, such as the Legión Cívica, the Alianza de la Juventud Nacionalista (later known as Alianza Libertadora Nacionalista), and the Legión de Mayo, among others. Some were decidedly elitist and rejected universal suffrage, but others sought to gain a foothold among the lower classes and called for their demands to be addressed from an antisocialist perspective. They sought to identify themselves with what was criollo as a way of rejecting the cosmopolitan tendencies of the left; some also defended their Hispanic heritage and Catholicism. All shared a taste for militarism and a preference for traditional family order and male authority. Several were antisemitic and were seduced by fascism and Nazism. As part of their rejection of liberalism, they also tended to be critical of the free market. They disseminated their ideas through various newspapers and magazines and gained considerable popularity.

The Church, which had its own tradition of questioning liberalism and valued its Hispanic heritage, joined them. In 1928, with the magazine *Criterio* (Criteria), it gave right-wing nationalism a forum; Monsignor Gustavo Franceschi stood out for his fascist and antisemitic preaching and for his praise of strong governments. In 1934, the Church demonstrated its strength with the celebration of the International Eucharistic Congress, during which it proved its capacity for mobilization in the streets of Buenos Aires. With its own press and powerful lay organizations, such as Acción Católica (Catholic Action), founded in 1928, it became an indispensable political actor and a bridge between right-wing nationalism and the armed forces.

Starting in 1934, certain sectors of this right-wing tendency developed a peculiar "revisionist" narrative of the past that supported their arguments. They sought to vindicate the role of the federalist caudillos and those of the country's interior, whom they regarded as the guardians of the true nation, which was criollo and Hispanic. They were particularly focused on extolling Juan Manuel de Rosas, portrayed as the leader of autonomous development and an organic social order. His defeat in 1852 had ushered in an era of national decline, dominated by the foreign-loving Porteño elites in the service of British interests (during this period, the right developed a peculiar anti-imperialism, more focused on rejecting the foreign for being a vector of liberalism than for its adverse economic effects).

From this standpoint, it did not seem coincidental that the leader of the Buenos Aires liberals, Bartolomé Mitre, had also been the historian who established a canonical interpretation of the past. His history, in their view, was an ideological misrepresentation. Among the revisionists, Manuel Gálvez from Santa Fe, Carlos Ibarguren from Salta, and Ernesto Palacio from Buenos Aires were the most prominent. It should be noted, however, that the impulse toward revising the past did not begin with this group, nor did it end with it. As explained in chapter 3, popular criollismo had already produced a defense of the *montoneras*, and there were later forms of revisionism that did not identify with right-wing ideas and were even intertwined with others of the left. In their various forms, over the long term they had a considerable influence on the way that Argentines imagined their past.

Given his attractiveness to a broad range of people, the gaucho became established during these years as an emblem of Argentine identity. For some sectors of the left, he was a rebellious and anti-oligarchic hero; for the right, he was a component of a nationalism anchored in criollo/Hispanic traditions, and for the general population, he had the emotional appeal he had always had. In 1939, the Buenos Aires provincial legislature finally gave the gaucho official cult status by establishing the "Day of Tradition," which in 1943 became a national holiday. (Governor Manuel Fresco and Minister of Education Gustavo Martínez Zuviría, both from the extreme right, were crucial in this recognition.) None of this prevented many other Argentines from continuing to regard everything that was criollo, *moreno* (dark-skinned), federalist, or from the interior—the gaucho included—as a source of backwardness and barbarism. Argentina reached the 1940s without having come to an agreement about how to define the national "we." In fact, there were now competing narratives that were openly antagonistic.

The Birth of Mass Culture

In the early twentieth century, the remarkable expansion of popular entertainment seen in the previous years continued. Criollo circuses toured the entire country. In the cities, theaters sprang up with shows of all kinds, especially *sainetes* and revues, with dancing and singing. In addition to the proliferation of cheap gaucho-themed publications, there were romantic novels published in weekly installments. But more importantly, the first four decades of the century also witnessed the emergence of a commercialized, mass culture. The first film screenings were held in Buenos Aires in 1896; silent films were soon produced locally, and by the 1910s they were a popular attraction. In the 1930s, with the advent of talkies, an important national industry developed in competition with the films from the United States that captured the majority of the audience. In 1929, there were 972 movie theaters nationwide, with 152 of them in the city of Buenos Aires, many of them in working-class neighborhoods, charging inexpensive admission. In the following years, the number of theaters and spectators would continue to multiply.

By this time, radio had already made its appearance, and by the late 1920s it was a rapidly expanding business. Twenty years later, there were already nineteen radio stations in the capital and another twenty in the rest of the country, with programming of all kinds, from music, criollo traditions, humor, and radio plays to news, political speeches, and sports shows. One out of every two families had a radio, which clearly illustrates the market penetration it had achieved. In the 1910s, records by local artists became available (they could be recorded in the country starting in 1919) and labels with their own catalogs appeared. This provided the opportunity for not only tango and jazz but also rural folk music to become a mainstream genre in the 1930s.

The 1920s also saw the consolidation of a new type of journalism geared toward the masses. The newspaper *Crítica*, founded in 1913, set the tone with a series of novel strategies to attract readers. Sensationalist news, crime stories, and sports coverage took center stage. It was the most widely read newspaper in Argentina and one of the most widely read in the world (in 1939, it printed a record of more than 810,000 copies in a single day).

Mass culture in Argentina was completely ahead of the curve. Only one year after the first cinematographic projection in Paris, films were already being exhibited and shot in the country. As of 1905, Rosario had the first movie theater dedicated exclusively to Latin American films (before that, they were shown in cafés as brief entertainment). Argentine films were exported to several countries in the region and even to Spain. And in 1917, the world's first animated film was produced in Buenos Aires. Argentina was also a pioneer in radio broadcasting with one of the first general-interest broadcasts in the world in 1920.

During these years, sports became a form of commercial and mass entertainment as well, especially soccer, which ceased to be reserved for British immigrants and the elite and instead became a passion of the masses. In the early twentieth century, it became popular among men from the middle and lower sectors, who started hundreds of small amateur clubs. It did not take long for the spectacle to be marketed. From the 1920s on, matches attracted more and more spectators willing to pay for tickets in stadiums that were now ready to receive crowds. The media broadcast the names and images of the most admired players, and it was soon possible to buy their pictures at newsstands. By then, the practice of offering payment to the most skilled players to prevent them from leaving for other clubs was spreading, which gave an advantage to the institutions that could raise the most money and pushed the others to follow suit or disappear. The process of professionalizing soccer was completed early in the following decade. Playing in small fields and paddocks remained open to all, but the creation of clubs and competition in major tournaments was out of reach for the vast majority.

The emergence of mass culture meant a decisive change in entertainment styles. The abundance of more sophisticated offerings pushed some expressions of earlier popular culture into the margins, such as Carnival, which began its slow decline. It also affected the way that cultural goods were produced and disseminated. Business ownership, advertising, and technology took center stage. Admittedly, in these early years, many of the businesses were still small and improvised, but the historical tendency was for them to gradually transform into capitalist companies. Artists were forced to adapt to market demands, which gave them new opportunities while imposing conditions on them at the same time.

A clear example of this can be seen in the evolution of tango: the marketing and dissemination of it among the "respectable" classes led to profound changes. From the early 1920s, it took on the form of tango-song: its lyrics ceased to be picaresque, and though they spoke of the underworld in elevated poetry, they also described "champagne" and cabarets, trips to Paris, and other episodes that had little to do with the plebeian. Due to the need to compete with the sound of jazz—by then very popular in Argentina—tango became harmonically more complex. On the back of this development, Carlos Gardel became an international star in the 1930s. He succeeded due to the unquestionable quality of his art but also because it was by then possible for him to record his voice and to star in successful films produced in the United States (which, in turn, forced him to partially abandon the Porteño *lunfardo* [slang], only understandable to local audiences).

The involvement of business owners also had a political impact. Whereas previously a party, trade union, or agitation group could print newspapers and pamphlets and compete with the newspapers of the elite for the public's attention, the competition became much more one-sided (as the Radicals found out when *Crítica* supported the 1930 coup). However, it is also true that the lower classes had some influence, albeit indirect, on the content of mass culture. Since the media and entertainment industries needed to sell their products, they inevitably had to take popular taste into account. This was crucial for local business owners, especially the film and record companies that had modest capital and found it very difficult to compete with American and European products. Therefore, their business strategy was to draw as much as possible on earlier popular culture—theatrical *sainetes*, criollismo, tango—in order to offer products with an authentic "local flavor," something that foreign record companies and studios could not provide. In that way, mass culture inherited some of the traits of those earlier expressions, including a few that were politically inconvenient for the wealthy classes, such as the rebelliousness of the gaucho or tango's contempt for the well-to-do.

As they did elsewhere, many of the cinematic melodramas had plots that encouraged social harmony and mutual understanding. But the first decades of Argentine films also abounded in the opposite: relatively "class-based" plots that depicted the wealthy as evil hypocrites, superficial, alienating, or oppressive, and the world of the poor as the repository of national authenticity, solidarity, and moral values.

As a result of both the vitality of leftist ideas and the peculiar bias of mass media products, the 1930s were characterized by a political life that was once again monopolized by the upper classes but accompanied by a culture rich in politically subversive content.

Political Alternatives and the 1943 Coup

Within this context, political closure became increasingly unsustainable. The opposition parties were pushing for a return to democracy and, at the same time, the workers' movement was displaying renewed vitality and initiative.

Violently attacked by the state, union activism peaked in 1919–21 but ended in divisions and a deadlocked struggle. By 1929, the movement was more fragmented than ever, with four different workers' confederations: the anarchist FORA, the trade unionists' Unión Sindical Argentina (Argentine Syndicates' Union, or USA), a Workers' Confederation closely aligned with the Socialist Party, and the Comité de Unidad Sindical Clasista (Committee of Class and Union Unity, or CUSC) created by the communists. However, trade unionism slowly reconstructed its unity. A few days after Uriburu's coup, talks that had begun earlier resulted in the founding of the Confederación General del Trabajo (General Confederation of Labor, or CGT), which would go on to unite the bulk of the movement.

Despite the repression, in 1936–37 the strikes reached peaks of considerable intensity and participation. During these years, they also expanded throughout the country: not only in the capital city and the provinces of Buenos Aires, Córdoba, Santa Fe, and Tucumán but also in areas that until then had been relatively uncommon settings for strikes, such as Entre Ríos, Formosa, Mendoza, Catamarca, San Juan, and Santiago del Estero. In response to the Taylorist fragmentation of the labor process, the traditional model of organizing unions *by trade* was gradually replaced with a single organization *per industry*, which grouped together all the workers of a particular activity, regardless of their respective trades and levels of skill. In this way, the movement succeeded in reunifying what management sought to divide. The rate of membership grew perceptibly, although unevenly; in some of the new industrial sectors, it was still very low.

During the 1930s, the state strengthened its mediating role, while at the same time it continued to use brutal repressive measures, albeit more selectively. Some of the first social policies date from those years and emerged more at the provincial than the national level. Governor Manuel Fresco was merciless with the communists, but he actively intervened to regulate the labor market, extend support measures, and organize union demands to channel them peacefully and isolate revolutionary currents. The province of Buenos Aires' Department of Labor increased its funding and expanded its personnel and forms of intervention, thereby becoming a real tribunal for the resolution of labor disputes (generally in favor of the workers). At the same time, Córdoba, governed by Amadeo Sabattini of the Radical Party, and Santa Fe, under the Progressive Democratic Party, developed similar policies. Thus, a new conception of the state began to emerge, not only as a "neutral" mediator between management and workers but also as a guarantor of the dignity and welfare of the latter (several female activists played a central role in promoting this vision).

This new orientation, along with the growing "Argentineization" of the labor force, strengthened the trade unionist and socialist sectors, more willing to interact with the state, at the expense of the anarchists, who in the 1930s lost prominence. However, this does not mean that the more class-conscious options disappeared: the popularity of the Communist Party grew steadily among the workers, especially in the industrial sector. After joining the CGT, the Communists went on to hold seventeen of the forty-five positions in its Confederal Central Committee as well as the vice presidency, which reflects the degree of their influence. Although their orientation distanced them from other political parties, the international context helped narrow the gap, especially after 1935, when the Communist International called for the creation of broad fronts against fascism. In this way, the dominant currents within the workers' movement converged on a central point: the need to have a more direct influence on what was happening within the state. And to do so, democratization was necessary. In 1936, this new impulse was clearly reflected in the major demonstration the CGT organized for International Workers' Day on May 1, with a clearly oppositional tone, in which it invited high-ranking leaders of the Radical, Progressive-Democratic, and Socialist parties as speakers. It was thus the driving force behind an unprecedented political action that in practice—although not yet formally—brought together the opposition.

The united electoral front against the liberal-conservatives and their allies finally took shape in 1942 with the creation of the first Unión Democrática (Democratic Union). Although the discussion on whether to join it caused a split in the CGT—there were sectors that did not support the move—it was clear that, within the workers' movement, there was a new willingness to become involved in high politics and in state administration. No one could have imagined that this willingness would soon find itself presented with such a strange and unexpected opportunity to carve out a new path.

The international context contributed other factors that conspired against the Concordancia government. Relations with the United States deteriorated significantly after it entered World War II. Argentina maintained its traditional neutrality, more to avoid jeopardizing its exports to Europe than out of sympathy with the Germans. In fact, for this same reason, Great Britain, which was also at war, showed no interest in enlisting Argentina's support, which in any case did not show much promise of great contributions in military matters. However, the United States now demanded unconditional support in the name of defending democracy against the threat of fascism (an urgency that many saw as an attempt to advance its imperialist interests). Continuing a long tradition of frustrating "Pan-Americanist" initiatives, in 1942 the Argentine foreign minister managed to thwart an agreement for all Latin American countries to enter the war as a bloc. Consequently, the American government implemented strong retaliatory trade measures against the country and opted for Brazil as its regional ally. The results were unsettling: the United States was helping arm the neighboring country, Argentina's traditional military rival. At the same time, the international struggle was also reflected in local politics: the opposition front used the rhetoric of democracy in mortal danger to attack the Concordancia government, which it associated with the Nazi menace threatening the world. In 1940, the coalition Acción Argentina, which brought together leaders of the main parties and prominent cultural figures, demanded that war be declared on the Axis. Nevertheless, President Castillo maintained neutrality, relying on the opinion of the military and nationalist groups. The situation took on an apparent clarity that was deceptive: apparently to be "democratic" was to oppose the fraudulent government but also to support the United States.

The pressure from the United States became intolerable and, with the elections approaching, Castillo announced that his candidate would be Robustiano Patrón Costas, a sugar producer from Salta, who was very conservative but at the same time strongly in favor of the Allies. This decision was of some relief to his foreign and domestic enemies, but it also displeased his few remaining supporters. And so, on June 4, 1943, the army, most in favor of remaining neutral, staged another coup d'état that deposed Castillo.

Like the previous coup, this one was also quite improvised: the initial de facto president, General Arturo Rawson, lasted only three days before he was replaced by General Pedro Pablo Ramírez, who, in turn, was replaced less than a year later by General Edelmiro Farrell. These last two were the visible face of the GOU, a secret society of nationalist officers operating behind the scenes.

Members of this group had two main concerns. On the one hand, they feared the influence that the Communists had acquired in the workers' movement. They foresaw, with good reason, that the advance of the Communists worldwide would intensify as soon as the war ended. The antipopular nature of the liberal-conservatives only served to add fuel to their fire: the country had to be prepared to resist their advance, and this required a state that was much more attentive to popular demands.

On the other hand, they were also concerned about Argentina's military weakness with respect to Brazil. In order to be in a position to defend itself in the event of a war with the neighboring country, in addition to national unity, there was a need for much greater economic development than Argentina had seen up to that point, particularly in heavy industry. And this required the state to take an even more active role in the economy.

One of the government's first measures was to implement religious education in public schools in order to counteract the message of the Communists, who were also subjected to increased persecution. The National Labor Department, renamed the Secretaría de Trabajo y Previsión (Secretariat of Labor and Social Security, or STP), was granted more powers and began to take numerous initiatives in favor of wage earners. Colonel Juan Domingo Perón, completely unknown at the time, was appointed to head the department. He soon gained notoriety for how quickly he organized relief for the city of San Juan when it was struck in early 1944 by an earthquake that killed more than nine thousand people.

During Perón's brief tenure, the workers' movement achieved unprecedented benefits and rights. The organizations under communist leadership endured ongoing persecution, and the government often unseated them by encouraging the creation of parallel unions. However, organizations that had a good relationship with the government were invited to participate in the elaboration of STP measures, which in turn benefited them with subsidies to extend their healthcare and social welfare programs. They saw the expansion of pension benefits, the creation of the *aguinaldo* (thirteenth-month bonus), an improvement in workers' compensation for on-the-job accidents, an increase in the number of paid vacation days, and the introduction of new job security clauses for several unions. The Laborer's Statute extended basic rights to rural workers, who had been unprotected until then. A freeze on leases also benefited small-scale farmers. Additionally, a new legal jurisdiction was created, with labor tribunals presided over by judges specially dedicated to protecting workers' rights.

Perhaps the most significant measure was the decree that regulated and extended the negotiation of collective bargaining agreements for each industry, something that few unions had achieved before then. The agreements would be enforceable and the STP was given the power to enforce them. The October 1945 Law of Professional Associations, which transformed this decree into permanent legislation, also granted broad union rights, including the protection of delegates and members against any retaliation from management. Prior to this, the few labor laws enacted by the state had been seldom and poorly enforced, especially outside the capital city. The vigorous action of the STP made them a reality and expanded them geographically.

These measures irked business owners because they brought about changes in their day-to-day dealings with their labor force. Workers began to feel that there was now a higher authority looking out for their interests that trumped that of their bosses. This naturally affected labor discipline, as fear and submission gave way to a more proud, even haughty, attitude on the part of laborers, white-collar employees, and workers. Business owners and estancieros could not stand this "undisciplined atmosphere" in the workplace, and starting in mid-1945, the major employers' associations began to speak out publicly, dragging in their wake those that represented small- and medium-sized producers and retailers.

Other middle sectors—such as teachers, offended by the reintroduction of religious education in schools, and professionals and students, fed up with government interventions in the universities—added their discontent. The political parties, who wished to return to democratic life, also contributed.

Although the de facto government, yielding to pressure, had reluctantly declared war on Germany, the American ambassador took an active role in the opposition, especially to the rising figure of Perón, who had been designated minister of defense and vice president in addition to his previous position. Many saw him as either a Nazi-fascist leader or a caudillo who was bringing back the barbarism of Juan Manuel de Rosas, or both at the same time. The main newspapers and the most prominent intellectuals added their own concerns. This fueled a formidable anti-Peronist reaction in 1945, which led to countless proclamations and, in September, a demonstration of 200,000 people that flooded the streets of Buenos Aires, the likes of which had never before been seen.

Cornered, the military government sacrificed Perón and prepared for the transfer of power back to civilian rule. On October 9, the colonel was forced to resign from his multiple positions and was confined on Martín García Island.

Liberal Argentina and Its Constraints

The Supreme Court declared the decree that had created the Labor Tribunals "unconstitutional," and a few weeks later employers refused to pay the new year-end bonuses. The reaction of the propertied classes had begun.

The Irruption of Peronism

Perón is remembered as a leader strongly identified with the workers and at odds with the upper classes. However, none of this characterized his first months in public office. "Social justice" and sympathy for the workers were hardly motivations for those who staged the 1943 coup. Perón's own ideas initially began with little more than the peaceful cooperation of the various social sectors under the firm leadership of the state, with no clear preference for the lower classes, nor antagonism toward the upper classes. His thinking was based on his military education, social Catholicism, and nationalism. He had attempted to win the support of the business community, the middle sectors, and the UCR, but to no avail. Only the workers showed him sympathy, although in 1945 many of the union leaders still regarded him with distrust.

On October 17, 1945, detained on Martín García Island, Perón was convinced that his political career had ended. However, that day the masses acted of their own accord and changed the anticipated course of history: in very little time, the previously almost unknown colonel would be catapulted into the nation's presidency. A hitherto unseen group of people occupied Buenos Aires' elegant downtown: they were poor and shabbily dressed; some lacked suit jackets and even shoes. Many were brown-skinned, internal migrants who had arrived in the capital city over the previous decade. Others were descendants of European immigrants or were themselves born abroad. They came from low-income neighborhoods and from the city's outskirts, where factories were multiplying and the poor lived crammed together. In La Plata, Tucumán, Zárate, Córdoba, and Salta, there were similar demonstrations.

In the unions, they could see the reaction of management coming. It was clear that without Perón in the government, the achievements of the previous months were at risk, but it was not as obvious that the workers should go out to defend him. Many continued to distrust his intentions and others felt that his career had come to an end, which made it inconvenient to pin their demands on him. Since October 14, the CGT had been debating what to do; the answer came two days later in a very divided vote. The workers' confederation called for a general strike on October 18, without a demonstration; the text of the announcement did not even mention Perón.

But the multitude of workers, encouraged by indications that the CGT had taken a lead in the struggle, decided not to wait and acted on their own. Very early in the morning, a day before the strike was to take place and without any announcement from any organization (with the exception of some rank-and-file unions), they took to the streets to demand Perón's release. Their unexpected presence flooding the Plaza de Mayo caused a strong impression: the enormous crowd gathered there had no intention of leaving the plaza without concrete answers.

As Perón seemed to be the only one capable of calming them down, there appeared to be no choice but to have him brought back from Martín García. After long hours of hesitation and negotiations, the colonel finally appeared on the balcony of the Casa Rosada to speak to the crowd. During the speech, he was interrupted several times by demonstrators and a kind of dialogue was established with the leader that from then on would be a typical feature of Peronist rallies. The October 18 general strike paralyzed the entire country. Never before had a labor action organized by the CGT achieved such overwhelming and widespread support.

It was in those forty-eight hours that the movement that would dominate national politics for decades to come was born. For the Peronist movement cannot be explained only through the figure of Perón but also in the interaction of his leadership with the presence of two other no-less-important actors: the organized workers' movement and grassroots-level action, which often overshadowed one another. The trade union movement had made important progress in unifying the struggles and demands of the lower sectors but was still far from having achieved it. In an unexpected way, the figure of Perón allowed the Argentine popular classes to move beyond the considerable fragmentation that still characterized them. Through Peronism, they became a unified political subject for the first time.

For a long time, there was a belief that Perón had drawn especially strong support from "new workers" who had recently migrated from "backward" areas of the country, while those with more urban and organizational experience had been reluctant to embrace the new leadership. Studies show that the colonel attracted supporters from both sides and counted many experienced trade unionists among his strongest defenders. Furthermore, although the workers' movement played a key role, the Peronist movement went beyond it; Peronism was something new and distinct, and it mobilized the popular classes in areas where there were no factories or trade unions. This convergence did not come without a cost for both sides; trade unionism lost in autonomy what it gained in influence, while the lower classes tied their fate to their leader and, in doing so, allowed themselves to be shaped to a considerable extent by his ideas.

Perón, for his part, had to maintain a public image of "tribune of the plebs," which he did not initially plan to adopt and which did not merge well with his own ideology. When the decisive mass mobilization on October 17 revived his political career, he found himself at the head of a much more plebeian movement than he would have liked. From that point on, his power depended on his ability to continue to mobilize worker support, which forced him to tolerate or even channel a class antagonism that was inconsistent with his personal beliefs.

Partially Perón's political project, partially the product of the self-interest of the labor leaders, partially the plebeian and galvanic contribution of the masses: it was all Peronism. That tension between the leader's will and the desires his followers invested in him is what made it such a contradictory movement.

It was not clear at first, however, who would lead whom. As soon as the successful October 18 strike was over, the union leaders felt victorious. They then conceived the project of creating their own party that would serve as the political arm of the workers' movement. They immediately set to work and in November founded the Partido Laborista (Labor Party), headed by Luis Gay, a longtime union leader. The idea was to win the elections scheduled for February, with Perón as their candidate. In order to do so, Perón, who lacked a party of his own, needed the support of the unions. But he did not want to be bound hand and foot to them, so he demanded they accept an alliance with the UCR-Junta Renovadora, a small group of politicians who had broken away from Radicalism. It did not take long for conflicts to arise between the two groups, which gave Perón greater authority as an indispensable mediator. The Peronist coalition also received the support of several right-wing nationalist groups (while others remained its adversaries) and of the Church.

The Labor Party put all its energy into ensuring victory in the elections, and in fact it was, by far, the party that secured the largest number of votes for the colonel (assisted in many districts by Radical leaders who joined its ranks). The anti-Peronist forces united behind the candidates of the Democratic Union, a coalition that grouped not only the UCR and the Progressive Democratic Party but also Socialism and the Communist Party. (Due to their disrepute, the liberal-conservatives were not included; some of them supported

Chapter 4

the coalition informally, while others backed Peronism.) The employers' associations and most of the press were also on their side.

The campaign was marked by significant polarization and an intense class struggle. The Democratic Union presented itself as the standard-bearer of civilization, freedom, and democracy, threatened by a candidate who, in their view, represented nothing less than the arrival of "Nazi fascism." Perón, for his part, sought to identify himself with the lower classes and criollo culture. In addition to improvements for the workers, he promised an agrarian reform that would deliver "the land to those who work it" (a promise he would never keep). He denounced the "oligarchy" as the enemy of Argentine interests and took advantage of the constant interventions of American ambassador Spruille Braden to present the election as a choice between "Braden or Perón." He thus portrayed himself as a defender of the lower classes and the Argentine people against imperialist aggression.

Perón achieved a narrow victory in February 1946, in elections that saw a record in voter turnout. The popular classes voted for him as well as a significant segment of white-collar workers, small-scale producers, and other middle sectors. Some local elites even supported him (especially in Córdoba and Santa Fe), attracted by his nationalism, his clericalism, or for having declared himself "a conservative, in the noble sense of the word."

The Labor Party had little time to celebrate its victory: shortly after the elections, Perón began making moves to take power from them. In May, he ordered the dissolution of the Labor Party and the rest of the groups that had supported it and their merger into a new Partido Único de la Revolución Nacional (Sole Party of the National Revolution), later renamed the Partido Peronista (Peronist Party), as if to leave no room for doubts. The thousands of supporting groups that had spontaneously emerged throughout the country became "Basic Units" of the Peronist Party. Some surprised Labor Party members tried to resist. But faced with mounting pressure and the loss of leadership, they gave up and finally, in June, complied with the directive. Those who refused to do so, such as Cipriano Reyes, ended up in jail.

The next step was to take control of the CGT, which jealously guarded its autonomy until 1947, when, through a campaign of false accusations launched by Perón himself, its leaders were forced to resign and were replaced by more compliant ones. The CGT's increased *political* subordination, however, did not mean the end of the power of trade unionism; on the contrary, its role as an agent of *economic* struggle was strengthened. The confederation no longer functioned as an entity that pressured the state from the outside but rather as an agent of pressure from within.

From then on, the CGT was to a large extent a means of relaying Perón's power to those below. But to be effective in that mission, it had to maintain its legitimacy among the workers, which gave it space to channel the demands coming from below. In fact, in 1946 there was an explosive eruption of strikes and conflicts throughout the country, which continued until 1948. The working class, through its unions, capitalized on the electoral victory and used strike actions to enforce and deepen its gains. Some of them were carried out despite Perón's wishes. The "internal commissions" within each factory expanded; their role was to defend the workers on site and to ensure that agreements with management were respected. These agreements now included special clauses—on seniority, promotions, punitive measures, incorporation of new personnel, and so forth—which limited employers' power in the use, organization, and disciplining of the labor force. These changes marked a profound redistribution of power in the workplace.

Furthermore, this new alliance with the state played an important role in the organization of the working class. The expansion of collective bargaining agreements required the unions to be well organized, which in turn fostered a greater unionization of workers. The number of union members grew by more than 370 percent between 1945 and 1950. With the incorporation of new entities representing most sectors of activity, the CGT achieved something akin to the unification of the entire labor arc. Deeply rooted in both the state and Peronism, by 1955 Argentina had one of the most powerful workers' movements in the world.

Achieving that status, however, had its costs. The enormous growth profoundly affected the internal life of most trade union organizations. Their size, along with the increasing complexity of the tasks involved, made multiplying the number of nonelected paid positions essential. In addition to their traditional roles, the unions began to attend to a wide variety of issues related to the well-being of workers, such as the provision of affordable food, tourist services, healthcare, and so on. In addition, complex collective bargaining required a corps of legal and technical advisors. In short, a rather extensive union bureaucracy began to pull its own weight in internal decisions. The leaders—now a professional class with full-time responsibilities—progressively distanced themselves from the daily lives of ordinary workers. Grassroots democracy became more of an exception.

Chapter 4

Less autonomous but at the same time more powerful, more distant from the grassroots but with a greater capacity for mobilization, the workers' movement occupied a central place and had a weight of its own within Peronism and, as part of that alliance, within the national landscape.

The First Term of Perón (and Evita)

Perón won the 1946 presidential election in all districts except Corrientes. This gave him something that Yrigoyen had not had: an absolute majority in the Chamber of Deputies and control of the Senate, where the ruling party held all the seats. In the following elections, Peronism won around 60 percent of the vote, which allowed the Peronist Party to hold on to and increase those seats. It was thus able to deactivate the countermajoritarian power of the liberal-conservative Supreme Court, which from the outset had been dedicated to blocking measures taken by the ruling party: through a swift impeachment trial, it was almost completely renewed.

Once the political and institutional obstacles were cleared, Perón had free rein to govern, which he did in a corporatist style, with a strong executive branch (in which military cadres had a highly visible presence) that made decisions in conjunction with the representatives of the main interest groups, especially the workers, businesspeople, and the Church. Without any doubt, this meant that the political parties and the parliament were no longer the gravitational center, but it was, in any case, a moderate corporativism, which did not involve formal changes either in the attributions of Congress or in the civic rights associated with the vote.

In 1949, Perón seized the opportunity to promote constitutional reform. In the elections called for this purpose, the delegates to the constitutional convention again obtained an absolute majority and the opposition decided to withdraw from the debates: the drafting of the new text was left exclusively in the hands of the Peronists. Contrary to the fears of many, they did not take advantage of the situation to draft a corporatist constitution: the liberal core of the 1853 constitution remained in place, although some of its countermajoritarian provisions were attenuated. The new text established direct voting for senators and for the president and vice president, for whom indefinite reelection was enabled. The reform established the promotion of "social justice" as one of the objectives of the state and gave a series of social rights constitutional status, including fair remuneration for work and access to adequate housing, recreation, social security, and healthcare. It also stipulated the national ownership of subsoil resources.

Perón's government introduced reforms that had a profound effect on social relations. Just as the United States had done under the New Deal, the state expanded its direct involvement in the economy. Similar to France and Great Britain, progress was also made in the nationalization of some of the country's key resources, such as gas, ports, telecommunications, railroads, and part of the electrical power supply. Shortly before Perón took office, the military government had also nationalized the Central Bank and created the Instituto Argentino para la Promoción del Intercambio (Argentine Institute for the Promotion of Trade, or IAPI), a centerpiece of Peronist economic policy. The IAPI bought grains, meat, and other primary goods directly from producers and then sold them to foreign buyers. This decoupled the local price from the international price, which reduced profits for producers but helped lower the price of products for Argentine consumers. The surpluses obtained by the state were channeled into the promotion of other sectors of the economy, mainly manufacturing. These resources, combined with the exceptional trade surpluses that World War II contributed to the Argentine coffers and the deepening of customs protectionism, gave the substitute industry, which was already growing rapidly, a crucial boost. They were also used to pay off the foreign debt that the country had been burdened with for decades. During these years, Argentina experienced the most rapid period of industrial expansion in its history.

These and other measures had a direct impact on the levels of employment and wages, which grew steadily. Real wages for urban workers grew by 60 percent between 1945 and 1949, which gave them access to consumption beyond what was strictly necessary for survival. Like a virtuous cycle—at least this is how it worked in the early years—better incomes translated into more consumption, which fed industrial growth, especially in small- and medium-sized businesses, which in turn generated more employment and better wages. Exports of manufactured products to neighboring countries declined, however, as a result of American trade policies deliberately aimed at punishing Argentina for having maintained neutrality in the war (they also succeeded in complicating sales of grain to Europe). Thus, the notable industrial growth of these years was oriented almost exclusively to the domestic market.

Additionally, the state took a much more active role in promoting the population's well-being. Rent freezes brought relief to tenants, and extensive housing construction programs for workers along with cheap credit helped many become homeowners (despite the fact that, due to the intense flow of internal migrants, *villas miseria* proliferated in the Buenos Aires metropolitan area). Age and disability pensions were expanded to an unprecedented extent, while the number of people with social security coverage rose from 1.4 to 2.5 million between 1945 and 1950.

The creation of the Ministry of Health in 1949 and the decisive efforts of its first minister, Ramón Carrillo, expanded hospital services, health campaigns, and vaccinations throughout the country. Access to education continued to grow, with a significant leap forward at the secondary level and then the university level, which became increasingly accessible to people from working-class backgrounds (thanks in part to the elimination of tuition fees).

With more rights and better salaries, the popular classes enjoyed more free time, which fueled various forms of entertainment and cultural expression, including some directly fostered by the government. Thanks to government promotion and the unions themselves, which established summer camps and hotels, access to tourism grew exponentially: the traditional seaside resort of Mar del Plata, which in 1940 had received 380,000 vacationers, had to make room for more than 1.4 million in 1955.

In short, the working class experienced the greatest peak of well-being in its history and society became less unequal: the proportion of the country's total income that remained in the hands of wage earners rose from 37 percent to 47 percent in 1950. Perceived as the result of a political process in which the lower classes also played a leading role, these improvements all contributed to a significant change in the way citizenship was conceived from that moment on: it was no longer just a matter of having the right to vote but also of having access to a minimum level of well-being.

Peronism also brought with it significant changes in gender relations. The participation of women from the popular classes had already been apparent in the 1946 campaign, when they had the audacity to sing, "Sin corpiño y sin calzón / Somos todas de Perón" (Ain't got no bra or knickers on / We are all down with Perón). In 1947, Congress finally signed women's suffrage into law.

Eva Duarte, better known as Evita, Perón's wife, was central to the women's suffrage initiative (much to the chagrin of feminist activists, whose years of struggle were given little or no recognition). From the outset, she had taken an interest in participating in government that was very unusual for first ladies. Her career was meteoric. In July 1948, she personally organized the Eva Perón Foundation, a large-scale parastatal structure, through which she succeeded in providing social aid to the poorest people in every corner of

Liberal Argentina and Its Constraints

the country, from medication, eyeglasses, and gifts for children to the construction of schools, housing, hospitals, and general stores. Through her own humble origins, she identified with the poorest, became the main ally of the CGT in the government, and lambasted the opposition and the "oligarchy" with more fury than Perón himself. At the same time, however, she made an effort to remove all political overtones from her actions: her figure took on a maternal and spiritual aura, far removed from what she herself called "politicking." Nevertheless, two years later she founded the Partido Peronista Femenino (Peronist Women's Party), the third and final branch of the peculiar tripartite structure of Peronism, which already had political and trade union branches. The new party consisted entirely of women and was protective of its independence.

The 1951 presidential election was the first in which women were able to vote. By then Evita had become a popular leader on par with the president himself and one of the most recognized in the world. Her candidacy for the vice presidency seemed obvious: the Peronist Women's Party was planning for it and the CGT demanded it in the famous "cabildo abierto" on August 22 of that year, a gathering of more than a million people on 9 de Julio Avenue, the largest demonstration in the country's history at the time and for a long time to come. In the end, due to the opposition of the armed forces, Evita was unable to run as a candidate, but the representatives of the Peronist Women's Party were, and they won twenty-three seats in the Chamber of Deputies, six in the Senate, and another seventy-seven in the provincial legislatures. It was the first time that women held such important positions, and only the Peronists enjoyed this honor: the UCR did not nominate any female candidates, while the other parties nominated women for positions for which they would not be elected. In 1955, the number of female legislators was even higher, placing Argentina, in this respect, ahead of most advanced countries (after Perón was ousted, the proportion of female legislators would only reach the same level in 1999 thanks to the Law of Quotas).

Ill with cancer, Evita died on July 26, 1952, at the age of thirty-three. Her wake was the most extensive and massive in Argentine history. Her brief political career left a lasting mark on gender relations. Although government discourse had conservative undertones that appeared to reinforce traditional stereotypes—motherhood as a duty, a "caring" role rather than a political one, subservience to the male leader—there is no doubt that the mere appearance of a leader like Evita and the participation of women in the movement weakened previously pervasive patriarchal tendencies. The Peronist years

Chapter 4

also brought about an affirmation of women in other respects. Improvements were made to the rights of "illegitimate" children, which to some extent mitigated a stigma that particularly affected women and children of the popular classes. Additionally, near the end of Perón's second term, advances were made toward the legalization of divorce (an achievement that would be cut short due to pressure from the Church).

Perón's government also brought about changes—though rather modest and ambiguous—in the relationship between the state and the indigenous peoples. In 1916, the Honorable Commission of Indian Reductions had been created to provide for their well-being, at least in theory. However, there was so much indifference that the commission wasn't actually established until 1927, and even then it failed to play any significant role. In Perón's time, the commission of *Reductions* was renamed the Office of Aboriginal *Protection* and granted more authority. For the first time, the state issued identity cards to indigenous people from various communities, which, combined with the provincialization of most of the national territories, made them citizens (a right to which, in practice, they still did not have equal access).

In 1946, several friendly overtures by the new president encouraged an astonishing political action on the part of the Kolla people, the "Raid for Peace," a long march that 174 Kollas carried out on foot from Salta and Jujuy to Buenos Aires to demand the return of their ancestral lands. Initially supported by the government, the action was a complete success: it aroused sympathy as it passed through half the country, attracted the attention of the press, and was received triumphantly when it finally arrived at the Plaza de Mayo. Perón met with the group at the Casa Rosada, promised to address their demands, and embraced several of them before the crowd on the building's historic balcony. It was an unprecedented symbol of recognition: it seemed that indigenous peoples had finally been given a seat at the national table.

But the action of the Kollas also marked the limits of the government's commitment to popular demands. While passing through the Humid Pampas, the Kollas had inspired small-scale farmers to replicate their march to ask Perón to fulfill the promise of agrarian reform, something much more difficult to satisfy than the request of a handful of northern communities. This worried the government, since it did not want to empower demands that it would later be unable to satisfy. Finally, the Kolla envoys, who did not want to leave Buenos Aires with nothing more than a promise, were taken by the police, amid beatings and tear gas, to a sealed train that took them back to the Puna.

Liberal Argentina and Its Constraints

The "Raid for Peace" would become one of the first milestones of the indigenist movement in Argentina, placing the issues of indigenous peoples on the public agenda for the first time. Nevertheless, at the time, the illegal and violent expulsion of the Kollas, which was carried out with complete impunity, set a dismal precedent.

In October 1947, in Formosa, the Pilagá people were the victims of one of the worst massacres of the twentieth century. A group of them, starving after returning on foot from their traditional pilgrimage to the sugar mills in Salta, where they had been unable to find work, requested help from the authorities and the assistance of Perón. The national government sent a convoy with food, which was delayed and arrived spoiled. Desperate, the Pilagás consumed it anyway and some fifty of them died of food poisoning. Meanwhile, rumors began to circulate in the town of Las Lomitas that the indignant natives were preparing to attack the white population. In response, without any apparent motive, the Gendarmerie opened fire on the contingent. More than 300 Pilagás were killed on the spot; the survivors tried to escape but were hunted down. The Gendarmerie pursued them for miles and killed another 200. When the massacre was over, between the dead and the missing, the total number of victims had reached approximately 750, many of them children, women, and the elderly. The newspapers collaborated, minimizing the incident (they reported "around four deaths") and claiming that the Pilagás had attacked Las Lomitas, which was false. Perón never ordered an investigation.

Culture and Politics in the Peronist Era

Perón's vision for his government centered on the doctrine of the "third position," in which he placed himself at the delicate midpoint between the abuses of capitalist individualism and communist collectivism (reflected in an international policy distanced from both the Soviet bloc and American imperialism). The state was to play a guiding role in order to achieve an "organized community" in which each class would carry out its role harmoniously and without antagonism to the others. This presupposed greater solidarity from those at the top, the willingness of those at the bottom to work in an orderly fashion, and more subjection of all to state decisions. (Among other things, this resulted in the virtual elimination of the autonomy enjoyed by universities, which were subject to strong interference.)

During these years, a powerful propaganda machine was launched to disseminate the images, ideas, and words of the president and his wife throughout the entire country. Millions of posters, pins, Peronist flags and coats of arms, pamphlets, and portraits were produced and distributed at the expense of the state. There was intense programming of radio shows and short films in cinemas (as well as on state television starting in 1951). Music festivals and works of theater with pro-government content were organized, and the scripts of national films were monitored. The government backed an acolyte press and exerted pressure on those that were not (some newspapers were shut down and, in 1951, *La Prensa* was expropriated and handed over to the CGT). At the same time, a liturgy of street demonstrations in support of the ruling party was implemented. Its main events were the Day of Loyalty every October 17 and the traditional May Day mobilization, redefined as the Workers' Celebration. Perón and Evita's speeches, the "Peronist March," and the banners and decorations exalting the leaders became a constant feature.

Thanks to this evangelism, a true cult of personality was gradually constructed. Perón and Evita presented themselves not only as political leaders but also as the incarnation of the Argentine people and, therefore, of the nation. Peronism thus acquired a more pronounced plebiscitary tone than Yrigoyenism: each election was presented as if the alternatives were to defend the nation (by voting for Peronism) or to support the "contrarians," who were considered unpatriotic and, therefore, lacking all legitimacy. To be against Perón was to be against the working people and Argentina. This message was not only preached from above. Since the popular classes had succeeded in becoming a political subject thanks to the movement, it was not surprising that they would feel that "the popular" was inextricably linked to Perón. And since during these years the state had made its presence felt in the reality of many lower-class inhabitants for the first time, especially in more outlying areas, it is possible that, for many, statehood itself became indistinguishable from the figures of Perón and Evita. The bonds that the popular classes established among themselves and with the leaders of the movement reached a powerful and enduring emotional intensity.

The state's discourse during these years was strongly nationalist and anti-imperialist. But it was not a xenophobic or elitist nationalism, like that of some right-wing groups. In fact, perhaps in order to get rid of the "Nazi fascist" label that the opposition had branded him with, Perón was particularly benevolent toward the Jewish community, and in 1949 Argentina was among the first countries in the world to recognize the State of Israel. Nor did he reject the pantheon of heroes that Mitre had established or adopt the cult to Rosas proposed by the revisionist intellectuals, who were paid little heed (some had joined the movement, while others were opponents).

Rather, it was a popular nationalism, similar to the one cultivated by FORJA, which had disbanded, with most joining Peronism. National greatness was associated with the defense of the dignity of the worker, the emblematic figure of the New Argentina that Perón claimed to be building. The oligarchy was criticized for its past as an exploitative and parasitic group focused on foreign interests, but at the same time its moral reeducation and reintegration into the organized community were proposed as entirely possible. In this non-antagonistic class struggle, Peronist discourse was closely connected to the values and visions offered by the mass culture of the previous decades. In fact, Peronism did not introduce any decisive changes in this regard: rather, it drew on this culture and exploited its political potential. Among other things, Perón sought to associate himself as much as possible with the figure of the gaucho, and it was common for him to use references to José Hernández's epic poem *Martín Fierro* in his speeches.

The tone of Perón's message oscillated between criticism of the wealthy and promises of class harmony. The task of dignifying the worker was not related to the elimination of social hierarchies, as it was in leftist visions, but rather to giving workers access to the well-being and respectability that only the well-off had enjoyed up to that point. But beyond Perón's intentions, during these years there were expressions of antagonism and a struggle for the recognition of the plebeian that would prove to be quite disruptive to those ideals of harmony. Nothing illustrates this tension better than the lyrics of the "Peronist March," which retained the phrase "fighting against capital" from the earlier song of a workers' group that served as its inspiration, representing a source of discomfort to Perón.

Even without its leaders intending it to, the irruption of Peronism also had an impact on social hierarchies and some of the values that the elites had been inculcating since the nineteenth century. The masses contributed a series of plebeian traits to the movement that had never before been present in Argentine politics. Suddenly, everything that had been invisibilized, silenced, or repressed by the dominant culture had surfaced and, to make matters worse, had become political.

On October 17, 1945, the poor men and women who lived in the margins of coquettish Buenos Aires invaded the city. They arrived with their shabby clothes and coarse manners and, against all rules of civility, frolicked in the plazas with their sweaty bodies in full view of everyone, cooling their feet in the water of the public fountains. The mere act of occupying the Plaza de Mayo and other parts of the city center with their poor and despised humanity became for them a political gesture.

The same defiant attitude was repeated with other dominant standards of respectability and "decency." For years, the poor had had to listen to sermons on cleanliness and proper dress; they had tolerated the images used in advertising, which reflected bodies and clothes that were not and could not be their own. Following the events of October 17, the anti-Peronists pointed to the clothing of some of the demonstrators as a sign of their lowliness and began to speak disparagingly of the *descamisados* (shirtless) who had paraded through the city. But the Peronists quickly reclaimed that expression and gave it a positive meaning. This lack of a garment became a symbol of the truly popular nature of the movement. Perón himself would affectionately refer to his followers as his *descamisados*. Even being part of the *chusma maloliente* (smelly rabble) was assumed with pride by some Peronists, like poet Juan Oscar Ponferrada. *Mis grasitas* (my beloved lowlifes), from a word meaning both "vulgar" and "greasy," was the memorable way in which Evita addressed the most humble, once again inverting a common insult and turning it into a political challenge to the "cleanliness" of those who despised them.

Education was also a battleground for this type of dispute. In 1945, students, academics, and intellectuals, from the position of authority that scholarship gave them, spoke out against Perón, whom they accused of manipulating his followers by taking advantage of their "lack of culture." In response to this attitude, a number of Peronists then coined the famous slogan "Alpargatas sí, libros no" (Boots, not books). During the events of October 17 in La Plata and Córdoba, there were demonstrations of hostility toward the universities. In subsequent years, there would be other displays of anti-intellectualism in Peronism.

To a certain degree, the ideals of respectability were also called into question. Young Peronists imbued the movement with the festive, irreverent, and coarse spirit that would come to characterize it, accentuated by the carnivalesque sound of drums during demonstrations. And what of the position that Evita gradually occupied? An illegitimate daughter and an actress (not a "respectable" profession at the time), who, to top it all off, was living with Perón, unmarried, her mere presence was a constant challenge to traditional values and, therefore, a source of irritation for some and admiration for others.

Through their actions, the plebs also politicized the question of ethnic origins and skin color. Suddenly one could hear people speaking in "Quichua or Guaraní" in the European city of Buenos Aires, as the newspaper *Clarín* noted with astonishment in 1945, or a Kolla "raid" from the north might appear. *Cabecitas negras* (little black heads) were what "respectable" people contemptuously dubbed all these unexpected presences and, by extension, all Peronists. The Peronists, however, were not yet defending their "brownness," let alone identifying as *cabecitas* (that would not happen until 1955).

The self-assertion of the Argentines who did not see themselves reflected in the image of a white and European Argentina left an interesting legacy at the level of popular and mass culture, in which visions of the Argentine people in implicit dissidence with those of the government had already been presented before. An interesting example can be found in music. Tango, which only a short time earlier had reached its golden age, entered a phase of slow decline in the late 1940s, while other rhythms of a more festive tone were gaining popularity among the masses. Alberto Castillo, for instance, reached his peak popularity after 1944 by incorporating *candombes* into his repertoire, with lyrics that made frequent reference to "los negros" (Black people). Another rhythm that gained enormous popularity among the lower classes was *chamamé*. Antonio Tormo from Mendoza broke all sales records in 1950 with his single "El rancho'e la Cambicha," which had a rhythm similar to *chamamé*, lyrics with words in Quechua and Guaraní, and references to the lifestyle of the popular sectors of the littoral region. In a more melancholic tone, folk music continued to produce figures such as Atahualpa Yupanqui or Buenaventura Luna, whose compositions spoke of the sufferings of the "razas viejas" (old races) and the mestizos.

During these years, the government did not explicitly defend "brownness" (although it did defend criollo identity): given the ideals of harmony and national homogeneity that Perón was promoting, it was disadvantageous to explicitly state that there were differences of origin or color among Argentines. However, the issue was sometimes addressed implicitly through the way the state visually represented the population. In some government posters—albeit a minority—the bodies personifying it were deliberately mestizo in appearance. There was also a version of the Peronist coat of arms in which the emblem of the intertwined hands showed the lower hand painted in a brownish tone and the upper one in a pinkish tone (as if to suggest that the desired class solidarity should also be an interethnic fraternity).

In this way, the Peronist era directly or indirectly generated a reclamation of the culturally plebeian, which gained legitimacy in political life. It should also be noted, however, that the state under Perón continued to promote ideals of respectability that were similar to those the elite had established in earlier periods, based on work and discipline, dressing smartly, education, traditional morality, and the submission of women to men, among other things. In fact, during these years the state exerted pressure—with some degree of success—in an effort to bring the norms of family life and sexuality of the popular classes, always less "ordered" than those of the bourgeoisie, more in line with them. (This included, among other things, a marked increase in police repression of male homosexuality.) The "heretical" component of Peronism—the reclaiming of the plebeian and the challenge to traditional values—coexisted in tension with these more conservative aspects.

Anti-Peronism and the "Middle Class"

As a result of the deep roots it had among voters, the emotional intensity it aroused among the lower classes, its plebeian traits, and several of the measures it promoted, Peronism produced a seismic shift in the political system. Since its emergence, it had attracted and incorporated leaders and voters of all backgrounds—from anarchists and socialists to Radicals and conservatives—and caused a realignment of the other political forces.

Following its defeat in 1946, the Democratic Union dissolved and the UCR entered a deep internal crisis. The liberal-conservatives disbanded and lost their national presence (even in some of the provinces that had previously been their strongholds). The Socialist Party and the Progressive Democratic Party suffered such a severe decline in their voter base that they became virtually irrelevant. Communism slowly lost the support it had gained among the workers. Right-wing nationalism was divided between those who supported Perón and those who abhorred him. The central axis of national politics ceased to be the opposition between Radicals and liberal-conservatives and instead became a confrontation between Peronists and anti-Peronists. Despite its internal crisis, the UCR became the first choice of the latter, taking advantage of many of the votes that the other parties were losing.

Although in 1946 anti-Peronism was still politically disorganized, the strength it had by then gained as a social and cultural reaction persisted and deepened, until it became a political identity as deep-rooted and influential as that of Peronism itself. In fact, neither can be understood without the other: formulated as early as 1945, *before* Peronism had even taken a precise form, anti-Peronism made a decisive contribution to shaping some of the specific characteristics of the new movement. The criticisms it had raised of the colonel's promotion that year focused on the danger of his being a "Nazi fascist" but also on other aspects of the leader and, more importantly, of his followers.

Much of the furious anti-Peronist reaction had more to do with disgust at the weakening of cultural norms and social hierarchies than with the fact that any purely economic interest was being affected. Those who attacked Perón often alluded in their criticism to racial and even moral and aesthetic questions of "proper education." The newspaper *Crítica*, for example, complained in 1945 that the plebs in the streets of Buenos Aires were an attack on "good taste and on the aesthetics of the citizenry spoiled by their presence." According to the conservative Adolfo Mugica, the country was living as if in a kind of "immense pandemonium of blacks." The nationalist Juan Carulla agreed: upon observing the demonstrations, "consisting, for the most part, of mestizos and even Indians," he expressed regret that Argentina "is becoming blackened." Sometime later, a Radical leader coined the famous expression "zoological flood," referring to them as if they were animals. Even the Communist Party spoke out to disparage the "thugs and crooks" of the "Peronist ruffians" who were a threat "to the home, to businesses, to modesty and honesty, to decency, to culture."

The outpouring of contempt for the lower classes during these years was so tremendous that it conjures up similar expressions by the elite in the nineteenth century, when setting out to "civilize" the country. And it is no coincidence: in both cases, the thorn in their side was the plebs straying outside their acceptable lanes. Américo Ghioldi, one of the most important leaders of the Socialist Party, revived Domingo Faustino Sarmiento's dichotomy of "civilization or barbarism" to call for a fight against that "primitive force" that had become visible, that new "caudillo of the civil war" like the one that the former federalists had inspired. If Peronism later began to emphasize its more plebeian and anti-intellectualist streak, if it later identified itself with the *cabecitas negras* and, much later, with the ideas of the revisionists, it was partly in reaction to this contempt.

In turn, Perón's ambition to embody the will of the working people and, therefore, of the Argentine nation once again influenced aspects of the anti-Peronist identity that emerged after their defeat in 1946. Until October of the year before, the anti-Peronists had been certain that they represented the whole of society, including workers. The sheer massiveness of the street demonstrations they staged and the fact that they even had the Communists on their side added to this conviction. And with respect to those who supported the colonel, they assumed that they were just a handful of thugs assembled for the occasion. The October 17 movement cast doubts on these certainties, which were later confirmed by their defeat in the election. The local power groups, the intellectuals, in other words, the traditional political players, faced an uncomfortable fact: more than half of the voters and the overwhelming majority of the lower classes had turned their backs on them. From then on, they viewed the Argentine people as split into two halves: one wholesome, the other despicable.

Faced with this bitter truth, and at the same time as a way of affirming their legitimacy in the face of a government that considered them a handful of unpatriotic oligarchs without any social roots, the anti-Peronists clung to a mode of identification that until that time had had little presence in Argentine society: they proclaimed themselves representatives of the "middle class." This represented a transcendental change in the way the country saw itself. As late as the early twentieth century, Argentine culture recognized only two major social strata: "respectable people" and the pueblo (common people). It was not conceivable at the time that the pueblo be divided into different classes.

This panorama slowly changed starting in 1919, the year in which the expression "middle class" was first used in public debates, something that until then had been rare in the vocabulary of Argentines. This took place in a very specific context. Tragic Week had just shaken the social order to its foundations and clearly shown that the rebellious workers enjoyed strong sympathy among a portion of the middle sectors. Seeing this, several right-wing intellectuals and politicians set out to incite "middle-class" pride as a way of weakening popular solidarity. They borrowed the expression from European debates, where it was used for the same purpose. They thus sought to convince white-collar employees that they were part of a different class, more respectable than that of manual laborers, and that their demands should not be merged.

However, the idea did not catch on at the time. The image that most Argentines had of the society they lived in continued to be rather binary, with the pueblo on the one hand and the oligarchy on the other. It was the irruption of Peronism that finally generated the incentives and impulses for a segment of the pueblo to imagine itself as an intermediate class between the poorest and the upper class. There were many reasons why someone from the middle sectors might feel offended. The defense of the worker, the new importance attributed to the plebeian, the affirmation of the mestizo and "brownness," the gains an entire union received collectively regardless of whether, individually, its members deserved them or had earned them: presenting oneself as "middle class" served to establish a line of distinction with respect to that Peronist working mass, scorned for its lack of education and sometimes also for its ethnic origins. And at the same time, it was useful as a way of distinguishing oneself from the handful of oligarchs that Perón criticized: to proclaim oneself as "middle class" allowed one to be anti-Peronist and, at the same time, to claim a legitimate place at the national table, which was precisely what the government withheld from its opponents.

The press and anti-Peronist activists were very insistent, starting in 1946, in summoning the "middle class" to action and endowing it with a sense of pride and the mission of putting an end to Peronism. A number of leaders and organizations associated with the Church, in particular Acción Católica, stood out in this area. As a result, during these years a significant portion of the population began to identify as "middle class." It was then that it became an identity that claimed a position of cultural and moral superiority over the Peronist plebs, whom they saw as uneducated, inferior, backward, and irrational. Those who perceived themselves as "middle class" often invoked notions of personal merit associated with virtue and hard work, which in turn were connected to stories of self-sacrificing immigrant grandparents who had made progress on their own merit, without handouts from any government. In a subtle way, this ethnic characteristic—that of being a descendant of Europeans—was contrasted with the mestizo heritage of the Peronist *cabecitas negras*, a lineage that supposedly explained their moral and intellectual limitations.

At the same time, these individual and family narratives of merit and advancement through effort tied in to the narratives about Argentina that the elites had proposed since the times of national organization. As socialist leader Ghioldi stated, given that everything "civilized" had come from European contributions and everything barbaric was a remnant of the criollo legacy, as Alberdi and Sarmiento had argued, the descendants of immigrants perceived themselves as bastions of civilization and modernity fighting against the forces of backwardness that remained entrenched among the lower-class and mestizo population and that had resurfaced in the present.

Anti-Peronist *political* identity was thus strongly associated with a *social* identity—that of the "middle class"—and with a particular narrative of national history that saw Peronism as a manifestation of the former barbarism emanating from the ethnic and cultural inferiority of the lower classes (especially those of the country's backward interior, from where the old caudillos and their *montoneras* had come and the *cabecitas negras* were arriving). The "middle class," the heart of modern, rational, European Argentina, felt it had been called on to play the lead role in national life, which Peronism had instead assigned, rather unexpectedly, to such a defective underclass. According to this outlook—similar to that of Sarmiento, to which it was heir—the country was irremediably divided into two irreconcilable halves.

Perón's Second Term and the 1955 Coup d'État

Rooted in this powerful social identity, anti-Peronism gradually found ways to regain its initiative after the fiasco in 1946. The electoral scenario was not favorable: in 1951, the president was reelected with more than 63 percent of the vote. Ironically, it would be the Church and the army, two fundamental supporters of Perón's political career, that would reunite a powerful front against him.

In 1949, the economy began to experience difficulties. The transfer of resources from the countryside to the city produced a drop in agricultural production and its decapitalization. This was compounded by the effects of American and European trade policies, which now favored their own farmers or directly excluded the country as a supplier. The expansion of light industry generated an increasing need for imported supplies. Since Argentina was not able to export (in part due to its own limitations but also owing to American trade sanctions), the foreign currency needed to bring these supplies in could only come from the now stagnant rural sector. At the same time, inflation levels began rising at an alarming rate and, with them, signs of discontent. Faced with this situation, Perón launched his Second Five-Year Plan with a program that privileged investment, agriculture, and heavy industry over the expansion of consumption and the "social justice" that had marked his first presidency. The plan meant that there would be less receptivity to demands for wage increases and more pressure for increased productivity and worker discipline. However, contrary to Perón's plan, economic hardships reactivated union struggles, and, starting in 1950, there was a new wave of strikes, some of them violent and declared behind the backs of the union authorities who answered to Perón. The government reacted to some of them with repressive crackdowns.

The crisis reached its worst peak in 1952, with a record annual inflation of 38 percent and a shortage of basic goods. To address this situation, the government implemented the Stabilization Plan, which involved a further intensification of the new, more orthodox, approach. Rural producers benefited from tax reductions and subsidies, and incentives were announced to attract foreign investment to the country. In a previously unthinkable move, the government once again secured foreign loans, and agreements were made with American oil companies that would invest in the country as part of a new policy of rapprochement with the United States. At the same time, collective bargaining was suspended and wage indexes for the following two years were fixed by decree as a way of capping salary increases. The right to strike was effectively suppressed.

As soon as the worst of the crisis was behind them, workers began to fight to regain lost ground. In several factories, union delegates managed to obtain wage increases despite the imposed freeze and forced their unions to ratify them. This type of activity infuriated Perón, who in 1953 strongly criticized the internal commissions and demanded they cease to act on their own and subordinate themselves to their unions. In spite of these warnings, the following year was marked by an explosion of labor conflicts, which revealed the government's limitations in controlling the workers' movement. In this context, business owners demanded that discipline be restored and demands be moderated. In March 1955, Perón called for a major Congress of Productivity, with the idea that the unions would reach an agreement with business owners along the lines of what the latter expected. The congress, however, turned out to be a complete failure. The CGT—which participated reluctantly—successfully resisted the advances of management.

As complications accumulated, Perón gradually became more authoritarian. Restrictions on the press were tightened. Opposition leaders were harassed and some spent time in prison. The state took official propaganda and the cult of personality to excessive levels. The "Peronist doctrine" was taught in military schools and was imposed on public-sector employees. Primary school readers were filled with praise of Perón and Evita. When, in 1951, the national territories of Chaco and La Pampa were declared provinces, they were respectively called the provinces of President Perón and Eva Perón (the city of La Plata was also renamed after the first lady). At the same time, the government went to great lengths to integrate the sectors of the population that did not participate in the workers' movement into Peronist trade union organizations. For management, it created the Confederación General Económica (General Economic Confederation, or CGE), which gained some ground, especially in the country's interior. For professionals and intellectual workers, the Confederación General de Profesionales (General Confederation of Professionals) was established in 1953, strongly resisted by the majority in these sectors. There were similar initiatives for high school and university students. The goal of the times seemed to be to Peronize everything.

This authoritarian shift generated resentment in various sectors. It was perhaps less alarming for the popular classes because they identified with Peronism but also because they had not experienced the benefits of freedom and republican guarantees in a truly tangible way in previous periods. The case was different for the middle and, of course, upper sectors, which during these years intensified their rejection of Perón and everything associated with him. Unable to defeat him through democratic means, the anti-Peronists became increasingly violent.

In September 1951, sectors of the army attempted to stage a coup d'état, which was quickly defused. In April 1953, young opposition militants resorted to terrorist methods: they planted bombs during a workers' demonstration in support of Perón, causing seven deaths and dozens of injuries. The enraged demonstrators set fire to the aristocratic Jockey Club and destroyed the headquarters of Radicalism, the Socialist Party, and the conservatives.

Finally, in late 1954, an unexpected situation prompted the reconstruction of the anti-Peronist coalition. Following the Vatican's guidelines, the Church had launched a campaign to promote Catholic professional and political groups, something that conspired against Perón's desire to be the sole driver of society. The president reacted with speeches against the Church and promoted laws and measures that ran counter to its interests (including eliminating the teaching of religion in public schools, which had been a significant source of irritation for the anti-Peronists). The ecclesiastical hierarchy called for resistance, mobilizing the extensive apparatus it controlled throughout the country. In May 1955, there were fervent demonstrations by Catholics; for the first time since 1946, a political movement challenged Peronism in the streets. The situation became increasingly tense.

On June 11, during the feast of Corpus Christi, an unprecedented crowd filled the Buenos Aires Cathedral and spilled over into much of the Plaza de Mayo. A group even headed for Congress, throwing stones at public buildings and pro-government newspaper headquarters, shouting "Death to Perón!" and "Long live Christ the King!" Five days later, there was another coup attempt, in which conspirators from the navy had no qualms about using their airplanes to drop bombs on the government supporters gathered in Plaza de Mayo, leaving more than 350 dead. As many were convinced that the Corpus Christi demonstration had been part of the military plan, Peronist groups set fire to several churches in retaliation. The unprecedented burning of churches finally united the entire opposition: even politicians and student groups traditionally opposed to the Church came out in defense of aggrieved Catholicism.

In early July, Perón attempted to cool the situation with conciliatory words, but it was too late. Faced with the prospect of a coup d'état, the workers' movement evaluated the possibility of creating popular militias to defend the government, which further irritated the military. Perón sought to defuse this possibility by calling for calm, although this did not prevent him from once again making verbal threats to the opposition, which had rejected en bloc his invitations for reconciliation.

On September 16, 1955, the move to overthrow the government finally began in Córdoba and was quickly joined by so-called civilian commandos, irregular groups of armed anti-Peronists. When it became clear that he had lost the support of the military, at least a significant part of it, and following another bombing, this time of Mar del Plata (with the threat of a repetition in the capital city), Perón opted to seek refuge in Paraguay without putting up any resistance. That was the end of the Peronist government.

The movement, however, was far from over.

5

The Pendulum

*Dictatorship, the Market, and Popular Power,
from Perón's Overthrow to the National Reorganization
Process (1955–1983)*

THE OUSTING OF JUAN DOMINGO PERÓN and the events leading up to it were a turning point in Argentine history. The airplanes dropping bombs on civilians in Plaza de Mayo crossed a threshold. Indeed, it is a rare event in world history for the armed forces of a country to bomb its own capital while not even at war. It was the beginning of a spiral of violence that would give way to increasingly brutal dictatorships, aimed not only at changing governments but also at dismantling the path by which the popular classes had managed to organize themselves and gain new rights.

With Perón in exile (he passed through several countries before settling in Madrid), Peronism would remain banned for eighteen years. Thus, the tentative political openness initiated in 1916 was completely abandoned. The political-institutional apparatus that the liberal elites had constructed in the nineteenth century had not been able to accommodate the demands of society. Like Hipólito Yrigoyen, Perón had encouraged hopes of democratization. His ideal of an "organized community" had promised to include the lower classes in national affairs. Even with its authoritarian features and corporatist components, it was a process that had involved opening up to democratic demands channeled through the country's institutions. Perón's government sought to achieve a superior synthesis by building on the foundations laid by the nineteenth-century elites, while at the same time making room for what they had excluded. But now, that all appeared to have failed. The fractures and tensions running through Argentine society had not only *not* been mitigated but were now exposed with blinding clarity.

Even more than it had been in 1945, during the 1955 Revolución Libertadora (Liberating Revolution)—as the coup was dubbed—the political landscape was divided along class lines. The employers' associations, the Church, and the main political parties (including the Radical and the Socialist parties) welcomed the coup and actively supported it. Almost all of the press and most of the organizations representing the middle sectors, along with leading academics and writers, also expressed their approval. But that was not all: a real mass movement flooded the streets to salute the military and furiously destroy the thousands of busts and portraits of Perón and Evita that were everywhere; in the months following, these multitudes would occupy public space several more times to show their support for the new regime. At the same time, the lower classes reaffirmed their Peronist identity and embarked on a lengthy resistance of unexpected intensity.

During General Eduardo Lonardi's brief nationalist government, the dictatorship went through a conciliatory phase, which ended two months later when General Pedro Eugenio Aramburu, a right-wing liberal with a more confrontational attitude, took office. The government took over the Confederación General del Trabajo (CGT), union leaders were persecuted, and measures were taken to divide and weaken the workers' movement. A decree was issued prohibiting any show of support for Peronism. Even pronouncing Perón's name in public became illegal. The same applied to Evita, whose corpse was kidnapped by the military and submitted to a lengthy and macabre manipulation (with the help of the Church, it would be kept hidden until 1971). Peronist artists, officials, and politicians were imprisoned. Several purges in the army removed officers who sympathized with the deposed government, and the institution remained more firmly in the hands of the liberal sectors. The task of the hour was to "de-Peronize" society, to erase all traces of the recent past.

There were also purges in the universities, and the most important positions were given to anti-Peronist academics. In the distribution of positions assigned to each segment of the front that supported the Libertadora dictatorship, the leadership of the University of Buenos Aires and other universities ended up in the hands of reformist sectors, including those tied to socialism. The decade that followed the coup d'état was possibly the period in which university life would flourish the most. Some of its most distinguished participants, such as the sociologist Gino Germani, collaborated with the mission of de-Peronization, recommending ways of bringing it to fruition or lending "scientific" validity to some of the preconceptions of the anti-Peronists, such as the affirmation that Perón's support had come from the poor and culturally "backward" people of the country's interior. The creation of the Consejo Nacional de Investigaciones Científicas y Técnicas (National Council for Scientific and Technical Research, or CONICET) in 1958 also contributed to boosting scientific development.

As in previous dictatorships, Congress was dissolved and, for the first time, the Supreme Court was also dismissed and replaced with a new one more in line with the new regime. Despite all this, the military government presented itself as a bastion of liberal tradition. It announced that it did not intend to remain in power, claiming that its objectives were none other than to restore liberties, harmony, honesty, and republican life. The military government identified itself with the tradition of Bartolomé Mitre and Domingo Faustino Sarmiento and drew analogies between the coup it had staged and the 1852 Battle of Caseros; Perón's government, in its words, had been the "second tyranny" (framing it as continuation of the first, that of Juan Manuel de Rosas).

Unlike previous coups, the activities of political parties were not only *not* prohibited (with the exception of the Peronists); they were invited to participate at various levels of government, something that most of them accepted. Although it had no authority to do so, the military decreed the 1949 Constitution null and void and held elections for a new constituent convention, whose representatives were chosen in 1957, with the main political party banned. Shortly after convening, half of the elected members withdrew (in a clear move to avoid substantive reforms), which left the assembly without a quorum and the constitutional text of 1853 and its amendments, with only one addition—Article 14 bis, which recognized a series of social rights, although only as nominal rights—not enforceable in court. Despite its lack of legitimacy due to its origins, this constitution was in force in Argentina until 1994.

Economic policy took an orthodox approach: some of the instruments of state regulation were eliminated—including the Instituto Argentino para la Promoción del Intercambio (IAPI)—the peso was devalued, and there were incentives for the rural sector. As a result of the suspension of collective bargaining, repression, and the 1956 economic crisis, there was a dramatic decline in wages.

The Resistance

In this new context of political closure, with no leaders in sight, marching on toward "resistance" was the slogan of the hour for the rank and file of Peronism. As soon as the coup took place, there were numerous instances of direct action and uncoordinated strikes, some of them very intense. In Rosario, there were riots that lasted a week, and at least fifteen were killed in the repression used to quash them (several testimonies speak of a higher death toll). On October 17, in Tucumán, soldiers were sent from house to house to force the workers to go to work. Thus began a long period of intense struggle known as the "Peronist Resistance," which lasted until 1973.

While some expressed their anger by beating drums or singing the Peronist march at soccer games, others began to form "Peronist commandos," small groups consisting mainly of young workers with little previous experience in political activism. They acted spontaneously in various cities and towns across the country, generally isolated from each other, clandestinely distributing propaganda or carrying out small attacks with *caños* (homemade explosive devices made with metal pipes). Later, they carried out sabotage and larger-scale attacks on oil companies, banks, police headquarters, power plants, bridges, and, occasionally, on the homes of those responsible for the repression, albeit with no fatalities at this point. Seeing that several different groups and commandos were attempting to lead the resistance, Perón proposed organizing it himself while in exile, with the help of John William Cooke, whom he appointed as his representative in the country.

In the first months, many of those who participated in the resistance hoped to be able to foster civil-military conspiracies, taking advantage of the fact that Perón still had comrades-in-arms who were devoted to him. On June 9, 1956, several commandos participated in a military revolt led by General Juan José Valle. The government was alerted in advance and quickly thwarted it. On Aramburu's orders, around thirty of those who took part—including Valle—were shot to death without a trial. A huge anti-Peronist crowd filled the streets following the shootings to reaffirm their support for the dictatorship.

The failure of the conspiracy meant that military strategy was no longer an option. From then on, the resistance would make use of more conventional methods and the workers' movement played a leading role. During these years, there was a reconfiguration of the movement's leadership, with the rise of a new group of rank-and-file delegates and several leaders who were more combative than those who had risen to prominence during the last years of Perón's rule, strongly accustomed to caution and submission.

With the CGT having been taken over and the old union leaders removed from the picture, new union activists were gaining organizational experience and, in February 1957, they managed to form a Comisión Intersindical (Inter-Union Commission). It was initially promoted by the communists but quickly attracted various Peronist-led unions. After a failed attempt to recover the CGT, and in order to distinguish itself from the thirty-two unions that were collaborating with the military government, the most combative sectors joined together as the "62 Organizations," which took over the leadership of the workers' movement. (A short time later, nineteen communist-led unions withdrew from the group, so the name was left to the Peronists.)

In the absence of a party, Peronist unions also became the main organizational hub of Peronism. This restructuring made it possible to carry out increasingly radical protest actions and led to the "La Falda Program," which proposed measures such as the "state control of foreign trade," the "liquidation of foreign monopolies," the "nationalization of natural energy sources," the "expropriation of latifundios," "worker control of production," and the economic unity of Latin America as a way of confronting imperialism.

The experience of these years of resistance had a profound impact on the ideas and sentiments of the workers and on Perón's supporters in general. Some of the earlier elements of Peronism were still present, including anti-imperialism and nationalism, the demand for "social justice," and the idea that the state should act as a guarantor of harmony between social classes. But the strong confrontations of these years also reinforced other more class-based components, which stressed the need for workers to have political autonomy and fueled them with hatred for the "gorillas"—as anti-Peronists were called—and businesspeople. And as the coup supporters were full of talk of republicanism and democracy but had no qualms about engaging in unprecedented violence and manipulating the laws and institutions as they pleased, a rather skeptical attitude regarding the usefulness of

The Pendulum

institutions and electoral politics also emerged. At the same time, there was a strong nostalgia that took hold among the popular classes for a past that was increasingly remembered as a mythical era of happiness and fulfillment presided over by the paternal and protective figure of Perón.

Additionally, since the Libertadora dictatorship had proclaimed itself the heir of Caseros, most Peronists during this period adopted a predominantly antiliberal and Rosista stance (including Perón, who, starting in 1957, embraced historical revisionism). It was also during these years that they began to identify with the figure of the *cabecita negra* and to openly criticize the middle sectors for their racism, their Europeanist fantasies, and their lack of understanding of national issues. A whole literature of denigration of the middle class and the *medio pelo* (social climbers) flourished, encouraged by Peronist intellectuals, such as Arturo Jauretche, Jorge Abelardo Ramos, and others on the national left, and later, on the new left, Juan José Sebreli, who became enormously influential.

Between Restricted Elections and Dictatorships (1958–1966)

The resistance complicated the dictatorship's plans, forcing it to call an election earlier than anticipated. The date was set for February 1958; Peronism would not be allowed to present candidates.

Unexpectedly, a sector of Radicalism complicated the proposed restrictions on Peronism. During Perón's years in power, the young Arturo Frondizi had become the top leader of the "intransigent" faction that led the Unión Cívica Radical (UCR) following the displacement of the "unionists." The disagreements between the two groups had intensified after the 1955 coup: the unionists and other Radicals supported the Libertadora administration, while Frondizi quickly distanced himself from it. After the UCR officially proclaimed Frondizi as its candidate, the split was confirmed: Ricardo Balbín, Arturo Illia, and other leaders formed the UCR del Pueblo (People's UCR), while Frondizi's supporters formed the UCR Intransigente (Intransigent UCR, or UCRI).

Frondizi devised a bold strategy in a bid to win a segment of the Peronist vote: through envoys, he secretly negotiated with Perón for the leader's public support in the upcoming election in exchange for a promise to immediately lift the ban on the party as soon as he became president. The agreement was successful and Perón ordered his followers to vote for the UCRI, thanks to which, in 1958, Frondizi won the presidency. It should be noted, however, that many sectors of Peronism refused to obey the order and called on supporters to cast a blank ballot, an option that accounted for 8 percent of the vote nationwide (and almost 30 percent in places such as Tucumán). In this unforeseen way, the consensus that all non-Peronists seemed to have reached three years earlier regarding the need to wipe Peronism off the map was finally put to rest. Of course, the military and hard-line anti-Peronists would never allow Frondizi to keep his part of the bargain. As long as Peronism was excluded from the elections, the Libertadora dictatorship would be followed by a series of weak civilian governments lacking in legitimacy, which were then successively overthrown by new dictatorships.

The Frondizi government proclaimed itself "developmentalist," inspired by the ideas of Rogelio Frigerio. It argued that the country could overcome its economic difficulties through autonomous policies and an intensive industrialization process (especially in heavy and basic industry), with the state playing a strong leading role. Science and technology were called on to play a central role in the planning and "modernization" of society and in its increased integration (disciplines such as sociology were to provide crucial support for the latter). One of Frondizi's main focuses was the need to attract foreign investment. The president himself negotiated contracts with foreign oil companies with very beneficial (and secret) clauses. The strong incentives he introduced in other sectors led to the rapid arrival of foreign multinationals to the country between 1959 and 1962, mainly American but also European. Most of them were dedicated to the petrochemical, steel, and automotive sectors and were based in Greater Buenos Aires, the city of Córdoba, and other major hubs. In contrast with previous periods, in which small- and medium-sized establishments had proliferated, during these years there was a process of consolidation in the manufacturing sector, creating larger companies that had more capital and were able to impose greater discipline and productivity on the labor force.

Notwithstanding his developmentalist visions, Frondizi sought to gather support from all walks of life and yielded to the pressures of various interest groups, reflected in the heterogeneity of his ministers. In 1959, the Ministry of Economy was assigned to Captain Álvaro Alsogaray, who would go on to become the most prominent neoliberal of the second half of the century and who had the support of the army (he had already been an official in the Libertadora dictatorship). Other positions and ministries were left in the hands of socialists and, naturally, Radicals, but also Catholics, conservatives, and right-wing nationalists. To each group Frondizi granted something, including private educational institutions, to which he gave the power to issue university degrees, something the Church had demanded but that more progressive students rejected. This triggered a conflict remembered for its main slogan, "Laica o libre" (Secular or free). Before ousting him, the armed forces made thirty-two public "suggestions," and all their demands were met.

Frondizi sought to contain resistance with some initial concessions to the workers and, in an attempt to win the complacency of the union bureaucracy, he ceded control of the *obras sociales* (health benefits funds), an enormous sum of money over which, from that point on, the unions would have discretionary management. Since the condition for this was to maintain legal standing—which the government could withdraw—this created powerful incentives for union leaders to be "reasonable." Yet, at the same time, they could not become mere civil servants at the service of the government: if they wanted to remain at the head of their organizations, they needed to continue to have some degree of support from the rank and file and also mobilize them from time to time, so that those at the top would not forget about the important task of containment they were performing. It was therefore a question of maintaining a delicate balance between pressure and compromise, between threats and good manners, between giving free rein to the struggle and bringing it back under control. Strike first, negotiate later: the bureaucracy became an expert in this strategy, which came to be known as "Vandorism," after its main proponent in the 1960s, the metallurgist Augusto Vandor, strongman of the 62 Organizations.

Nevertheless, discontent often spilled over to the state as well as to the union leaders. In late 1958, Frondizi announced a plan backed by the International Monetary Fund (IMF), consisting of a severe devaluation, a wage freeze (the real value of wages was reduced by 20 percent), and an increase in public utility tariffs, among other things. At the time, the dollar was beginning to be a cause for concern, not only for investors but also in the press read by the general public. Furthermore, the plan included the privatization of certain state agencies, among them, the Buenos Aires meat-packing plant Lisandro de la Torre. Moving forward with this plan generated one of the most significant trade union conflicts of the decade: nine thousand workers seized the plant in January 1959, until the 62 Organizations were forced to call a general strike. The struggle lasted two and a half months, despite intense repression and dissuasive maneuvers by union bureaucracy, before finally ending in defeat.

In 1959, many other conflicts emerged and there was a significant peak in strikes. Frondizi responded to them with an iron fist: he decreed a state of siege whenever he considered it necessary; detained trade unionists and prosecuted them under military authority; and militarized railway stations, warehouses, and repair shops. Through the Conintes Plan, he placed the armed forces in charge of coordinating tasks related to repression within the country. As a result of his economic policies and the crackdown on the workers' movement, income distribution worsened during these years: the share of the GDP remaining in the hands of salaried workers dropped from 49 percent in 1954 to 40 percent in 1962.

The increased repression managed to calm the waters after 1959, but it did not succeed in saving the government. Fulfilling the commitment he had made, Frondizi authorized Peronism to compete in the legislative and provincial elections in March 1962. The previously banned movement won in most districts (albeit not in the city of Buenos Aires), and labor leader Andrés Framini was elected governor of Buenos Aires province. The results prompted the annulment of the electoral act and a new coup d'état.

On March 29, the military overthrew Frondizi. However, this time it did not take power but instead transferred it to the provisional president of the Senate, José María Guido. Called on to govern until the end of the deposed president's term, he surrounded himself with a decidedly "gorilla" cabinet. Federico Pinedo was once again put in charge of the Ministry of Economy and introduced another brutal devaluation. He was soon replaced, once again, by Álvaro Alsogaray, who dictated policies similar to those he had applied only a short time earlier. The political situation was back to square one.

In reality, it was more complicated now than before, due to existing divisions within the army. By 1960, the United States was already fully involved in the Cold War and was extremely concerned with the possibility of the Soviet example spreading to Latin America following the success of the Cuban Revolution. The US government pressured the continent's armed forces to align themselves in the global struggle and to make their key objective "internal security," a euphemism to indicate that they ought to engage in the eradication of communism (if necessary, overthrowing governments that were not doing enough).

The Argentine military embraced this vision and gave itself the mission of protecting not only the national territory but also a set of values and beliefs that were considered intrinsic to Argentina, the "Western and

The Pendulum

Christian" way of life—as the military called it—threatened by the communist advance. However, this objective was superimposed on the previous one: to remove Perón's influence from society. How could the two plans be combined? During Guido's interim presidency, the conflicts over this question were so intense that two military factions, the Azules and the Colorados, reached the extreme of confronting each other in the streets, tanks and all, before the astonished gaze of the Porteño population. Both groups were equally anti-Peronist. What distinguished them and pitted them against each other was that, for the Colorados, Peronism was a class-based movement and therefore paved the way for communism, meaning that it had to be suppressed as a matter of urgency. For the Azules, on the other hand, if handled well, Peronism could be used as a force to resist the advance of communism. They opposed interrupting the legality of the state and instead sought to find a way to integrate Peronism into political life, removing, of course, its more subversive aspects. The Azules, whose most prominent leader was General Juan Carlos Onganía, prevailed. In any case, under pressure from the navy—which had not intervened in the dispute—the most hard-line anti-Peronist positions continued to dominate among the officers.

Meanwhile, the economic situation deteriorated and labor conflicts remained intense. In addition to the traditional work stoppages, starting in 1962, factory takeovers became a widespread form of struggle. Management demanded they be quashed without hesitation. From then on, the use of terror tactics against the rank and file of the workers' movement became increasingly frequent (one of its first victims was the young delegate Felipe Vallese, who was kidnapped, tortured, and "disappeared" in 1962).

The normalization of the CGT in 1963 ratified the leadership that the 62 Organizations and their strongman, Vandor, had already assumed. The independence that the Vandoristas gradually acquired—becoming less and less concerned with fighting for Perón's return and more focused on consolidating their own power—worried the leader in exile. Indeed, since the 1955 coup, the risk of what was known as "neo-Peronism" had already become apparent to him. In fact, no sooner did the coup take place than some of the leaders or former leaders of the movement, such as Juan Atilio Bramuglia in the province of Buenos Aires and Vicente Saadi in Catamarca, had started to create their own parties to capitalize on Peronist loyalties beyond the figure of the leader. A short time later, Felipe Sapag did the same in Neuquén. None of them lasted very long, except for the powerful Movimiento Popular Neuquino (Neuquén Popular Movement). "Peronism without Perón" was naturally not a prospect that interested the leader: his primary concern was therefore to maintain the *verticalismo* (rigid hierarchy) within his movement, which compelled him to constantly maneuver and negotiate.

In July 1963, it was time for the general elections that would put an end to Guido's interim government. As Peronism was still banned, Perón called on his supporters to cast blank ballots, which handed the victory to the Radical "of the People," Arturo Illia, who became president with only 25.8 percent of the vote, a strong reflection of the popularity of the general in exile.

The pendulum of economic policy swung sharply once again: Illia took more statist measures, protecting local industry and strengthening wages and the domestic market. He suspended the controversial oil contracts that Frondizi had signed and took steps to control the sale of pharmaceuticals. These measures earned him the dislike of major businesspeople and the export sectors. His policies initially yielded good results and output increased significantly (especially in the industrial sector). But with such limited legitimacy, he was unable to solve the underlying problems, which subsequently led to a drop in production and an increase in inflation and unemployment, which climbed to 10.6 percent.

Given this context, the workers' movement continued on its path of radicalization. As a defensive measure against suspensions and layoffs, between 1963 and 1964 factory occupations proliferated but this time with the managers being held as "hostages." This type of measure became especially popular among workers in the mechanics, textile, printing, and metallurgical industries, driven by the rank and file, often skirting union leadership. Soon, however, the CGT appropriated this form of protest. In May 1964, the union carried out a seven-day plan of factory takeovers with hostages, coordinated throughout the country, which paralyzed some eleven thousand establishments. At the end of that same year, Perón made an attempt to return to the country, but his plane was detained in Brazil: Operation Return, as it was called, had failed.

With the unions stronger than ever, Vandor's intention to take advantage of the political opening offered by Illia—enabling the Peronists to compete under other party names—increased tensions with Perón. Relations between the two were generally poor, tempered by brief periods of peace sustained through tenuous agreements. In any case, the animosity of the business community and the government's decision to allow Peronists to participate in the elections led Illia's government to the same fate as Frondizi's.

From Onganía's Coup to the Popular Uprisings

Following Perón's downfall, the ruling classes had failed to establish a coherent political and economic project capable of stabilizing the situation on both fronts. In order to achieve this, it became increasingly clear to them that they had to deactivate the labor movement and align themselves behind the same austerity program with greater pressure on productivity, something they tended to call "economic modernization." And this meant finding a way to de-Peronize the country, an undertaking at which the Libertadora dictatorship and Frondizi had already failed.

The coup d'état that ousted Illia on June 28, 1966, set out to resolve this impasse once and for all. Led by General Juan Carlos Onganía, the so-called Argentine Revolution had the support of the employers' associations, a segment of the political leadership, the media, and the Church. Unlike in previous dictatorships, Onganía declared that he intended to govern for an extended period of time, as long as it took to thoroughly reorganize the republic, establish order, and clean up the economy. To achieve this, he spared no repressive measures: he dissolved Congress, and all expressions of political life were banned for an indefinite period of time. Federalism was effectively eliminated through the imposition of military governors appointed by the capital. University autonomy was suppressed and severe crackdowns were carried out on university campuses, culminating in the "Night of the Long Batons" in July 1966. Students and academics were beaten by police who stormed into the University of Buenos Aires, destroyed laboratories and libraries, and jailed numerous students and professors, in an attempt to combat an alleged "Marxist infiltration." This episode marked the beginning of a period of decline in research and university life. An entire generation of brilliant scientists was forced to emigrate. Onganía also imposed strict surveillance on morality, which involved monitoring the length of women's skirts and men's haircuts, the harassment of couples kissing in public, and censorship of the arts and the press.

The government's plans for the "rationalization" of production included massive layoffs, which in turn generated intense resistance, especially among the sugar workers in Tucumán and the Buenos Aires dockers. Worker unrest was exacerbated by the designation of Adalbert Krieger Vasena at the head of the Ministry of Economy. A liberal who had close ties with major businesspeople and the United States, he had already served as a minister under the Libertadora dictatorship. Krieger Vasena applied an anti-inflationary plan that included a wage freeze, a strong devaluation of the peso, cuts in public spending, and tariff increases, along with renewed incentives for the establishment of transnational companies. The pendulum was swinging back toward orthodoxy.

But the new minister's program did not aim, as others would later, to reduce the entire manufacturing sector for the benefit of agro-exporters. In fact, he imposed export duties on the agricultural sector and continued channeling resources to promote industrial development, although this was done not by strengthening consumption but by specifically targeting funds toward certain supposedly "modern" companies and sectors. At the same time, he reduced customs tariffs and protections for regional economies, in an attempt to eliminate uncompetitive companies and activities.

The combined effect of Krieger Vasena's policies along with the previous ones implemented by Frondizi generated a marked change in the country's economic profile. The main beneficiaries were the most consolidated companies, which grew at the expense of medium and small ones. The process of the foreign takeover of industry intensified. The upper classes became more heterogeneous, due to the rise of powerful "captains of industry" with international ties as well as, for the first time, the growing influence of the executives of large companies. Furthermore, starting in the early 1960s, the agricultural and livestock sector in the Pampas, which had declined during the Peronist period, began to recover and entered a major expansionary cycle that would last for two decades. Growth was particularly strong in agriculture, which moved into lands previously used for raising cattle, aided by increased mechanization, the introduction of hybrid seeds that improved yields, and the growing use of agrochemicals and fertilizers. The opening up of new markets (including those in the Soviet bloc) brought profitable export opportunities. The profile of producers in this sector became more heterogeneous as well, with the appearance of landless contract farmers, quite different from the earlier small-scale farmers settled on their plots of land who had become established in the previous century.

Rural exports, foreign investments in industry, and IMF loans eased the balance of payments, and Krieger Vasena's plan achieved some overall success, albeit only in the short term. However, the plan's focus was detrimental to many, starting with wage earners. Urban development during these years increased the flow of internal migrants to the main urban areas, and they were now joined by contingents of Paraguayan, Chilean, and Bolivian workers. Greater Buenos Aires experienced an explosive expansion that would take it from 1.7 million inhabitants in 1947 to almost 5.4 million in 1970. The working-class neighborhoods and shantytowns multiplied. The wage outlook became more heterogeneous: some managed to secure good jobs in the "modern" industrial sector, but most were employed in the less profitable construction and service sectors.

The CGT reacted to Krieger Vasena's program by launching an action plan that was quickly quashed by a government crackdown, which this time included stripping several unions of their legal status and the suspension of collective bargaining. Under this new scenario, Vandorista tactics collapsed: it was simply not possible to obtain concessions from a government that was making a show of its intransigence. Resistance thus shifted to a more localized level within each plant and was organized by the rank and file, often independent from the union bureaucracy. In March 1968, this process finally produced a division within the CGT, leading to the creation of the CGT de los Argentinos (CGT of Argentines, or CGTA), which confronted the bureaucracy, criticizing it harshly for its "dialogist" attitude. Some of the unions most punished by the government's policies, such as those representing civil servants, telecommunications, railway, and sugar industry workers, came together in this new workers' federation. Led by Raimundo Ongaro, the CGTA established an agenda that transcended merely sectoral demands, presenting proposals for anti-dictatorial and anti-imperialist policies and a transition to socialism. Another difference with the official CGT was the new organization's willingness to forge alliances with non-working-class sectors. It thus managed to attract intellectuals, artists, students, and priests to the movement and developed labor actions in conjunction with the student movement and left-wing groups.

There was an unexpected surge in intensity in the radicalization of the workers' movement and of society in general starting in 1969, with the appearance of a new form of collective action: *puebladas* (popular uprisings). These were massive demonstrations that sometimes grew into real rebellions capable of bringing entire cities to a standstill. What is unique about these uprisings is that not only workers but also other sectors of the population were involved in the same struggle. This was especially true of university students and, to a lesser extent, small-scale retailers, professionals, and even homemakers. The demands and motivations that triggered each uprising varied greatly, as did the sectors that led them. The arbitrary measures of the military government and the effects of its economic policies facilitated the joint expression of the discontent of each social group based on a minimum common *political* denominator: opposition to the dictatorship. Occasionally, these were accompanied by class-driven, anti-imperialist, or even anti-capitalist programs and expectations.

Between 1969 and 1973, there were at least fifteen large-scale popular uprisings, all in the country's interior. The first, in May of 1969 were known as the Correntinazo and the first Rosariazo (in Corrientes and Rosario, respectively) and were sparked by the demands of university students. As if resonating like echoes, other "azos" followed in Córdoba (where there were two) and in Tucumán (three), as well as a second one in Rosario and others in El Chocón, Chaco, Cipolletti, Casilda, General Roca, Mendoza, and Trelew.

By far the largest was the Cordobazo that took place on May 29 and 30, 1969, which led to a full-scale popular insurrection. The decisive actors in this case were the workers in the automotive and electric power unions and university students. The unions—led by the Peronist Elpidio Torres and the independent Marxist Agustín Tosco, respectively—had a growing list of reasons for discontent over the deterioration of wages and working conditions. For their part, the students were fed up with the dictatorship's interventions and "purges" at the university.

The uprising began with a general strike and a workers' demonstration in downtown Córdoba; the protesters were joined by columns of students. They were met with harsh repression, resulting in one death. This infuriated the protesters, who attacked the police. With the help of members of the middle sectors, who also joined in, they managed to force the police to retreat. A large part of the city ended up occupied by the rebels, who set up barricades. The government did not hesitate to send in the army to suppress the rebellion. Unexpectedly, however, the troops were confronted by snipers stationed on rooftops. They were few in number—Peronist, Marxist, and even UCR activists, poorly armed and uncoordinated—but they managed to hinder the advance of the soldiers. Additionally, people threw objects of all kinds from balconies and rooftops. Argentina had not seen an insurrection of such magnitude since the Tragic Week of 1919.

The army launched a final offensive and managed to regain control of the city, with a death toll of twelve, according to the official report (the actual figure may have been as high as sixty). Union leaders and dozens of demonstrators were imprisoned, some with lengthy sentences. But the insurrection brought about Krieger Vasena's immediate downfall and left Onganía's days numbered: a year later, his own comrades-in-arms forced him to step down.

A Shift to the Left

The Cordobazo acted as a turning point between the period of the resistance and a more radical period that emerged with the new decade. Its magnitude inspired enthusiasm among young people, who enlisted en masse in the various leftist organizations throughout the country. The global context also contributed to the urgency of the situation. The new wave of leftism in Europe, the civil rights struggles in the United States, the decolonization movements in Asia and Africa: the 1960s were years of a strong desire for change and revolutionary energy throughout.

In Latin America, national liberation struggles merged with an intense yearning for a life beyond capitalism, spawning movements of unprecedented vigor. In 1959, Cuba managed to light the fuse of a social revolution that was soon on the path to building socialism. And by 1968, it became clear that the Vietnamese were defeating the most powerful army in the world. Suddenly, overthrowing the bourgeoisie and imperialism looked like a completely possible mission, well within reach.

In Argentina, this shift to the left took place through both the revitalization of Marxist ideas and the move of some sectors of Peronism toward more radicalized positions, which in turn facilitated a circulation of ideas and political activists in both directions. The universities became a hotbed of enthusiasm and activism, and, with anti-imperialism as a common denominator, new points of contact were enabled between popular nationalism and Marxism. The traditional left-wing groups split several times, thanks to the attractiveness of national-popular perspectives and global realignments, and several new ones emerged.

John Cooke himself traveled to Cuba in 1960 and reached the conclusion that the fight against imperialism demanded a more clearly anti-capitalist and revolutionary posture. In this way, Cooke came to support guerrilla warfare as a viable form of struggle and "national socialism" as the objective. This would inevitably end up distancing him from Perón, who, a short time earlier, had designated him as his successor.

It was in this context that the earliest guerrilla organizations were formed. In 1959, the Uturuncos were the first, operating for a year in the backcountry of Tucumán and Santiago del Estero before they were disbanded. The small organization grew out of one of the many "commandos" that had emerged in the previous two years; in this case, it consisted of former union leaders, community leaders, and members of the Tucumán Peronist Youth. Around the same time, other young Peronists of modest means began organizing armed actions in urban areas. In 1960, Gustavo Rearte, a young soap worker who had survived the 1955 bombing of Plaza de Mayo, led a guerrilla group in an assault on a military unit to procure weapons, for which he and other leaders were jailed.

Three years later, the first Marxist guerrilla movement, the very small Ejército Guerrillero del Pueblo (People's Guerrilla Army) led by journalist Jorge Masetti, made its debut, attempting to gain a footing in a rural area of Salta as part of a broader plan conceived by Che Guevara. None of these initiatives succeeded in generating sufficient followers. Neither did other leftist organizations that did not subscribe to the armed struggle. All of them, at that time, remained small expressions of little relevance.

This situation, however, changed rapidly following the Cordobazo. The forces on the left—both Peronist and several Marxist ones as well—began to grow considerably as thousands of young people, especially from the middle sectors, joined their ranks. The groups that increased the most were those that proposed armed struggle.

By the end of the decade, there were already more than fifteen guerrilla organizations. Although only a tiny percentage of the population participated in them, there was widespread support for their actions, at least in the early years. A survey in late 1971 showed that 45 percent of those questioned in Greater Buenos Aires approved of their methods, a percentage that climbed to 53 percent in other places, such as Córdoba. In September 1973, another survey showed that 30 percent of secondary school students had a positive perception of the armed groups, while another 22 percent expressed a "tolerant" view. Of the guerrilla groups, only five achieved relative prominence, but they soon converged into two main groups, one Peronist and the other Marxist: Montoneros and the Ejército Revolucionario del Pueblo (People's Revolutionary Army, or ERP).

The Montoneros announced their existence in 1970 with the kidnapping and execution of former president General Aramburu, an act that won them great popular sympathy. Its founders held nationalist views that had gradually shifted toward the Peronist left in response to the climate of the times, but also—as for so many other young Catholics in those years—due to the influence of the Movement of Priests for the Third World. A minority sector of the Catholic Church, the movement believed that the option for the poor as preached by the Gospel must be expressed through a firm condemnation of capitalism and a rapprochement with socialist ideals.

The Montoneros initially avoided indiscriminate violence and direct confrontation with law enforcement. They focused on attacking multinationals, disseminating propaganda, and carrying out operations to obtain weapons. Starting in 1972, they had a solid relationship with the Peronist Youth, which that same year had finally established itself as a unified student and community-based organization (rather than a workers' organization). In the following two years, they managed to gain a foothold in the popular sectors, creating organizations that responded to their leadership, such as the Juventud Peronista Regionales (Regional Peronist Youth), the Movimiento Villero Peronista (Peronist Shantytown Movement), the Movimiento de Inquilinos Peronistas (Peronist Tenants' Movement), and the Juventud Trabajadora Peronista (Young Peronist Workers), among others.

By then, the organizations of the Tendencia Revolucionaria (Revolutionary Tendency)—as it was known—were already capable of mobilizing more than a hundred thousand people in the streets (although not all were tied to the Montoneros and only a small minority were armed combatants). Nevertheless, although they did not lack union delegates and a presence in some of the workers' struggles, they never achieved sufficient integration in the trade unions to rival the power of the bureaucracy. With a leadership that came from the middle and even upper sectors, they tended to idealize the Peronist movement and to imagine Perón with a revolutionary drive. This vision led them to underestimate the deep roots the bureaucracy had within the trade union movement and the solid alliance that they had with Perón. At the same time, they disregarded Cooke's insistence on the need to turn Peronism into a revolutionary party connected to the workers' movement. In their view, all that remained to be done was to get the "gorillas" and the oligarchs who oppressed the people, and the traitors who allowed them to do so, out of the way. It was nothing that their organization could not achieve on its own.

Perón himself helped fuel that vision: on several occasions, he issued statements implying that he favored more radical positions, including "socialism." This was not because his convictions had changed—he was still as anti-left as he had ever been—but it was a strategic move, to counterbalance the power of the Vandoristas and neo-Peronists. Many rank-and-file Peronists, however, took his statements at face value and genuinely believed that "the Old Man" was moving to the left. When that position began to turn dangerously against the trade union bureaucracy as a whole—in June 1969 a group, possibly from the Peronist left, assassinated Vandor, and in the following years the Montoneros would do the same with other trade unionists whom they accused of betraying the workers—Perón closed ranks with the more traditional trade unionism.

Although the ERP was even less integrated with the popular classes than the Peronist guerrilla, it did manage to establish some roots among the workers. The ERP emerged out of the Partido Revolucionario de los Trabajadores (Revolutionary Workers' Party, or PRT), founded in 1965 in the merger between a small Trotskyist group with weak roots in a few cities and a student group of Latin Americanist and indigenist ideas in the country's northwest. When, in 1968, the PRT split in two, the larger group decided to opt for armed struggle and, two years later, formed the ERP.

The small organization grew dramatically starting in 1973: the most optimistic calculations estimate that two years later, at its peak, it included roughly five thousand activists and collaborators (of which a very small percentage was fully dedicated to armed activities). Among them, women may have accounted for as much as 40 percent of members, quite a notable percentage that nevertheless was not reflected at the level of the leadership, which was overwhelmingly male. Like the Montoneros, they were almost all very young. However, unlike them, the ERP was both an urban and a rural guerrilla. Between 1974 and 1976, members pursued the *foquista* strategy in the backcountry of Tucumán, in the belief that a small revolutionary cell could help trigger popular rebellion, while also seeking to engage urban workers in the cities. By 1975, the organization had established cells in roughly four hundred factories in Greater Buenos Aires. However, most of its senior leadership came from the middle sectors.

This tendency toward increased radicalization was reflected not only in the emergence of armed groups but also in social and political organizations of all kinds. After 1970, the workers' movement, which was already on this path, saw the emergence of a more openly class-based tendency, especially visible in Sitram and Sitrac, the new autoworkers' unions of Córdoba that defended class independence, promoted grassroots democracy, and encouraged the struggle for socialism. Some of their top leaders were Marxists. There was a similar process of radicalization starting in 1973 among the growing number of shantytown dwellers who formed the Frente Villero de Liberación Nacional (Shantytown Front for National Liberation) and the Movimiento Villero Peronista (Peronist Shantytown Movement), associated with the left wing of Peronism.

In rural areas, campesinos and small-scale family farmers also engaged in unprecedented forms of struggle. The countryside saw important changes beginning in the 1950s. The intensification of capitalism brought with it a process of "depeasantization," the disappearance of small family farms that had little capacity for accumulation. In contrast with what had happened during the first half of the century, the total number of farms now *decreased* throughout the country. Those that survived were generally midsized or larger and in a better position to take advantage of technical innovations that favored increased productivity. In this context, starting in 1970 there was an intense process of organization and struggle, especially in the country's northeast, with the appearance of Agrarian Leagues demanding antitrust measures, land distribution, accessible credit, the establishment of minimum prices for cotton and other products, and solidarity with indigenous demands. The declarations of several of their leaders revealed a growing class consciousness and an intense desire to converge with the anti-bureaucratic and anti-government struggles of the workers and students. Some sectors aligned themselves with the Peronist left.

Indigenous peoples also formed part of the atmosphere of struggle and the dreams of liberation that marked these years. The defense of the legacy of "brown" and indigenous peoples, part of the culture of affirmation of the "national and popular" at the time, resonated with them. As a result, in 1970 a group of indigenous peoples in Buenos Aires created the Comisión Coordinadora de Instituciones Indígenas de la Argentina (Coordinating Commission of Indigenous Institutions of Argentina). Around that time, the Mapuches did something similar in Neuquén, where they organized the Confederación Indígena Neuquina (Neuquén Indigenous Confederation). Responding to the same impulse, the Tobas and the Wichis would soon create the Federación Indígena del Chaco (Indigenous Federation of Chaco).

In 1972, the first Parlamento Indígena Nacional (National Indigenous Parliament) was convened, with representatives from seven provinces, marking a turning point in the joint organization of various indigenous peoples. These initiatives laid the foundation for later demands regarding the legal recognition of communities, land ownership, cultural affirmation, historical rights, and better working conditions, which would galvanize the movement in the years to come.

Despite all these developments, it is important to note that a large portion of the population, perhaps even the majority, did not participate at all in the shift to the left and instead maintained a strong rejection of anything that deviated from liberal or conservative principles, along with a powerful

Chapter 5

anti-Peronism. In its political ideas and its visions of what Argentina was or should be, society continued to be strongly divided during these years.

Youth Participation and Cultural Changes

The shift to the left was closely related to another unprecedented phenomenon that became apparent during these years: the emergence of a profound *generational divide*. Of course, there had always been conflicts between the young and the old. But young people now burst into public life, developing a culture of their own that, for the first time, radically rejected many of the values and customs of the older generation. Class conflict, which pitted the popular sectors against the powerful, thus overlapped with a growing discord between young people and an adult world that was increasingly alien and intolerable to them. This youth rebellion intersected with the social struggles in complex and varied ways. In some respects, they developed following independent or even conflicting paths. But more often they mutually reinforced each other. For many of the young people who threw themselves into political life in these years, the desired future was not only a world without capitalists, imperialism, and repression but also the promise of a more authentic, free, spontaneous, unprejudiced, and creative life than the one that awaited them if they followed in their parents' footsteps.

The restlessness of young people was an international phenomenon. The central role they had played in the popular uprisings of 1969 conjured up inevitable associations with similar movements that had taken place a few months earlier in Paris, Mexico, Berkeley, and Prague. The rapid expansion of secondary school education also played a role. While in 1940–41 only 23.1 percent of those who finished primary school had continued their studies, by 1965–66 the percentage had risen to 74 percent. Not only did most adolescents from the middle sectors have access to secondary school education, but a good proportion of those from the upper strata of the popular classes did as well (including many women). For first-generation secondary school graduates, this higher level of education allowed them to renegotiate greater authority within their households.

At the same time, the Argentine educational system—in which private schools still played a very minor role—facilitated contact between young people from the popular classes and the middle sectors, and as a result the expansion of the new youth culture transcended class barriers. Lastly, overtures from politicians at the time may also have contributed to the emergence of "youth" as a group with distinctive characteristics. Perón himself encouraged the participation of young people from early on; starting in the mid-1960s, he insisted on the urgency of a "generational shift" that would bring in "new blood," clearly inviting them to dispute the authority of their elders.

Thousands of young people, even if they were not activists of a particular group, participated in a vertiginous process of cultural change that, whether they intended it to or not, had political consequences since it called into question various forms of authority, in both the private and the public spheres. International phenomena, such as the hippie movement, and others with a more specifically local character, such as the extraordinary popularization of psychoanalysis, helped shake up traditional practices.

From the 1960s onward, there was a palpable loss of interest on the part of students in the content taught at school, with a subsequent questioning of the authority of teachers and administrators. Young people also questioned some of the moral standards and sexual mores of their parents. Women gained ground in several social spaces (although they continued to endure male domination of all these spaces); by the mid-1960s, for instance, women accounted for 30 percent of university graduates, a percentage that had barely reached 5 percent three decades earlier. Starting in 1960, relationships between young people gradually became more relaxed and, to some extent, more egalitarian, moving away from rigid patterns of sexual repression and female subordination. Virginity was no longer an indispensable virtue for marriageable women, and common-law unions and children out of wedlock (which had always been a palpable reality among the most disadvantaged) became more frequent and lost some of their stigma. The introduction of the contraceptive pill allowed women greater autonomy in the pursuit of pleasure. These changes, of course, were not uniform: in many families, more conservative habits were still imposed and women had many more limitations placed on them than men when it came to enjoying their sexuality.

Continuing a long tradition, the 1960s and 1970s witnessed the emergence of new, generally small, feminist groups, such as the Unión Feminista Argentina (Argentine Feminist Union)—to mention just one—and women participated massively in left-wing political activism, including armed groups, although very few managed to reach positions of leadership.

Even though attacks, persecution, and contempt for sexual minorities continued to be the norm, there was sufficient questioning of traditional morals during these years to give rise to the appearance of Nuestro Mundo (Our

World), an organization of homosexuals fighting against discrimination, the first of its kind in Latin America. Created in 1967 by a small group of workers with union experience, it later converged with a group of intellectuals, forming the Frente de Liberación Homosexual (Homosexual Liberation Front, or FLH) in 1971. As part of the shift to the left, the FLH proposed free sexual choice as one of the inevitable objectives of the revolution to come.

Perhaps the most visible aspect of the irruption of this new youth culture was related to clothing norms. Beginning in the 1960s, colorful garments gradually replaced the more muted tones typical of men's clothing in previous decades. "Unisex" fashion was a sign of greater egalitarianism between men and women. But it was jeans, more than any other garment, that were most clearly identified with young people. Introduced in 1958 by an inexpensive local factory, jeans quickly spread among lower-middle and working-class young men in the main cities (men from the middle and upper sectors also started wearing them but preferred imported brands). A few years later, women also embraced them, and by the early 1970s they had become a kind of "uniform" for young people, especially political activists and those involved in a counterculture movement.

Along with clothing, music also became an emblem of youth. Since the 1950s, there had been a veritable explosion in the popularity of folk music. For many of the young people who were becoming more involved in politics, this music served as a way of connecting with the popular and federal aspects of the country. Growing anti-imperialism also fostered an appreciation for Latin American music, especially protest songs and/or songs with indigenist content.

But the most significant novelty of these years was the appearance of rock music, which marked a divide between the tastes of the young and the old (largely at the expense of tango, which declined sharply in popularity). Rock music was introduced to Argentina in late 1956, and by 1960 there were already local bands singing in Spanish; soon their records were selling by the thousands. Record companies quickly saw the economic potential of this "new wave." However, once commercialized, youth culture lost much of its rebellious edge. To counter this trend, a "national rock" movement emerged in the late 1960s that challenged traditional moral values and called on young people to reject social norms. Through music, it urged them to preserve their authenticity and freedom rather than become the "suits" that society needed, obedient and focused on family, work, and consumption.

By the early 1970s, the most important artists were attracting audiences of several thousand, from social backgrounds that combined the middle sectors and the working class. It was a true counterculture; fans identified themselves not only by the way they dressed but also by the length of their hair, which soon became one of the emblems of youth. Starting in the late 1960s, both were the subject of constant conflicts at schools and in public spaces. In secondary schools, administrators applied unusually strict disciplinary measures in a vain attempt to preserve uniforms and short hair, which were rejected by a growing minority of students. In the streets, long-haired men had to tolerate frequent homophobic insults. Although it had nothing to do with sexual orientation, the appearance of these young men was an indication that the essence of masculinity was being redefined, which was upsetting to those who were accustomed to more traditional roles. The police detained them whenever possible and did not hesitate to organize raids at concerts. In those years, the use of marijuana gained prominence; even though it was not a very widespread habit at the time, it was banned starting in 1971.

The cultural rebellion of young people merged with politics in complex ways. Although the left often shared the same spirit of rebellion, the two were not always compatible. The PRT-ERP, for example, was known for the frankly puritanical values it instilled in its members: it condemned adultery as "bourgeois" behavior unbecoming of political activists. Although the number of women participating in political organizations was significant, machismo still tended to be the norm, no matter how radicalized members were in other respects. Homosexuality—regarded as a lack of manliness—was not readily accepted (queer political activists generally had to hide their identity). The FLH tried approaching the Montoneros and Marxist groups, but none of them were receptive.

In music and styles of dress, there were similar rejections. The peak of youth politicization, between 1972 and 1974, coincided with the peak of vitality within rock culture, which also became a form of protest music. In March 1973, the most famous bands of the time gave a concert to support Perón's return, which was attended by twenty thousand people. However, many political activists rejected what they contemptuously referred to as "the hippies," whom they criticized for adopting North American behaviors and for not being committed to the struggles of the time. Disruptive and experimental art, such as that promoted by the Di Tella Institute starting in 1958, was criticized on similar grounds.

Unlike the early decades of the century, when the left had been at the forefront of cultural change, it now seemed to have adopted, in many ways, a relatively conservative disposition. That is not to say that many political activists were not part of the rock counterculture (in fact, many became more politicized thanks to the education in rebelliousness it provided). Nor is it true that the art world failed to show any sign of political commitment. The massive exhibit *Tucumán Arde* staged in Rosario in 1968 was a good example of this, among others. The crossovers and intersections between both worlds were intense.

However, the extent of this youth rebellion, whose effects were more limited among the more modest sector of the popular classes and outside the big cities, should not be exaggerated. New sexual habits did not end the conservatism of the patriarchal family order, rock music did not displace *chamamé* or other forms of folk music (especially not melodic folk songs), and leftism did not end religious beliefs or traditional political preferences. In Córdoba, popular *cuarteto* music became even more popular. And starting in 1960, in Buenos Aires and other places, the presence of *cumbia*, a rhythm with African and indigenous roots that came from Colombia, could already be felt and would only grow in popularity. At that time, neither *cuarteto* nor *cumbia* were interested in political issues, nor did they challenge the culture of the status quo.

The appearance of television—the first broadcast took place in 1951 and by the middle of that decade it had achieved a sizeable audience—offered a new and very powerful means of disseminating cultural messages, which were generally conformist. Soap operas and stories of model families (always middle-class, Porteño, and fair-skinned) abounded—like the successful *La familia Falcón* (The Falcón family), launched in 1962—reinforcing traditional moral values and conveying the idea that happiness was to be found in domestic spaces and paternal order rather than in collective political exploits. Television was also a medium for broadcasting the products of American culture, whose symbols and messages had an impact on local culture. (In contrast, Argentine cinema dedicated considerable space to social criticism and leftist militancy.)

Cámpora's Brief Moment

In the years following the Cordobazo, history seemed to accelerate. Manual laborers and white-collar workers, shantytown dwellers, campesinos, small-scale rural producers, farm workers, students, and many people from the middle sectors expressed their grievances and discontent in multiple ways. They often crossed paths protesting in the streets, sharing not only their anger but also their ideas and forms of struggle. Dreams of a socialist future took root in a growing number of people. The international context encouraged the winds of change; in 1970, Salvador Allende became the president of Chile, announcing a socialist revolution through democratic means.

With the fall of de facto president Onganía in 1970, the broad antidictatorial movement had finally proven that it had sufficient strength to remove a government from power. It was able not only to influence the government's decisions but also to bring about its downfall. Despite their heterogeneity, the popular classes threatened to become a unified political subject in their opposition both to the government and to the ruling elites. It did not take much foresight to realize that the growing discontent indicated a need to find a political solution that would put an end to the dictatorship.

It was with this objective in mind that General Roberto Levingston took office that same year. His first minister of economy, liberal in orientation, introduced another drastic devaluation. After the failure of that policy, the portfolio passed into the hands of Aldo Ferrer, an economist from the other side of the spectrum, who believed in the need for strong state intervention to promote development, causing another swing of the pendulum and an abrupt change of direction. Under attack by big business for his heterodox economic measures and following a new popular uprising in Córdoba, the "Viborazo," in 1971, Levingston was forced to pass the presidency to General Alejandro Lanusse, who was determined to completely abandon the goals that the military regime had set in 1966 and instead limit himself to ensuring a dignified withdrawal.

The new dictator thus proposed the Gran Acuerdo Nacional (Great National Agreement, or GAN), with the goal of creating a transitional government that both the UCR and Peronism would support. The idea was to involve Perón in the negotiations in the hopes that, while in exile in Spain, he would stop encouraging the more radicalized tendencies. However, Perón did precisely the opposite: in one of his speeches, he gave his blessing to the guerrillas. The various popular movements and organizations unanimously rejected the military's proposal.

Meanwhile, government repression again reached horrifying levels. On August 22, 1972, nineteen members of guerrilla organizations who were prisoners on a military base near Trelew, having been recaptured after an attempted escape, were shot dead on orders from the navy. That same year, the chaos of the economy, the rebellions in factories, intense strikes by middle-sector unions, the occupation of universities, and several popular uprisings in the country's interior finally forced the government to abandon its GAN strategy and to urgently call for elections. The anti-Peronists had hoped that the "Perón issue" would resolve itself through his physical demise—in 1972 the leader was already seventy-seven years old—but this scenario had not materialized. It was clear that the only way out was to allow him to return so that he himself could reorganize his movement, in order to prevent it from falling completely into the hands of the CGT or the Peronist left.

Since Perón did not accept the condition Lanusse imposed of immediately returning to the country, he was unable to run as a candidate in the elections. Instead, he decided that his party, heading a broad front, would be represented by Héctor Cámpora, who assured him unconditional loyalty. The call for elections, at least in the short term, had the effect the military had hoped for. The Montoneros suspended their armed struggle, and shortly afterward the ERP declared a partial truce and announced that it would not attack government targets (in reality, this did not change much as they continued to target the military and businesspeople). The popular uprisings practically disappeared. A great deal of energy and expectations were focused on the election.

Contrary to what the military anticipated, Cámpora won 49.5 percent of the vote with a very wide lead over his UCR contender, and on May 25, 1973, he was sworn in as the new president in a ceremony attended by top dignitaries from revolutionary Chile and Cuba. The feeling of impending change was so intoxicating that a large part of the massive crowd that celebrated the inauguration in the streets went on to Devoto prison and liberated numerous political prisoners held there. (There were similar actions at other prisons across the country.) Peronism's Revolutionary Tendency suddenly held considerable influence in the state apparatus, including two ministries, eight deputies of its own, five governors who sympathized with the Montoneros, and the rector of the University of Buenos Aires.

The withdrawal of the military gave rise to a wave of grassroots struggles, especially characterized by the seizure or occupation of establishments, not only factories but also hospitals, schools, municipalities, tenement houses, theaters, hotels, radios, television channels, et cetera. In just twelve days, in early June, there were more than five hundred occupations of all kinds throughout the country.

The new government's first measures seemed to confirm the winds of change. José Gelbard, appointed as minister of economy, promoted a "social pact" between the employers' associations and the CGT, which established guidelines for economic reactivation and income redistribution, including a general increase in salaries (before freezing them) and the establishment of maximum prices for goods of mass consumption. In addition, Gelbard promised to send a package of laws to Congress that included the nationalization of bank deposits, state control of foreign trade, a tax reform that levied more taxes on those with the highest incomes, an agrarian law that established a tax on land income and favored small producers, and a new policy that imposed strict regulations on foreign investments. Few of these proposals—which management and the elite viewed with great concern—were signed into law, but they still consolidated Cámpora's image as a president of change. The shift to the left seemed to have finally reached the state. Nothing could stop it now (or at least that was the hope that many harbored).

Perón's Return

The "Cámpora spring," however, lasted only forty-nine days. Few imagined that Perón himself would be the one to deactivate these promises of change. From the day he returned to the country there were signs that he had no intention of allowing his movement's Revolutionary Tendency to continue to grow. On June 20, 1973, a crowd estimated at more than a million people gathered at Ezeiza airport to welcome the old leader. It was the largest gathering in the country's history; approximately half of those who were present marched under the banners of the Peronist Youth and the Revolutionary Tendency.

But what should have been a party turned into a massacre. Right-wing Peronist groups, commanded and financed by officials close to Perón himself, opened fire on the crowd, resulting in at least 13 deaths and more than 360 wounded. The ominous signs did not end there. Cámpora soon had to resign and new elections were called. On September 23, Perón won by an overwhelming 62 percent of the vote. His third wife, María Estela Martínez ("Isabel"), accompanied him as vice president, as proposed by the party's right wing, which lacked a social base but held growing influence. The CGT leadership played a central role in the campaign; ironically, it became increasingly rigid and hierarchical as Perón demonstrated his readiness to remove two thorns in the leadership's side: the guerrillas and *clasismo* (revolutionary trade unionism). Given that they shared the same enemies, the trade union bureaucracy grew closer to the small groups on the Peronist right and they began to act in coordination.

For his part, Perón made it clear in his speeches that there was a need to generate "antibodies" in order to eliminate the most radicalized sectors from the movement. Days after he became president, the police raided the main bookstores in Buenos Aires and seized books by leftist authors. From very early on, Perón also began to openly criticize the leaders of the Revolutionary Tendency, especially after the Montoneros assassinated José Ignacio Rucci, general secretary of the CGT, one of the leaders of the Peronist right wing, and a close associate of Perón, in September of that year.

The calls for a "purge" that he then launched coincided with the creation of a new paramilitary group, more powerful than any other: the Alianza Anticomunista Argentina (Argentine Anti-Communist Alliance, or Triple A), led by Perón's personal secretary and minister of social welfare, José López Rega, and by Alberto Villar, appointed head of the Federal Police. (It has never been proven that Perón himself endorsed its creation, but there are indications that suggest this was the case.) Starting in late 1973, for two years the Triple A assassinated leading figures on the left—both Marxists and Peronists. The exact number has never been determined, but estimates point to a minimum of four hundred assassinations and possibly as many as a thousand. They also threatened many others and forced them to emigrate. Additionally, Perón ordered the resignation of several governors and all the representatives with close ties to the Revolutionary Tendency. The break with the Montoneros finally occurred during an event commemorating May Day in 1974. That day, in a battle of slogans launched back and forth, the profound differences in the movement became clear; while some chanted, "Perón, Evita, la patria socialista" (Perón, Evita, the socialist homeland), others replaced the ending with "la patria Peronista" (the Peronist homeland). The Revolutionary Tendency's columns finally got on Perón's nerves by chanting, "¿Qué pasa general? / Está llena de gorilas / el gobierno popular" (What is going on, General? / The popular government / is full of gorillas), to which the leader responded by calling them "stupid" and "immature." Hearing these insults, the nearly sixty thousand supporters the Tendency had brought to Plaza de Mayo turned around and left, making the separation obvious.

Underlying the repressive nature of Perón's government were growing economic difficulties, similar in many ways to those that had marked the end of his second presidency. Since then, a similar cycle of crises had recurred approximately every three years, followed by austerity policies that usually included devaluation and a reduction in public spending and in credit, the

The Pendulum

combined effects of which always generated a decline in consumption and, with it, a drop in manufacturing output.

The industrial decline would finally end up "resolving" the bottlenecks that periodically arose in the balance of payments, whenever import expenditures (for a variety of inputs but essentially to buy the machinery and materials required by the factories) exceeded export revenues, which were only provided by the rural sector. Following the decline of the industrial sector, balance was restored and the cycle began again with a new phase of growth. Cyclical crises, combined with political instability, had led to abruptly changing and rather erratic economic policies. In response to personal pressures and preferences, each government had benefited a specific sector of the economy.

There was a complete absence of long-term, sustained measures. Nevertheless, the industrial outlook was not bad; in spite of the crises and labor conflicts, manufacturing output was developing and the sector as a whole grew steadily between 1963 and 1975. In the early 1970s, machinery, vehicles, and steel and chemical products were even exported. Despite certain difficulties, import substitution was bearing fruit, although there were still traditional sectors—such as textiles, household appliances, footwear, and foodstuffs—that remained inefficient and dependent on state protection.

Perón kept Gelbard in the Ministry of Economy and maintained the social pact he had proposed. Although the focus of his program was to protect the domestic market, he also sought to stimulate rural and industrial exports, which in those years had good prospects, alleviating the balance-of-payments issue. The economy was soon on a path toward growth, and inflation, which had been rampant in 1972, had been brought to a halt. The popular classes recovered the share in income distribution they had had in 1950 and that had only deteriorated since then; by 1974, the proportion of the country's total income that remained in the hands of wage earners was once again above 44 percent. In late 1973, however, the difficulties resurfaced. The state had considerably increased its expenditures, which exacerbated the problem of the fiscal deficit. Gelbard had initially managed to prevent businessmen from generating inflation to counteract the wage increases obtained by the workers. Their agreement was, however, very tenuous.

In 1974, an unfavorable international context sparked by an increase in oil prices began to affect the Argentine economy. As the worldwide recession was accompanied by inflation, the businesspeople who used imported goods redoubled pressures to end the price freeze. And as the government gave in and authorized increases, this inevitably led to greater demands for wage hikes, in a cycle that gradually eroded the pact with each passing day. The union bureaucracy tried to contain the demands, which led to a proliferation of conflicts in which the rank and file overpowered the leaders. These often took the form of "wildcat strikes": self-organized struggles using direct action (including hostage taking or the positioning of tanks with flammable liquids around a factory as self-defense). These small factory rebellions formed part of a radicalization of the workers' movement, gradually giving more power to rank-and-file groups, such as internal commissions, bodies of delegates, and strike committees, which sometimes managed to form "anti-bureaucratic" lists that successfully competed in some union elections.

Perón, who had long understood that the power gained by the rank-and-file workers undermined his own (even when the workers declared themselves to be loyal Peronists), reacted by expanding the powers of the bureaucracy and helping it maintain control. The union leadership, for its part, intensified its "gangster-style" practices, employing armed thugs to intimidate "fractious" workers (even occasionally collaborating with paramilitary groups). In the short term, however, neither the new legal powers nor the violent methods were consistently effective in defusing rank-and-file struggles. In March 1974, one of the most impressive of these struggles, the "Villazo," took place in Villa Constitución, Santa Fe, one of the largest metallurgical centers in the country. It was a genuine popular uprising to support a workers' strike, which ended in a resounding victory for the workers.

At the same time, government repression began taking on unprecedented forms. In late February 1974, in the rebellious Córdoba, where the automotive workers had obtained higher wage increases than was desirable, the head of the provincial police, Domingo Navarro, led a coup d'état with the help of union bureaucracy shock groups. As a result of this "Navarrazo" (as it was known), the governor, who had close ties with the Revolutionary Tendency, was ousted. Perón, far from condemning the action and restoring the deposed official, decreed a state intervention in the province and, to replace the governor, appointed a military officer who implemented a policy of intense repression. Dictatorship thus took root in one of the country's major provinces.

None of these measures were sufficient, however, to curb the rapid erosion of the social pact. In a context of growing inflationary pressures, the major collective bargaining negotiations of 1974 failed. Caught in the crossfire, the CGT scrambled to obtain increases that were modest enough not to jeopardize the pact but high enough so that the rank and file would not completely bypass it. The situation appeared so dangerously close to spinning out of control that, in June, Perón threatened to resign. Three weeks later, he died of a heart attack.

Perón's death on July 1, 1974, at the age of seventy-eight, moved the popular classes like few other events in national history. Hundreds of thousands of people turned out to pay their respects to him at the National Congress. Despite the course his government had been taking and the country's growing difficulties, the poor mourned him inconsolably, just as they had with Evita.

Perón's death left the country devoid of the only leader with sufficient authority to contain the explosive tensions that had been brewing. Isabel, completely lacking in experience, took office as president, a position in which she was an easy target for the pressures of the right wing and business interests. Businesspeople immediately launched an attack (especially those from the rural sector, who pushed for all the measures that had been proposed to tax land income and fight against the latifundia to be dropped). Gelbard was forced to resign, which put an end to the attempt at economic cooperation. The social pact was replaced with policies that increasingly favored big capital, especially financial capital.

The economic difficulties, which were already apparent in the second half of 1974, became more pronounced during the following year. Production fell abruptly, inflation reached very high rates, the trade deficit became unbalanced, and the foreign debt began to accumulate. Real wages, which had still been on the rise in 1974, fell by 4.1 percent in 1975.

While all this was taking place, the rank and file in the workers' movement continued to gain increasing independence and to spearhead radical struggles. The government responded by increasing its repressive measures, while the Triple A intensified its attacks against union delegates and grassroots political activists. Montoneros resumed its clandestine activities and, among other actions, assassinated one of the heads of the paramilitary organization, Superintendent Alberto Villar. On November 6, 1974, Isabel declared an indefinite state of siege and, in early February 1975, ruled that the army would be in charge of domestic repressive measures. The provinces of the northwest were placed under the control of the military, which organized the so-called Operation Independence in Tucumán, soon quashing the *foco* (revolutionary cell) that the ERP had established there a few months earlier. The army did not limit itself to fighting the guerrillas but instead took advantage of the situation to exterminate numerous activists and militants of unarmed organizations in several towns and cities. The use of torture, detentions in clandestine centers, and "disappearances" became commonplace in the area. Dictatorship thus took hold of another province.

The onslaught of repression was not only directed at the guerrillas and the rank and file of the workers' movement. Starting in August 1974, the Ministry of Education was taken over by the right wing. The government took control of the universities and a declared fascist was appointed as the rector of the University of Buenos Aires. He supported the expulsion of numerous professors and the imprisonment of hundreds of students. The Triple A, for its part, redoubled its assassinations of intellectuals, journalists, politicians, and leftist lawyers. The state also took measures aimed at controlling youth rebellion, even in areas without any obvious relationship to politics. Before Perón's death, a decree bearing his signature banned the over-the-counter sale of contraceptives and eliminated all state support for activities related to birth control; women were called on to resume their "natural duty" of motherhood. In September 1974, Congress passed a new narcotics law with tougher measures for drug use. Rock concerts were once again plagued by raids, which had become more sporadic since 1973.

Meanwhile, the inflationary spiral intensified and, with it, tensions among wage earners. During the March 1975 collective bargaining negotiations, workers won substantial wage increases, but the government unexpectedly changed course and refused to ratify them. In early June, a new minister of economy, Celestino Rodrigo, implemented a set of brutal measures that would go down in history as the "Rodrigazo" because of the tremendous harm they caused to the majority of the population. The value of the dollar doubled, the costs of fuel and power increased dramatically, and caps were lifted on prices that had previously been controlled. Wage negotiations were suspended and postponed until 1977. The plan's objective was to reduce domestic consumption in order to rebalance the trade deficit. It also sought to reduce the fiscal deficit. In practice, the plan meant a massive transfer of income in favor of bankers and the export sectors, especially agribusiness, and to the detriment of wage earners and small local traders and businessmen. It was the first time that a Peronist government had adopted such a markedly antipopular policy.

The response from workers was immediate. Strikes and factory occupations erupted everywhere, especially in Córdoba, Santa Fe, and Greater Buenos Aires. A wide range of unions joined the struggle, not only manual workers but also teachers, transport workers, civil servants, journalists, doctors, healthcare workers, judicial workers, and so on. Faced with intense pressure from the rank and file, the CGT was forced to call a general strike on

June 27, albeit accompanied by a mobilization *in support* of the president. The rank and file, however, completely overrode the leadership; that day a hundred thousand people marched to Plaza de Mayo, demanding that the collective bargaining agreements be ratified and that Rodrigo and López Rega resign. Since the government refused to give in, a wave of spontaneous protests flooded the country. The CGT building was surrounded daily by workers' demonstrations demanding it take the lead in the struggle.

Finally, the workers' federation had to concede and called a forty-eight-hour general strike on July 7 and 8, which paralyzed the country. It was the first general strike against a Peronist government; the workers' movement questioned not only management but now also the government. And it did so with such force that it managed to bring about the resignations of López Rega and Rodrigo, as well as the repeal of most of their recent measures (an achievement that nevertheless did not take place soon enough to save thousands of small- and medium-scale businesspeople, retailers, and self-employed workers from ruin). Large-scale businesspeople and the export sectors, for their part, employed unprecedented pressure tactics, including a series of agrarian strikes and a deliberate meat shortage caused by withholding livestock, and finally, in February 1976, a lockout.

Meanwhile, the Montoneros—who since September 1974 had resumed armed actions—were expanding rapidly; by 1975, they had about five thousand combatants and militants, organized in a military structure with ranks. By then, the negative effects of an excessive tendency toward militarization were already evident. Their attacks and political "executions" were increasingly indiscriminate. The need to strengthen their military power complicated their relationship with the workers' movement. Something similar happened with the PRT-ERP, which also experienced a growing tendency toward militarism. Living underground and the expectations nurtured by their own ideology isolated them in a world of their own, far removed from the daily reality of ordinary workers; the organization showed little sensitivity to changes in the political scene. Its armed actions increasingly overlooked any consideration of opportunities, victims, or consequences.

Who Cuts the Gordian Knot?

The defeat of Rodrigo's pro-management plan ended up convincing businesspeople in the export and finance sectors of the imperious need to definitively crush the social movement in order to reorganize Argentine capitalism in line with their needs. It was not only the fear that massive mobilization could lead to a socialist outcome. Even if this had not been within the realm of possibility (something that was far from obvious at the time), the constant wage struggle, the limitations that workers placed on attempts to increase productivity, the ease with which they were able to wrest policies in their favor from the state: these all threatened the stability and future viability of large-scale businesspeople's desired economic system.

Changes on the international stage added further pressure. The period of conflict and economic turmoil between the two world wars had ended with the Bretton Woods Agreements signed by the leading Western countries in 1944. The pact set a new global financial order in motion, with the dollar as the exchange standard. New institutions ensured optimal conditions for the flow of capital. The International Monetary Fund, established the following year, would be in charge of maintaining financial stability and monitoring countries to ensure they reduced state regulations, opened up their economies, and maintained orthodox monetary policies. The World Bank, created the same year, would offer them loans for capitalization. Starting in 1947, the pressure for free trade was reinforced with the General Agreement on Tariffs and Trade (GATT, the forerunner of today's World Trade Organization), which would begin forcing each nation to reduce protections for its industries.

It was, in short, a whole architecture of global governance, controlled by the wealthiest countries and corporate lobbies, that took power away from national governments. It did not emerge from the popular vote, nor was it subject to any citizen control. In fact, intellectuals, such as the neoliberal Friedrich Hayek, who conceived some of the entities that helped shape this order, argued that markets should be protected from any interference by democratic politics.

The orthodox economic model that fostered this network of institutions clashed for some time with alternative approaches that recommended a more active role for the state, especially in underdeveloped countries. But the combined pressures of the world market, international organizations, American diplomacy, and local actors gradually reversed the tendency that national economies had of closing in on themselves. In the 1970s, the world capitalist system embarked decisively on the path of what later came to be known as "globalization."

International corporations and wealthy nations demanded with increasing insistence an end to the state protection of national economies and the granting of total freedom to businesses to move their investments wherever they wished without any restrictions. As a result, poor nations were forced to compete to offer the lowest wages, charge the lowest taxes, and provide extraordinary opportunities without asking too many questions. Workers' movements everywhere were weakened and inequality was on the rise.

The new global order also gradually made its way to Argentina. It was dictatorships that decided that the country would participate in these new economic governing bodies: the Libertadora approved the country's entry into the IMF and the World Bank, and Onganía into the GATT. At the same time, local liberal leaders, such as Álvaro Alsogaray and Federico Pinedo, connected with some of the leading figures of neoliberal thought, such as Hayek, and began to disseminate their ideas on the need to reduce the role of the state to a minimum and leave the market to its own devices. The problem was that a significant part of the Argentine industrial sector was not in a position to compete; if the economy were opened up, many companies would inevitably go bankrupt. This did not matter much to the financial sectors or the exporters, who wanted to reappropriate the funds that were being used to protect "inefficient" industry.

There was a political undercurrent that strongly resisted adopting the measures that these sectors demanded. Starting in 1945, domestic market-oriented industrial development and pressure from social movements had combined to create a society with one of the best levels of income distribution and lowest unemployment on the continent. Any economic measure that undermined "inefficient" industry would also affect the employment and income levels of workers. The interests of the popular classes and of small- and medium-scale local producers partially coincided; it was beneficial for both not only to support the protection of the domestic market but also to halt the "modernizing" policies promoted by international capital, a sector of large-scale local businesspeople, bankers, and agro-export interests. This partial convergence of interests had slowly given way to the formation of defensive political alliances that, by involving not only a powerful social movement but also part of the bourgeoisie and the middle sectors, were unbeatable (frequent commonalities between the CGE and the CGT and the multiclass support for Peronism were the most visible indications of this).

To a large extent, the country's political instability in the previous decades was related to this; the most economically powerful groups could only govern by resorting to coups d'état, which in turn were unable to overcome the resistance of civil society. However, at the same time, this resistance was not powerful enough to defeat the interests of major finance and export capital.

The situation represented a sort of stalemate, in which no one could firmly take the reins of the republic. The economic pendulum was its most obvious symptom. The growing spiral of violence seemed to announce that the decisive outcome in favor of one side or the other would come by force.

Politics and economics were thus strongly intertwined; to adjust one, it was necessary to deal with the other as well. From the perspective of the ruling classes, there was a need to profoundly reorganize social ties, to force small- and medium-scale entrepreneurs to adapt to the new scenario or perish, to quickly discipline the working classes, to break the bonds of solidarity that united them with part of the middle sectors, to restore social hierarchies—in short, to destroy the bases that fed into the enormous vitality of popular politics. To use a term that certain figures on the right began to use at that time, it was necessary to put an end to "populism." And it was increasingly clear that Isabel was not up to the task and that, in order to achieve their objectives, the limitations imposed by democratic laws and institutions would have to be removed, at least for a while. The prospect of dictatorship once again loomed inexorably on the horizon.

The Dictatorship's Advance

The dictatorship had slowly imposed itself while Perón was still in office. The "Navarrazo" had established a limited dictatorship in Córdoba, and, under Isabel, the northwest had already been placed under military command. Immediately after Rodrigo's fall, plans for the establishment of a nationwide dictatorship became evident. Isabel herself paved the way in a last-ditch attempt to maintain a semblance of legality. With the approval of the CGT, she turned to the armed forces to ensure governability and placed a military officer with broad powers in charge of the Ministry of the Interior. By September, the army had already taken control of fourteen provinces and was increasingly involved in government decisions. In October, the army was authorized by decree to "annihilate the activities of subversive elements" throughout the national territory. That the "subversion" to be annihilated was not only the guerrillas was clear. The media insistently presented the military as the best solution to put an end to the "industrial guerrillas" in the factories, according to the misleading expression circulated in those days by UCR leader Ricardo Balbín and other figures.

Finally, on March 24, 1976, a military coup planned well in advance toppled the government with little difficulty. The new dictatorship had the active and almost complete support of the financial and business sectors, the United States and the IMF, the Church, and the main media outlets. It also received the passive support of a significant part of the population, tired of the daily backdrop of political violence and economic crisis, in the belief that the military would bring the longed-for return to order. The name chosen for the new regime by those who staged the coup—Proceso de Reorganización Nacional (National Reorganization Process)—was indicative of their true intentions. Although they came to power under the pretext of fighting the guerrillas (which by that time had already been largely dismantled), their objectives were much broader: they sought to lay the foundation for a profound change in the country's blueprint.

The strategy of the National Reorganization Process was twofold. During the term of the first de facto president, General Jorge Rafael Videla, in particular, the military unleashed a wave of repression, unparalleled in the country's history: a systematic plan of kidnapping, torture, and "disappearance" of thousands of people. The entire operation was carried out in the shadows, hidden from the public; more than seven hundred clandestine detention sites were established throughout the country, the majority of which were also torture centers. The "task forces" that carried out the kidnappings and torture often stole their victims' possessions and sometimes even forced them to sign over the deeds of their properties. Hundreds of children kidnapped with their parents or born in captivity were appropriated by their captors, passed on to their captors' friends or relatives, or abandoned in institutions, deprived of their identity.

The total number of victims of executions and forced disappearances has never been accurately determined. Based on estimates by the military itself and confidential documents, the human rights movement calculated at the time that the total number could be as high as thirty thousand. Despite the difficulties involved in recording the disappearances—the dictators called for silence on the topic and ordered the destruction of all related documentation—so far around nine thousand disappeared have been documented by first and last name, although the total number is unquestionably higher (there are known cases of families who preferred not to report kidnappings). The victims were scattered throughout the country but were mainly concentrated in the regions where the social struggles were most intense. Of the documented cases, 17.9 percent were white-collar workers and 30.2 percent blue-collar workers; the vast majority were young people between sixteen and thirty years of age. Of the total, 30 percent were women, many of whom were systematically raped during captivity, a further means of asserting military power through the brutal imposition of male authority. Prisoners who were Jewish or gay were often subjected to particularly sadistic treatment.

The victims were not only political activists. Many rank-and-file union delegates shared the same fate. (In 1976, the business forum Idea recommended informing on delegates, and there are strong indications that some companies, such as Mercedes Benz or Ingenio Ledesma, collaborated with the authorities by handing over "black lists" of workers who were too demanding.) Student representatives and teachers, nuns and priests committed to helping the poor, lawyers for political prisoners, independent journalists and academics, dissident artists, and people in general who in any way participated in the vast movement that had developed in the previous years were targeted as well.

In addition to the number of disappeared, there were also roughly nine thousand detainees held in ordinary prisons and at least twenty thousand people forced to go into exile (some estimates double that number).

The magnitude and nature of the extermination made this dictatorship incomparable to previous ones; it also made it the bloodiest dictatorship in South America. The objective of the planned repression was to eliminate the most important social figures and paralyze the rest of the population with terror in order to destroy any resistance and "depoliticize" the country. The government even tried to prohibit any form of gathering in the streets. The traditional Carnival festival was banned by decree. In Córdoba, *cuarteto* music was completely removed from radio and television, and dances were often interrupted by raids.

The repression also aimed to "clean" public space of any plebeian presence; in 1977, for instance, the de facto governor of Tucumán issued orders for all panhandlers in the provincial capital to be loaded into trucks and abandoned in a deserted wasteland, while in Buenos Aires bulldozers "whitened" the city, removing the shantytowns from sight.

Immigrants from neighboring countries were subjected to various forms of harassment (including deportation), and tighter restrictions were imposed on their entry into the country in order to preserve—according to one official—the "quality" of the population. Youth empowerment, counterculture, and dissident sexualities were attacked relentlessly. Around eight thousand "suspicious" teachers were dismissed from high schools and universities. Hundreds of artists, intellectuals, and writers were forced to remain silent or limited themselves to quietly sustaining their activities underground.

While the military cleared the way using state terrorism, a group of specialists closely tied to the interests of the export and financial sectors took charge of the economy. They sought to replicate the path that the "Chicago boys"—young graduates of the University of Chicago, a beacon of economic orthodoxy—had been trying out in Chile under Pinochet's ferocious dictatorship, one of the first neoliberal experiments in the world.

The minister of economy was José Alfredo Martínez de Hoz, former president of the Argentine Business Council; those involved in the coup had secretly been working with him since 1975. He embodied the continuity of the ties between the Argentine ruling class and state violence; he was a descendant of the family of the eponymous estanciero who founded the Rural Society in 1866 and later received an enormous share of the land annexed during the Conquest of the Desert. The teams that accompanied and succeeded him bore the distinctive mark of the so-called establishment, a group of liberal economists with close ties to the business world and the United States who repeatedly held positions in the civil service. Martínez de Hoz himself had already served as a minister in Guido's government. Ricardo Zinn, one of his advisors, had held positions under Frondizi, Levingston, and Lanusse and had designed the "Rodrigazo" (he would later act as an advisor for Carlos Menem's privatizations and as a mentor to Mauricio Macri, during their respective presidencies). Roberto Alemann, minister of economy starting in late 1981, had already held that position under Frondizi and had been Guido's ambassador to the United States. His successor, José María Dagnino Pastore, had been Onganía's minister of economy. Adolfo Diz, who had received his doctorate in economics from the University of Chicago under the guidance of Milton Friedman—one of the world's leading proponents of neoliberalism—was appointed head of the Central Bank; he had previously been executive director of the IMF and had served as a government official under Onganía.

This group's alliance with Videla was facilitated by a subtle change in military ideology. Since the armed forces adopted the National Security Doctrine, the thrust of their nationalism had been shifting. It was no longer, as it had been in the past, about promoting an antiliberal organic order, nor about achieving national greatness through pharaonic industrial plans. It was aimed at something more modest: curbing communism and ensuring that the country belonged to the "Western and Christian" bloc led by the United States. This weakening of the antiliberal and industrialist component was not the case for all officers—many remained loyal to previous ideas—but it did apply to some of those who led the dictatorship, such as Videla and his minister of the interior, Albano Harguindeguy, enabling a new alignment with the sectors that viewed the market as the great disciplinarian of a society whose disorder—according to the thinking of those in uniform—contributed to the dissemination of subversive ideas. In fact, the discourse that accompanied this coup was not authoritarian, elitist, or corporative, as it had been in previous dictatorships, but rather liberal-republican; what they had come to do, in Videla's words, was to put an end to "populism," demagogy, and corruption and thus create the conditions for "an authentic republican democracy" as outlined in the constitution.

The dictatorship's economic program was strongly supported by the United States, the IMF, and the banks, which allowed Martínez de Hoz to remain in his position for five years, an unprecedented duration given the country's typical instability. Its main features were heavy overseas borrowing that increased the foreign debt by more than 700 percent (especially in favor of the IMF), the unrestricted entry of capital and deregulation of financial services, a currency devaluation, a generalized reduction of the customs tariffs that protected local production, severe cuts in some areas of public spending, a reduction of direct taxes on capital (compensated by higher taxes on consumption) and of the social security contributions of employers, the privatization of 120 of the 433 state-owned companies that existed at the time, and the decision to transfer entire areas of some of the remaining companies into private hands and manage them in a way that rendered them inefficient.

The combined effect of these policies was devastating. It was the first dictatorship that was decidedly hostile to industry (although this animosity was not unanimous among the military) and the first that coincided with the orthodox free-trade vision of the exporting sectors, which was at the same time the preferred approach of the main advocates of global capitalism. The industrial sector, which despite all the previous upheaval had been growing, shrank by about 20 percent due to the disappearance of numerous companies, unable to compete with the imported products that flooded the market.

Many small commercial establishments also went bankrupt. A few concentrated local and international business groups, such as Techint and Bunge y Born or those with ties to the Bulgheroni, Macri, Perez Companc, and Fortabat families, were able to monopolize the bulk of the economic power. Those that produced commodities (such as oil derivatives, aluminum, cellulose, or cement), managed to gain a foothold in the financial sector, and established a privileged relationship with the military government were especially successful. The focus of the economy shifted to the financial sector. By 1982, the GDP per capita was 15 percent less than it had been in 1975.

With the disappearance of jobs and the limitations placed on union activity, the real value of wages plummeted by 40 percent. Income distribution became more regressive; the wage earners' share of the GDP fell from 45 percent in 1974 to 34 percent in 1983. During the same period, unemployment and underemployment rates—which were very low in 1974—increased, as did informal labor and unstable forms of self-employment. On the other hand, numerous government provisions led to the loss of specific rights for workers.

Businesspeople's approval of the new extermination campaign and the economic measures was such that in 1979, when a scandal over human rights violations prompted questions from the international community, a hundred or so organizations—including the Stock Exchange, the Rural Society, the Argentine Chamber of Commerce, the Argentine Business Council, and the Association of Argentine Banks—came out to jointly declare their unconditional support for the regime (some even demanded that if there was to be a return to a civilian government, it should be through a restrictive vote).

Beyond these sectors, a good portion of society viewed the military favorably, and there was another segment that continued to support it even after suspecting or learning of its criminal actions. After the chaos of 1975, the reestablishment of state authority came as a relief, and many replicated it at the micro level; during these years, there was an increase in authoritarianism in the workplace, schools, and domestic life, which was fostered from above but also applied spontaneously by ordinary people. With few exceptions, the press collaborated in justifying the use of repression and concealing the dictatorship's crimes as well as in promoting respect for authority at all levels. The top leaders of the UCR and other groups—including some Peronists—were fairly cooperative with the military during the first five years.

Despite the prevailing terror, the ambiguity and collaborationism of the leaders, and the manipulation of the media, some sectors of the population found ways to resist the dictatorship. The workers' strikes returned in 1978. Although they were generally brief, the following year they lasted for longer. On April 27, 1979, a committee formed by several of the leaders of the CGT called for a National Day of Protest, which achieved a turnout of about 40 percent. From that point on, workers' struggles were on the rise. In 1980, there were several factory occupations, a few significant strikes, numerous brief "surprise strikes" (to avoid crackdowns), and the clandestine coordination of some of the unions on a national scale. In the middle of the following year, there was a veritable wave of strikes, and the CGT summoned the courage to call a national strike on July 22, demanding better wages and the "full application of the rule of law," which was very well attended.

At the end of that year, the workers began to take to the streets again with massive demonstrations in which there was no lack of chants against the military; the main political parties began to resurface and formed a multiparty alliance to demand, albeit timidly, the end of the tutelage of the armed forces. On March 30, 1982, the CGT summoned workers to the Plaza de Mayo, and clashes with the security forces in the city center lasted until nightfall. Simultaneously, in almost all the cities of the interior there were similar demonstrations.

The few public gatherings still permitted were occasionally scenarios for demonstrating discontent as well. Chants against the military became commonplace at rock concerts, which during 1976 and 1977 saw a growing turnout. Soccer was a more ambiguous terrain. The dictators paid enormous attention and dedicated substantial funds to organizing the World Cup, which Argentina hosted in 1978 and which ended with the victory of the national team, providing a local and international opportunity for the military to showcase itself as the administrator of a new and successful country (Videla himself was present at the final match). However, soccer would not always bring joy; two years later, General Roberto E. Viola, Videla's successor, was met with loud jeering when he visited Rosario Central's stadium.

With Ronald Reagan's inauguration as president of the United States in January 1981, the international scene gave the dictatorship some respite. The new president maintained excellent relations with the Argentine dictators and ceased to cause the kind of discomfort that his predecessor had with his questioning about human rights violations. Nevertheless, despite all the support it received and the forced silencing of the population, the military did not manage to put the economy in order. In fact, its policies exacerbated the existing problems. The crisis and rising inflation quickly dissolved the support it had initially garnered. In 1981, there was another sharp devaluation, and inflation exceeded 100 percent (in 1983, it would exceed 400 percent). It was around that time that the habit of buying dollars to protect savings took root among those Argentines who had the means to do so, as well as the custom of dollarizing contracts and prices.

While most people were being hit by the crisis, in 1982 the government implemented measures whereby the state took over the debts in dollars that large companies had contracted abroad. This meant a huge transfer of public money into the pockets of a handful of businesspeople, including several banks, the cement company Loma Negra, the Macri Group, Bunge y Born, and the oil company Perez Companc. The foreign debt multiplied and, by 1983, 40 percent of the state's income went toward interest payments. The deficit increased sharply and external lenders began to condition the continuity of their financing. Additionally, during the same period, the expansionary cycle that agriculture in the Pampas had been enjoying came to a halt.

By then, the disagreements between the three armed forces that had been present from the beginning—they had divided up the ministries and public offices that they managed, each as they saw fit, with poor coordination between them—became impossible to hide. Moreover, the impunity enjoyed by both the repressive groups and the military hierarchy soon gave rise to a whole industry of illicit activities, ranging from extortive kidnappings to the organization of mafia networks for arms or drug trafficking. Corruption spread to all levels of the state. This was compounded by rivalries between factions within the army, which contributed to the misgovernment. General Viola, from the sector considered "soft," was removed from the presidency by the military junta and replaced with "hard-liner" General Leopoldo Galtieri. Hoping to rally some support, on April 2, 1982, the new president set out to retake the Malvinas Islands, which led to an absurd war with Great Britain (the dictators had previously been on the verge of unleashing another war with Chile over disagreements on the demarcation of the border in the Beagle Channel).

Far from leading to the recovery of the islands, Galtieri's bravado interrupted diplomatic advances and earlier moves by Britain toward the restitution of sovereignty over the territory to Argentina. In the short term, however, it seemed to bear fruit; a huge wave of nationalist enthusiasm swept all political and social sectors and muted criticism of the government. However, defeat was not long in coming: Argentina was forced to surrender after only forty-five days of combat. The adventure left a total of 649 dead on the Argentine side—most of them eighteen- and nineteen-year-old conscripts from some of the poorest areas of the country—plus 255 on the British side and three islanders. The poor performance of the armed forces on the battlefield gave the dictatorship an approaching end date. While the conflict lasted, the media had broadcast news reports announcing a resounding Argentine victory. From one day to the next, the stunned population suddenly became aware of the disastrous reality. Indignation was immediate. The war, moreover, put an end to the friendship with Reagan, who, predictably, had to support his British allies.

The End of the "Years of Lead"

After the defeat of the Malvinas, Galtieri was forced to leave office. With the military leadership plunged into growing disarray and internal quarrels, the presidency was left in the hands of General Reynaldo Bignone, who was determined to speed up the process of returning power to civilian rule. Up until the war began, the dictators had discussed plans for a future transition in which the armed forces would retain a decisive political role, and the traditional political parties, responsible for the previous "populism" and misrule, would be replaced by new ones. They hoped that one of these new parties would embody the project of the National Reorganization Process and win popular backing. But now all those plans were laid to rest. While the "hardliners" fantasized about regaining a strength they had clearly lost, Bignone tried to negotiate an orderly withdrawal that would at least guarantee impunity for crimes committed.

Meanwhile, discontent was on the rise. In late 1982 and in March of the following year, there were general strikes, which were well attended not only by workers but also by small-scale retailers and other sectors of the middle class. In the last months of 1982, there were also spontaneous neighborhood protests in the Buenos Aires suburbs against tax increases. The struggle in defense of human rights that some organizations had started alone in 1977, such as the courageous Mothers of Plaza de Mayo—looking for answers regarding the whereabouts of their missing children—and other organizations of victims' family members, began to attract more attention and quickly gained momentum in the streets. The Grandmothers of Plaza de Mayo had embarked on the long search for their stolen grandchildren. And within this context, the political parties began to take on an oppositional attitude not seen in previous years.

Nevertheless, it was not political or popular pressure that pushed the dictatorship into retreat, as had happened in 1973, but its own inevitable collapse on all fronts. Since early 1983, it had been in free fall. The economy was collapsing and the handling of the state was increasingly chaotic. The regime had lost almost all its local and international support (it was around this time that the United States began to be more cautious in sponsoring coups d'état, and throughout Latin America there was a shift toward civilian governments). Even from within the Catholic Church—which until then had demonstrated a frankly collaborationist attitude—critical voices began to emerge. Only the business organizations that had supported the dictatorship in the previous

The Pendulum

years upheld their support until the very end. In this context, Bignone was forced to call elections for October that year.

The months of the electoral campaign went by in a climate of political reawakening and extraordinary enthusiasm. The traditional political parties, rejected only a short time earlier, received a tidal wave of new members; 30 percent of the electoral roll joined a party, mainly the Justicialist Party (better known as the Peronist Party) but also the UCR in very high numbers. In 1981, Ricardo Balbín, historical leader of the UCR and very cooperative with the military, had passed away, so the leadership of the party was left to the charismatic Raúl Alfonsín, who adopted a more oppositional stance. The orderly leadership election in which he was chosen as the party's presidential candidate contrasted with the chaotic nature of the Peronists' leadership election, in which the various factions of Peronism confronted each other, at times with physical violence. In this case, the trade union sectors asserted their influence and the winning candidate was Ítalo Luder, who was surlier than his opponent and bore the stigma of having been a member of Isabel's government.

The electoral campaign was lively. While the Peronists largely stuck with their traditional slogans and aesthetics, Alfonsín managed to connect well with a new social climate that, in the wake of the experience of the 1970s and the dictatorship, longed for a more consensual and nonviolent approach to politics. His speeches were not anti-Peronist, although they did denounce the existence of a "union-military pact." Additionally, he announced that, if elected, he would repudiate the self-amnesty law the military had issued to protect itself (as opposed to Luder, who considered it untouchable). The Radical slogan, "Somos la vida" (We are life), in contrast with the Peronist slogan, "Somos la rabia" (We are rage), said it all.

The results of the election were quite unexpected. Alfonsín won with 52 percent of the vote and ten points separating him from Luder. For the first time, Peronism had been defeated in clean elections, a sign that a historical cycle was coming to an end. The UCR triumphed even in the Peronist stronghold of Buenos Aires province with a fairly unknown candidate, which indicates that a significant portion of the lower classes, who this time had chosen not to vote for their usual party, had turned to the UCR.

After Bignone handed over command to the president-elect in December 1983, the military withdrew in humiliation. It was leaving without having fulfilled most of its objectives. It had not achieved the civilian continuity it had imagined, with a government led by a new right-wing party that represented military interests. In fact, no right-wing party in 1983 achieved any relevant level of support. Peronism had been defeated—which was no small feat—but by the UCR, which the military considered part of the "populist" problem. Worse still, the UCR was in the hands of a leader like Alfonsín, who gave it a decidedly progressive and anti-military tinge and who once again announced an economic policy based on strengthening the domestic market and the purchasing power of wage earners. Furthermore, Peronism still maintained significant electoral strength and controlled the Senate. Nor had the strength of the unions waned to the extent that the dictators had expected.

Nevertheless, the National Reorganization Process had two valuable achievements from the point of view of the business sectors that supported it. When the dark veil that had fallen over society was lifted, little was left of the powerful left-wing movement that had previously played a leading role in Argentine politics. Terror permeated the entire population so deeply that it managed to transform the political culture and ties between people in a lasting way. And in terms of the economy, the changes were irreversible. Since Martínez de Hoz's administration, Argentina had become an enormously vulnerable country dependent on the international financial system. The foreign debt—which before the National Reorganization Process had hardly been relevant—had become unpayable and an instrument for the permanent outflow of surpluses abroad. The mandates and conditions of the IMF and large-scale local businesspeople and bankers would, in the future, place a heavy mortgage on the possibilities of returning to an economic model that would be more favorable to most of the population.

The National Reorganization Process had not managed to establish a stable and well-functioning new economic order, nor had it found a way to create a right-wing political force capable of attracting the popular vote, nor had it been able to sweep the "populist" parties out of the way. Instead, it had tied the state's hands and feet, ensuring the state would no longer be able to take a path other than the one indicated by the financial and export sectors. The stalemate of the previous decades ended with the triumph of these groups. The military left humiliated in 1983, but the sectors of the elite that had driven it to take power in 1976 could feel satisfied.

6

Democracy Devalued

*Between the Promises of Democracy and Neoliberalism,
from Alfonsín to Macri (1983–2019)*

IN 1983, very few people understood how much Argentina had been transformed by the dictatorship. To begin with, the most evident change was in the political culture. And it was associated less with the military legacy than with the victory of the Unión Cívica Radical (UCR). There was, however, a complex relationship between these two things. In his own way, Raúl Alfonsín offered the potential to inaugurate a new era that would leave behind the Peronist Argentina of disorder and social conflict. During the campaign and throughout his government, in place of the previous great collective yearnings—social justice, national development, and socialism—Alfonsín bestowed new legitimacy on a more modest aspiration: democracy. "With democracy one eats, heals, and educates" was one of his most famous slogans, in which he sought to endow the very word *democracy* with a certain social and progressive content. The imperative now was to embrace democracy and strengthen republican institutions and culture as a vital and satisfactory prospect for the country. His most enduring legacy was precisely in this area: it was in these years that Argentine society—which had not shown significant signs of appreciation for democracy in the past—began to value it more than it ever had before.

Alfonsín's project called on society as a whole to unite behind this objective and to leave aside the confrontations of the past. But the citizens who were being asked to support this project of democratic civility were the same ones who had fueled deep class conflicts and a spiral of violence only a few months earlier. For this project to gain a foothold, the citizenry would have to be re-educated; in fact, a new democratic subject would have to be constructed. To this end, Alfonsín and the political and intellectual figures who accompanied him took elements from various sources and combined them into a powerful narrative. On the one hand, they drew on the UCR's long civic tradition and on several classic motifs of liberal republicanism: respect for the rights and guarantees established by the constitution; the importance of suffrage and the pluralistic debate of ideas; and the pursuit of consensus through institutions rather than through corporative negotiation between interest groups, which had been the norm in the previous decades. To these elements they added the idea that there were "human rights" that should take precedence over any other consideration, an older notion, of course, but one that the opposition to the dictatorship had brought to the forefront of the discussion.

The effectiveness of these notions stemmed from the way in which they were intertwined with a new narrative known as the "theory of the two demons." It was not Alfonsín's creation—it emerged from voices within the human rights movement before the end of the dictatorship—but it was his government that turned it into a state doctrine. The theory proposed that the responsibility for the violence of the previous years rested exclusively with the military commanders and the leadership of the guerrilla organizations. It was these two rather small groups, one on the right and the other on the left, that had unleashed the horror, and, in that sense, they were equally responsible for it. They were condemned in moral terms, without much attention being paid to their political projects and social supports. The rest of the population had been trapped between them and was a passive victim of their violence. The responsibility and participation of society as a whole were thus ignored, so as to leave it free of guilt and blame and ready to embrace the democratic cause.

As a result, two crucial issues were overlooked: the high level of civilian support there had been for the dictatorship (especially from the business sector) and the fact that another equally significant part of the population—and not only the guerrilla leaders—had fought for a new world without worrying much about respecting democratic formalities. With all this forgotten, repudiation could be swiftly condensed, making it possible to move forward with a quick condemnation and a turn of the page.

The vision proposed by Alfonsín's government proved tremendously persuasive for a society that wished to leave the past behind as soon as possible. The global context also played its part: this was an era of a shift to the right, abandoning the utopias and rebellious ideals that had characterized the previous two decades. The model of progressive democratic civic responsibility proposed an explicit condemnation of both the military's atrocities and the fanaticism of the guerrilla leaders, though in a more paternalistic way it also distanced itself from the naive "young idealists" who were victims of one or the other. It was also no longer the moment to put corporative interests above those of the country: it was now time to put an end to the overreaching of the trade unions and the typical Peronist rhetoric of struggle and resistance. It was time for dialogue and consensus, not for the use of force or conflict. The new democratic Argentina had nothing to do with the military or guerrilla past, or with the Marxist or Peronist past.

This new narrative ushered in by the return to democracy was inevitably reflected in social identities. Faith in the worker as the central figure of a longed-for change, which in previous years had motivated both the left and Peronism, lost ground. The new ideal of civic responsibility was implicitly embodied in the "middle class." Indeed, Alfonsín's victory was interpreted as the victory of that class, supposedly putting an end to the undue influence of the plebeian element in national history. Many assumed that with the triumph of the middle class, there would be a return to a "normal country" governed by moderation, rationality, social peace, and respect for institutions. Even the political vocabulary reflected this, with a tendency to replace references to *el pueblo* (the people) or *los trabajadores* (the workers) with others such as *la gente* (folks), a category that left no room for imagining social differences between individuals.

There are indications that this perspective also permeated the world of the popular classes. The defeat of the revolutionary movement, the loss of credibility of Peronism and the Confederación General del Trabajo (CGT), and the expectations generated by Alfonsín's victory likely contributed to the spread of a middle-class identity among them as well, which came at the expense of working-class pride. As a result of this political and cultural defeat, the democracy inaugurated in 1983 was paradoxically founded more on the waning of the popular classes as a political actor than on their participation. Many imagined that this decline in involvement would strengthen the new democratic civic spirit. But subsequent events would show that the effect was the opposite: it was the citizenry itself, popular sovereignty in general, that was emptied of meaning.

Alfonsín's Decisive Moment (1983–1989)

On December 10, 1983, Raúl Alfonsín took office accompanied by an enormous surge of enthusiasm that placed expectations of profound change—as the government's rhetoric itself promised—on the democratic transition. The vigorous way in which the new president went about dismantling the apparatus of impunity that had been set up by the armed forces before their departure generated a sense of empowerment in many, the idea that this time democracy was finally imposing itself over military power. As soon as he was sworn in, Alfonsín repealed the self-amnesty decreed by the military and set up the Comisión Nacional sobre la Desaparición de Personas (National Commission on the Disappearance of Persons, or CONADEP), consisting of independent professionals, that several months later produced a chilling report on the crimes of the dictatorship. Entitled *Nunca más* (*Never Again*), it quickly became one of the most influential texts in Argentine history; "Never Again" was from that moment on a slogan that expressed an unwavering commitment to democracy.

What followed was unprecedented: in 1985, by order of the president, the nine members of the first three military juntas that had been in power starting in 1976 and several other high-ranking officers were put on trial in a civilian court. The judges determined that there had been no "war" that could justify their actions, and they were thus classified as crimes against humanity. Five high-ranking commanders were sentenced—some to life—and sent to prison. The trial was the first of its kind, globally, and set a standard for other cases of human rights violations: it was the first time a nation had succeeded in convicting its dictators in its own courts. For the sake of balance and in line with the idea of the "two demons," Alfonsín issued another decree stipulating that the leadership of the Montoneros and the Ejército Revolucionario del Pueblo (ERP) would be put on trial, and they also ended up convicted.

With the convictions of both "demons," Alfonsín sought to conclude the process of examining the past. But the "Trial of the Juntas," as it was known, generated an unexpected dynamic. The human rights movement began to antagonize the government and pressured it to prosecute all those responsible (it also raised the overlooked question of the complicity of the business and financial sectors). Throughout the country, judges began to investigate the responsibilities of other top-ranking military commanders and even of intermediate commanders, causing growing nervousness in the barracks. Alfonsín reacted with a measure that was to be the first step on a path toward disenchantment: in 1986, he succeeded in getting Congress to approve the Ley de Punto Final (Full Stop Law), which set a deadline for filing new accusations. While he was preparing another law that would limit the responsibility of midlevel commanders, there was a military uprising.

During Easter Week 1987, Lieutenant Colonel Aldo Rico occupied the barracks of the Campo de Mayo military base together with other rebels referred to as *carapintadas* ("painted faces," in reference to the camouflage paint they used). This time they were not seeking to stage a coup but to demand an end to the trials and vindication for the repressive actions of the armed forces. The uprising was not replicated in other barracks, but nor were the rest of the armed forces willing to suppress it, which left the government in a difficult position. At the same time, there was a massive popular reaction in defense of democracy. Tens of thousands of people took to the streets across the country. A crowd flooded Plaza de Mayo and marched to Campo de Mayo, the army's stronghold. All the political parties and organizations of all types vigorously backed up the president. It was a decisive crossroads for the nascent democracy.

Alfonsín reacted hesitantly. He accepted the rebels' demand to travel personally by helicopter to meet with them and promised to take measures to limit the scope of the trials. Upon his return to the Casa Rosada, he addressed the crowd gathered there using terms that appeared to justify the actions of the *carapintadas* and reported that they had laid down their arms. He wished everyone a "happy Easter," assured them that "the house is in order," and urged them to go home. Days later, he presented Congress with the Ley de Obediencia Debida (Due Obedience Law), which stipulated that military personnel up to the rank of colonel could not be tried, since they were considered obligated to comply with any order that their superiors gave them. Like the Full Stop Law, it passed with the vote of a segment of the Peronist Party. Alfonsín's attitude and the "impunity laws"—as the human rights movement called them—generated deep disappointment: the illusion that the mobilization of ordinary people and the general will could defeat the forces of power was decisively shattered. The magic of that 1983 moment had been extinguished.

Furthermore, Alfonsín's concession did not even serve to ensure calm in the barracks; in fact, the government's weakness gave the rebels even greater impetus. Rico staged another uprising in 1988, and his fellow *carapintada* Mohamed Alí Seineldín did the same later that year and again in 1990. However, the restraint that the armed forces showed in repressing seditious members within their ranks was completely absent in January 1989, when they deployed all their power to crush a small leftist group, the Movimiento Todos por la Patria (All for the Fatherland Movement), when it attempted to seize the military barracks at La Tablada. In this case, the armed forces even secretly shot some of the people they had captured alive. After this episode, Alfonsín once again gave in to the military and created a National Security Council that effectively allowed the armed forces to participate in matters of domestic security, something that was prohibited by law.

In other areas, the Alfonsín administration showed similar vacillations, with partial advances, setbacks, and missed opportunities. Relations with the Church were very poor; from the outset, the ecclesiastical hierarchy was wary of the investigations into human rights violations that would inevitably show—as they did—their involvement in the repressive plan. They rejected the trials of the members of the military and called for "reconciliation"; they also made a habit of criticizing the nascent democracy, in whose progressive spirit they saw signs of the spread of immorality. In spite of this opposition, freedom of expression was broadened and the president succeeded in getting two crucial laws passed legalizing divorce and enabling shared parental rights. But he failed to introduce the educational reforms he had in mind when he convened an ambitious National Pedagogical Congress, which ended up dominated by Catholic groups. Nevertheless, university life and culture in general flourished, partly due to the return of artists and intellectuals who had gone into exile. Theater, television, literature, essays, and cinema—with the successful films *La república perdida* (*The Lost Republic*) and *La historia oficial* (*The Official Story*), among many others—all focused on the horrors of the dictatorship.

Alfonsín also attempted to change the set of laws regulating union life in a way that would limit the power of the bureaucracy and at the same time weaken the unions. The top leadership of the CGT closed ranks to resist him. Opposition from a sector of Peronism, which controlled the Senate, made the reform impossible, so the government radically changed course and tried to win the support of the trade unionists with concessions, even incorporating them into government positions. Given the context of economic austerity, none of this prevented the CGT, led by Saúl Ubaldini, from adopting a generally confrontational attitude that included calling thirteen general strikes.

Relations with major businesspeople were equally tense, and attempts to assert the state's authority were even more inconsistent. Alfonsín criticized the so-called *patria financiera* (domestic interests profiting from financial speculation, the main beneficiaries of the liberalization process), and when he took office he had assured that each of the loan certificates that the companies had transferred to the state when it decided to nationalize private foreign debt would be analyzed, as there was a suspicion that many of them were forged. He had also proposed to review bankruptcies, subsidies, and fraudulent transfers of companies that had been approved by the dictatorship (the most scandalous case was that of Papel Prensa, the country's main paper mill, whose owners had been forced to cede the property to the three leading newspapers, *Clarín*, *La Nación*, and *La Razón*). Although none of these things happened, the heterodox beginnings of Alfonsín's government and the possibility that he might go ahead with all of this earned him obvious disfavor from the business sector.

In foreign policy, he was an active president. His greatest achievements included the resolution of the dispute with Chile over the demarcation of the border in the Beagle Channel (with a settlement endorsed through an unprecedented referendum) and the free-trade agreement signed with Brazil in 1991. The latter would give rise to the Mercado Común del Sur (Southern Common Market, or MERCOSUR), one of the most important economic blocs in the world, which would go on to include Uruguay, Paraguay, and later Venezuela. With respect to American policy, Alfonsín initially adopted an independent stance, but this attitude soon became less evident. When he took office, Alfonsín passed up the opportunity to repudiate the foreign debt taken on by the dictatorship, something that would have been politically risky but technically possible due to the doctrine of "odious debt" that the United States itself had already applied on several occasions. He threatened to form a "debtors' club" with other nations to negotiate from a better position, but this idea was never implemented. The American government gave him broad support throughout his administration.

The area where he showed the greatest hesitation was the economy. When the Alfonsín administration began, the economy was stagnant and the main variables were out of control. The public coffers were empty, the country was on the verge of default, onerous foreign debt repayments were approaching, and inflation was still very high. During the first year, with Bernardo Grinspun as minister of economy, Alfonsín implemented policies to promote consumption and stimulate the domestic market similar to those Arturo Illia's government had adopted in the 1960s. There was a brief reactivation of the economy and wages improved. But the risk of hyperinflation and pressures from the IMF and the business sector pushed Alfonsín in a different direction. In 1985, he appointed Juan Sourrouille to replace Grinspun and gradually began to shift toward more orthodox policies. With the so-called Austral Plan, he applied "shock therapy"; prices, salaries, and tariffs were frozen, and the peso was replaced by a new currency: the austral.

These measures managed to halt inflation and stabilize the main variables. However, by late 1985, inflation was once again on the rise, and the government, continuously under IMF supervision, began to explore ways of deepening the reforms in terms of greater fiscal austerity, further deregulation of the economy, privatization of several state-owned companies, reduction of agricultural export duties, and the influx of foreign capital. At the same time, in an attempt to calm social tensions and gain the support of the business sector, in 1987 Alfonsín incorporated representatives of economic corporations into his government and a trade unionist into the Ministry of Labor, which once again reflected the weakness of the state.

Unlike the 1985 elections in which the UCR had achieved a significant victory, in the 1987 legislative elections it suffered a serious setback: it lost control of the Chamber of Deputies and most of the provinces it governed, including the province of Buenos Aires, which hastened the government's loss of authority. In August 1988, following the failure of the Austral Plan, a new package of measures was announced called the Spring Plan, which intensified the orthodox approach with new price and wage freezes and announcements of dramatic austerity measures.

The rhetoric that accompanied this progressive shift once again focused on the need for structural reforms and the state's inefficiency as the reason for the shortages (in fact, although it never materialized, a plan was made for the privatization of several state-owned companies). However, none of this was enough to stabilize the economy; in addition to the national government's financial difficulties, many of the provinces were also experiencing hardships, especially Salta, Tucumán, La Rioja, Catamarca, and Chaco, where the situation was becoming desperate. Meanwhile, problems with the electric power supply, which resulted in constant programmed outages, exacerbated negative public sentiment and further discredited the state-owned companies.

In early 1989, following the announcement by the IMF and the World Bank that they would start restricting loans to Argentina, the economy collapsed. The government authorized a sharp devaluation, and inflation spiraled out of control, reaching levels rarely seen before anywhere in the world; it rose to a staggering 3,620 percent per annum. Prices increased so quickly that wages lost their value a few hours after they were paid. The rates of poverty and extreme poverty climbed to previously unheard-of levels: 47.3 percent and 17.5 percent, respectively.

The 1989 elections took place in the midst of this inflationary chaos, having been moved up to May for the sake of the ruling party. As his government collapsed, the progressive vision Alfonsín had put forward lost support. Early in his term, discontent had fueled the growth of a leftist party, the Partido Intransigente (Intransigent Party), which in 1985 had won just over 6 percent of the vote. However, this trend was soon reversed with the help of a constant stream of voices encouraging an interpretation of the crisis that fed into the right wing's agenda. Starting in 1987, the media had embarked on a systematic campaign for the need to dismantle "statism"—which was targeted as the main culprit of the hardships—liberalize the economy, and put an end to "abusive" labor rights. The market, left to its own devices, would resolve all the problems. Alfonsín himself added credibility to these ideas in his speeches, albeit in a more moderate way.

In election after election, Álvaro Alsogaray's Unión del Centro Democrático (Union of the Democratic Center, or UCEDE), which boasted a neoliberal program, had been gaining traction (in 1989, it would win almost 10 percent of the vote for its legislators). Given this context, Alfonsín proposed Eduardo Angeloz, the governor of Córdoba, who was far from progressive, as his party's presidential candidate. During the campaign, Angeloz announced that he would implement orthodox economic policies and would undertake a severe fiscal adjustment if elected. Roberto Alemann, who had already held the position during the dictatorship, was rumored to be the proposed minister of economy for his future cabinet.

But it was Peronism that capitalized on the discontent, although it was not the same Peronism that had been defeated at the ballot box six years earlier. In 1987, a faction of "reformists" had displaced the trade unionists and the most "stale" Peronists from the leadership of the Partido Justicialista (Justicialist Party, better known as the Peronist Party). It was presided over by leaders such as Antonio Cafiero, Eduardo Duhalde, Carlos Grosso, and José Manuel de la Sota. They understood that in the wake of previous defeats, Peronism was now at a crossroads where it had to either evolve or perish. It had to be "deplebicized" and adopt a party apparatus with formal rules and a more "modern" leadership, acceptable to the middle sectors and the spirit of democratic civic-mindedness that had been established. The reformists had forged alliances with several leaders who were well established in their respective provinces (such as Carlos Menem from La Rioja) and cultivated a good relationship with major businesspeople (some of them, such as Franco Macri, financed their ascent). Cafiero appeared to be the natural candidate of this group, but in the leadership elections—something completely new to the movement that Juan Domingo Perón had founded—Menem unexpectedly defeated him and became the presidential candidate.

Carlos Menem ran in the 1989 elections with a fairly traditional Peronist platform, promising a *salariazo* (substantial wage increase), Latin American unity, and stimulus for industry, as part of a front that included the Intransigent Party and other progressive and leftist parties. His speeches were strongly nationalistic and messianic in tone. His mannerisms and campaign aesthetics were unrefined; indeed, with his ample sideburns and long hair, he played at resembling old federalist caudillos such as his fellow Riojans Facundo Quiroga and Chacho Peñaloza. When the votes were counted, he emerged triumphant with just over 47 percent, which appears to indicate that rather traditional-looking Peronism still had a good hold among half of the population. Even so, Angeloz received 37 percent of the vote, reflecting the electoral weight of those who, in spite of everything, continued to be Radicals or considered the UCR as the only viable alternative for their anti-Peronism. Not insignificantly, whatever their reasons, they were willing to support a candidate with a real chance at winning who, for the first time in history, was running with a neoliberal platform (Alsogaray, for his part, won just over 7 percent of the vote).

With hyperinflation rampant and a portion of the population gripped by desperation, in late May 1989, a few days after the elections, there was an intense wave of looting in stores, the first large-scale food riots in Argentina's modern history. In response, the government declared a state of siege and arrested the leadership of the Partido Obrero (Workers' Party), a small Trotskyist group, which it accused, without any proof, of having organized the assaults. The handover of the government had to be moved up six months because the outgoing president, who no longer had any power, could not get the situation under control. Alfonsín stepped down in total disrepute, having become an emblem of bitter disillusionment.

From Menem to the Alianza: The Triumph of Neoliberalism

During Alfonsín's years in office, the world had changed. With Margaret Thatcher in power in Great Britain and Ronald Reagan in the United States, pressures in favor of the free market became more aggressive than ever before. In 1989, shocked, the world witnessed the collapse of the Berlin Wall and, two years later, the demise of the Soviet Union. Capitalism now reigned undisputed. At the same time, developed countries began to dismantle the social welfare mechanisms that previous social democratic or progressive governments had established. In the words of an American intellectual, "the end of history" had arrived: globalized free market capitalism demanded to be recognized as the culmination of human evolution. "There is no alternative," Thatcher proclaimed. The so-called Washington Consensus translated that imperative into the reforms that Latin American countries were expected to adopt, the ten commandments of orthodox economic policy championed by the IMF and the World Bank.

The dictatorship had already made a vigorous attempt to restructure Argentina's economy and society along neoliberal lines. But the work had been left unfinished. After his heterodox start, Alfonsín had also taken a step in that direction but did not make much progress. Although weakened, trade unionism still had a good share of power. And more importantly, the state still retained the capacity to regulate various aspects of market functioning and controlled entire areas of the economy. All of that had to come to an end.

In the midst of the traumatic experience of hyperinflation, there were some who realized that they could take advantage of the situation. The extreme distress caused by the total collapse and the feeling that the social order itself was at risk encouraged people to set aside their specific interests and embrace any measure that promised stabilization. The disrepute into which the entire political system had fallen also made people more receptive to discourses promoting privatization. Years later, certain scholars found that the proponents of neoliberalism had used the same strategy in other places, and they dubbed it the "shock doctrine": when a chaotic situation plunges the population into fear and confusion, it then becomes possible to proceed with "bailout measures" that in normal times would never be accepted. If used intelligently, chaos can become a great ally. In fact, in the case of Argentina, although the evidence is not conclusive, it is possible that the most consolidated business and financial sectors induced hyperinflation in order to bring the political system to its knees (not only the outgoing president but also whoever won the 1989 elections, especially if it was Carlos Menem, who was campaigning with ideas and slogans that ran contrary to the preferences of the establishment).

Instead of a coup d'état, some scholars see it as a "market coup." It is difficult to prove whether it was deliberate or not, but the fact is that in the period leading up to the elections, rural producers delayed export operations and others withheld tax payments, which generated financial problems. This was compounded by the behavior of large companies that did not liquidate foreign currency and produced currency runs as they abandoned the austral en masse to take refuge in the dollar.

Whatever the case, hyperinflation was followed by a program of the most drastic neoliberal austerity measures on record. More than half of the electorate had not validated it with their vote but had to accept it as an inevitability. Argentina embarked on this course, in what was a complete electoral swindle. Upon taking office, Menem shaved off his caudillo-like sideburns, changed his simple clothes for Armani suits, and surprised everyone with measures that were diametrically opposed to those he had announced. He also teamed up with Álvaro Alsogaray, a fervent anti-Peronist who, ironically, would become one of his staunchest allies. Prior to the elections, he had discreetly cultivated ties with the corporate group Bunge y Born, and his first minister of economy was the firm's vice president. This was the first of a series of orthodox finance ministers, the most famous of whom was Domingo Cavallo, who had overseen the Central Bank during the previous dictatorship. Cavallo held the position for more than five years—he narrowly surpassed Martínez de Hoz's record—and was succeeded, during Menem's second term, by Roque Fernández, a "Chicago boy" who came from the UCEDE.

After a period of turbulence (which included more looting, more hyperinflation, and the expropriation of fixed-term deposits exchanged for bonds to be cashed within ten years' time), the economy began to stabilize. With the consent of a large part of the trade union hierarchy and almost the entire Peronist Party, most of the tariff protections for industry and a significant portion of the subsidies were eliminated or reduced in record time (although certain subsidies were maintained on a discretionary basis for those who had government contacts). Practically all state-owned companies were also privatized, including the massive oil company Yacimientos Petrolíferos Fiscales (YPF). In addition, banks were authorized to set up Administradoras de Fondos de Jubilaciones y Pensiones (Retirement and Pension Fund Administrators, or AFJP), which offered individually funded private retirement schemes.

Cavallo succeeded in bringing inflation to a complete standstill with a bold shock program, including the convertibility of the national currency, which was changed back to the peso. For the next ten years, there would be no devaluations and one peso would be equivalent to one dollar. The value-added tax (VAT) levied on consumers was extended to include food products and progressively increased from 13 percent to 21 percent, while property, investment, and income taxes remained almost unchanged, making the country's tax structure more regressive. The dismantling of the state's regulatory capacity was almost absolute. Financiers and investors benefited from previously unheard-of rights and guarantees to engage in activities as they pleased, without controls or restrictions.

The consequences of these policies were devastating. Tens of thousands of state employees were laid off. Entire branches of the railroad were closed as part of its privatization—the rail network shrank from 21,800 miles to only 5,000 miles—and as a result, entire communities were transformed into ghost towns. Competition from imported products exacerbated the process of deindustrialization initiated during the dictatorship. Numerous bankruptcies of small- and medium-sized companies and businesses left tens of thousands of laborers, workers, technicians, and former owners in the street. Greater Buenos Aires was the hardest hit area: during the 1990s, it lost 5,508 industrial plants and, in the first five years alone, the manufacturing sector eliminated 200,000 jobs. By 1995, unemployment and underemployment had reached 33.8 percent.

Just as during the dictatorship, the winners were the large local and transnational businesses—especially those producing export commodities—government contractors, and, of course, the financial sectors, groups that all gave Menem their enthusiastic support. Well-known journalists and the owners of media outlets also supported him; in an unprecedented event, they called on the population to participate in a demonstration in favor of the government, which turned out to be massive. Starting in 1991, new laws were introduced with devastating consequences for labor rights. Under the pretense of needing to "make jobs more flexible," conditions were generated to encourage subcontracting, outsourcing, self-employment, and temporary jobs. In practice, this meant the expansion of undercover labor relations and casual employment. Unreported employment increased sharply from 26.5 percent in 1990 to 35 percent in 1999. There was a tendency toward an increase in the length of the workday, often without a corresponding increase in wages. During these same years, the so-called cost of labor fell by 62 percent: employers' social security contributions were reduced and the regulations on occupational illnesses and work-related accidents were changed to the detriment of wage earners.

Neoliberal policies also exacerbated regional imbalances and the tendency toward the reprimarization of the economy. The elimination of export taxes on agricultural exports generated significant growth in the sector but in a way that accentuated the concentration of profits in the hands of a few and a tendency toward monoculture. The spread of genetically modified seeds and the use of glyphosate—approved in 1996 in record time by the secretary of agriculture, Felipe Solá, without any local studies on their potential health impacts—generated an unprecedented expansion in soybean production, which overtook other crops and livestock production. This was especially exploited by the *pools de siembra*, groups of investors, sometimes not even directly connected to the rural sector, who rented land and machinery and placed a professional in charge of production. Exchange-rate policies, the increase in the cost of land, and the need for large investments to keep pace with technical improvements complicated the lives of small- and medium-scale producers, many of whom incurred debt and eventually went bankrupt.

At the same time, new "zero-tillage" technology resulted in labor savings of up to 30 percent, reducing employment opportunities for farm laborers. More suitable for poor-quality soils, soybean cultivation hit campesinos and indigenous peoples particularly hard, as they were pressured to abandon their land. It also dramatically exacerbated environmental deterioration by motivating the indiscriminate felling of the few remaining forests in many areas, which, in turn, led to soil erosion and flooding. The massive use of herbicides damaged native flora and degraded soil quality, and there are strong indications that it is the cause of higher rates of cancer and respiratory diseases among the rural population. Consequences like this were not only seen in agriculture. In the 1990s, the government granted permits to foreign companies to carry out open-pit mining in various parts of the Andes Mountains, thus exposing communities to water and soil contamination.

Nevertheless, Menem's program did succeed in triggering growth in some sectors of the economy. As a result, between 1991 and 1994, the poverty rate was reduced to 30 percent (according to the current methodology used by the Instituto Nacional de Estadística y Censos [National Institute of Statistics and Census of Argentina, or INDEC]), much lower than during the 1989 crisis but well above levels in the 1970s. With inflation under control—in 1994, it returned to levels comparable to those of developed countries for the first time in twenty years—the ability to pay for purchases in installments was reintroduced, generating a brief frenzy in consumer spending and an illusory sense of an economic upswing. The government managed to place bonds with foreign investors, which ensured liquidity, although the cost was an abrupt increase in the foreign debt. Supporters of neoliberalism around the world spoke of the "Argentine miracle" and offered it as proof that the Washington Consensus was working.

These initial achievements, which were magnified by the capital inflow from the privatizations and foreign debt refinancing the IMF had granted while its prescriptions were being applied, concealed a growing imbalance in the trade deficit and a rise in unemployment, allowing Menem to win reelection in 1995. A year earlier, he had managed to gain authorization for a second consecutive term through a constitutional reform, which had been facilitated by an agreement with Alfonsín as part of the so-called Olivos Pact, giving Menem the votes he lacked to push it through Congress. Menem's victory was a milestone of great significance in national history: it was the first time the upper classes' preferred candidate came to power in clean elections in which the electorate was aware of the candidate's intentions. Never since the establishment of democracy in 1916 had the wealthiest and most powerful sectors secured the freely given consent of the majority of the population for the policies and politicians that represented them. It was a historical irony that the person to achieve such an accomplishment was, in fact, a man of Peronism. It seemed to announce that the long phase that began in 1945 was coming to an end.

Menem himself reinforced this idea through his narrative of a longstanding crisis requiring a refoundational change for the nation. "I come to unite the two Argentinas," he said in his inauguration speech, the Argentinas "of Rosas and Sarmiento, of Mitre and Facundo, of Peñaloza and Alberdi, of Pellegrini and Yrigoyen, of Perón and Balbín." He accompanied this declaration with a series of gestures that sought to settle enduring feuds: he embraced Admiral Isaac Rojas, one of the most high-profile of the "gorillas" who had ousted Perón in 1955; he subscribed to the liberal creed but also repatriated the remains of Juan Manuel de Rosas, whose portrait was featured on the twenty-peso banknote. Additionally, through a series of pardons, which generated widespread social rejection, the military officers convicted of crimes against humanity and the leaders of the *carapintadas* were released from prison, along with former guerrilla leaders.

His government's neoliberal policies were accompanied by a rapprochement with the United States, a country with which Argentina was maintaining "carnal relations," according to the metaphor used by Menem's own diplomatic corps. The support of the United States was sustained and reciprocated, and Menem became the first Peronist president to travel to Washington. Foreign debt obligations were renegotiated on more favorable terms, and Argentina was recognized as a "non-NATO ally," which represented a surprising reversal after more than a century of complicated relations.

Commensurate with this new status, Menem sent military forces to collaborate with the war that the United States launched on Iraq in 1990, a participation that was unprecedented for Argentina. It may have been due to this involvement that Buenos Aires was the target of two international terrorist attacks, the worst in its history, although exactly who was responsible for them has never been established. The first, in 1992, was against the Israeli Embassy; the second, in 1994, targeted the Asociación Mutual Israelita Argentina (Argentine Jewish Mutual Aid Association, or AMIA), causing eighty-five deaths. The government's investigation of the latter quickly led to accusations of Iran based on flimsy evidence, which served American interests. With respect to the perpetrators' local connections, there was a chain of suspicious cover-ups orchestrated by high-ranking officials in the Menem government (quite possibly under his orders, although definitive proof has never been found) and in the judiciary, which were maintained by subsequent administrations.

The AMIA cover-up was only one of several cases of illegal actions, shady negotiations, and corruption that marked the Menem years. Among the most notorious were the smuggling of arms to countries at war (and blowing up the Military Arms Factory in Río Tercero to cover up the operation, causing damage to the city, seven deaths, and more than three hundred wounded), the payment of a number of bribes—especially in the process of privatizing state-owned companies—and a string of alleged suicides and questionable deaths in connection with all the above. The executive branch weakened all agencies overseeing its actions as well as the independence of the judiciary through control over or bribery of federal judges (a task that was generally left in the hands of the intelligence services). Along similar lines, Menem promoted the expansion of the Supreme Court from five to nine members, which allowed him to secure an automatic majority; he also granted it the power of *per saltum*, allowing it to take over any case being handled by a lower court and make whatever decision it deemed appropriate. The powers of Congress were eroded through frequent decrees of necessity and urgency and laws delegating broad powers to the executive branch. The ultimate symbol of the undermining of these powers was in 1992 with the so-called *diputrucho* (fake representative) scandal when a random person was seated in Congress in order to achieve the necessary quorum to privatize Gas del Estado (State Gas Company).

Despite this institutional deterioration, the 1994 constitutional reform did provide the opportunity to introduce several amendments that resulted in an expansion of rights and guarantees. Among others, indirect voting and the electoral college system were abolished: representatives at all levels of government were to be directly elected by voters. New mechanisms were also established to ensure the separation of powers and improve oversight of public officials (including the option for popular consultations). The city of Buenos Aires, which up to that point had been governed directly by the national government, was declared autonomous and able to elect its own mayors. The reform acknowledged the preexistence of the indigenous peoples and recognized their right to own communal lands and preserve their culture. Environmental and consumer rights were also established and new provisions were made for the defense of democracy.

In 1994, at the president's initiative, compulsory military service was eliminated. A few years earlier, a law had been passed with the support of the executive branch establishing a quota of 30 percent of legislative positions for women. With meager representation in previous administrations, the presence of women in Congress finally began to reach a more balanced level.

A second term gave Menem the opportunity to intensify his policies. However, in addition to the domestic challenges, beginning in 1994, a series of financial collapses in peripheral countries, especially Mexico, triggered capital flight to more secure markets. For a time, the government managed to stave off the crisis with new support from the IMF, which only added to the foreign debt. But in 1995, the GDP fell once again and the decline was evident (this time, due to convertibility and the recession, it was not accompanied by inflation but by an unprecedented process of deflation in real prices). Many companies went bankrupt and, among those left standing, the process of foreignization was accentuated: locally owned companies, which accounted for 56.6 percent of sales in 1994, only represented 30.3 percent four years later.

Starting in 1998, Argentina entered economic free fall. The unemployment rate reached astronomical levels, and the levels of poverty and extreme poverty rose sharply once again. Dissatisfaction with the situation led to the victory in the 1999 elections of the Alianza (Alliance), an opposition coalition formed by the UCR and the Frente País Solidario (Front for a Country in Solidarity, or FREPASO), itself a coalition consisting of Peronists dissatisfied with the new orientation of the Peronist Party, Socialists, Christian Democrats, the Intransigent Party, and other minor groups. The Alianza was headed by the Radical Fernando de la Rúa. Despite the expectations of change, however, the economic policy of this new government remained the same. What is more, in 2001, de la Rúa reappointed Domingo Cavallo as minister of economy. Cavallo thus accomplished the feat of having formed part of a military dictatorship and two civilian governments, one Peronist and one Radical, which had all indiscriminately left economic policy in his hands.

A Pivotal Moment

After more than a decade of neoliberalism (preceded by the policies implemented during the dictatorship), Argentina had undergone such a profound transformation that little remained of the society that those who had been youth or adults in the 1970s had known. At the heart of all the changes was the enormous growth in inequality. In the city of Buenos Aires and surrounding areas, in 1974 the wealthiest 10 percent of the population had an average income 12.3 times greater than that of the poorest 10 percent. By October 1989—just before Menem's inauguration—the gap had already expanded to 23.1 times. In May 2002, during the peak of the crisis generated by Menem's policies, the figure climbed even higher: the wealthiest then earned an average of 33.6 times more than the least fortunate 10 percent. Thanks to military repression and neoliberal policies, the upper classes had managed to appropriate a much larger portion of socially produced wealth. And it should be noted that these figures do not allow us to see the minority of the "super-rich": if we measured the gap between them and the poorest, the result would be much more dramatic. These changes had an impact not only on the fate of the wealthiest and the poorest but on the entire social pyramid. Figure 6.1 shows the change over time in the six income brackets of metropolitan households.

As figure 6.1 shows, between 1974 and 2004 the proportion of extremely poor, poor, and lower-middle-income households grew sharply, while the percentage of middle- and upper-middle-income households declined. The vast

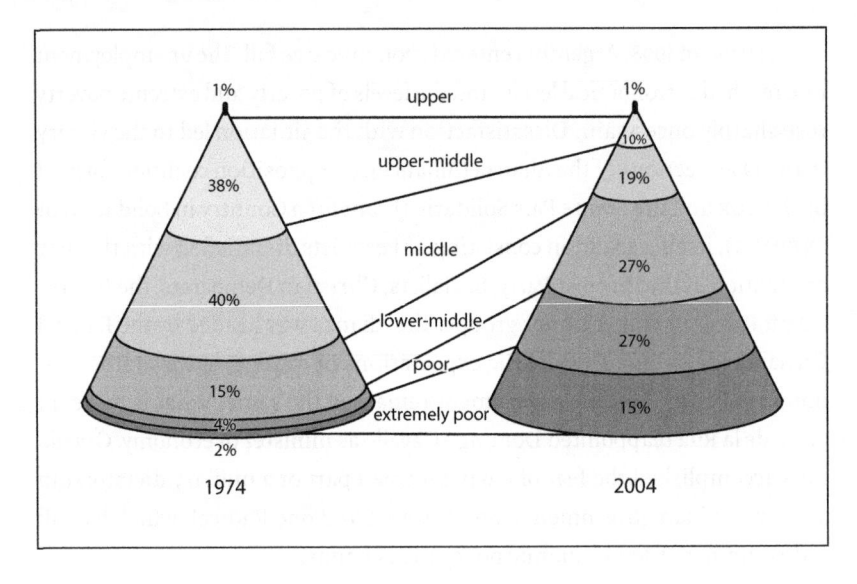

FIGURE 6.1. Income pyramid in the Buenos Aires metropolitan area, 1974 and 2004. Artemio López and Martín Romeo, *La declinación de la clase media argentina*.

majority of the population saw their social condition worsen. In fact, starting in the late 1980s, the phenomenon of the "new poor" emerged: many of the poor recorded in the statistics were people who only a short time earlier had enjoyed a more comfortable economic situation and belonged to the middle class. Although there are regional variations, the statistics available for the country as a whole show a similar trend. In short, in only a few years, Argentina went from having a social structure similar to countries that today are considered "advanced" to one that brought it closer to the less developed ones. In terms of the proportion of people living below the poverty line, again in the metropolitan area, in 1974 the figure was only 4.5 percent. By 1980 it had climbed to 8.4 percent and would double again four years later. During the peak of the 1989 crisis, it reached almost 48 percent. It fell to less than half of that after the recovery, but it would once again break through the 40 percent barrier in 2001 to reach, in October 2002, the incredible peak of 57 percent at the national level.

At the same time, the gap widened between the country's most prosperous and most disadvantaged regions. In various ways, the statistics speak of a country with greater poverty, inequality, and fragmentation. This fracture was especially visible in the phenomenon of *barrios cerrados* (gated communities), where those who could afford it chose to live separately from the rest of society. Relatively uncommon until the mid-1990s, they have since proliferated in Greater Buenos Aires, Córdoba, Rosario, Mendoza, and elsewhere.

Life for the general population underwent profound transformations. Due to high unemployment rates and the new prevalence of generally unstable and short-term jobs, worker pride and identity gradually came to be seen as part of a distant memory; the youngest did not even have that memory. Men, who used to affirm their masculinity as household breadwinners, felt out of place as they lost their jobs, and women were forced to go out into the labor market en masse or make do any way they could to feed their families. The traditional notion of "respect" that women and young people were expected to show for the "head of the household" had become hazy and was called into question. But this time that questioning was a reflection not of broader freedoms but of the fear and reproach generated by the loss of a certainty with nothing better to replace it. Family ties suffered, and violence inside and outside the home intensified.

These years also saw a marked rise in the feminization of poverty. Women from the popular classes and impoverished middle sectors were forced to enter the labor market on a massive scale in order to support the family economy. While in 1974, 22 percent of the wives of skilled manual laborers had their own economic activity, by the early 1990s the percentage had risen to 37 percent and continued to rise. The jobs they had access to were mostly in the service sector and were the lowest paid. Unemployment hit them harder than men. Additionally, the difference in salaries for the same job continued to be very pronounced. At the same time, the proportion of female workers who were the main household providers and the proportion of households headed by women alone increased.

But neoliberalism not only brought with it a new economic model: it was a project that involved a deep reformulation of all aspects of social life. One of the most obvious changes was in the role of the state. The prevailing belief at the time was that everyone was responsible for ensuring their well-being using their own means. All public services were to be cut back. As a result, the public health, welfare, and education systems were dramatically defunded. During the Menem administration, the national government transferred the responsibility for schools and other public institutions to the provinces without the accompanying funds to support them. The middle sectors gradually abandoned the public education system, which during this period ceased to be a space for interaction between different classes as it had been in previous decades. The public pension system was left underfunded due to lower contributions but also thanks to the creation of the AFJP, based on individual capitalization, which would prove to be a great fiasco (except for the financial sector, which for years earned commissions of up to 30 percent of workers' contributions).

The combination of the withdrawal of the state and the high rates of unemployment and informal employment meant that a much larger proportion of the popular classes found themselves without healthcare coverage or education. A study in the mid-1990s revealed that only 50 percent of young people in the lower social strata who were of secondary school age attended school. Of the half that did not, only 25 percent had a job, meaning that a huge number of young people did not have access during the day to activities that would help them progress or integrate. For many, these were times of great solitude and distress. The consumption of narcotics spread at a dizzying rate. Along with alcohol, abuse of marijuana, cocaine, and eventually highly lethal cocaine paste came to be part of the daily habits of many young people from the popular classes (and from the middle sectors as well).

At the same time, in order to keep the growing phenomenon of poverty and extreme poverty under control, the national, provincial, and municipal governments developed targeted assistance policies. From the first attempts with the National Food Program launched by Alfonsín in 1985 to the unemployment benefits implemented by Menem during his second term, welfare policies multiplied. The approaches the state used to address the needs of the popular classes were no longer focused primarily on the expansion of rights or benefits that citizens could claim collectively. The focal point of social policy was no longer workplaces but rather neighborhoods. The new social policy identified potential sources of conflict in order to provide specific assistance that would keep conflicts contained and under control. The prospect of eliminating poverty became a mere rhetorical formula: rather than eliminating it, the state sought to manage it.

Given that the number of state employees was progressively being reduced, the state took advantage of existing nonstate organizations and informal self-help networks in order to implement its welfare policies. It was not only nongovernmental organizations (NGOs) and churches that were used as a channel for the allocation and distribution of assistance; social activists and grassroots organizations were also invited to play the same role. This strategy was particularly successful in the districts under Peronist control. The "Basic Units" and local leaders turned out en masse to manage the resources coming from the state in each neighborhood. Over time, many of the "natural" neighborhood and grassroots leaders ended up becoming mediators or *punteros* (political bosses) at the service of the welfare apparatus.

The flip side of this process was the rapid expansion of clientelism, that is, personal favors (financed by the state) given in exchange for electoral support. In this way, a new network of territorially based personal ties began connecting the state with the popular classes. This blurred the boundaries between state, private, and partisan. Eduardo Duhalde, who was elected governor of Buenos Aires province in 1991, managed to set up a vast welfare structure by resorting to the services of ten thousand female volunteers, the famous *manzaneras* (block delegates), who channeled state resources working closely with the Peronist Party's Basic Units. Starting in the late 1980s, extensive clientelistic networks were organized in Santa Fe, La Pampa, San Luis, Santa Cruz, Formosa, Misiones, and Salta, and to a lesser extent in other provinces.

Politics also underwent other notable transformations that steadily brought them closer to business principles. Alfonsín was a pioneer in this sense, using marketing tools to promote his candidacy in 1983. Since then, image consultants and opinion polls have been used to a growing extent as market studies to "place" candidates, just as brands do with their products. For their part, business groups embarked on an aggressive policy of colonizing political parties by financing campaigns and training political leaders through foundations and think tanks. In some cases, they even went to the extreme of "buying" a place on the ballot (as Alberto Pierri did in the Peronist Party in the province of Buenos Aires). Some trade unionists also began to combine union representation with economic ventures; the term *sindicalismo empresarial* (entrepreneurial unionism) has since been used to refer to this phenomenon.

Viewed from above, Peronism in the 1990s had become unrecognizable. The right-wing, clientelist, and liberal Peronism of Menem's era more closely resembled the Conservative Party of the 1930s than the plebeian and galvanic movement that had erupted in 1945. Viewed from below, however, the image that emerged was different. A good part of the party's rank and file—possibly more than half, according to some surveys—disapproved of Menem's policies throughout his administration and held rather "statist" ideas. Despite this, there was no massive abandonment of the Peronist Party. Many rank-and-file leaders believed that Menem was implementing transitional stabilization policies, after which he would return to a more typically "Peronist" model. In the meantime, during these years they took refuge in a kind of "micro-Peronism," promoting social justice in their particular neighborhoods in whatever way they could and disengaging themselves from the actions of the national government. Thus, Peronism managed to maintain a deeply rooted extensive informal structure within the world of the popular classes.

Although Peronism's rank and file did not drift as far to the right as its leadership, the expansion of clientelism nevertheless influenced the movement's identity. Historically, Peronism had relied on the active figure of the workers and the narrative of their struggle against the oligarchy for the defense of the rights and dignity of those below them. But there had always been another, more passive lead figure in Peronist discourse: the poor, the dispossessed who could not fend for themselves and therefore deserved the protection of the state (which in the early days of the movement was embodied in the maternal figure of Evita).

Historically, Peronism had taken the form of both a struggle against privilege and assistance to the underprivileged. But now, following the de-unionization of the Peronist Party and its shift toward clientelism, this first component was weakened. Peronism was becoming less of an invitation to fight for dignity and against injustice and instead a promise to assist the poor without blaming anyone for poverty. The "best" Peronist was no longer the most committed to the struggle, nor the most rebellious, as it had been during the resistance, but simply "whoever who gives the most." The opposition to "those at the top" became less clear (and now it was the politicians who "did not give" who were despised rather than the upper class). Peronism was gradually being transformed from a political counterculture into an ideology of welfarism and passivity.

The dismantling of the state also had an impact on the deterioration of the security apparatus. The defunding of the police and low salaries only reinforced the temptation to use the uniform for personal enrichment. "Self-financing" activities increasingly shifted from simple requests for bribes to the outright organization of criminal networks dedicated to theft or drug trafficking. The police officers involved soon established connections with authorities of the judiciary and others with political power in order to ensure their impunity. Forms of "clandestine collection" thus served not only the police but also some prosecutors and judges as well as some segments of clientelist politics. This "gray zone," in which state officials and the underworld intermingled, developed most extensively in the regions most devastated by neoliberal policies, such as Greater Buenos Aires and in the outskirts of other major cities, where the vulnerability of the population provided fertile ground for establishing areas for dealing drugs or recruiting people willing to join criminal gangs.

In a context marked by extreme corruption in the police, political, and business sectors, criminal activities became an acceptable option for a growing number of people from other classes as well. Between 1985 and 2000, property crime increased by a factor of 2.5 in relation to the total population. The highest peaks were recorded during the years of greatest economic crisis. The use of violence in crime also grew, albeit only slightly, much less than the increase in property crime. The rate of violent deaths rose to a level above the historical average but was still comparable to that of many European countries and well below the Latin American average.

Nevertheless, a general feeling of insecurity took hold of Argentine society, which by the beginning of the new century was among the most fearful in the world. To a large extent, this happened because the press and certain political sectors began to exploit the issue ideologically, linking crime to other forms of "disorder" in society, in order to justify the need for adopting harsh measures to restore the supposedly lost order. Without any supporting evidence, during the Menem years a number of voices in government and the media blamed immigrants from neighboring countries for the increase in crime.

In part because of this, the failure of Alfonsín's progressivism and the years of neoliberalism gave rise to the emergence of extreme right-wing movements that won popular support for the first time. In a country with a charmless democracy in which political illusions had been dispelled, where politicians appeared to divide up the spoils of the state among themselves, and the abandonment and loss of traditional ethical values had given way to the idea that "anything goes," the open peddling of authoritarianism slowly became more attractive.

The most prominent example was the resounding success of the Fuerza Republicana (Republican Force) party in Tucumán, created by General Antonio Bussi, who was the de facto governor of the province during the dictatorship. The new party won the governorship in 1995, displacing a local form of Peronism. Following the uprisings he had led, Aldo Rico also founded a right-wing party, Modin, which became the third-most-important party in the province of Buenos Aires. It was with this party that the former colonel was elected mayor of San Miguel, a city in the province of Buenos Aires, in 1997 (and later went on to join the Peronist Party).

The sum of all these changes represented a watershed in Argentine history. The vision of a society with the potential to integrate those who came from the poorest sectors was fatally shattered during these years. In the political model proposed by neoliberalism, the notion of "social citizenship," involving access to guaranteed basic rights, no longer existed. Social life underwent a notable process of "decollectivization" as all instances of socialization that were available to people of modest means were weakened or disappeared. For the unemployed or those with unstable jobs, trade unions no longer offered a channel for collective influence in high politics. And political parties, colonized by the business world, represented even less of an option. Immersed in poverty, the most disadvantaged sectors could not even participate in national life as consumers, which advertising increasingly insisted was the way to "form part of it." The model that remained was that of very low-intensity political citizenship or outright exclusion (i.e., *to not form part of it*, noncitizenship).

Identities and Mass Culture in the Era of Neoliberalism

The expansion of neoliberalism had profound repercussions. The value of the state and the collective was diminished in favor of the individual and the private. While the "modern" and successful businessman was portrayed as the figure that would lead the country out of the crisis and as an example to imitate, many of the cultural messages, especially in advertising and a segment of mass culture, gave new validity to the most extreme individualism. Notions of potential happiness were associated with taking care of one's own affairs, earning money, being up for anything, breaking the mold, pursuing one's own desires, and completely disengaging from any collective responsibility. It was about being a "winner" and staying away from the "losers." Through advertising, people were called on to act without thinking, to follow their passions without considering the costs, to consume without contemplating the future; the slogan was "Just do it."

The weakening of the state's role as integrator and the end of the "wage-based society"—that is, of employment as the mainstay of people's life projects—generated a whole series of other effects on culture. Contact with work became more fragmented and intermittent, which meant that the labor identities that had been the backbone of the working-class world languished. To some extent, being a citizen lost concrete meaning, and, for many, this led to a crisis in their sense of belonging to a national community. What community, what class, what movement was it possible to feel part of in this context? In the 1990s, the answer to this question was no longer entirely obvious. This crisis in the traditional notion of belonging created the potential for everyone to seek new ways to feel they were part of some kind of community, either by joining a new one or by trying to make room for smaller and more specific communities within the Argentine nation. Identities became more fragmented, specific, and ephemeral. More local and other more "globalized" identities began to compete with the nation as the main frame of reference.

Entertainment activities, consumption patterns, and involvement in more localized groups gained relevance when it came to constructing a sense of belonging, especially among young people. Soccer was one of the spaces that was best suited to this. From the outset, it had contributed to the formation of identity groups, but during these years the team jersey was one of the last remaining symbols capable of stirring collective emotions (not coincidentally, it was that of the national team that enabled the expression of a nationalist fervor that had become rare outside sports). The value attributed to defending one's team became so great that a new term was coined to describe it: *el aguante*. To remain loyal to the team in good times and in bad, to go to the stadium and always cheer them on, and to fight with rivals if necessary became a mandate for every true soccer fan (which, in turn, led to episodes of violence among the fans that reached an intensity rarely seen in previous decades). The new legitimacy that this passion acquired in those years paved the way for many women to become soccer fans, something that had previously not been perceived as acceptable given dominant notions of femininity.

In fact, soccer culture and the ethics of *el aguante* became a shared language that permeated other domains. It could be found, for instance, in a new musical subgenre known as *rock barrial* or *rock chabón*. In the previous decade, the rock world had undergone important changes. While in the 1970s it had been a unified movement that was committed (however weakly) to the country's situation, by the 1980s it had become fragmented and to a large extent depoliticized. The diva attitude and sophistication that some of its top stars had developed increased the distance with the public, especially those with some desire for rebellion. A branch of pop music that appeared during Alfonsín's government even seemed to celebrate happiness and superficiality.

Given this context, *rock barrial* emerged as an alternative for a growing number of young people from the popular classes and impoverished middle sectors. Musically, it was quite simple and its lyrics spoke nostalgically of the world of childhood, affirmed the ethics of neighborhood loyalty, lamented the end of the working world, and critically expounded on the poverty and corruption of the moment. These songs were politicized but in a different way from those of the 1970s: the issue was no longer the pressure to integrate into a society of "suits" but rather exclusion. The most important novelty, however, was the audience, which followed bands like soccer hooligans follow their teams and participated to an unprecedented degree in their concerts. The identities that *rock barrial* fans took on expressed an opposition to commercialism in music and to the world of the *chetos* (posh), despised for their affluent origins as well as their inauthentic or "fake" attitude.

But *cumbia* was the rhythm that captivated a good part of the popular classes throughout the country (except in Córdoba, where it did not manage to unseat *cuarteto*) and then spread its influence to the middle and upper classes. During the 1980s, it experienced remarkable commercial expansion. Hundreds of dance clubs opened, especially on the outskirts of major cities, and some of the artists in the scene achieved great notoriety, particularly in the 1990s when *cumbia* gained a place in the mass media. Its lyrics spoke of everyday topics: love, jealousy, money, sex, happiness. Some of the most popular were picaresque.

Toward the end of the 1990s, a subgenre emerged that changed everything. In an attempt to express the reality of life for the poor but also to gain the attention of record labels, a group of young artists, some from very humble backgrounds, developed a new style. Drawing on elements of the gangsta rap that had been sweeping the United States, they wrote *cumbias* with testimonial lyrics referring to episodes from the lives of the most marginalized sectors: violence, drugs, incarceration, and repression. Their songs expressed a plebeian pride, criticizing the discrimination they were subjected to and speaking out against the *chetos* and the wealthy, the police and corrupt politicians. *Cumbia villera*, as it was called, soon became extremely widespread, halted only, in part, when in 2001 the state prohibited the media from broadcasting it, claiming that it was inciting drug use and crime.

Neoliberal fragmentation also led many to look to religion as a way to replace their evanescent sense of belonging and to shore up the weak bonds of solidarity among people. Surveys show a sustained growth in religious belief. The image of the Catholic Church improved in these years and arguably the number of those who identified with it increased. However, since Catholicism was so closely associated with the nation, a growing number of people sought an outlet for their religiosity outside of Roman Christianity.

Indeed, it was certain Protestant denominations and movements— Pentecostal churches in particular—that offered many the promise of rebuilding the destroyed communal bond. Since the 1980s, the number of evangelical faithful, insignificant half a century earlier, has multiplied rapidly. The forms of worship, much less concerned with ritual, more accessible to the average person, and—especially among the Pentecostals—focused on the promise of healing and miracles, were highly attractive to the most marginalized sectors of the population. By the late 1990s, there was a church every few blocks in Greater Buenos Aires, and it is estimated that almost 20 percent of the area's poorest inhabitants had converted to the new faith.

Around the same time, Afro-Brazilian religions, particularly Umbanda, were also spreading, and cults of popular saints not recognized by the Catholic Church flourished. Each region had its own, but the one dedicated to the Gauchito Gil, which expanded at an exponential rate in the 1990s, eventually spread through the entire country (a 2008 survey revealed that 44 percent of Argentines believed in his powers). Argentina ceased to be a Catholic nation with a few religious minorities and became a country of many denominations.

The weakening of the state's capacity for integration also paved the way for a profound questioning of the myth of the white and European Argentina. Starting in the 1990s, for the first time in the twentieth century there were signs that "Blackness," traditionally an insult or a source of shame, was becoming an emblem of defiant pride among the popular classes. It was especially noticeable in *cumbia* and *cuarteto*, whose followers defended their identity as *negros cabeza*—in reference to their dark complexion and modest means rather than to any African ancestry—and made a habit of disparaging the *chetos/rubios* (posh/fair-skinned). At the same time, there was also renewed enthusiasm among the country's indigenous peoples determined to recover their cultural practices and gain visibility and respect. A notable process of re-ethnicization took place, including the reappearance of groups such as the Rankulches, Huarpes, and Selk'nam, which had been declared to have been wiped out. After a century of invisibility, a number of Afro-Argentine groups also reemerged and once again organized themselves in representative associations. Among the popular classes, the identities of immigrants from neighboring countries were strengthened as well, and they began to fight for their rights and against the xenophobia that had flourished since the dictatorship.

From Fragmentation to the Reconstruction of Resistance

The sweeping changes of the neoliberal era left the general population socially fragmented and completely vulnerable. The traditional political parties supported the changes, while the CGT offered no resistance whatsoever since Menem's inauguration. For its part, following its defeat under the dictatorship, the left was unable to gain a foothold in either the trade unions or the elections. In the 1989 elections, a coalition of Communists and Trotskyists from the Movimiento al Socialismo (Movement for Socialism, or MAS) had won 2.45 percent of the vote, a small percentage but much higher than usual. However, internal discussions soon ended up destroying the MAS and dissolving the alliance. The 1990s, characterized by the ultimate victory of the ruling classes, swept by like a raging tornado. Amid the desolation, however, the popular classes were reconstructing bonds of solidarity and inventing new ways of doing politics.

The first series of Menem's privatizations, up to 1991, were marked by intense union resistance, especially from state employees, telecommunications workers, and the community of San Nicolás in Buenos Aires province, dependent on the steel company Somisa, which laid off more than six thousand workers. Several governors were forced to resign due to the unrest in their provinces. After that year, there were fewer conflicts, partly because repeated defeat generated a sense of discouragement but also because the government had managed to bring the economy under control and had embarked on skillful negotiations with the trade union bureaucracy to deactivate the protests.

Only the unions hardest hit by the austerity measures, public-sector workers and teachers, continued to resist, with the Asociación de Trabajadores del Estado (Association of Government Employees, or ATE) and the Confederación de Trabajadores de la Educación de la República Argentina (Confederation of Education Workers of the Argentine Republic, or CTERA) taking the lead. The latter initiated several protests, with the most visible being the installation of a white tent in front of Congress in 1997, where it remained for two years. Teachers in the province of Neuquén also took measures that were unprecedented in their radicalism. And there were intense struggles during these years in other parts of the country as well. In 1993, public-sector workers in Santiago del Estero staged a popular uprising, known as the "Santiagueñazo," in which they set fire to the main offices of the three branches of government and hounded local politicians accused of corruption. In Jujuy, public-sector workers also refused to give their government any respite: between 1990 and 1994, five governors were forced to step down as a result of massive demonstrations. State employees staged vigorous resistance in Río Negro, Córdoba, and San Juan, among other places. For the first time, retirees also took to the streets to make their demands heard.

The CGT was slow to take up the struggle, and in the meantime there were interesting realignments. A dissident wing, led by trucker Hugo Moyano, created the Movimiento de Trabajadores Argentinos (Argentine Workers Movement, or MTA), which confronted the government, without departing from the framework of the CGT. But the most significant development was the creation of a new entity, the Central de Trabajadores de la Argentina (Central Federation of Argentine Workers, or CTA), which sought to group the workers' movement outside the CGT and in opposition to the Peronist Party. It was formed in 1992 with the support of ATE and CTERA. Unlike the traditional federation, its authorities were chosen through the direct vote of members, and it included not only workers but also tenants' organizations, small rural landowners, and the unemployed.

The CTA was the driving force behind several general strikes and two of the most important milestones in the resistance to neoliberalism during these years. The first was the "Federal March," which, setting out from various points across the country, succeeded in gathering a huge crowd in Plaza de Mayo on June 6, 1994. The second was the Frente Nacional contra la Pobreza (National Front against Poverty, or FRENAPO), created in 2001, which sought to promote a law obligating the state to guarantee a universal basic income to ensure that no one would fall below the poverty line. Although it was never passed, tens of thousands of volunteers helped organize an informal plebiscite held in mid-December throughout the country, which collected more than 3 million signatures in support of the project. Along with the CTA, another new trade union organization emerged in 1994 that would very soon take on great relevance, the Corriente Clasista y Combativa (Classist and Combative Current, or CCC), with ties to the Partido Comunista Revolucionario (Revolutionary Communist Party, or PCR).

But the most surprising development was the appearance of a massive movement of the unemployed known as *piqueteros* (picketers). The movement emerged in 1996–97 among those laid off from YPF, the state-owned oil and gas company, in Cutral-Co and Plaza Huincul (Neuquén) and in Tartagal and Mosconi (Salta), all dependent on the company and facing the prospect of becoming ghost towns. Organized in assemblies and autonomous "multisectoral" groups, with no ties to unions or political parties, the inhabitants began to block highways as a means of protest. The national government initially responded with repression but was eventually forced to improvise a more extensive assistance program than it had in past situations, consisting of monthly payments to those who had lost their jobs in exchange for hours of service. By 1997, there were already two hundred thousand beneficiaries of these "Trabajar plans," which began to function like an unemployment subsidy.

The unemployed and other social groups in the rest of the country soon began to imitate this approach. One study counted 685 blockades throughout the country between 1993 and October 1999; of these, 36.8 percent were carried out by wage earners (some of them unemployed, although, in fact, the majority were employed). Another 47.6 percent were organized by small- and medium-sized landowners, agricultural producers, retailers, and students, especially toward the end of this period. Among the unemployed, the *piquetero* movement grew at a dizzying rate between 1999 and 2001 and reached a scale with few precedents in world history. Since the factory and the union had ceased to be points of reference for the majority, the new movement found its strength at the territorial level.

Neighborhoods became the space of choice for reconstructing bonds of solidarity and political cooperation. Community self-organization—fostered by state assistance—was the fulcrum of the emerging movements, which were sometimes able to imbue this self-organization with renewed politicization, at least partially freeing it from clientelistic constraints. Their political affiliations varied, reflecting a trend that was also seen in other sectors of the popular classes: Peronism continued to be the dominant political identity during these years, but it no longer monopolized support (especially among younger people). There were several organizations that brought the *piqueteros* together: the main ones were those that formed part of the CTA and the CCC, but the autonomist Movimientos de Trabajadores Desocupados (Movements of Unemployed Workers, or MTD) also appeared, some of them influenced by Marxist activists, Third World priests, or leaders who had distanced themselves from Peronism. Along with them, other groups formed with ties to various leftist parties—the Workers' Party, the Socialist Workers' Party, the Socialist Workers' Movement, and the old Communist Party—and still others that were independent. In 2001, they all attempted unity with two big "*piquetero* assemblies" in the municipality of La Matanza, involving delegates from across the country, but the different approaches and party loyalties made it impossible. Women played a major role in the movement: more than 50 percent of the *piqueteros* were women, despite the fact that the overwhelming majority of leaders were men.

Other sectors also developed new forms of resistance. Starting in 1998, workers began occupying factories that had been financially gutted by their managers and reactivating them. In the years to follow, there were more than 160 of these *empresas recuperadas* (worker-run enterprises).

The various rural areas of the country also generated new forms of organization and confrontation. In the Pampas, the resistance of the most impoverished small-scale farmers was spearheaded by the unprecedented

Movimiento de Mujeres Agropecuarias en Lucha (Movement of Agricultural Women in Struggle, or MMAL) starting in 1995. Created in La Pampa, the MMAL soon managed to expand to Santa Fe, Río Negro, Neuquén, Formosa, and Córdoba. Using direct action, members managed to stop land auctions and evictions. By 1986, the Movimiento Agrario Misionero (Agrarian Movement of Misiones) had already been revived, and in subsequent years campesino organizations emerged in provinces where there had not previously been any tradition of protest, such as the Movimiento Campesino de Santiago del Estero (Campesino Movement of Santiago del Estero, or MOCASE), founded in 1989 to resist the evictions that accompanied the expansion of the agribusiness frontier. In Córdoba, Formosa, and Salta, there were similar initiatives. For the same reasons, as well as to reclaim their ancestral lands, several indigenous peoples joined the struggle, especially in Salta, Chaco, Neuquén, and Formosa.

During these years, there were also large-scale protests against institutional repression, *gatillo fácil* (unjustified killings by police and other authorities), and impunity. The Ingeniero Budge massacre in Greater Buenos Aires (1987), the crime of María Soledad Morales in Catamarca (1993), and the murder of conscript Omar Carrasco in Zapala, Neuquén (1994), were a few of the episodes that generated massive demonstrations. The 1990s also witnessed the first environmental protests involving entire communities. Starting in 1995, the construction of the Corpus Christi dam in the upper Paraná River mobilized the majority of the population of that part of Misiones that was to be affected by the flooding. Around the same time, resistance to open-pit mining also emerged. In 1997, the town of Belén, in the province of Catamarca, began to organize protests against the La Alumbrera mine, which had been established a short time before, with great promises of public works and jobs that never materialized. The first to take to the streets were a group of the unemployed who, imitating *piquetero* methods, blocked access to the mine to demand the jobs that the company had promised. By 2000, other social sectors had joined in, adding their own demands, including a forceful condemnation of the contamination produced by the mining activities. In the decade that followed, many communities throughout the Andes would follow Belén's example, each organizing their own "citizen assemblies" to stop open-pit mining.

Ecological concerns were also at the root of one of the most surprising and massive forms of self-organization during this period. Following the initiative of a small group of activists promoting organic food production, the use of alternative energy sources, and recycling, in 1995, some twenty residents of Bernal, in the south of Greater Buenos Aires, started a "Barter Club." Each person brought something they produced or had left over—pies, empanadas, clothing, artisanal products, et cetera—to weekly gatherings with the idea of exchanging them for other products without using money. Soon others imitated them and the barter clubs attracted a growing number of people who had lost their jobs and lacked money. They then invented their own "social currency" to facilitate indirect exchange on a larger scale, which allowed the clubs to expand into a truly self-organized network that grew at an exponential rate. By 2000, there were already 1,800 hubs across the country with more than 800,000 participants, a number that would triple the following year. As the state withdrew and the capitalist market collapsed, an unexpected experiment in social, horizontal, and solidarity-based self-organization provided a real and inclusive alternative.

The 2001 Rebellion

After Fernando de la Rúa became president in 1999, all expectations of change were shattered. In order to face the crippling foreign debt with a stagnant economy, the president took another huge loan, presented as a "financial buffer," from the IMF. Nevertheless, it was immediately channeled into foreign capital flight. The conditionalities of the disbursement meant a further intensification of the neoliberal austerity measures. Moreover, the government's coalition soon began to erode, particularly after the scandalous approval, in April 2000, of a labor reform that further curtailed workers' rights. It was reported that several legislators had received bribes, paid by the executive branch, in exchange for their votes. Vice President Carlos "Chacho" Álvarez, who was also the head of the FREPASO party, initiated an investigation, but the Radical and Peronist senators closed ranks to prevent it from moving ahead. Seeing that he had lost the support of the president, Álvarez resigned. The Alianza was practically destroyed.

In March 2001, in a final attempt to mitigate the economic crisis, de la Rúa once again summoned Cavallo to take charge of national finances. Along with the secretary of economic policy, Federico Sturzenegger, Cavallo approved a "mega-swap" of debt bonds for others with longer maturities and higher interest rates, proposed by a group of international banks. It was clear that the operation was not going to mitigate the crisis. Instead, it generated millions of dollars in commissions for the participating bankers and resulted in a much larger public debt. (All those involved, in what was considered the largest swindle in history, were later prosecuted. In 2016, however, they were exonerated in a controversial court decision.) Cavallo also launched a "zero-deficit" plan that included a 13 percent cut in the salaries and pensions of all public-sector employees and retirees. The provinces received less in transfers from the national treasury; several of them found themselves in critical situations and were forced to print emergency bonds, locally valid currencies that enabled them to pay salaries; the *patacón* in Buenos Aires province was the one with the greatest circulation, but most districts had their own.

Predictably, in the October 2001 legislative elections, the Alianza suffered a crushing defeat to Peronism. But something unprecedented also happened: 22 percent of citizens opted to protest the vote by casting a blank ballot or spoiling their ballot, while another 22 percent abstained from voting altogether. This was their way of expressing a loss of trust in politicians, regardless of the party to which they belonged. In addition to the economic crisis, there was now a crisis of legitimacy, not only of the government but of the entire political system. Since companies and the wealthy were taking their deposits abroad and small-scale savers were storing them under their mattresses, to help banks face the stampede of deposit withdrawals, in early December, Cavallo implemented the famous *corralito*, which limited the amount of money that could be withdrawn from bank accounts to a minimum. But none of that was enough. When the IMF announced that it was suspending disbursements to the country, the financial system collapsed completely.

It was the worst economic crisis in Argentina's history, the culmination of years of neoliberal measures. As a consequence of its effects, 54 percent of the population soon fell below the poverty line (27 percent below the extreme poverty line) and the unemployment rate exceeded 20 percent. Thousands of people from the popular classes or impoverished middle sectors were left completely vulnerable; many managed to survive thanks to the barter clubs (at that time, those who participated were able to acquire up to 40 percent or more of their daily needs through this system). Others joined the ranks of an impressive army of *cartoneros* who scoured the city and the garbage dumps every night in search of recyclables to sell.

However, the catastrophe fueled reactions of resistance and solidarity that sparked an unexpected turn in national politics. In December, the demands of the various sectors affected were rapidly coalescing into a network that would give rise to a massive and extended rebellion with few parallels in national history. On December 12, thousands of *piqueteros* blocked roads in Greater Buenos

Aires, Rosario, Tucumán, and Mar del Plata, demanding that the president and Cavallo resign, while public-sector workers, teachers, taxi drivers, students, and others carried out a variety of protest actions across the country. That afternoon, a massive demonstration of retailers took place in the capital and other cities. As the *corralito* had also frozen workers' salaries, the two factions of the CGT and the CTA declared a general strike on December 13 to demand the end of this measure. Retailers and middle-sector unions also joined the strike. There were numerous marches everywhere, some leading to serious clashes with the police. In addition to the protests, looting started on December 14 and spread to eleven provinces. By the end of this wave of protests, there were eighteen dead at the hands of police or store owners and hundreds of wounded. Although the looting was a genuine popular reaction and it had long been part of the repertoire of the defensive struggles of the popular classes, several well-documented cases reveal the complicity of local political leaders and the police, who withdrew from designated areas or even participated in the attacks on businesses.

On December 19, 2001, the situation took an unexpected turn. In the evening, following a speech by de la Rúa in which he announced a state of siege and no solution to the crisis, groups of Buenos Aires neighbors spontaneously started banging pots and pans outside their homes. By ten o'clock at night, hundreds of thousands of people were banging their pots and pans in a strange symphony of protest. No one was carrying political placards; those who tried to display a banner were forced to put it away. Meeting at the main points of the city, many marched to Plaza de Mayo at midnight. Thousands of people carried out similar events in Rosario, Paraná, Tucumán, and other parts of the country. Disconcerted, the president sought to appease the popular outrage by announcing Cavallo's resignation. But it was not enough. The next morning, when the government ordered a crackdown on the demonstrators who had remained in front of the Casa Rosada since the night before, a crowd surrounded the Plaza de Mayo. After several hours of battles with the police, de la Rúa finally decided to step down. Demonstrations had taken place simultaneously in Santiago del Estero, Entre Ríos, Córdoba, Mendoza, Neuquén, and other places. The repression during those two days left at least thirty-eight people dead in different parts of the country, five of them in Plaza de Mayo.

Although some wanted to interpret it as a Buenos Aires "middle-class revolt" triggered by the *corralito*, it was in fact a popular rebellion, pluralistic and diverse in its social makeup. It formed part of a series of events initiated by both the middle sectors and the popular classes across the country. "¡Que se vayan todos, que no quede ni uno solo!" (Out with them all, each and every one of them!)—a *political* rather than an economic slogan—was the main chant that united those participating in the rebellion. Several dozen demonstrations—including *escraches* (public denunciations), roadblocks, *cacerolazos* (pot-banging protests), and popular uprisings—took place after December 2001, headed by the same diverse range of social groups. Their slogans and demands often combined the aspirations of each. They might demand an end to the *corralito* but also the payment of salary arrears and increased subsidies for the unemployed. They were concerned about the financial difficulties of retailers and small-scale producers but also about the defense of public healthcare and education. Such demands soon melded with other broader and more structural demands, including a universal hatred of banks and the questioning of multinationals, of the privatization of public utility companies, and of the neoliberal policies promoted by the IMF.

Throughout the country, the unrest led to calls for a change in the authorities. The crowds in the streets also demanded the resignation of the Supreme Court and even protested Channel 13, after it and other media outlets decided not to broadcast news about one of the main *cacerolazos* during those days, in an attempt to encourage demobilization. The demonstrations targeted the main pillars of the social order: the three branches of government, companies and banks, international financial organizations, and the media.

The year following the rebellion saw unprecedented forms of self-organization, resistance, and solidarity. The worst moment of the crisis awoke the best instincts of cooperation, creativity, and public interest among part of the population; these were extraordinary times. People with no previous political experience and others who were more experienced joined together in unprecedented forms of radical direct action, ranging from *escraches* against politicians and occupations of buildings to attacks on multinationals and road blockades. The banks in Buenos Aires had to operate behind boarded-up windows for a year due to frequent attacks by savers. The most active were undoubtedly a minority, but a large portion of society sympathized with them. Immediately after de la Rúa's fall, during a dizzying succession of interim presidents, "popular assemblies" began to emerge spontaneously in different cities across the country. In the city of Buenos Aires and surrounding areas alone, there were close to 150 of them. Throughout 2002, they would prove to be tremendously active, calling for dozens of massive *cacerolazos*, discussing how to replace professional politicians with forms of direct democracy, exploring economic solutions to the crisis, and establishing strong ties of solidarity with other social movements, such as the *piqueteros* and the *empresas recuperadas*, which were also flourishing at the time.

The willingness to come together in the same rebellion, despite and beyond social differences, resulted in moving demonstrations. On January 28, for example, there was a massive joint march of *piquetero* organizations to Plaza de Mayo. The march received the support and solidarity of the Buenos Aires assemblies, and thousands of people from the middle sectors applauded the procession of the columns of the poor through the city center. That day, the heterogeneous crowd chanted, "Piquete y cacerola, la lucha es una sola!" (Picket and pot, divide us you cannot). And it was not merely an expression of desire: in those extraordinary times, there were intense contacts and joint struggles between the impoverished middle sectors, laborers, and the unemployed. There was the feeling that a "new politics," as it was called at the time, was on the horizon.

The Effects of 2001 and the Recovery from the Crisis

The winds of change arrived, albeit in unexpected ways. The complex combination of popular pressure and expectations, local and international economic constraints, and the readjustment of the political system generated a period of unpredictability that led to new political identities and parties, the brilliant rise of new leaders (and no less spectacular falls), and government measures that had previously been unthinkable. The FREPASO practically disappeared and the UCR embarked on a long decline. Greatly discredited, the Peronist Party was fragmented and, for a time, in no position to determine its leadership. With the traditional party system thus dismantled, opportunities opened up for new parties to seek to occupy government positions and for the rise of leaders who previously had no clout of their own.

Starting on December 20, there was a succession of five presidents in only thirteen days. After the fall of de la Rúa, the president of the Senate took over provisionally and quickly summoned the Legislative Assembly, which elected as president Peronist Adolfo Rodríguez Saá, at that time the governor of San Luis, without a national following. The massive public outcry produced when Rodríguez Saá offered a position in his government to a former Menemist with a well-known history of corruption along with the lack of support from other Peronist Party leaders led to his downfall after only seven days in office. In that brief period, however, he did implement one crucial measure: before an enthusiastically applauding Congress and amid anti-imperialist speeches, he declared the unilateral suspension of foreign debt payments. This scene would have been inconceivable only a few weeks earlier: Argentina was defaulting, and, to the dismay of international financial interests, it was doing so with pride. After Rodríguez Saá's untimely resignation and another very brief interim president, on January 2, the Legislative Assembly appointed Eduardo Duhalde as the new president. Duhalde was a strongman within Peronism in Buenos Aires province but had the support of a multiparty majority. De la Rúa had beaten him by ten points in the presidential race two years earlier and now, with even less popular support, the Congress named him the new president.

In the midst of the economic collapse and with social movements occupying the streets, Duhalde was forced to make a series of decisions that he would not have made in any other context. Convertibility was officially repealed with a devaluation of the currency from 1 peso per dollar to 1.4, accompanied by the "asymmetric pesification" of dollar-denominated deposits and debts. They were compulsorily converted into pesos but in a way that avoided shifting the cost entirely onto the weakest: debtors would pay one peso for each dollar owed, but banks had to recognize $1.40 for each dollar of the savers. To benefit the banks, the IMF proposed resorting to a "controlled hyperinflation" that would completely liquidate the value of the pesified contracts, but this path was politically untenable. The devaluation was passed on to prices, but inflation did not spiral out of control and soon returned to relatively low levels.

Duhalde decreed a freeze on public utility tariffs and reintroduced export duties so that the state would keep a portion of the profits of some exporting sectors, especially agriculture. With the funds obtained through this measure, the moratorium on foreign debt, and emergency loans from international agencies, the nation launched a massive program of subsidies for the unemployed. Whereas in December 2001, barely 1 percent of the population was receiving state aid, this figure now rose to more than 6 percent, which meant that 2.5 million people were receiving subsidies. Businesspeople and international organizations had to let all these measures pass without their usual resistance, for fear of igniting popular discontent.

By the end of 2002, the financial reorganization made it possible to end the *corralito* and discontinue the use of quasi-currencies in the provinces. Meanwhile, increased consumption, a halt in capital flight, high international prices for soybeans, and the reduction of imports as a result of devaluation triggered a recovery. The economic situation began to decompress. But the political crisis remained. The enormous sum of subsidies distributed during

2002 was almost entirely channeled through municipalities, which gave the Peronist clientelist apparatus a fabulous tool with which to restore its dominance. In very little time, the Peronist Party would recover part of the power it had lost to the new social movements and would regain its place as the most powerful party in national politics. It still retained, however, a significant loss of prestige and was struggling to overcome its internal divisions.

In a bid to regain control of the streets, in June 2002 the government embarked on a repressive crackdown. In response to the blockade of an access bridge to the city of Buenos Aires, the police staged a scene to justify a ferocious attack on the more autonomous *piquetero* organizations, which resulted in the deaths of two young people—Maximiliano Kosteki and Darío Santillán—and numerous wounded. With the help of the main newspapers and television channels, an attempt was made to convince the public that the deaths had been the result of confrontations between the *piqueteros* themselves. But photographs of the events exposed the farce, and a massive protest in response meant that the government's days in power were numbered. Duhalde was forced to move up the call for the general election and to refrain from running as a candidate. The hope was that the elections, set for April 2003, would help the political system regain some of its legitimacy.

The problem was that without Duhalde's candidacy, it was not clear who would lead the Peronist Party. None of the contending figures within the party appeared to stand a chance, so there was a risk that his archenemy Carlos Menem would represent the party in the elections. Menem had lost an enormous amount of prestige, which made his defeat a certainty, but he still had enough support to win the leadership election over other unknown figures.

Faced with this complicated scenario, Duhalde suspended the leadership election and introduced a change in the electoral rules that allowed several candidates to run under the name of the Peronist Party. As a result, Menem, Rodríguez Saá, and Néstor Kirchner, a little-known politician from Santa Cruz, entered the race. Duhalde had tried to persuade the governor of Santa Fe, Carlos Reutemann, to run since he felt he had a good chance of winning. But when he refused, Duhalde endorsed Kirchner.

In the end, the three Peronist candidates competed against each other, and against Ricardo López Murphy—a right-wing liberal economist that the establishment managed to rapidly position with the help of the media—and Elisa Carrió, a former Radical who had recently founded the Afirmación para una República Igualitaria (Affirmation for an Egalitarian Republic, or ARI) party, which at the time had a center-left orientation. Some social movements called for abstention, but by then the window of opportunity for change that had opened in 2001 was rapidly closing due to the demand for a return to "normality." Voters went to the polls unenthusiastically, and in the first round the vote was divided among all the candidates. Menem was in first place but with barely more than 24 percent. Kirchner was in second place, having obtained 22 percent of the vote with a campaign focused on criticizing neoliberalism. The other three contenders received between 14 and 16 percent each. The UCR also presented a candidate but received only 2.34 percent, an almost irrelevant share of the vote and yet another indication of the collapse of the traditional parties. The left, even adding up the results of its various groups, came in below that figure.

Leading up to the runoff election, it became clear that the votes obtained by Menem were his upper limit. Dozens of organizations and leaders from across the country called on people to vote for Kirchner, less out of an appreciation for the candidate than to block Menem from a third term in office. The former president came with the promise of harsh repression and a return to ultraliberal austerity policies, including the potential for total dollarization through the elimination of the national currency, a drastic path that Ecuador had taken in 2000 and that Menem had floated as a possibility.

Faced with the prospect of losing by an overwhelming margin in the second round—polls showed his opponent at 70 percent—Menem decided to withdraw his candidacy. Thus, with only 22 percent of the vote, someone virtually unknown when the campaign began, who had not even achieved the representation of his party as a whole, was elected to the Casa Rosada—another unexpected outcome of 2001.

The Emergence of Kirchnerism (2003–2007)

When Kirchner took office, the economy was in the early stages of an incipient recovery that over the following years gained surprising momentum. During his term, inflation remained low and the GDP grew between 8 and 9 percent per year. By 2005, production had rebounded to the precrisis level of 1998, and it would continue to grow for the next decade. Its driving forces were industry oriented to the domestic market, automotive exports to Brazil, and exports of industrial commodities (steel, aluminum) and agricultural products (particularly soybeans, which are widely consumed in Asian markets).

The main factors that enabled this performance were those established after de la Rúa's fall, largely to appease the discontent: the fiscal surplus (increased by export duties and the lack of foreign debt payments), the expansion of consumption (encouraged through social spending), and the trade surplus (fueled by the devaluation and excellent international prices for food products). It was also aided by a series of measures aimed to stimulate the local production of goods that had previously been imported. The continuity of this economic policy was embodied in the continuity of Duhalde's minister of economy, Roberto Lavagna, who remained in his position until late 2005.

The increased prosperity was reflected in a reduction in unemployment and poverty and the recovery of the purchasing power of wages, which in 2008 reached and then surpassed their pre-2001 levels. The improvement was also aided through the resumption of collective bargaining negotiations in 2005 and by policies aimed at sustaining the level of employment and restoring some of the labor rights violated by the "flexibilization" measures of previous governments. Subsidies to public services continued, which meant higher indirect income. After 2006, there was also a policy aimed at aggressively expanding pension rights, which led to a rapid doubling in the number of retirees. (Soon after, a biannual system for updating pensions was introduced, which gradually improved their purchasing power.)

There remained, however, complex problems to be solved. The most pressing issue was the default. The government embarked on a long and tense negotiation with international bondholders, and in 2005, 76 percent of them accepted a 75 percent reduction of the principal owed—an unprecedented level in the history of restructurings—and the exchange of their papers for others payable in longer terms and under more favorable conditions for the country. In 2010, another group would follow suit, bringing the acceptance of the deal proposed by Argentina to 92 percent of the bondholders. Most of those who rejected it were the American-based "vulture funds" that had purchased the bonds at a low price following the default and kept litigating in order to try to collect their claims without any reduction. In the eyes of the international community, the government's firmness in these negotiations was undoubtedly more justified (and unavoidable) given the memory of the 2001 rebellion.

In late 2005, the government also announced the full payment, in cash, of the debt with the IMF. It justified the measure as a way of recovering the state's sovereignty and no longer having to comply with IMF recommendations, which were always orthodox. During the following decade, Argentina did not receive its supervision missions, take on any new loans, or accept its recommendations, a novelty in the last half century of history. The cost of this was that Argentina's access to international loans, not only from private investors but also from financial institutions, would be extremely limited.

The emphasis on sovereignty was also evident that year at the Summit of the Americas held in Mar del Plata. The presidential meeting focused on moving forward with the creation of a Free Trade Area of the Americas (FTAA) that the United States was pursuing in order to facilitate business with American companies. An extensive network of social movements throughout the continent opposed it, and Argentines held their own massive demonstration in Mar del Plata to reject it. With that pressure as a backdrop, a group of more popularly oriented presidents surreptitiously agreed to block the American proposal. Néstor Kirchner, as summit host, played a key role in the success of this mission, which also included Hugo Chávez of Venezuela, Luiz Inácio Lula da Silva of Brazil, and Tabaré Vázquez of Uruguay. In what was a historic crossroads, the American president left empty-handed and the FTAA project was buried. During this period, MERCOSUR emerged stronger and in 2006 accepted Venezuela as a full member (its incorporation would take a few more years). Argentina also strengthened its bilateral ties with other powers, such as Russia and China.

These positions were accompanied by a significant change in discourse and political outlook in a country where, until a short time earlier, it seemed that the only option was to adhere to the free market. Kirchner sought to tune in to the demands of the "new politics" of the 2001 rebellion and adopted a tone that was critical of neoliberalism and moderately nationalist. He argued that the state should once again play an active role in the economy, albeit without hindering market functioning or the flow of foreign investment. It had to work jointly with the local business community to strengthen the domestic market and, at the same time, improve the situation of workers. During Kirchner's term in office, nuclear development was reactivated, the Río Santiago Shipyard was revived, and the postal service (which had accumulated a sizeable unpaid debt with the state while in the hands of the Macri Group) was renationalized, as was the company that supplied water to the capital city and the surrounding areas. The budgets for education, universities, and science and technology expanded considerably.

Along with this economic and social vision, Kirchner sought to associate himself with the most progressive traditions of national politics. He advocated a strong revival of the generation of young leftists of the 1970s, of which he had been a part. At the same time, he vigorously defended the human rights movement, establishing a close and friendly relationship with many of its organizations, and took a series of measures to ensure the criminals of the last dictatorship were prosecuted.

In 2003, on his initiative, Congress annulled the Full Stop and Due Obedience laws. They had already been repealed in 1998, but this annulment had a retroactive effect, making it possible to prosecute all members of the military who had been involved in human rights violations, regardless of their rank. Within this new climate, a number of judges also declared the pardons that Menem had issued unconstitutional (which the Supreme Court later confirmed), thereby enabling proceedings against the dictatorship's top commanders. Furthermore, in a highly significant gesture, on March 24, 2004, the anniversary of the military coup, Kirchner personally went to the National Military College and ordered the head of the army to remove the portraits of the dictators Videla and Bignone that still adorned its walls. This image was immediately transformed into a powerful symbolic milestone: military power was now completely subordinated to civilian power.

This progressive tendency was also reflected in the renewal of the Supreme Court. In 2003, it still consisted of the Menemist "automatic majority": several judges with rather poor records had issued rulings of questionable legality to suit specific interests (among other things, they had intervened to shield Mauricio Macri from being prosecuted for smuggling auto parts). Moreover, since Duhalde's government, they had used the threat of annulling crucial measures of the executive branch as a bargaining tool. Following on the heels of public demonstrations being held against the Supreme Court, Kirchner pushed for the impeachment of several of its members. Four finally resigned and two others were dismissed by Congress, after which the president nominated and obtained approval for four new members. Independent and with solid backgrounds, several of them were known for their progressive standpoints. Two were women, which gave the Court an unprecedented gender balance. A new public consultation system was implemented to appoint justices, and the Supreme Court returned to its historical number of five.

With respect to the continually intense level of demonstrations in the streets, the government's behavior was ambivalent. With the *piquetero* movements that expressed their support, it established a cordial relationship of political alliance. Some of their leaders were appointed to minor positions within the government. In Jujuy, the Túpac Amaru organization, led by Milagro Sala, a Kolla woman of modest origins, achieved considerable regional expansion with government support. Those who maintained antagonistic positions, however, were demonized. Regardless, during the Kirchner years, the use of repression by the security forces in controlling street demonstrations was severely curtailed. This did not prevent episodes of police violence, including episodes with deadly consequences, but they were comparatively fewer than in previous periods. On the other hand, in 2004, an unexpected and massive demonstration led by a businessman whose son had been murdered by criminals called for a toughening of the state's punitive powers, and Kirchner gave in to this demand. Cases of *gatillo fácil* were fewer than in 2000 or 2001 but nevertheless remained high.

On the political front, there were many novelties. In keeping with the new political aspirations of 2001, Kirchner initially distanced himself from the Peronist identity of his origins. The "Peronist March" was not sung at his campaigns or rallies, and, for a time, his electoral ballots dispensed with the traditional Peronist Party coat of arms. The party, on the other hand, remained fragmented and lacked clear leadership. In fact, in the 2005 legislative elections, Cristina Fernández de Kirchner, the president's wife, who had an extensive political career of her own, successfully defeated Hilda Duhalde, wife of the former president—who by then was very much at odds with Kirchner—in a race in the province of Buenos Aires in which the latter was the official representative of the Peronist Party.

What was then becoming known as "Kirchnerism" announced that its objective was *transversalidad* or "cross-party politics." The aim was to dissolve Peronism into a new political force that would regroup the progressive sectors of other parties, especially the UCR. The idea generated resistance within the Peronist Party and only advanced half-heartedly. Kirchner managed to attract a fairly good proportion of influential members of Radicalism—including several governors and historical leaders, known since then as Radicales K (K Radicals)—to his space, the Frente para la Victoria (Front for Victory). A number of politicians from other left or center-left parties also joined him. But as Kirchner's term in office wore on, he increasingly relied on the Peronist Party apparatus, which ensured him a territorial presence that was hard to relinquish. He then tried to give his old party a new and decidedly progressive identity, something it had not had before. But some of the most discredited figures of the past—including Aldo Rico—soon reappeared within the context of his policy of alliances. The re-Peronization of the government irritated non-Kirchnerists, without managing to generate much enthusiasm among its own voters.

The 2007 general elections confirmed the open nature of these political realignments. Cristina Fernández de Kirchner headed the ruling party's ticket, accompanied by Julio Cobos, the governor of Mendoza and a Radical.

They won with 45 percent of the vote, at a significant distance from the main opposition coalition, Elisa Carrió's Coalición Cívica (Civic Coalition), which received 23 percent of the vote. This time Carrió was accompanied by the Socialist Party, which that year, in Santa Fe, won the first governorship in its long history. Still in the midst of its debacle, the UCR chose to nominate an extra-party candidate of Peronist origin, Roberto Lavagna, who had been a minister in Kirchner's government only two years earlier. He received 16 percent of the vote. The sum result of all the forces perceived as "progressive" or left-wing exceeded 88 percent of the vote, which gives a sense of the political shift that the 2001 crisis had generated in society. Openly right-wing parties, or those perceived as such, received only a minimal portion of the vote.

However, in the city of Buenos Aires there was another novelty in the opposite sense: with 45 percent of the vote, Mauricio Macri became the new mayor. The well-known businessman, previously close to Menemism, had entered politics only four years earlier and had just founded the Propuesta Republicana (Republican Proposal, or PRO), the party that brought him to power. In Buenos Aires and several other large urban centers, the growth of a strongly anti-Kirchnerist tendency was already noticeable by that point.

Cristina Fernández de Kirchner's Presidencies

Cristina Fernández de Kirchner took office on December 10, 2007. The continuity of public policies with respect to Néstor Kirchner's government was reflected in her decision to retain his chief of cabinet, Alberto Fernández, and the majority of his ministers. With the most pressing issues of the crisis already addressed, the new president announced that she would seek to consolidate the foundations for growth and improve institutional quality.

Complications arose immediately. In October 2007, years of irresponsible management by American banks led to a financial crisis, the effects of which were felt around the world. The 2008 crisis was the worst in global capitalism since 1929: almost all countries entered into recession, credit and international trade slowed down, poverty rose everywhere, and inflation accelerated. Its fallout lasted for several years.

Ironically, Argentina's financial isolation turned out to be an advantage: it was not dependent on loans, and its banks were not shaken. However, the global crisis did have an impact on trade. Latin American countries were severely affected, including Brazil, which had to drastically devalue its currency, affecting Argentina's exports to its main trading partner. This situation was compounded by severe droughts in 2008–9, the worst in fifty years, and another almost as severe in 2011–12, affecting local crops and livestock. The Argentine economy, which had its own problems, suffered a sharp downturn in 2008 and 2009; it recovered in 2010 but then experienced another downturn in 2012, and, from that point on, evolved slowly and unevenly. In order to reduce the effects of the crisis, the government increased public spending, which weakened two of the pillars of the Kirchnerist model, the "twin surpluses": fiscal and trade.

Even before the effects of the crisis were felt, an unexpected confrontation had shaken the political scene. International corn, soy, and grain prices had been rising steadily since 2005 and reached an unusual peak in early 2008. The exorbitant values generated extraordinary profits for producers, while at the same time pushing up domestic food prices. To curb the latter and to take advantage of this boom, the government raised export duties from 28 percent to 35 percent and, in March 2008, decided to apply a sliding-scale system of tariffs that would rise or fall according to variations in the international prices of these products.

To protest this measure, the main agribusiness associations initiated a lockout accompanied by roadblocks and a threat to generate deliberate shortages of products in cities. What began as a sectoral problem soon united the entire political opposition and led to the first serious challenge to Kirchner's government. On March 25, thousands of opposition supporters, mostly from the middle or upper sectors (many with no connection to agribusiness), staged *cacerolazos* in several cities to support the rural enterprises. Although they invoked the spirit of the 2001 *cacerolazos*, the unity of those earlier days was absent: this time the chants did refer to a specific sectoral issue ("El campo no se toca" [Hands off agriculture]). And, as the newspapers themselves acknowledged, in that demonstration and in the several very massive ones that followed, racist insults against *los negros* who supported the government abounded. The mainstream media encouraged the protest and thus galvanized a powerful anti-Kirchnerist movement that revived many of the motives of classic anti-Peronism.

The government refused to back down and the conflict dragged on for three months, during which crowds of pro-Kirchner supporters also took to the streets. Public debate became more vitriolic and heated than ever before. This dramatic crossroads produced a clear change in government discourse, which became as markedly binary and bellicose as that of its rivals. The government and like-minded leaders compared the opposition movement to the demonstrations that had supported the Libertadora dictatorship, accusing them of having destabilizing intentions. Long-forgotten vocabulary from the 1970s also made a reappearance, with epithets hurled at "the oligarchy" and at the middle class for hanging on their coattails. The Kirchnerists presented themselves as defenders of the lower classes, and at the same time, in a novel way, they served as a means for the issue of ethnic-racial differences among Argentines to surface in public debate. Even the Kirchners themselves played with the idea that those opposing the government were "whites" who despised "brownness."

In a bid to settle the conflict, Fernández de Kirchner decided to rework the proposed modification of the export duties as a bill that she sent to Congress for its consideration. Following a heated debate, it passed in the Chamber of Deputies. When it came to the vote in the Senate, accompanied by intense street demonstrations, there was a tie. The decision fell to the president of the Senate, who by constitutional provision is the vice president of the nation and representative of the executive branch. Unexpectedly, Julio Cobos voted against the bill, which turned him into a celebrity and the hero of the anti-Kirchnerists for several weeks. The government criticized this "betrayal" but accepted defeat and restored the export duties to their previous levels. The conflict was over. As a result of the discredit generated by this situation and the economic hardships, in the 2009 legislative elections, Kirchnerism saw the worst performance of its brief history. Anti-Kirchnerist Peronism worked with right-wing parties in the province of Buenos Aires to seriously defeat Néstor Kirchner, who headed the list in that district.

Kirchnerism emerged from this moment of weakness with a transformation that surprised both supporters and opponents. Instead of reconciling and moderating its hegemonic ambitions, the movement radicalized the social content of its proposal with a more marked criticism of corporations and the upper classes and put even more effort into identifying with the lower classes. It more firmly embraced the emblems and the traditional liturgy of Peronism. However, at the same time, of the entire legacy of Peronism, it made a particular effort to retrieve the brief period in which Cámpora was president, the sole and ephemeral time in which the movement took on a leftist position that transcended the political boundaries its founder had established. This shift was accompanied by a marked change in government rhetoric, which began to draw on ideas, vocabulary, and symbols of the 1970s as part of an epic struggle against the enemies of the people. A new internal branch of Kirchnerism—which not coincidentally was dubbed La Cámpora—

acquired a vertiginous notoriety and spaces of power. This shift in discourse made it possible to reconcile the legacy of Peronism with the illusion of transcending and surpassing it that still resonated from 2001.

At the same time, Fernández de Kirchner's government took the public by surprise with a series of measures that generated enthusiasm among a broad sector of the population. In mid-2008, she obtained parliamentary approval for the renationalization of Aerolíneas Argentinas (Argentine Airlines), which at the time was undergoing a crisis due to the asset-stripping maneuvers of its Spanish administrators. Toward the end of that same year, she secured congressional approval to eliminate the system of private pension fund administrators and bring them back under state management. Although this change was aimed at solving the government's financing issues, it also addressed the complete failure of the private system, which had only benefited the banks. However, the most significant measure was the 2009 decree that created the Universal Child Allowance, a monthly stipend to meet the needs of children that had a huge impact on the poorest households. Unlike social plans, it was the extension of a right; access to it was transparent and involved no political intermediation.

After the clash with the agribusiness sector, the government found itself in a bitter dispute with the Clarín multimedia company, which was fueling the opposition's positions. At the time, Argentina had an extremely concentrated media structure. Grupo Clarín owned the most widely circulated national newspaper as well as several newspapers in the country's interior, dozens of magazines, the most important over-the-air channel and several dozen cable channels, some of the most popular radio stations, and companies manufacturing paper, telephony, and broadband. As long as Clarín kept criticism at a moderate level, this quasi-monopoly had not bothered the Fernández de Kirchner government (which had, incidentally, favored Clarín's expansion).

However, everything changed in 2008. As part of the government's new ethos, the following year Fernández de Kirchner secured approval for a new Audiovisual Media Law, which, in line with the regulations of the most advanced countries, aimed to prevent media concentration. It included antitrust clauses that forced Grupo Clarín and other multimedia companies to divest some of their licenses and ensured space for community-based radio and television stations. Clarín tenaciously resisted the measure, obtained court-sanctioned delays in applying it, and embarked on what one of the newspaper's editors called "war journalism" against Kirchnerism. The government responded with frequent verbal attacks on the multimedia company and with the sponsorship of a whole array of supportive public and private media outlets that attempted to counteract the messages disseminated by Clarín. From that point on, the state-owned TV Pública and other news agencies acquired a very pronounced pro-government tone, and the president made growing use of national networks to ensure coverage of her speeches. Public debate became extremely bellicose, and significantly less attention was paid to the actual veracity of the news.

In 2010, the government surprised the public with another unexpected measure. Once again with the approval of Congress, the Equal Marriage Law was passed, granting same-sex couples the right to legally marry. And in 2012, the Gender Identity Law was introduced, enabling people who did not identify with the sex they were assigned at birth to be reregistered in all public identity documents according to their self-perceived gender, a law that placed Argentina ahead of the rest of the world in this area.

The "Camporista" shift of the government and the number of progressive measures that it managed to promote in a short period of time restored its popularity, especially among young people, who, starting in 2008, flocked massively to Kirchnerism. During these years, political activism in support of the government reached a peak of emotional and political intensity. In this new incarnation, Peronist identity recovered to a large extent the place it had lost as a result of the 2001 crisis and even expanded among middle sectors that had never before identified with it.

The first confirmation of this change in direction was the bicentennial celebration in May 2010. Despite the indifference and skepticism of the press, almost 3 million people crowded the streets of Buenos Aires to participate in the various events organized by the national government. The messages featured in the carefully organized events constituted a novelty with respect to the way that the state had represented Argentine identity in the past. As part of the central event, a succession of floats presented a narrative of the past in which indigenous peoples, Afro-Argentines, mestizo identity, and social struggles occupied a very prominent place.

Another notable crowd gathered in October 2010, to bid farewell to Néstor Kirchner when he unexpectedly died. The president's grief generated a wave of empathy toward her that also helped dispel some of the previous misgivings.

In the 2011 presidential elections, Fernández de Kirchner was reelected in the first round with 54 percent of the vote, a result only surpassed by Perón. It was the first time since the Hipólito Yrigoyen era that the same political party managed to govern for three consecutive terms. The Frente Amplio

Progresista (Broad Progressive Front), led by the Santa Fe socialist Hermes Binner, was in a distant second place with 17 percent of the vote. The UCR won another meager 11 percent of the vote. The main contender in the previous presidential elections, Elisa Carrió, experienced a dramatic decline: only 1.8 percent of the electorate voted for her. The party system was still in a tumultuous state: although Kirchnerism now firmly controlled the Peronist Party, two other Peronist candidates tried their luck independently. The opposition remained fragmented and unstable. Once again, the electorate was overwhelmingly positioned between center and center-left; no right-wing force obtained any relevant percentage.

After the elections, the difficulties on the economic front became more apparent. Public spending increased due to the cost of sustaining the economic recovery, the burden of public subsidies to keep utility tariffs low, and the growing expense of oil and gas imports to make up for the shortage of local energy production. Since external financing remained virtually inaccessible, the state resorted to issuing currency and added further pressure to the inflation rate, which after 2010 frequently breached the 20 percent annual line. The need for foreign currency by both the state and private companies, in addition to an increase in capital flight, drove the dollar higher. Once again, the old problem of foreign exchange constraints resurfaced.

In late 2011, the economy was affected by an unexpected legal complication. On December 7, a New York judge issued a capricious ruling threatening to confiscate Argentina's payments to creditors who had entered into the foreign debt restructuring if the country did not agree to pay the handful of speculators who had decided not to negotiate at the same time. The ruling placed the country in a catch-22 situation. According to the contractual terms, if the vulture funds were paid the full amount they were claiming at the time, without deductions, the other creditors would be entitled to demand equal treatment, which would mean the complete collapse of the restructuring. If they were not paid, the new judicial ruling prevented the country from honoring its commitments, placing it once again in default (this time involuntary) and sacrificing all the normalization efforts of the previous years.

Argentina upheld its refusal to comply with the New York judge's ruling, and the government embarked instead on a defensive judicial battle in the American courts and elsewhere. It also launched an international offensive that won the country one of its most resounding diplomatic achievements: several nations explicitly supported Argentina's position, and, by a wide margin in September 2015, the United Nations (UN) approved a protocol for restructuring sovereign debts with "anti-vulture" clauses that had been proposed by Argentina and rejected by the United States and a handful of its allies. International pressure grew, but it did not immediately succeed in changing the hostile judicial scenario. Argentina remained unable to access external financing, the need for which became increasingly urgent. The conflict itself sowed doubts about the future of the economy, affected investment decisions, and fueled capital flight.

Fernández de Kirchner's government dealt with the economic turbulence by intensifying the heterodox approach it had been applying since the beginning. In order to keep the exchange rate within a reasonable range and tackle foreign currency flight, in November 2011 she set a limit on the amount of dollars that private individuals were allowed to buy; this so-called *cepo cambiario* (currency exchange restriction) lasted until the end of her term in office. In early 2012, a new bureaucratic system forced importers to request authorization before importing goods, a veiled way of protecting national industry. And since the crisis in energy production was, at least in part, the responsibility of the Spanish company that had bought YPF during Menem's administration and failed to make the necessary investments to explore new fields and bring them into operation, in 2012, through a law passed in Congress, the state expropriated 51 percent of its shareholding package. Although YPF remained a joint stock company, it was now run by a manager appointed by the government, who soon got it back on its feet.

Employers in various sectors were pressured not to cut costs by laying off personnel. The government also extended social spending and labor rights policies that had a positive impact on income levels (and therefore on consumption). Among the most noteworthy were the 2013 policy that brought the working conditions of domestic workers in line with those of other wage earners and a new series of pension moratoriums in 2014, making pension coverage almost universal. While only 66 percent of the elderly had access to that benefit in 2003, that percentage now rose to 97 percent and included homemakers, recognized for their unpaid labor. This was accompanied by a program of hundreds of thousands of low-cost loans for building or expanding housing and incentives to facilitate access to plots of land for this purpose.

Although the worst effects were mitigated or deferred, the economic difficulties continued. The heterodox profile of these policies was reaffirmed through the appointment of Axel Kicillof as minister of economy in late 2013, although he did begin his tenure with a devaluation of the peso from 6.8 per dollar to 8. This measure immediately resulted in higher inflation—which peaked in 2014 at more than 35 percent—and a drop in wages. As a result, in 2014, relations with the unions deteriorated and the CGT held its first general strike of the Kirchner era. A series of policies aimed at encouraging purchases in installments and controlling the prices of basic products partially offset the losses in purchasing power. Wage levels improved in 2015, and inflation, which prior to the 2015 elections was around 23 percent, fell significantly that year.

Genders and Sexualities: A Dramatic Change

The approval of the divorce law under Alfonsín and the Equal Marriage and Gender Identity laws under Fernández de Kirchner bookended a dizzying process of sociocultural change in terms of sexualities, family, and gender. Starting in the 1980s, film, and later television, the press, and mainstream music, began giving space to positive images of homosexual relationships (initially between men, and later also between women). In the following decade, transgender people slowly found a place in commercial theater and on television, where they were included for the first time without the exclusive intention of denigration. These developments were indicative of a change at a more general level, which made dissident sexual and gender identities and choices progressively more acceptable.

Activism by sexual minorities played a crucial role in this transformation. The experience of the Homosexual Liberation Front had been cut short by the dictatorship, but the movement reappeared in full force as soon as democracy was reestablished. In 1984, the Homosexual Liberation Movement was founded in Rosario and the Comunidad Homosexual Argentina (Argentine Homosexual Community, or CHA) in Buenos Aires, two of the most solid initiatives among several that emerged in those years. The late 1980s and early 1990s saw the advent of exclusively lesbian organizations and, in 1991, the first for the defense of transgender women. Though not free of tensions, these groups were building alliances and bolstering public demands.

In July 1992, the first Gay-Lesbian Pride March was held in Buenos Aires, coinciding with those taking place in other countries. Some 250 people, most of them wearing masks to avoid being identified, marched to Congress with the slogan "Freedom, equality, diversity." The march has been repeated every year since then. The turnout grew moderately until 2000, and after that year, exponentially. By 2008, tens of thousands were marching with their faces uncovered in the capital city as well as in other cities throughout the country. In

2015, according to organizers, the crowd gathered in Buenos Aires numbered two hundred thousand people.

At about the same time, feminism was expanding, and for the first time it became a mass movement with deep roots in all classes. The movement was spearheaded by various organizations, but its most visible expression was the National Women's Gatherings. The first was held in Buenos Aires in 1986 and was attended by around six hundred women with the aim of making gender oppression visible and discussing ways of confronting it. It was an open and nonhierarchical space for workshops and discussions, independent of any institution or organization. Moving each year to a different city, the successive gatherings voiced demands and organized initiatives with respect to quotas for women in public office, gender-based violence, reproductive health, and the right to abortion. The number of participants grew each year, reaching twelve thousand in 2001. By then, women from diverse backgrounds were participating: homemakers, laborers, rural workers, students, *campesinas*, political party activists, professionals, indigenous peoples, and *piqueteras*.

Through the ties formed at the gatherings, a National Campaign for the Right to Abortion was organized in 2005, which built on the work of a whole series of initiatives that had been underway since the return to democracy. Demands were also made in conjunction with movements of sexual minorities, and lesbian, trans, and bisexual women were gaining greater prominence. By 2015, the number of attendees at the National Women's Gathering had reached sixty thousand, and the demand for the right to abortion was being raised in public debates with unprecedented insistence. Nevertheless, it was not echoed by the Kirchnerist leadership, which refrained from presenting the issue before Congress.

Starting in 2015, the women's movement held frequent demonstrations and presented an increasingly sharp critique of the patriarchy. In June of that year, it filled the streets in surprisingly massive numbers. In the wake of a series of gruesome murders of young women, the rallying cry of "Ni una menos" (Not one [woman] less), echoing the "Ni una más" (Not one more) used in Mexico, began to circulate. Demands were made for an end to femicides and better enforcement of the law on gender-based violence that had been passed in 2009 but remained poorly implemented. The response was overwhelming: around two hundred thousand people marched in Buenos Aires, most of them women. Many cities throughout the rest of the country had similar demonstrations.

Other massive demonstrations followed that year and in the following years, and the movement came to be headed by an assembly of leaders of grassroots organizations and other activists. "Ni una menos" also went international and was replicated in many countries. In Argentina, it spilled over to other sectors and expressed solidarity with workers, the poor, the human rights movement, indigenous peoples, and oppressed minorities of all kinds. (In 2016, this movement proposed and organized an unprecedented "women's strike" that was replicated internationally.) All of this, in turn, amplified the demand for the right to abortion to a much greater scale. In a short period of time, the feminist movement had succeeded in questioning previously untouched cornerstones of the patriarchy, denouncing not only femicide and unequal rights but also the multiple forms of violence in relationships and even in language itself.

The Limits of Kirchnerism and Macri's Victory

By the end of the third consecutive Kirchner administration, the country appeared transformed, albeit with very clear contrasts. The most substantial and indisputable improvements were in the expansion or restitution of social, labor, and civil rights and the defense of human rights. In this respect, Kirchnerism represented a turning point in recent history and a clear reversal of the tendencies that had been established in the 1990s.

Another area of undoubtedly positive change was that of scientific development. The creation of a new Ministry of Science, Technology, and Productive Innovation in 2007 was a clear indication of the attention and support that Kirchnerism gave this area. In the 1980s, as a result of decades of public spending, Argentina had reached the point of being able to manufacture and export nuclear reactors and, a short time later, produce its first satellites. However, during that decade and the following one, these programs were defunded to the point that they were nearly frozen (some were dismantled under pressure from the United States, such as the ballistic missile manufacturing program, which was very advanced), and the country lost a significant number of its scientists and technologists to emigration. During the Kirchnerist era, this trend was reversed: Argentina managed to put the first locally manufactured geostationary satellite into orbit and exported nuclear reactors to countries such as Australia and the Netherlands, which positioned it among only a handful of nations capable of producing this type of goods. There were also important advances in nanotechnology, biotechnology, and the software industry. The Consejo Nacional de Investigaciones Científicas y Técnicas (CONICET) benefited from unprecedented funding, and the country's scientific production improved significantly in all international rankings. The Kirchner years also stood out for their support for cultural production, with very visible achievements, especially in the audiovisual field.

In terms of the economy, there were both high and low points. The 2003–11 period saw one of the highest GDP growth rates in Argentina's history (and the highest since the centennial); following this, the pace slowed without a drop in production, except for a slight decline in 2014. Agricultural production for export reached a record in 2010. Soybeans, in particular, were a crucial driver of this performance, with international prices trending upward. At the same time, industry made a remarkable recovery. Unlike other Latin American countries that also grew during the same period, Argentina did so without reprimarizing its economy: along with agriculture, industry and the service sector were a driving force of this expansion, and they did not lose their share in the GDP.

All these achievements were accomplished without relying on international loans. In fact, there was a strong process of debt reduction: the public debt went from representing 116 percent of GDP in 2003 to 45 percent in 2014; moreover, its structure changed, with a much larger portion of it denominated in pesos and owed to departments of the state itself (rather than private parties and international organizations). In 2015, on the other hand, the Central Bank's reserves were close to twice what they were in 2003 (although half the level they had reached in 2010).

Nevertheless, the improvements in the economy did not manage to solve some long-standing limitations, such as the difficulties the manufacturing sector had in exporting and the resulting dependency on foreign currency caused by the primary sector. Restrictions on the external front and maneuvers to secure dollars were once again evident during Fernández de Kirchner's second term in office. Other problems became more pronounced. A lack of investment led to a serious crisis in the energy supply. Agricultural growth exacerbated the trend toward monoculture, and the brutal expansion of genetically modified soybeans led to soil deterioration; the use of agrochemicals continued to increase and, with it, so did health problems among the population.

The expansion of mining in the Andean zone and, later, of fracking in Patagonia brought few benefits to the communities in question and instead left them with an irreversible environmental liability with long-lasting effects. The massive use, in both activities, of carcinogenic and highly toxic chemicals added to the growing health problems in these regions, although they were also left out of the public agenda. Additionally, these extractive activities saw an increase in the violence against indigenous peoples and the affected populations who resisted them. Despite all this, in her speeches, Fernández de Kirchner supported the multinationals behind them, including Monsanto.

There were similar contrasts in other social welfare indicators. There were some clear improvements. The proportion of registered workers increased and unemployment fell markedly until 2011 (then it slowed down and rose slightly toward the end of her term). Poverty decreased consistently until 2013, increased slightly the following year, and decreased again in 2015: the proportion of the poor in the overall population, which was above 60 percent at the beginning of the Kirchnerist cycle (calculated according to the new methodology used by the INDEC since 2016), had decreased to 28 percent by 2015.

Income distribution became more egalitarian between 2003 and 2015, when it was more equal than it had been at the peak of the 1990s (although it was still very unfavorable compared to Argentina in the 1970s). And there were improvements in many social indicators, from infant mortality to education, housing, and health. Nevertheless, society remained deeply fragmented. Improvements for the popular classes were uneven, visible for white-collar workers but much less so for the unregistered or unemployed. Deep pockets of poverty, exclusion, and marginalization continued to be a part of the social landscape.

The most negative aspects of the period were evident at the institutional level. In the 2009 legislative elections, the ruling party placed "testimonial" candidates, who did not plan to take office if elected, at the top of its lists, violating the very core of popular sovereignty (the practice was not repeated in subsequent elections). Other Kirchnerist policies seriously affected the normal functioning of the state. The most severe case was the intervention of INDEC and the manipulation of official statistics starting in 2007. Inflation data were systematically "retouched" downward until 2014; the poverty series was also discontinued, in order to disguise economic difficulties. This generated considerable disrepute for INDEC and for the government in general. On the other hand, it also weakened the ability and independence of state agencies to ensure the honesty of their officials. Likewise, there was undue pressure on the Consejo de la Magistratura (Council of the Magistrature) regarding the appointment of acting judges, and the clandestine network of contacts between the intelligence services, judges, and journalists, which several presidents had taken advantage of since Menem's era, continued to be used for political purposes.

Democracy Devalued

Corruption reached the highest echelons of the state apparatus: a minister and a national secretary were convicted on such charges during Fernández de Kirchner's administration, and other officials, including the president herself and her last vice president, are still facing trials as this book goes to press.

In the last two years of Fernández de Kirchner's government, political polarization, which was not new, took on an unusual and bitter intensity. Government supporters and anti-Kirchnerists expressed such mutual resentment that it can only be compared to sentiments at the time of Perón's overthrow. This animosity was even noticeable in intellectual circles, which were divided between government supporters and anti-Kirchnerist groups. The press gave it a name: society was divided by *la grieta* (the rift).

Kirchnerism headed into the 2015 elections with the wear and tear of twelve years in government as well as fallout generated by its own shortcomings. There was a growing disconnect between its fiery leftist rhetoric and reality, which reflected little progress in a progressive sense. Economic difficulties hampered the passion that the epic was capable of arousing. In the last two years of her presidency, Fernández de Kirchner appeared self-absorbed and was unable to propose a candidate for continuity. Resigned, she entrusted the mission to the only option who performed well in the polls, the governor of Buenos Aires, Daniel Scioli, an anodyne figure with a moderate profile who did not arouse much enthusiasm among his own people. And the enthusiasm he might have aroused among independent voters was diminished when the president insisted on one of her most loyal collaborators as his candidate for vice president. Thus, as the elections approached, it became increasingly difficult for Kirchnerism to continue claiming the role of standard-bearer of the change that had been longed for since 2001. In fact, during the electoral campaign, it presented itself as the defender of the status quo rather than as an agent of change. It called for protecting what had already been accomplished. It had ceased to look toward the future, falling back instead on self-complacency for past achievements.

The government's adversaries exploited this weakness relentlessly. Opposition leaders, the mainstream media, and a number of public figures from various fields embarked on a daily demonization of everything that was Kirchnerist. Their interventions were marked by an emotional and strongly Manichean rhetoric. In addition to the motives of classic anti-Peronism, this rhetoric was guided by two concepts: "populism," which they denounced in increasingly urgent tones, threatened to destroy "the republic" and, along with it, democracy, freedom, institutions, the rule of law, and even people's lives.

Seen in these terms, there was no room for half measures: one had to be in favor of the (good) republic and against (evil) populism. Kirchnerism, for its part, responded with its own equally binary alternative: one was either with "the people" or with "the oligarchy" and "the corporations." The campaign's strongly emotional appeal complicated the rational debate of ideas. Instead, accusations of all sorts prevailed.

The issue of corruption dominated the campaign. Other accusations against the government were added to the cases already pending in the courts, and they multiplied during the electoral period. Some were clearly fabricated, others perhaps not (they are still making their way through the courts), but all were heavily amplified by the media. At the last moment, the Kirchnerist candidate for governor of Buenos Aires province was accused of being a drug trafficker implicated in murders, an accusation that was widely echoed in the press, although no evidence was ever given. Renowned intellectual figures even went as far as to claim that the government resembled Adolf Hitler's dictatorship, that it was preparing a self-coup, that it had set up a terror apparatus, and that it was organizing armed militias (none of this was true).

The most spectacular accusation was launched in early 2015 by the prosecutor in charge of the AMIA investigation, Alberto Nisman, when he surprisingly claimed that Fernández de Kirchner had orchestrated an international plot to cover up for a group of Iranians he considered responsible for the 1994 attack. The accusation was immediately taken up by the opposition to fuel the electoral campaign. Its bases were very flimsy and, as the days went by, it began to collapse: several judges and jurists found the allegation capricious, and one of the key witnesses, a former head of Interpol, considered it an outright lie. Several journalists reminded the public that Nisman had been reporting to the American Embassy, according to information that had surfaced in a massive leak of documents from the United States five years earlier. The prosecutor was summoned to deliver a report to Congress. Mere hours before his appearance, however, he was found dead in his apartment with a gunshot wound to the temple.

The opposition immediately used his death for political purposes and accused the government of having assassinated him. The judicial investigation—including the Supreme Court experts, at odds with Fernández de Kirchner at the time—found no evidence that another person had been with Nisman at the time of his death and pointed to suicide as a plausible explanation. In spite of this, journalists and leaders of the opposition continued to foster the theory of homicide. The complicity between political leaders, the media, sectors of the judiciary, and the intelligence services in conducting judicial procedures and spreading information that was damaging to the government, whether true or false, proved notable at the time.

The electoral campaign took place in this strained political climate. In the years leading up to the elections, it was not clear who would lead the opposition space, whether it would be a progressive or a figure from the UCR, or perhaps Sergio Massa, who led a dissident Peronist party and had good projections in the polls. Many were pinning their hopes on the mayor of Buenos Aires, Mauricio Macri. His party, the PRO, had been assembling its own leadership, consisting of businesspeople and members of economically liberal NGOs, along with several others who came from traditional parties. But its roots outside the capital city were very weak: in the 2013 legislative elections, the PRO had not been in a position to present a list of its own in the race for the province of Buenos Aires, Argentina's main electoral district. In 2015, they did not even have valid legal status there, so they had to compete under another name. And in most of the country's interior, they had barely established a foothold and lacked candidates. Moreover, in 2014, polls still showed Macri as having a very negative image among the population, and relatively few viewed him in a positive light. In a country with rather progressive values, the businessman was still associated with the right wing and shady business dealings, and his close ties with Menemism had not been forgotten.

Macri's chances began to improve in mid-2014 due to the climate that led to *la grieta* and, ironically, because Kirchnerism chose to target him as its main adversary. (Compared to an uncharismatic right-wing businessman—they thought—Peronism would prove unbeatable.) Thanks to pressures to unify the opposition, early the following year Macri surprised the public with an alliance with Elisa Carrió and, shortly thereafter, with the UCR, which provided him with an indispensable political apparatus on a national level. The confluence of these forces would have been inconceivable only a year earlier. The media, which still hesitated between supporting Macri or Massa, leaned in Macri's favor. The opposition alliance was christened Cambiemos (Let's Change), in order to connect with the widespread desire to transcend the old politics and dissatisfaction with the unfulfilled promises of Kirchnerism.

Until 2001, Macri had evaluated offers to enter politics under Menemism. And during that period, he had presented himself as a "center-right conservative." However, he now launched a skillful campaign in which he tried to appear progressive (or even "leftist," as one of his advocates proposed). He promised that he would preserve or deepen the progressive socioeconomic changes promoted by Kirchnerism and that his government would focus on remedying the previous government's institutional shortcomings. According to the discourse of *la grieta*, he emerged as the defender of "the republic" under threat.

Cambiemos grew significantly in the last stretch of the campaign. In the August primaries, only 23 percent of voters had opted for Macri as their preferred candidate (the coalition as a whole won only slightly more, 28.57 percent, which reflects the very low percentage his two rivals, Carrió and the UCR's candidate, obtained in the primaries). From that point on, the campaign took on a frenetic pace. By the October general elections, Cambiemos had already reached 34 percent; Scioli remained in the lead but with less of a difference than anticipated.

Leading up to the runoff, the country was on edge. The Kirchnerists redoubled their efforts and their opponents did the same. The media support for Macri was tenacious and unabashed. The idea of holding a televised debate between the candidates, something common in other countries but unprecedented in Argentina, had taken root following the suggestion of several children of prominent businesspeople combined with overwhelming media pressure. The face-off between the two main contenders was indicative of the crossroads: Scioli spent his time warning the population about his rival's true intentions, while Macri attacked him on the issues of corruption and the lack of transparency. The Cambiemos candidate explained that his economic policies would not only *not* reverse the achievements of Kirchnerism but would far exceed them. He made all sorts of promises (which he did not keep) and focused on refuting Scioli's warnings (among them, that Macri would apply austerity measures and a devaluation, which was precisely what he did as soon as he took office).

The media collaborated by reporting on what they called the "fear campaign," mocking the warnings about the direction that a potential Macri government would take and encouraging voters to seek "change." For the first time in these elections, social networks and the internet also became a fundamental battleground.

The final results were extremely close: Macri won with 51.4 percent of the vote against 48.6 percent for Scioli. The percentage of the former had been boosted by the very high 71.52 percent of the vote received in the province of Córdoba, whose inhabitants were responding to years of Kirchnerist mistreatment, as well as by the unexpected 48.8 percent that Macri obtained in the Peronist stronghold of the province of Buenos Aires, where María Eugenia Vidal triumphed. A previously little-known figure, her popularity had grown rapidly due to her own charisma, but she had also been helped by the accusations of drug trafficking that had been launched against the Peronist candidate. Looking at the change in results between the primaries and the final round of the election, it is clear that in a very short time there had been a massive increase in the number of voters who, without being committed Macristas, had opted for this alternative. Accepting the invitation expressed in the very name of the PRO's alliance, they opted for what they considered "a change."

Macri's victory and the brilliant rise of the PRO marked a real turning point in Argentine history. It was the first time that a third force came to power, one that did not come from Peronism or the UCR, the parties that had dominated national politics over the previous hundred years. With the near absorption of the UCR into Cambiemos as its junior partner and the almost irrelevant results obtained by the other non-Peronist groups, it appeared that the period of disorganization of the political system that had begun in 2001 was coming to an end. One of its extremes appeared to be consolidated (Peronism, on the other hand, would immediately enter a new phase of dispersion). However, more importantly, it was the first time since the liberal-conservatives lost power in 1916 that the upper classes had a party entirely of their own capable of winning elections.

Macri's Government (2015–2019): A Return to Neoliberalism

The transfer of power was a clear example of the bellicose and intolerant character of political life at the time. Mauricio Macri and Cristina Fernández de Kirchner could not agree on the details of the ceremony. And without the ceremony, there could be no inauguration. To resolve this impasse, at the president-elect's request, a judge issued an unusual ruling that shortened his predecessor's term by a few hours and temporarily transferred power to the president of the Senate, so that he could hand over the attributes of power to Macri. Fernández de Kirchner took the opportunity to avoid attending the ceremony, which reinforced the image that many had of her as an intractable person incapable of respecting republican ways.

The cabinet of ministers and senior officials that Macri appointed when he took office were mainly from the business sector; those from the UCR were few and of lower rank, which signaled that it would essentially be the PRO that would govern. It quickly became clear that Macri's economic policy was swinging back to orthodoxy and free trade. The vision behind it was clearly neoliberal, although the style was somewhat different from that of Menem's times. In order to establish a solid foundation this time for the neoliberal project, the government claimed it was important to generate not only economic reforms but also a "cultural change": the rather progressive values of Argentine society had to be altered. According to surveys conducted in previous years, egalitarianism and the idea that the state should be its guarantor were deeply rooted among Argentines, who historically—and especially after the experience of 2001—tended to distrust the market and the wealthy.

The project of "cultural change" consisted in shifting these fundamental values toward others that represented quite the opposite, the values of *emprendedurismo* (entrepreneurship)—another of the new government's key words—which emphasized the role of the individual focused on work and personal development. The path to well-being was no longer to be found in the expansion of collective rights guaranteed by the state but in the merit of each individual, which would be duly rewarded by the market. Abandoning political demands and devoting oneself to private affairs with a more "entrepreneurial" attitude would, presumably, result in improvements for the country as a whole.

Of course, generating a change like this in mainstream culture would be a slow process that would require significant time under the aegis of the PRO. In view of the limitations imposed by the electorate, the government announced that there would be no shock policy this time but rather a strategy of gradual change. This so-called gradualism was implemented to avoid adverse reactions among the population that would trigger an early change of government. Thus, from the outset of Macri's government, politics, economic measures, and the cultural project were intertwined.

On the economic front, Macri inaugurated his presidency by lifting all restrictions on the purchase of dollars, allowing the exchange rate to fluctuate freely. All regulations on the inflow and outflow of capital were eliminated: even short-term speculative inflows would be permitted. After a brief negotiation, the debt claimed by the vulture funds was paid in cash and, with it, the embargoes that prevented the country from taking on new loans were lifted. On the trade front, the para-tariff barriers and quotas that the previous government had established to protect domestic industry were dismantled and import tariffs on many products were lowered. Agricultural and mining exporters were rewarded with the elimination of export duties (they were maintained only for soy, with the promise that they would be gradually lowered to zero).

As these measures meant heavy losses for the public coffers, they were accompanied by others that sought to restore the balance. Despite a campaign promise, income tax for workers was not eliminated; in fact, the number of those required to pay it was increased. In violation of another promise, state subsidies for transportation and energy were immediately cut, resulting in significant increases in the cost of public services, which were periodically repeated.

Additionally, there were budget cuts in many areas of the state, accompanied by layoffs. Among the hardest-hit sectors were science and technology—for which increases had been promised—and culture. (In 2018, as part of a new round of cuts, the ministries in charge of these two areas were eliminated along with several others, including health.) At the government's initiative and in the midst of a fierce crackdown on protesters, in 2017 Congress approved a pension reform that changed the way pensions were calculated, causing their value to fall.

Inflation was a problem from the outset. As soon as the elections were over, businesses began to mark up their products, which reversed the previous downward trend. The liberalization of the dollar led to an increase in its value, which was initially moderate and then accelerated, but was passed on to prices regardless. The elimination of export duties and subsidies pushed up the cost of food and fuel. Macri placed Federico Sturzenegger, memorable architect of the 2001 mega-swap, at the head of the Central Bank. Sturzenegger took a monetarist approach to the issue, raising interest rates to unprecedented levels and offering treasury bills in pesos with very high yields in an attempt to withdraw money from the market and discourage the purchase of dollars. Inflation did not stop rising. Rather, a bubble of bills was generated, which the state found increasingly difficult to pay.

The government hoped to encourage a "flood of foreign investments." But when that didn't happen, it covered the deficit by taking on foreign debt, which was mostly used for expenditures. For this and other policies, it secured the approval of Congress (with the support of a good proportion of the Peronist legislators). The debt expanded rapidly until, in early 2018, international investors began to question the country's ability to repay and turned off the tap.

Cornered by the deficit and the rising dollar, in May, Macri surprised the public with the announcement that the country would once again borrow from the IMF and announced an agreement for a $50 billion loan, to which another $7 billion was later added. It was the largest loan ever granted by the IMF, and Argentina became the emerging country to have taken on the most debt since 2015. The disbursement came with its usual conditions of increased austerity and changes to several laws, including pension laws. Once again, sovereignty in economic decisions was jeopardized.

This shift in economic policy was accompanied by an abrupt change in foreign policy. Argentina cooled its multipolar ties and firmly realigned itself with the United States, which at the time had set out to recover lost ground in Latin America and embarked on an aggressive dispute with Russia and China to assert its geopolitical supremacy. Diplomatic advances on the vulture funds issue were forgotten. After endorsing the parliamentary coup that ousted Brazilian president Dilma Rousseff in 2016 in alliance with other right-wing governments in the region, Macri sabotaged efforts toward Latin American integration.

In 2017, he advocated for and achieved the suspension of Venezuela as a member of MERCOSUR, and, the following year, along with his Brazilian counterpart and others, withdrew Argentina from the Union of South American Nations (UNASUR), established ten years earlier, dealing it a lethal blow. In sync with Jair Bolsonaro, the extreme right-wing president who had recently come to power in Brazil, Macri announced in 2019 that MERCOSUR had reached a preliminary free-trade agreement with the European Union (its terms remained secret) and that Argentina and Brazil would move forward with talks along the same lines with the United States.

The combination of these measures had a devastating effect on the main economic variables. As in the days of the dictatorship and the Menem administration, the export and financial groups enjoyed significant profits, but the industrial sector shrank severely. The increased cost of utilities, high interest rates, the opening up of trade, and the decline in consumption led thousands of businesses and companies of all sizes to go bankrupt. Argentina was in recession for three of the four years of Macri's term and the GDP fell sharply; measured on a per capita basis, by 2019 it had receded to the level it had been ten years earlier. The increase in imports during the first years affected the trade deficit and as a result there was more pressure on the dollar, which climbed vertiginously. When Macri took office, the dollar was trading at just over 9 pesos (just over 12 pesos on the black market); by the end of his term, it had reached 63 pesos. As a result, inflation rose steadily: by 2019 it stood at 53.8 percent year-on-year, the highest in twenty-eight years.

In a vain attempt to curb the devaluation, the Central Bank burned through most of the dollars it had received from the IMF, the majority of which ended up funneled abroad. Little of that capital remained in the country; what did remain was serious indebtedness. The public debt went from representing 52.6 percent of GDP in 2015 to 91.6 percent in 2019 (other districts under the PRO administration, such as the province and the city of Buenos Aires, experienced similar processes of indebtedness). The servicing of the loans was already impossible for the next government to cover, while the long-term loans committed the country to disbursements up to a hundred years into the future. Macri's own government had to partially default on debt payments toward the end of his term, and, in order to stop the outflow of dollars, he was forced to reinstate an even more restrictive *cepo cambiario* (currency exchange restriction) than during Fernández de Kirchner's government.

During this period, Argentina became one of the world's worst economic performers. Toward the end of Macri's presidency, the plans for "gradualism" and order were outpaced by the situation, and the government had to suspend infrastructure investment programs and improvise emergency measures (including the reinstatement of agricultural export duties in September 2018).

Social policy, aimed at curbing protests, was very active. When Macri took office, he extended eligibility for the Universal Child Allowance to the children of self-employed workers; a short time later, he made the controversial decision to eliminate disability benefits for a significant number of beneficiaries. Early in his presidency, he also established a minimum pension for all senior citizens, although as a counterpart, he canceled the pension moratoriums that until then had enabled access to a full-value retirement pension. However, most social policy was not channeled through expanded rights but through forms of targeted intervention similar to those that had become common in the late 1990s. Social plans for the unemployed proliferated and reached more people than during Fernández de Kirchner's government, which had reduced them.

However, none of this managed to curb the social impact of the economic downturn. Unemployment rose to 9.7 percent and the purchasing power of wages fell by nearly 20 percent; unreported employment also grew, and working conditions worsened overall. Poverty increased in the first half of 2016, declined somewhat the following year, and increased again to around 38 percent in 2019. Inequality became more pronounced. The Ministry of Social Development maintained close ties with the leaders of social movements, channeling much of the social assistance through them, and the Ministry of Labor did the same with trade unionists. The measures managed to keep protest at fairly moderate levels, despite the decrease in the purchasing power of social plans, pensions, salaries, and the Universal Child Allowance.

In 2017, a multiparty majority passed a new law, introduced by opposition groups, guaranteeing gender parity in national legislative bodies. The following year, the government missed a unique opportunity to broaden women's rights. Unexpectedly, in 2018 Macri encouraged his party's legislators to allow the abortion rights bill that the feminist movement had for years been presenting in vain to be debated in Congress.

It is not clear why he did this: at the time, he was personally against women being able to voluntarily terminate their pregnancies and made no effort to rally parliamentary support for it. Some saw the initiative as an attempt to divert attention from growing economic difficulties or to capture some support from the feminist movement. In any case, the bill finally reached the floor, accompanied by massive street demonstrations across the country demanding its approval (there were also demonstrations against it, though they were much less intense).

After a dramatic session on July 14, the bill passed in the Chamber of Deputies with a slim majority, marking a historic milestone. The following month, however, it was defeated in the Senate by a margin of 38:31. A clear regional bias was evident: the regions where the Church still holds the greatest power, the provinces of the northwest and part of Cuyo, were the ones that tipped the scales against the bill, along with the city of Buenos Aires, where most of the senators of the ruling party were Catholics.

The vote divided all the blocs, though unevenly: the parties that most strongly backed the rejection were the UCR and the PRO, while the majority of Kirchnerism was very much in favor of the bill. Senator Fernández de Kirchner, who in the past had declared herself against the right to abortion and had made hostile remarks on feminism, surprised the public with a favorable vote and a change of perspective regarding the movement (she attributed this to her daughter's influence). The enormous expectations that the debate had generated in society and the frustration at the outcome proved to be a strong blow for the women's movement, which nevertheless remained active.

Hopes for an improvement in institutions and republican life were also frustrated. The Macri administration started with an auspicious measure: it placed a skilled professional at the head of the INDEC who, after a few months, recovered the credibility of government statistics.

In other areas, however, decisions were rather detrimental to institutional quality. The fight against corruption focused on cases involving the previous government, but in the handling of its own cases there was complete leniency. Shortly after taking office, Macri and several of his top officials were

Democracy Devalued

involved in the international Panama Papers scandal: the leaks showed that they had companies in tax havens that they had not declared to local tax authorities. The press treated the issue with indifference and the justice system closed several investigations into the matter in record time. Other officials, including the head of espionage and Macri himself, were involved in a variety of acts of corruption that were also not properly investigated. The president's personal friends benefited from public works contracts in a manner similar to the accusations against Fernández de Kirchner, and there were numerous cases of conflicts of interest with officials who came from the business sector making decisions that benefited the companies they came from.

For his part, Macri issued a decree to adjust an aspect of the Anti-Money Laundering Law, which had been approved by Congress in 2016, so that it would exclude direct relatives of government officials. Thanks to that decree, one of the president's brothers, a member of the same family holding company, was able to declare millions of dollars of unknown provenance. In other districts governed by the ruling party, there were also important corruption cases, such as election contributions made under false names for María Eugenia Vidal's campaign.

There was no notable improvement in republican life with respect to other issues either. Immediately after Macri took office, he used an emergency decree to suspend the Audiovisual Media Law enacted by Congress. The authorities of this area (which by law should be independent and their election should not coincide with presidential terms) were forcibly removed and replaced by others loyal to the executive branch. Grupo Clarín was immediately allowed to resume its expansion, which reinforced the already heavy concentration in the media. Additionally, the policy for government publicity and advertising was redirected in a manner that was particularly beneficial to the newspapers, radio stations, and television channels most sympathetic to the government (particularly those belonging to Grupo Clarín). At the same time, a veritable witch hunt took place in the state-owned TV Pública, Radio Nacional, and the news agency Télam. A major purge saw a number of journalists fired, accused simply of being Kirchnerists. Private media also displaced several figures with the same rationale, thus making communications and public debate much less pluralistic. The government used state databases to send personalized messages to the population and invested considerable resources in advertising on social networks. With respect to the latter, several opinion and fake news campaigns powered by legions of automated users were detected, and the government was accused of being behind them.

In terms of policies on the use of repressive measures and human rights, there were significant setbacks. The Ministry of Security was placed in the hands of Patricia Bullrich, who had held senior positions in the de la Rúa government and, before that, had formed part of Menemism. Bullrich changed the protocols governing response to social protests for security forces, reinstating the use of firearms and generally encouraging hard-line tactics. As a result, cases of *gatillo fácil* and institutional violence jumped significantly and crackdowns on demonstrations became more brutal, something that several groups, especially Mapuche activists, experienced firsthand. Bullrich and Macri both went to lengths to publicly defend officers responsible for homicides in what were clear cases of abuse of authority. And specters of false or unverifiable threats to national security were periodically conjured up in order to justify repressive measures.

The government maintained a tense relationship with the human rights movement, which included systematic efforts to discredit it through mid-level officials and like-minded journalists and intellectuals. With unusual urgency, they revived the "theory of the two demons," trivialized the question of the disappeared, and even blatantly defended the last dictatorship. Despite the demands of some within the government, there were no policies aimed at directly hindering the trials of the military officers responsible for the repression during the last dictatorship, although support from various departments was discontinued.

Following a proposal by the Supreme Court justice most closely aligned with the government, in a split decision in 2017, the highest court approved a request to reduce the sentences of a group of prisoners convicted of crimes against humanity. The measure was publicly celebrated by the executive branch but quickly reversed after a massive demonstration in Buenos Aires and a wave of repudiation by organizations and prominent figures from throughout the country and abroad.

The worst institutional decline was seen in the relations between the executive branch and the judiciary. Macri began his presidency by filling two vacancies in the Supreme Court using an unprecedented decree that allowed him to bypass mandatory congressional approval. The two candidates had solid backgrounds but a more conservative profile than the rest. The Court had to refuse to swear them in so that the government would agree to send their nomination papers to the Senate, as required by the constitution. (The Senate ended up approving them under pressure, as they had already been formally appointed.) Additionally, the head of the Public Prosecutor's Office—a supposedly autonomous body—was harassed by the government on a daily basis until she chose to resign. With this, the executive added further influence over prosecutors to its resources, which already included the loyalty of several federal judges.

Dating back at least as far as the Menem administration, the executive branch has had influence over the federal justice system, often through the intelligence services. But previous governments had mostly used this influence to limit investigations of their own people. During Macri's government, the judiciary was used as a battering ram against the opposition. A number of federal judges stood out as notable in their ability to generate cases or duplicate existing ones in order to incriminate Kirchnerist leaders or simply parade them through the courts in front of the television cameras. This was also done to gain the right to tap their phones and record their conversations. Starting in 2015, wiretaps illegally obtained or saved were leaked to the press with growing frequency, which systematically served to discredit Macri's opponents. Hundreds of hours of the personal conversations of dozens of prominent figures within Kirchnerism were released to the public, who learned not only about potential crimes they may have committed but also about their private lives. No government action was taken to limit the practice; on the contrary, Macri reinstated confidentiality regarding the use of intelligence funds, which had been limited by his predecessor. (The Supreme Court barely intervened in 2019 with a lukewarm admonition after some of its members were spied on.)

As part of this new political climate, plausible acts of corruption pending trial were indistinctly mixed with allegations that were new or rehashed for the occasion, some of which were clearly spurious. Due to a new doctrine produced by a magistrate with close ties to the government, certain judges began to make extensive use of pretrial detention—previously applied only in exceptional cases—to jail former government officials or political leaders immediately after indictment, before their guilt had been proven. This power was used in combination with the novel construct of the "repentant participant," established by a 2016 law, to coerce testimonies that could be useful to these cases.

This profound deterioration of the rule of law was noticeable everywhere but especially in Jujuy, where the provincial Supreme Court was expanded to guarantee an automatic majority for the Cambiemos governor. The local justice system was immediately used to place the Kirchnerist social justice leader Milagro Sala under pretrial detention and to keep her in prison for

Chapter 6

years. This measure was denounced by the UN, the Organization of American States, and the world's main human rights NGOs as arbitrary and in violation of basic rights.

In the climate of bitter polarization that accompanied *la grieta*, the government's republican failings were overlooked by its supporters, who also tended to interpret the economic downturn as an effect of the "burdensome legacy" of Kirchnerism. In fact, as the grand illusions that Macri had generated among part of the electorate came face-to-face with reality, *la grieta* was exacerbated.

Supporters of Kirchnerism saw their worst predictions about the government confirmed and grew more bitter toward its followers and the press for their double standards and insincere concerns for the health of the republic. On the other hand, Macrism maintained a firm and sizeable base that found reasons to sustain its hatred of Kirchnerism, blaming it for Macri's missteps, or even—projecting further back into history—blaming the "seventy years of Peronism" that had ruined the country, according to a slogan popularized by the government. Macri and his officials contributed to these tendencies by choosing to address the challenges they faced through extreme confrontation with Kirchnerism and other figures who were supposedly hindering national progress, especially trade unionists. They also blamed their difficulties on several supposed traits of Argentine culture in general, such as *viveza criolla* (criollo astuteness), reliance on the state, and excessive attention paid to the poor and to collective rights or egalitarianism.

This Macrista approach served to intensify something that had already become evident in previous years: people were becoming emotionally distanced from the Argentine nation, perceived as a permanent obstacle to individual fulfillment, as if it were something alien that weighed on their lives. As Macri's main advisor argued, "the enemy is us, our way of life, our customs." The mainstream media also played their part in exacerbating the polarization, in channeling discontent toward those cultural traits and elements, and in feeding national self-denigration—as if, having exhausted the promise of a bright future, the hope was that the urge to embrace the model they were proposing could instead come from contempt for what this country is.

The Reorganization of Peronism and the 2019 Election

Given all these factors, during the final stretch of the PRO government, a sector of the electorate with decidedly right-wing, even authoritarian, ideas, anxious to eliminate "populism" from the scene by any means possible, was given greater presence and visibility. With a view to the 2019 elections, Macri announced that he would run for reelection, and several of his actions were aimed at this segment in particular. A portion of those voters were attracted by an alternative option, an extreme neoliberal, conservative, and authoritarian tendency, which initially supported Macri but later broke away with harsh criticisms. Its main proponents were the economists Javier Milei and José Luis Espert, who had made themselves known thanks to their constant presence in the media and intense engagement in social networks.

Following its defeat in 2015, Peronism had been left divided and found itself in a complex situation. The Kirchnerist branch, under the leadership of Cristina Fernández de Kirchner, remained the most important. The presence of the former president on a ballot guaranteed a third of the vote—a figure that no other Peronist came close to. Yet at the same time, she provoked strong rejection among the rest of the population, which made her an unviable option or, at least, a very risky one.

The effects of Macri's government generated increasing pressure to seek unity; given that the polls revealed no other alternative, several traditionally anti-Kirchnerist leaders of the Peronist Party began to consider backing Fernández de Kirchner as the candidate of a united front that, nevertheless, might lose. Some sectors of Peronism did not rule out the possibility of opting for other candidates.

It was within this context that in May 2019, Fernández de Kirchner made the surprise announcement of a formula in which she would run as vice president, ceding the position of president to Alberto Fernández. The candidate was none other than the former cabinet chief of Néstor Kirchner's government and of the first year of that of his successor. In 2008, Fernández had distanced himself from the government through harsh criticism and had remained in the anti-Kirchnerist Peronist camp until shortly before the surprise announcement. The strategy appeared to be clear: the idea was to generate a formula that would shift the axis of *la grieta* with the combination of Fernández de Kirchner and a politician who was perceived as moderate and an independent thinker, and who was not associated with the most questionable aspects of the previous governments. Alberto Fernández's candidacy also paved the way for an agreement with Sergio Massa, the main representative of anti-Kirchnerist Peronism, who agreed to head the list of candidates for representatives in the province of Buenos Aires. Peronism thus embarked on a path of reunification after more than ten years of divisions.

The move initially upset the Cambiemos alliance, which realized that its strategy to antagonize Kirchnerism had become more complicated. In an inverse move, Macri decided to offer the candidacy for vice president to Miguel Pichetto, head of the senators' bloc of the Peronist Party. Pichetto had gained notoriety for his authoritarian and xenophobic statements and his alignment with Macri's economic policy. In this way, Macri hoped to attract part of the Peronist vote, possibly without losing the loyalty of his more right-wing voters. The UCR, which had hoped to position a vice president of its own, once again accepted being relegated to the margins. Thus, in an unusual event from the point of view of the separation of powers, the ruling coalition ran with a formula that included the person who represented its rival party in the Senate.

The primaries in August represented a major setback for the ruling party: Alberto Fernández won almost half the vote and left Macri sixteen points behind. This shake-up further disoriented the government. The immediate result was a currency run that severely devalued the peso and led to a new surge in inflation, with a consequent increase in poverty. Macri improvised a series of minor redistributive economic measures, but it was too late.

In the October general elections, the Peronist front won in the first round by 48.24 percent of the vote, against the 40.28 percent obtained by the ruling party. In the province of Buenos Aires, María Eugenia Vidal, the PRO's best ticket, was defeated by a wide margin against Axel Kicillof, who won more than 52 percent. By then, the economy had once again plunged into a deep crisis.

The outcome of the 2019 elections presented a novel scenario. The cycle initiated by the 2001 crisis, with the disorganization it had generated in the system of political parties, now appeared to have come to an end. On the one hand, in spite of the dismal results of its first experience in power, the PRO retained a considerable portion of the electorate and its UCR allies were maintained at a very secondary level. All indications are that from now on it will occupy the place previously held by Radicalism as the main draw for the anti-Peronist vote, with the added fact that a good portion of that electoral base—and this is a novelty—now expresses and embraces a more openly right-wing stance. The cycle of the overwhelming hegemony of "progressivism" that began in 2001 seems to have come to an end. On the other hand, Peronism has regained its unity with a rather moderate lineup, in which it is hard to distinguish the more disruptive approach that Kirchnerism had taken. A new bipartisanship appears to be firmly established.

Democracy Devalued

Epilogue

Argentine History over the Long Term

FIVE CENTURIES OF HISTORY. Five centuries of dramatic changes that led to Argentina's current form. Violence and conquests, exterminations and resettlements, resistance and revolutions, imposed traditions and surprising cultural creations, communities that disperse and reassemble, and successive attempts to construct a political and legal order capable of adapting to an ever diverse and heterogeneous population. Progress and setbacks. Brilliant moments of fraternity and of enthusiasm for the collective, and dark times of oppression and despair. All occurred against the backdrop of a world capitalist order that imposes its own imperatives. Retracing the path taken, the traces this has all left on the country are recognizable vestiges of bygone times and of more recent ones as well.

From the colonial order, perhaps the most lasting impact is the hierarchy established among people according to their ethnic origins and physical appearance. Today, descendants of Spaniards, subjugated Indians, Africans initially brought over as enslaved people, the criollos born of the intermingling of them all, and the more recent influx of immigrants from Europe and other regions around the world are bound to each other in all sorts of ways. But in these ties, one can distinguish feelings of superiority and contempt bequeathed by the colony. More than two centuries after the caste system was abolished, which opened up a space of unprecedented legal equality, the class structure of Argentine society still asserts itself on the basis of ethnic-racial differences. Just as in the era of the conquistadors, today the dominant classes still tend to be predominantly white and of European descent, while the poorest and those who are relegated to the worst jobs tend to bear traces of other origins on their skin and in their faces. They are also the most likely to be subjected to state violence. This colonial trait persists with regard to gender as well, reflected in the expectation many men hold of easily accessing the bodies of indigenous girls for casual sex when they go out to *chinitear*, as it is called in the northern provinces. Or the expectation of low-paid domestic labor. Or both at the same time.

Recent genetic studies show that most Argentines today have multiple ancestry. Simplifying this by focusing on only three origins—there are many others—most have indigenous and European ancestors. In fact, an estimated 70 percent of the Argentine population has indigenous ancestry, almost always in conjunction with European ancestry. Whether it is a single indigenous ancestor in the distant past or several and very recent, their genetic contribution is present in more than two-thirds of Argentines today. Along with one or both origins, approximately 8 percent of the inhabitants also have some ancestry from sub-Saharan Africa. There is no doubt that this data reflects an intense process of *mestizaje*, which nevertheless has not involved a little over a quarter of the country's inhabitants, whose genetic markers point to exclusively European ancestry.

These percentages, however, do not give us a sense of the weight of each component in the population as a whole. To give a hypothetical example, millions of inhabitants could share genetic markers from a single indigenous woman who lived four hundred years ago, whose descendants have since borne children only with Europeans. In that case, the current population as a whole would have some genetic traits from that remote ancestor but many more from European ancestry. If the example were different and the contributions of both origins had continued to blend over those four centuries, the relative weight of the genetic markers would be more balanced. Returning

Epilogue

to the current Argentine population, although most individuals bear traces of indigenous genetic contributions, it is estimated that on average in the population's gene pool, European origins represent 66 percent, indigenous origins 31 percent, and African origins 3 percent.

Nevertheless, there are considerable geographic and socioeconomic variations in these percentages: in the most disadvantaged provinces and urban peripheries, and among those with the worst jobs, the non-European component tends to be much higher. In contrast, those of exclusively European ancestry are mostly concentrated in the Pampas and tend to benefit from the best economic opportunities. Map E.1 shows the known averages for some locations.

The heterogeneity and disparities revealed in these data, along with state violence against indigenous peoples and the constant repetition of racist insults in daily interactions and political debates, clearly speak of a society that continues to find it difficult to deal with ethnic differences in a more or less egalitarian manner.

This disconnect was compounded through the narratives proposed by the political and intellectual elites who organized the country. Domingo Faustino Sarmiento's idea of history as a struggle of (European) "civilization" against (native) "barbarism," Bartolomé Mitre's vision of progress radiating from Buenos Aires to an interior that only offered backwardness and disorder, and the positivist intellectuals who blamed the country's ills on racial mixing all contributed to strongly degrading those whose bodies, origins, cultures, or places of residence were less European, less white, less central. The strange myth of the melting pot that would have resulted in a white and European "Argentine race" pushed them into the nation's margins and into outright invisibility. There is no doubt that these visions contributed their share of violence and intolerance to national political life every time citizens exercising their rights produced undesirable effects in the eyes of the wealthier classes or of those who trusted in their projects. This is evidenced in the combination of classism and racism first used to discredit Yrigoyenism, then the Peronist *cabecitas negras*, and, today, the *negros* who fuel "populism."

However, Argentina has also been rich in critical views and cultural *mestizaje* of all kinds, some of which explicitly or implicitly clash with government discourse. In reaction to these exclusionary narratives, Argentine culture has produced alternative visions of the nation and the *nosotros*, the collective "we" that inhabits it. The revival of the gaucho through popular *criollismo*; the dissident readings of history offered by various revisionisms; the reclaiming of

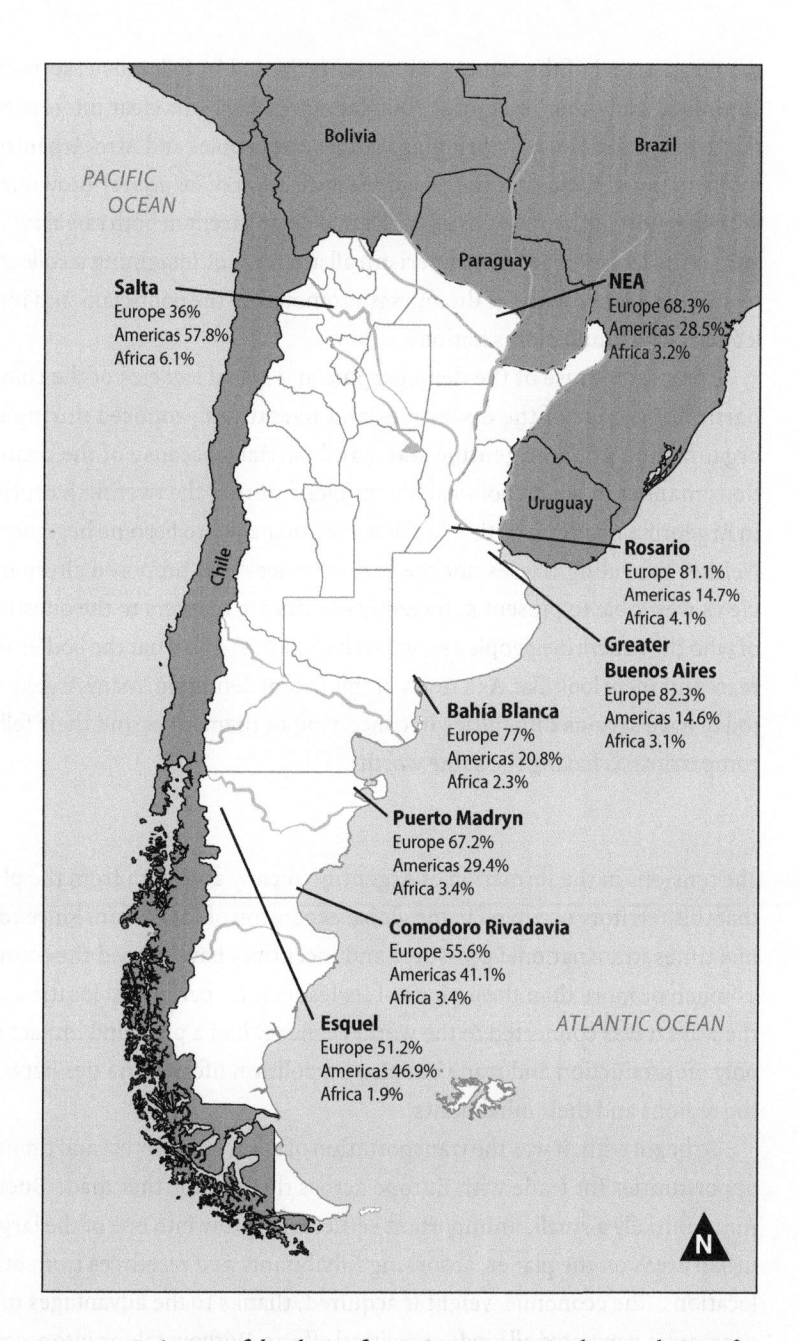

MAP E.1. Estimates of the share of genetic ancestries in the population of various Argentine locations in the early twenty-first century, according to continent of origin. Adapted from Francisco Raúl Carnese, *El mestizaje en la Argentina*.

the mestizo and of the country's interior proposed by folk music, sectors of Peronism, and other provincial political movements; the clear interest over the last several decades in bringing indigenous peoples and Afro-Argentines to the national table; and the proud identification of *los negros*/"brownness" with the most authentic essence of the pueblo apparent in both *cumbia villera* and in the latest form of Kirchnerism: all are ways of imagining a collective "we" in dissidence with the discourses promoted by the politicians and intellectuals who founded this nation.

Partially because of the demographic and social legacies of the colony, partially because of the discourses and narratives proposed during the organization of the Argentine state, and partially because of the contentious manner in which political life unfolded during the twentieth century, in Argentina no vision of this "we" has ever managed to become hegemonic. Neither the ruling classes nor the various voices that proposed alternative views were able to present sufficiently convincing answers to the questions of who the Argentine people are, what their past is, and what the bodies that represent them look like. As a result of this lack of definition, many Argentines today have serious difficulties in conceiving of themselves and their fellow compatriots as having the same worth.

The tensions in the formation of Argentine society also stem from the place that this territory occupied in the global expansion of capitalism. Since colonial times, transnational pressures and incentives have shaped the country as much or more than the actions of its leaders. Its peripheral location and the ways it was connected to the world economy had a profound impact not only on production and trade but also on political life and the ties between the regions and their inhabitants.

To begin with, it was the transportation of silver from Potosí and then the opportunities for trade with Europe across the Atlantic that made Buenos Aires, initially a small, unimportant settlement, grow into one of the largest urban areas on the planet, absorbing inhabitants and resources from other locations. The economic weight it acquired, thanks to the advantages of its geography, generated all kinds of political effects. Without taking into account the influence the city-port gained in the international market, it is impossible to understand the successive conflicts between the capital city and the provinces that began at the time of independence and were precariously resolved through the country's peculiar institutional configuration. Argentina sought to compensate for its deep centralism with a federal system that does not work well with the genuine inequality in the distribution of resources and power. The development of global capitalism thus unfolded in a way that strongly conditioned the possibilities of building a nation with more equally distributed opportunities.

It was also the powerful force of the capitalist world system that, in the nineteenth century, led the country to focus its development on the production of meat and grains. The agro-export model most certainly generated significant income for the nascent republic, but at the same time it deepened the internal regional imbalance. Wealth, human resources, and infrastructure were further concentrated in Buenos Aires and the Pampas, while the rest of the country lagged behind. The overwhelming majority of European immigrants settled in that area, accentuating the ethnic fragmentation of the territory. Furthermore, the type of production that was favored and the way it was organized caused income distribution to rapidly evolve toward a greater concentration of wealth. The country that set national organization in motion benefited its inhabitants very unequally.

Once the agro-export development model was in place, it was very difficult to change. Argentina was incorporated into the international division of labor as a supplier of foodstuffs and an importer of technology and higher value-added products. Given the unequal competition from countries that had been focused on manufacturing for more than a century and had already captured other markets, Argentina's industrial development would be hindered. Early manufacturing growth, which was not insignificant, ran up against the difficulty of capitalizing without having access to foreign markets. The enormous distance that separated the country from the main consumer markets did not help either.

After the 1930s, when the limitations of the agro-export model had become obvious, the state began to intervene in the economy to support industrialization, among other things. However, this introduced a whole new series of tensions, since the resources for it came from an agro-export sector that was not always willing to provide them. The struggle over foreign currency between sectors has been and continues to be an inescapable aspect of the domestic situation and one of the sources of the country's political instability.

In addition to the economic constraints imposed by global capitalism, there were also geopolitical ones. The fact that the United States replaced Great Britain as the hegemonic power in the twentieth century was not a minor detail for the country. Argentina's nascent industrialization, the fact

Epilogue

that the Americans were also food producers, and the early distaste among Argentina's leaders for the imperialist advances of the United States meant that bilateral relations were tense from the beginning. From 1945 onward, the United States frequently interfered in national politics and introduced diplomatic, trade, and investment measures that deliberately sought to disadvantage Argentina. The support the United States gave to the coups d'état and the more liberal or right-wing sectors of Argentine politics—directly or through the IMF—also contributed to economic and political disruption.

Like the rest of Latin America, Argentina's subordinate position in the concert of nations meant that it was subjected to a constant flow of goods and capital to the north, which complicated the local population's prospects for well-being. In a progression that began with metals in the eighteenth century and the harvest of the quebracho forests in the following century, and that continues with open-pit mining, lithium, and fracking today, natural resources have long been extracted for use by other geographical regions. The ecological and social effects of these activities have been very harmful, without clear evidence that they have left any lasting benefits in return. The country has also been fertile ground for constant financial plundering through the eternal servicing of foreign debt, from the Baring Brothers loan to the maneuvers that enriched local bankers and vulture funds during the Mauricio Macri administration. Starting in 1975, domestic factors contributed to this financial drain, at the hands of those who fueled capital flight.

Figure E.1 shows the exponential increase of the foreign debt in the three neoliberal cycles. But it also shows how debt and capital flight were closely connected, since the dollars that came with the former were often those that ended up being captured for the latter: money that leaves as soon as it enters, debt that remains. Argentina's wealthy classes are among those responsible for the most capital flight in the world.

And, just as in the days when it used to sell leather and buy textiles from Manchester, the country now tends to export soybeans and products with little processing and import others with higher added value, which also entails an outward flow of surpluses.

In addition to the disadvantages that all this meant for the population, Argentina's semiperipheral place in the world system added particular tensions. Its economy was developed enough to aspire to its own independent policies but too small to sustain them over time under the imperatives of the global capitalist order. The external focus of part of its ruling classes and its leadership weakened the state and strained political life.

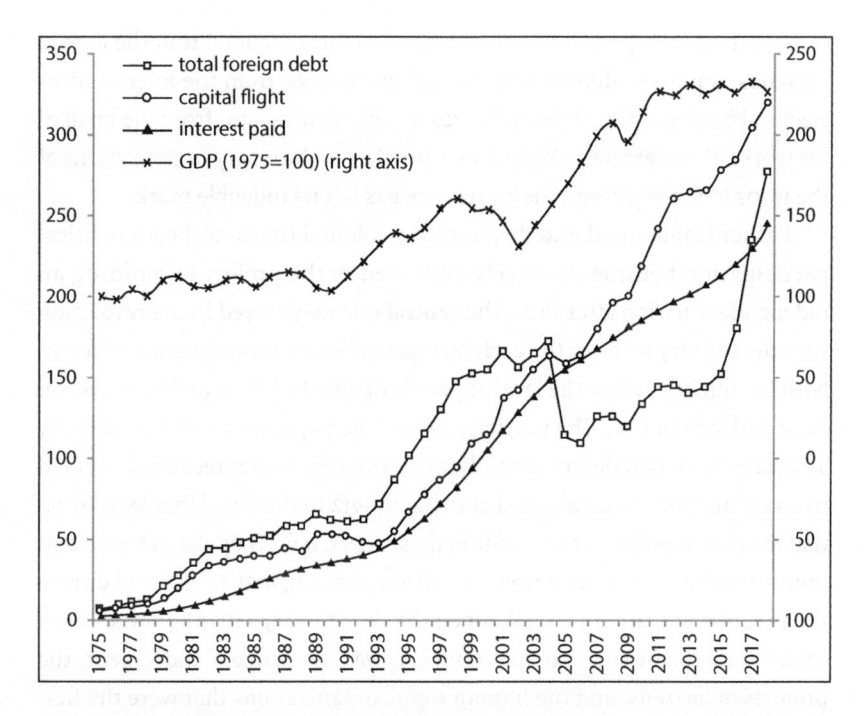

FIGURE E.1. Evolution of the cumulative stock of total foreign debt, capital flight, and interest paid (billions in current US dollars), Argentina, 1975–2018. Leandro M. Bona, *La fuga de capitales en la Argentina* (updated by the author).

Thus, the tendencies of the world capitalist order helped shape Argentine society in ways that made it more difficult, in some respects, to use its resources reasonably and to build harmonious and democratic ties among its inhabitants. It was not the only factor, of course. But neither its impact nor its continuity into the present day can be ignored.

In the face of fragmentation and the situation of subalternity that a highly unequal social system placed them in, within the successive, often exclusionary, political systems, ordinary people strove to build a sense of community and demanded the right for control over their own lives. Although power was not generally in their hands but in those of other sectors, the popular classes and the various oppressed groups managed to leave their mark on society as it developed. If anything characterizes Argentina in comparison with other countries, it is the capacity of its subaltern classes to influence the nation's fate, mobilizing in public spaces, forging solidarity with other sectors, and constructing unexpected social and political movements. From the armed paisanos of independence to the federal *montoneras*, from the Buenos Aires electoral battles of the 1860s and 1870s to early Radicalism, from the birth of the workers' movement to Peronism, from the revolutionary organizations of the 1970s to the *piqueteros*, their presence has left its indelible mark.

Rather fragmented and disjointed in colonial times, plebeian political participation became decisively entwined in the project of building an independent nation after 1810. The central role they played in the revolution gave the country some of the early egalitarian features that characterized it, both in equality before the law for people of all ethnicities and in universal male suffrage in 1821. The participation of the popular classes was directly associated with new democratic advances, from the guarantees implemented to guard against electoral fraud starting in 1912 to the first labor legislation that the state was forced to concede in those years. It was popular pressure that motivated the expansion of welfare policies, starting in the 1930s and during the Peronist era, and that challenged the dictatorships that followed. Even under state terrorism, starting in 1976, it was the workers' movement, the protests of citizens, and the human rights organizations that were the first to speak out and call for an end to the dictatorship. It was also popular pressure that resisted the advance of neoliberal policies during the Carlos Menem administration, that began to question mining and soybean extractivism, and that opened up unimagined political horizons in the aftermath of 2001.

And if Argentina managed to hold its ninth uninterrupted presidential election in 2019—something unprecedented in its unstable history—it was undoubtedly due to the tenacity with which various groups and sectors defended democracy after 1983 and succeeded in defeating, in the streets, the policies of impunity with which various governments sought to benefit the perpetrators of the coup d'état. Similarly, the reclaiming of criollo and nonwhite identities, in terms of both culture and public policy, cannot be understood without considering plebeian mobilization on the part of indigenous peoples and Afro-Argentines.

Meanwhile, overcoming opposition from men of all classes and ethnic groups, it was women who initially proposed women's suffrage and the establishment of equal civil rights for both genders. And today, they, along with sexual and gender dissidents, are the ones who are pushing the rights agenda forward at other levels.

In a variety of ways, the multiple forms of resistance by subaltern groups to authoritarianism, economic exploitation, the patriarchy, racism, the commodification of culture, and the devastation of the environment have left a profound mark on national history.

The fact that the changes associated with popular protagonism were generally of a progressive nature was no guarantee that society would inevitably evolve in that direction. On the contrary, many of the democratic and social conquests were fragile and were occasionally reversed: some sporadically, others in more lasting ways. The country's evolution can be read as a history of constant struggles with results that have been varied, at times unexpected, and always changeable.

From colonial times to the present, the use of class and state violence against subaltern groups has been continuous. At some points, it reached unprecedented levels of brutality; at others, there were more benevolent leaders, but it was meted out incessantly. Following national organization, there were several moments in which popular sovereignty was obstructed and politics remained entirely in the hands of the upper classes. This happened through fraud, in 1880–1916 and 1932–43, and through the military coups that inevitably transpired to counteract the power won by citizens through the vote or by workers through their unions. The military regimes almost always ruled in favor of the upper classes, particularly the bourgeoisie of the export and financial sectors, and the measures they took were antipopular.

Popular sovereignty was also curtailed in informal and less visible ways. Indeed, market forces have always forced changes or measures that would never have been validated at the ballot box. This was especially apparent in the 1970s with so-called globalization, when large transnational companies and corporations everywhere gained decisive power over nation-states. It is important to note, however, that in Argentina their agenda was not imposed solely through economic mechanisms. They were also assisted by political entities (albeit ones free of any democratic control), such as the IMF, and by local sectors that repeatedly intervened to push forward policies rejected by the citizenry.

Over the long term, popular protagonism has generally tended to favor the expansion of rights and greater equality. If at some points in time or in some aspects it contributed to the opposite—such as when it opposed freedom of religion in the first half of the nineteenth century—these were few and far between. On the other hand, the periods in which the upper classes managed to accumulate greater power and shut down or devalue the political game had the opposite effect. Statistics show that the development of the livestock export economy after 1815 was associated with a gradual increase in inequality,

Epilogue

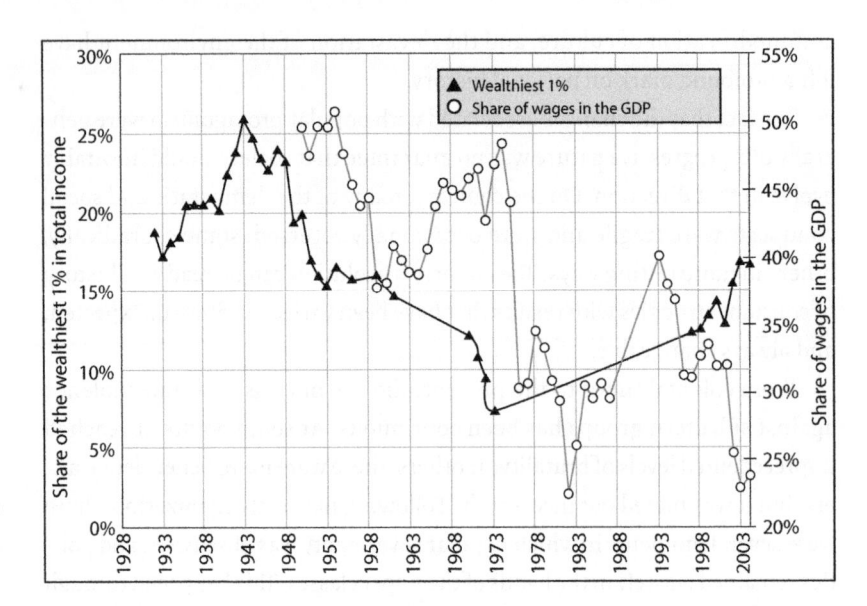

FIGURE E.2. Share of the wealthiest 1 percent of the population in total income and share of wages in the GDP, Argentina, 1932–2004. Facundo Alvarado, "The Rich in Argentina over the Twentieth Century."

which became more pronounced after 1855. The period of greatest political closure, which began in 1880, coincided with an enormous leap in income disparity. By the centennial, Argentine society was more unequal than ever: the enormous growth of the previous decades had benefited the wealthiest more than any other group.

The situation in the following century is even clearer. As figure E.2 shows, the moments of the greatest concentration of wealth in the hands of the wealthiest 1 percent of the population coincide with periods of political closure and/or pro-business economic policies that, in turn, led to a lower share of wage earners in GDP distribution. On the other hand, the two moments of greatest equality, around 1950 and 1974, were associated with periods of significant popular mobilization and heterodox policies (as well as the cycle of declining inequality that took place in the decade following 2002).

Contrary to the assertions of some economists, the increased egalitarianism of those periods did not conspire against growth (at least not in comparative terms). The evolution of Argentina's GDP per capita up to 1975 was comparable to that of today's wealthy countries; it was during that year that the real decline of the local economy began as a result of neoliberal policies. If

Epilogue

TABLE E.1. Evolution of Argentina's GDP per capita and comparison with that of the United States

	1885	1913	1929	1945	1975	2001
Argentina's per capita income (in 1990 dollars)	1,770	3,251	3,763	4,018	7,885	7,940
Argentina's per capita income as a percentage of that of the United States	54%	64%	57%	36%	48%	29%

Source: Pablo Gerchunoff and Lucas Llach, *El ciclo de la ilusión y el desencanto*.

we take the case of the United States—and the comparison is disadvantageous because the yardstick is the world's most powerful nation—the scenario is quite clear (see table E.1). Between 1885 and 1913, at the height of the agro-export boom, Argentina grew more than the United States. In the following three decades, 1913–45, the trend was reversed and the local GDP gradually lagged behind that of the United States. In contrast, in the thirty years after 1945, Argentina doubled its per capita income and expanded its product at rates higher than the United States as well as the United Kingdom, Australia, and New Zealand (although they were surpassed by some European countries). It was not until 1975 that the local economy suffered an abrupt decline and lost ground in comparison with not only the most advanced countries but also practically the entire world. The improvement in income distribution after 2003 was also accompanied by pronounced growth in GDP per capita at rates that surpassed those of the United States (the trend reversed after 2015).

Above all else, the neoliberal policies imposed after 1975 marked a watershed in Argentina's decline, as poverty indicators also attest. Figure E.3 presents the percentage of the population living in poverty, calculated according to the methodology that INDEC adopted after 2016 to make the series consistent. As the graph shows, Argentina had relatively low poverty levels around 1974, and it was after that point that they rose dramatically and irreversibly. The two peaks in the series—corresponding to Raúl Alfonsín's hyperinflation and the 2001 crisis—are directly related to the effects of the policies previously implemented by the military and Carlos Menem–Fernando de la Rúa, the two moments in which the dominance of the interests of the upper classes

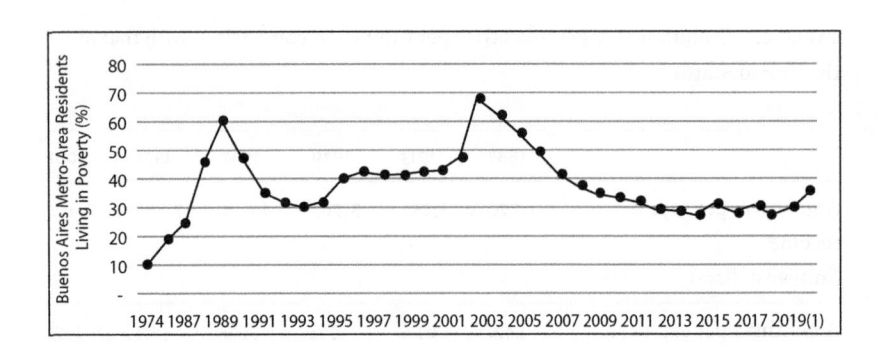

FIGURE E.3. Poverty levels in the Buenos Aires metropolitan area, from 1974 to mid-2019. Prepared by Daniel Shteingart especially for this book. The estimate for 1974 may be slightly understated due to the different demographic structure at the time.

in the national policy agenda were the clearest. The same can be said for the new upward trend of the Macri period. Without claiming to infer universal laws, Argentina's trajectory over the past eighty years shows that there was no contradiction between social mobilization, improvement in income distribution, and growth.

For the reasons outlined in this chapter, the Argentine elites failed to establish a true cultural and political hegemony. The visions they proposed and the models of the country they promoted were never entirely convincing. The political groups they promoted did not attract solid support among ordinary people. In its absence, they used coercion from the outset and military force starting in 1930 as a means of access to a government that the ballot boxes denied them. After 1955, this constant compulsion to resort to coups and brutal repression triggered a spiral of violence that would end up plunging the country into one of the worst experiences of state terrorism on record.

In the second half of the twentieth century, instability and repression were associated with successive attempts to impose orthodox liberal economic measures that society rejected and that ended up being politically unfeasible (often resulting in economic catastrophes). Due to their capacity for resistance and the partial overlapping of interests with part of the middle sectors and the small- and medium-scale business sector, the subaltern classes managed to block these attempts, without necessarily having more solid alternatives to defend. The financial and export sectors stubbornly stuck to the same type of orthodox measures, in a pendulum that swung from one approach to the other. After 1955, Argentina was unable to sustain stable economic policies: Neither good nor bad. Neither improvised nor planned. Neither orthodox nor heterodox.

A recent study undertook the task of analyzing for the first time the tenures of each minister of economy from 1955 through 2018. It reviewed their measures on several fronts and classified them as either "orthodox"—if they followed IMF or World Bank recommendations—or "heterodox," that is, the ones that were not aligned with that vision and instead adopted a developmentalist alternative or one more oriented toward stimulating the domestic market.

The results of the study are revealing, as shown in figure E.4. The dominant feature of the economic policy is the extreme oscillation between the two approaches, with thirty changes of course over the entire period, sixteen of which were abrupt, from one extreme to the other. Until 1989, the average duration of a single approach was just fifteen months, before it would give way to the opposite. Starting with Menem, the cycles lasted longer, with an average of seven years and two months before the pendulum swung in the opposite direction—complete instability.

Overall, the orthodox policies were the most dominant in terms of the length of time they were in effect. Of the sixty-three years analyzed, orthodox policies were in place for thirty-two years and heterodox for twenty-six (periods of "mixed" measures in which no specific approach can be distinguished account for the remaining five years).

What is interesting is that there was not necessarily a relationship between the type of economic policies and the governing party. Orthodox measures clearly prevailed during the dictatorships. Under democracy, both Peronists and Radicals have applied policies of one type or the other at different times (even during the same administration). Of the overall time during their respective mandates, 38 percent of the Peronist Party's periods were of orthodox policies, while the UCR and allied parties applied them 52 percent of the time. Beyond the party that implemented them, a statistical comparison of the relationship between policy approaches and their results shows that orthodox policies have been associated with a decrease in real wages and lower economic growth and that the volatility of the policies has always had a negative impact on investment and growth, regardless of who was in office. In short, in order to understand the performance of the Argentine economy, the specific party is far less important than the specific approach to economic policy.

Epilogue

Therefore, examining the course of Argentina's policies over the long term, there can be no doubt that the predominant vision has been a liberal one. The entire period of national organization, from 1853 onward, was guided by free-market ideas. The state acted decisively to lay the foundations of a capitalist economy, but beyond that the market reigned without any significant regulation for seventy-eight uninterrupted years until 1931, when governments began to apply interventionist policies. During that period, there were no subsidies for industry, foreign exchange controls, interference in foreign trade, export retentions, or anything of the sort. There was not even a Central Bank to manage monetary policy. The result was an economy that not only did *not* bring prosperity to the majority but did not even reach a macroeconomic equilibrium that would allow it to function smoothly. In fact, it was that realization that prompted the ruling elites of the "Infamous Decade"—who were liberal-conservative—to experiment with interventionist alternatives, similar to those that were being applied in many other places around the world at the time since the free market had not been yielding good results in the rest of the world either. If we were to add the entire period in which the market functioned without any significant regulation to the periods after 1955 in which economic policy was guided by an orthodox liberal vision, we would have to conclude that 111 of the 166 years of the organized institutional life of this country have been dominated by that ideology.

With fluctuations and inconsistencies, heterodox policies prevailed between 1931 and 1943 and then, in a more structured way and with a more nationalist vision, until Juan Domingo Perón was ousted. There were twenty-three years in which the public agenda was not dominated by liberal-style measures, although it was not dominated by a single consistent and continuous policy either. However, once the crisis of 1930 had passed, it was one of the periods of greatest growth and prosperity in history. After 1955, the pendulum constantly swung back and forth, with lengthy orthodox experiments during the last dictatorship, under Menem, and under Macri. In all those years, there was only one opportunity for a prolonged heterodox attempt and that was during Kirchnerism.

There is no doubt that instability made sustained growth extremely difficult: each oscillation undid what the previous one had done and attempted to start over again. In a scenario like that, there was no possible rationality in the economic decisions of individuals or companies. As for the results of the various economic approaches, the fact is that none of them has yet been able to show convincing achievements. The orthodox experiment undertaken

Epilogue

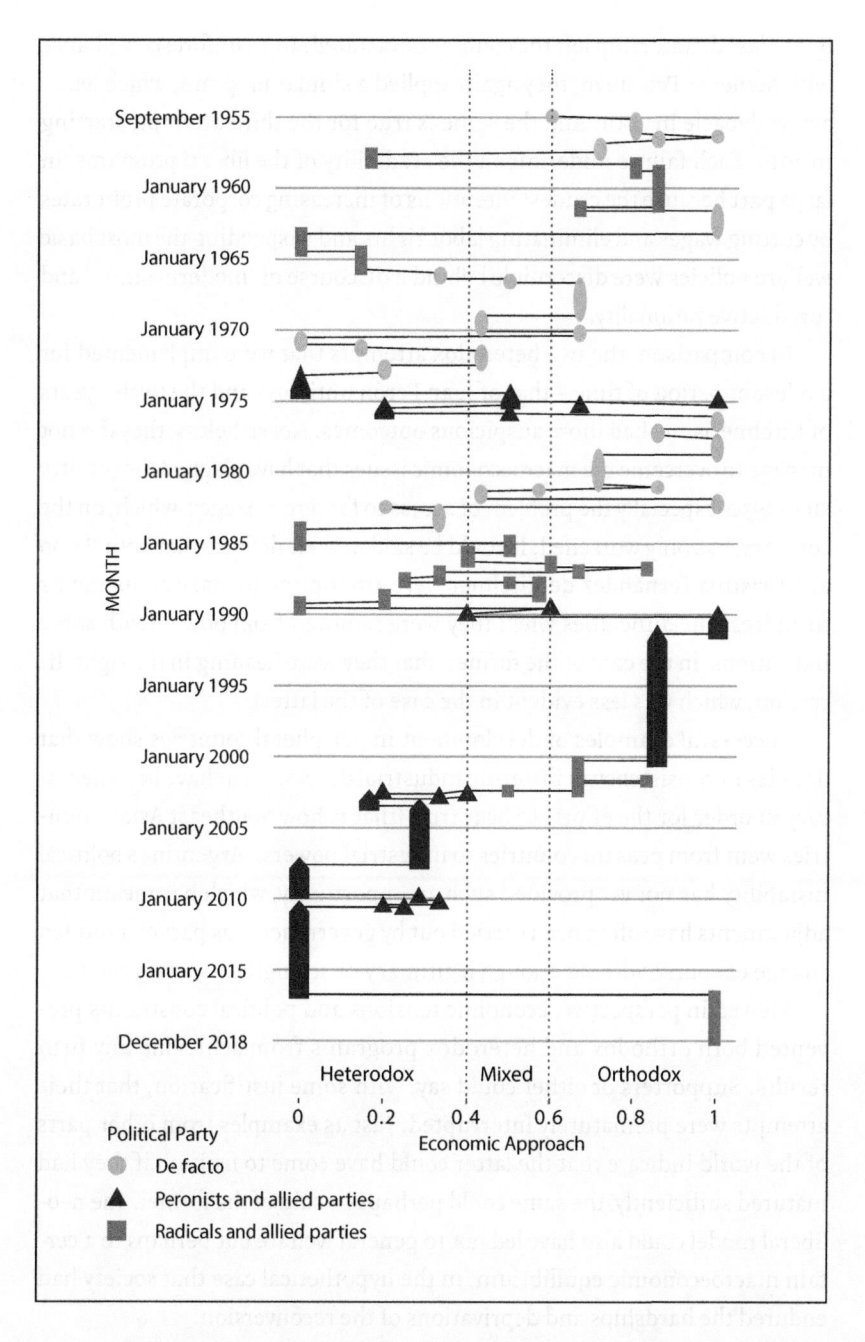

FIGURE E.4. Type of economic policy approach by political party, 1955–2018. Valeria Arza and Wendy Brau, "El péndulo en números."

by the last dictatorship left the country devastated. In an unforeseen alliance with Menem's Peronism, they again applied a similar program, which led to a new debacle in 2001. And the same is true for the third attempt, starting in 2015. Each failure undermined the credibility of the liberal programs, in large part because the crudest intentions of increasing corporate profit rates by cutting wages and eliminating labor rights and suspending the most basic welfare policies were discernible behind a discourse of "modernization" and "productive rationality."

In comparison, the two heterodox attempts that were implemented for a relevant period of time—that of Juan Perón until 1955 and the twelve years of Kirchnerism—had more auspicious outcomes. Nevertheless, they did not manage to overcome the macroeconomic issues that have plagued the country since 1930, especially the problem of access to foreign currency, which, on the contrary, has only worsened. It could be said in their defense that both Perón and Cristina Fernández de Kirchner were attempting to make adjustments to address the difficulties when they were removed from power (with some indications, in the case of the former, that they were heading in the right direction, which was less evident in the case of the latter).

Successful examples of development in peripheral countries show that decades of consistency in fostering industrial development have been necessary in order for the efforts to bear fruit (that is how Southeast Asian countries went from peasant countries to industrial powers). Argentina's political instability has not yet provided such an opportunity, which has meant that adjustments have often been carried out by governments as part of a sudden change of course without enough legitimacy or strength to sustain them.

Viewed in perspective, economic tensions and political constraints prevented both orthodox and heterodox programs from achieving any firm results. Supporters of either could say, with some justification, that their attempts were prematurely interrupted. Just as examples from other parts of the world indicate that the latter could have come to fruition if they had matured sufficiently, the same could perhaps be said of the former. The neoliberal model could also have led not to general welfare but perhaps to a certain macroeconomic equilibrium, in the hypothetical case that society had endured the hardships and deprivations of the reconversion.

But the symmetry of the failures and the conditions that could have prevented them ends when one introduces the question of democracy and the right of citizens to freely define the path they want to take together. This is where the legitimacy of insisting on one economic approach or the other is far from being the same because the impulse toward orthodox models has come more from the upper classes and the pressures of global capitalism than from the desire of the electorate. Certainly, a significant portion of today's voters share these ideas. But, to date, they have yet to form a clear majority. The attempts to impose neoliberal programs have either come from restricted governments and dictatorships or from other governments that won the elections, like Menem and Macri, by hiding their true intentions (or, in any case, as an endorsement for the continuity of a fait accompli, as in the elections of 1995 and 1999). It may be that the Argentine population has not yet found an alternative path and a political party capable of carrying it out in a consistent manner. But it is clear that liberal-oriented programs have already been rejected many times, in the streets and at the polls (although this has not diminished the obstinacy with which the export and financial sectors, the politicians of that ideology, and the agencies of global capitalism have continued to insist whenever they have the opportunity).

Several fault lines have traversed (and still traverse) Argentine society: its productive structure and regional imbalance, the heterogeneous ethnic profile of its population, its gender and class inequalities, the rival narratives about its historical trajectory, and its contrasting economic approaches. Although the origins and logics of these fault lines are different, they have occasionally come together and mutually reinforced each other. After 1945, a new dichotomy was added to them all, dividing the political landscape into two opposite poles: Peronism versus anti-Peronism. Having become identities and possibly even genuine worldviews, they deeply marked national politics over the past seventy years. Like the others, this fault line combined with the rest in complex and sometimes unexpected ways, adding its own frictions to a society that had long been in tension with itself.

Given the heterogeneity of the elements and ideas that constitute it, it is often said that Peronism is incomprehensible. However, in trying to understand it, it is important to remember that this trait is also shared by anti-Peronism. Both poles attract people from the left and the right. Someone can just as easily be a conservative and authoritarian Peronist as anti-Peronist. And the same goes for those who are progressive or even left-wing: some have been attracted by Peronism and some detest it.

The Peronism-anti-Peronism axis cuts across the left-right axis in a way that often confuses unsuspecting observers; between the two, they form a

Epilogue

political code that is very specific to Argentina. This confusion was present from the beginning: in 1945, communists, socialists, liberals, and conservatives came together in their rejection of Perón. Some were concerned that he was a right-wing demagogue; others that he promoted the interests of the workers too much. In the same way, in its early days, Peronism combined a commitment to the workers and to the poor that was typical of the left with elements more typical of the right, such as nationalism and an appreciation for the military, the reestablishment of religious education in schools, and anticommunism. It therefore attracted people from both the right and the left, as well as others, regardless of political leaning, who believed in a strong state capable of intervening in the economy and encouraging class harmony.

What made the Peronism-anti-Peronism axis more enduring was the way it combined with preexisting fault lines and the history of confrontations it has inspired ever since. From the beginning, anti-Peronism viewed the new movement through the lens used by the liberal elites a hundred years earlier: it saw the same poorly eradicated "barbarism" of the past reemerging at the hands of a "caudillo." It also drew on the racist and Porteño-centric interpretation proposed by intellectuals of previous decades: it was the *negros* of the country's backward interior who were once again complicating everything. Thus, anti-Peronism fed into existing tensions regarding the definition of a collective Argentine *nosotros*. Imagining it as white, European, and modern, anti-Peronism was incapable of doing anything but considering the Peronists—not just Perón—an illegitimate presence that had to be eliminated if Argentina were to be Argentina.

Therefore, when socialists, communists, and progressives joined forces with the liberal-conservative upper classes to try to stop Perón's advance in 1945, the rupture this caused was deep. For the workers, for someone to be considered on their side, it was no longer enough to merely talk about social rights, the working class, or socialism. From their point of view, that could be mere discourse, since in reality, those who paid lip service to those ideas often ended up aligning themselves with the wealthiest, making gestures of contempt toward the "uneducated" plebs.

For this reason, the Peronist movement developed its own alternative code to identify who was on which side. Along with concrete proposals made by politicians, the use of specific vocabulary, a series of symbols, and, above all, a particular aesthetics became important. Those who were on "the people's side" could be recognized first by their support for Peronism, their use of party emblems, their constant evocation of Evita and Perón, and the simple and contentious, emotional and occasionally tawdry style that the supporters of the new movement tended to display. A Peronist could be recognized, above all, by their lack of concern for mixing with and being seen among people of plebeian style and appearance. In the eyes of the masses, the aesthetics of Peronism and the way one appeared in public became an equally or even more important way of identifying allies and enemies than the traditional distinction of left and right. Those who embraced this aesthetic were saying that, through it, they recognized the existence of the plebs and showed their willingness to be on their side, even at the risk of being perceived as *negros* by anti-Peronists. And that was no small thing.

The anti-Peronists also paid close attention to aesthetic considerations. Along with the slogans and government proposals, those who cultivated a neat, austere, and urbane style of speech and dress, who were careful to maintain an educated and rational (rather than emotional) image, and who avoided being seen with populist-style leaders, were indirectly saying that they had little to do with the plebs and that they adhered to the values of the "respectable" half of the nation. To be smartly dressed, soft-spoken, and "well mannered" in a scenario that also included plebeian politics was a statement of principle: it was a subtle way of denying them any recognition. This sort of coded language, full of clues and symbols occupying the space of what was not being explicitly said, dominated Argentine politics.

This view of Peronists as not simply a political group one disagreed with but as a residual presence embedded in the nation, something alien, ominous, and morally and aesthetically reprehensible, fueled fantasies of annihilation from early on. There is no doubt that the cycle of state violence that began in 1955 with the bombing of Plaza de Mayo was facilitated by that combination of anxiety and irritation produced by the feeling of sharing the national space with an undesirable half that should not be there, those *cabecitas negras* who came from who-knows-where and were a source of backwardness and irrationality. Could that incredibly brutal event have taken place if the population that was bombed had not been considered inferior, not a legitimate part of an "us"?

The rejection that Peronism and Peronists generated among broad sectors helped justify banning them for eighteen years. But it was also used to gain support for government measures that sought to undo some of the policies implemented under Perón, or even those from as early as the 1930s when the state began to intervene in the economy. Successive attempts to deregulate markets, control union life, and change labor laws were justified in terms of the need to dismantle the Peronist legacy. Anti-Peronism thus often slipped into a more generically antipopular attitude.

As two sides of the same coin, if the existence of Peronism justified broader antipopular attitudes, the outbursts and violence of anti-Peronism also helped the Peronists. From 1955 to the present day, Peronism has regenerated and survived less because of the intrinsic attractiveness of its ideas—which are, in fact, quite changeable—than because it has become a symbol that enables people to rally together to resist the kind of policies that the anti-Peronist bloc promotes when it is in power. It works that way precisely because it is the symbol that, in turn, the anti-Peronists use to mobilize support in their favor, as if it were a game in which it is always advantageous to identify with the enemies of our enemies.

At no time has this been more evident than in the intense re-Peronization that has taken place over the past several years. When the voices that promote orthodox economic policies today disparage an entire country that they refer to as "Peronia," characterized by having not only Peronist inhabitants but also labor rights, trade unions, unemployment subsidies, a Universal Child Allowance, public-sector employment, free education, investment in culture, and a pay-as-you-go pension system—supposedly all obstacles to progress that must be removed—they also inadvertently invite those who view these things not as obstacles but as indispensable elements for a desirable country to identify with Peronism.

Since 1945, Peronism and anti-Peronism have formed a political system of their own. Their actions and the distorted visions of the present and the past that each of them puts forth feed off each other because it is clearly false that all the country's ills are due to "seventy years of Peronism," according to the recently popularized count (as if the Peronists had always applied the same policies and the military and other parties had not governed the country for half that time). If to be a prosperous country it were enough to have export wealth, a largely European population, solid institutions, and freedom from Peronism, then Uruguay should have a much stronger economy than it currently does rather than a per capita GDP similar to that of Argentina, as is the case. There is no doubt that the Peronist governments had many shortcomings. But they cannot be seen as the sole cause of the country's problems. Likewise, to consider anti-Peronism—as many of its opponents do—as the single and perpetual force that has led the country in antipopular directions requires forgetting more than one episode in the history of the Peronist Party itself, such as the "Rodrigazo" or the ten years of Menem's neoliberalism, which led to the worst crisis in recent memory. A more careful reading of Argentina's difficulties—such as the one this book attempts—must go beyond that antinomy.

A great historian, the late Tulio Halperin Donghi, proposed the idea that the second half of the twentieth century had been the "long agony of Peronist Argentina." In his view, Perón had established a model for the country that was economically unfeasible but had such powerful social foundations that it would take decades for it to finally collapse. His thesis is certainly thought-provoking. However, using the same argument, an alternative interpretation can be proposed: that since 1890 we have been witnessing the long agony of liberal Argentina because there are many reasons to suspect that the model for the country established at that time was equally unviable and has since been slowly breaking down.

Of course, in order to sustain either of the two interpretations, one must believe that there was a "normal" and viable path from which Argentina at some point deviated—a path of prosperity and harmony that would have been within reach, had it not been for certain leaders whose decisions were misguided. For many years, comparison with other scenarios could lead one to think that this was the case: the instability and uncertainty of Argentine development and the precariousness of its basic agreements seemed to stand in contrast with the apparent stability of "normal" countries. And yet a quick glance at the present state of the world casts doubt on this certainty. It is by no means evident that the planet is evolving toward greater harmony and prosperity, nor that its situation is stable and its future predictable—in fact, quite the contrary. Perhaps Argentina's abnormality is not, after all, so abnormal but only more premature and pronounced. Could Argentina be a mere chapter in the long agony of capitalism as a global system, an episode unfolding in a particularly peripheral corner of a world that has long been heading toward madness?

Whatever the case, Argentina entered the twenty-first century with all its fault lines exposed, both historic and more recent, intersecting and constantly generating intense and unexpected effects. Moreover, it did so with growing doubts about its place in the world, questioning whether it is or ever really was the exceptional white and European enclave in a mestizo and "brown" Latin America or rather a fundamental part of it. It is clear that economic adversities, the distressing questions that Argentines have about their own country, and everyday divisiveness nurture hardships that are less severe in other parts of the world. But it is no less true that these discomforts also feed that surprising cultural and political vitality that never ceases to reveal itself in the streets and in public debates and in that obstinacy through which Argentine society has sustained, despite its worst adversities, values of solidarity and egalitarianism and a hunger for justice that in other places are scarcely perceptible: As if by disrupting Argentines, they were forcing them to remember that happiness is not a purely individual matter. As if to remind them that the good life will not come from each individual taking refuge in the comfort of their own affairs but rather from the determination with which they support the collective.

SELECTED BIBLIOGRAPHY

This book is a compilation of knowledge generated by historians over the course of decades. The author has contributed historiographical interpretations, the general narrative plot, the writing style, and his criteria for the selection and prioritization of information. With the exception of several topics of the late nineteenth and twentieth centuries, to which he has devoted himself as a researcher, the rest of the contents are based on the findings of others. While it would be very challenging to be exhaustive, below is at least a mention of those to whom he owes the greatest debt.

Chapters 1 and 2

Acree, William. *Everyday Reading: Print Culture and Collective Identity in the Río de la Plata, 1780–1910.* Nashville: Vanderbilt University Press, 2011.

Assadourian, Carlos S., Guillermo Beato, and José C. Chiaramonte. *De la conquista a la Independencia.* 2nd ed. Historia Argentina 2. Buenos Aires: Paidós, 2010.

Chiaramonte, José Carlos. *Ciudades, provincias, Estados: Orígenes de la Nación argentina (1800–1846).* Buenos Aires: Ariel, 1997.

Di Meglio, Gabriel. *Historia de las clases populares en la Argentina, desde 1516 hasta 1880.* Buenos Aires: Sudamericana, 2012.

Di Meglio, Gabriel, and Raúl O. Fradkin, eds. *Hacer política: La participación popular en el siglo XIX rioplatense.* Buenos Aires: Prometeo, 2013.

Estruch, Dolores. *El ejercicio del poder en el Jujuy colonial: Enlaces y tensiones entre la jurisdicción civil y eclesiástica, siglo XVI–XVIII*. San Fernando: La Bicicleta, 2016.

Fradkin, Raúl, and Juan Carlos Garavaglia. *La Argentina colonial: El Río de la Plata entre los siglos XVI y XIX*. 2nd ed. Buenos Aires: Siglo Veintiuno, 2016.

Garavaglia, Juan Carlos. *Construir el Estado e inventar la nación: El Río de la Plata, siglos XVIII–XIX*. Buenos Aires: Prometeo, 2007.

Gelman, Jorge, ed. *La historia económica argentina en la encrucijada: Balances y perspectivas*. Buenos Aires: Prometeo, 2006.

Goldman, Noemí, ed. *Revolución, república, confederación: 1806–1852*. Nueva Historia Argentina 3. Buenos Aires: Sudamericana, 1998.

Goldman, Noemí, and Ricardo Salvatore, eds. *Caudillismos rioplatenses: Nuevas miradas a un viejo problema*. Buenos Aires: Eudeba, 2005.

González Bernaldo, Pilar. *Civilidad y política en los orígenes de la nación argentina: Las sociabilidades en Buenos Aires, 1829–1862*. Buenos Aires: Fondo de Cultura Económica, 2008.

Halperin Donghi, Tulio. *De la revolución de independencia a la confederación rosista*. 4th ed. Historia Argentina 3. Buenos Aires: Paidós, 1989.

Halperin Donghi, Tulio. *Revolución y guerra: Formación de una elite dirigente en la Argentina criolla*. 3rd ed. Buenos Aires: Siglo Veintiuno, 2014.

Ludmer, Josefina. *Gaucho Genre: A Treatise on the Motherland*. Translated by Molly Weigel. Durham, NC: Duke University Press, 2002.

Mandrini, Raúl. *La Argentina aborigen: De los primeros pobladores a 1910*. Buenos Aires: Siglo Veintiuno, 2008.

Míguez, Eduardo. *Historia económica de la Argentina: De la conquista a la crisis de 1930*. Buenos Aires: Sudamericana, 2008.

Myers, Jorge. *Orden y virtud: El discurso republicano en el régimen rosista*. Buenos Aires: Universidad Nacional de Quilmes, 1995.

Rex González, Alberto, and José A. Pérez. *Argentina indígena: Vísperas de la conquista*. 2nd ed. Historia Argentina 1. Buenos Aires: Paidós, 2007.

Salvatore, Ricardo. *Wandering Paysanos: State Order and Subaltern Experience in Buenos Aires during the Rosas Era*. Durham, NC: Duke University Press, 2003.

Santilli, Daniel. *La desigualdad en la Argentina: Apuntes para su historia, de la colonia a nuestros días*. Rosario: Prohistoria, 2019.

Tandeter, Enrique, ed. *La sociedad colonial*. Nueva Historia Argentina 2. Buenos Aires: Sudamericana, 2000.

Ternavasio, Marcela. *Historia de la Argentina, 1806–1852*. 3rd ed. Buenos Aires: Siglo Veintiuno, 2015.

Wasserman, Fabio. *Juan José Castelli: De súbdito de la Corona a líder revolucionario*. Buenos Aires: Edhasa, 2011.

Yankelevich, Pablo, ed. *Historia mínima de Argentina*. Mexico City: El Colegio de México; Madrid: Turner, 2014.

Chapter 3

Adamovsky, Ezequiel. *El gaucho indómito: De Martín Fierro a Perón, el emblema imposible de una nación desgarrada.* Buenos Aires: Siglo Veintiuno, 2019.

Alonso, Paula. *Entre la revolución y las urnas: Los orígenes de la Unión Cívica Radical y la política argentina en los 90.* Buenos Aires: Sudamericana, 2000.

Bandieri, Susana. *Historia de la Patagonia.* Buenos Aires: Sudamericana, 2005.

Barrancos, Dora. *Mujeres en la sociedad argentina: Una historia de cinco siglos.* Buenos Aires: Sudamericana, 2007.

Bohoslavsky, Ernesto, and Germán Soprano, eds. *Un Estado con rostro humano: Funcionarios e instituciones estatales en Argentina, desde 1880 hasta la actualidad.* Los Polvorines: Universidad Nacional de General Sarmiento, 2010.

Bonaudo, Marta, ed. *Liberalismo, estado y orden Burgués (1852–1880).* Nueva Historia Argentina 4. Buenos Aires: Sudamericana, 1999.

Botana, Natalio. *El orden conservador.* 2nd ed. Buenos Aires: Sudamericana, 1985.

Bragoni, Beatriz. *La agonía de la Argentina criolla: Ensayo de historia política y social, c. 1870.* Mendoza: Editorial de la Universidad Nacional de Cuyo, 2002.

Brailovsky, Antonio Elio, and Dina Foguelman. *Memoria verde: Historia ecológica de la Argentina.* 6th ed. Buenos Aires: Sudamericana, 1997.

Briones, Claudia, ed. *Cartografías argentinas: Políticas indigenistas y formaciones provinciales de alteridad.* Buenos Aires: Antropofagia, 2005.

de la Fuente, Ariel. *Children of Facundo: Caudillo and Gaucho Insurgency during the Argentine State-Formation Process (La Rioja, 1853–1870).* Durham, NC: Duke University Press, 2000.

Delrio, Walter. *Memorias de expropiación: Sometimiento e incorporación indígena en la Patagonia, 1872–1943.* Bernal: Universidad Nacional de Quilmes, 2005.

Devoto, Fernando. *Historia de la inmigración en la Argentina.* Buenos Aires: Sudamericana, 2009.

Devoto, Fernando, and Marta Madero, eds. *Historia de la vida privada en Argentina.* 3 vols. Buenos Aires: Taurus, 1999.

Djenderedjian, Julio, Sílcora Bearzotti, and Juan Luis Martirén. *Expansión agrícola y colonización en la segunda mitad del siglo XIX.* Historia del capitalismo agrario pampeano 6. Buenos Aires: Teseo, 2010.

Eujanian, Alejandro. *El pasado en el péndulo de la política: Rosas, la provincia y la nación en el debate político de Buenos Aires, 1852–1861.* Bernal: Universidad Nacional de Quilmes, 2015.

Falcón, Ricardo. *Los orígenes del movimiento obrero (1857–1899).* Buenos Aires: Centro Editor de América Latina, 1984.

Gallo, Ezequiel, and Roberto Cortés Conde. *La república conservadora.* 3rd ed. Historia Argentina 5. Buenos Aires: Paidós, 1990.

Geler, Lea. *Andares negros, caminos blancos: Afroporteños, Estado y Nación. Argentina a fines del siglo XIX.* Rosario: Prohistoria, 2010.

Gil Lozano, Fernanda, Valeria Pita, and María G. Ini, eds. *Historia de las mujeres en la Argentina*. Buenos Aires: Taurus, 2000.

Hora, Roy. *Historia económica de la Argentina en el siglo XIX*. Buenos Aires: Siglo Veintiuno, 2010.

Ladeuix, Joaquín, and Pablo Schiaffino. "El gigante con pies de barro: ¿Fue la Argentina realmente rica? El capital humano durante la primera globalización en una perspectiva comparada." *Revista de Historia Económica / Journal of Iberian and Latin American Economic History* 40, no. 3 (2020): 1–35.

Lobato, Mirta Z., ed. *El progreso, la modernización y sus límites 1880–1916*. Nueva Historia Argentina 5. Buenos Aires: Sudamericana, 2015.

Losada, Leandro. *La alta sociedad en la Buenos Aires de la Belle Époque*. Buenos Aires: Siglo Veintiuno, 2008.

Oszlak, Oscar. *La formación del Estado argentino*. Buenos Aires: Ed. de Belgrano, 1982.

Palacio, Juan Manuel, ed. *Historia de la Provincia de Buenos Aires*. 6 vols. Buenos Aires: Edhasa, 2012–15.

Rocchi, Fernando. *Chimneys in the Desert: Industrialization in Argentina during the Export Boom Years, 1870–1930*. Stanford, CA: Stanford University Press, 2006.

Rocchi, Fernando. "El péndulo de la riqueza: La economía argentina en el período 1880–1916." In *El progreso, la modernización y sus límites 1880–1916*, edited by Mirta Z. Lobato, 15–69. Nueva Historia Argentina 5. Buenos Aires: Sudamericana, 2014.

Sabato, Hilda. *Historia de la Argentina 1852–1890*. 2nd ed. Buenos Aires: Siglo Veintiuno, 2012.

Suriano, Juan, ed. *Nueva historia Argentina*. 10 vols. Buenos Aires: Sudamericana, 2000–2005.

Terán, Oscar. *Historia de las ideas en la Argentina: Diez lecciones iniciales, 1810–1980*. Buenos Aires: Siglo Veintiuno, 2008.

Yankelevich, Pablo, ed. *Historia mínima de Argentina*. Mexico City: El Colegio de México; Madrid: Turner, 2014.

Chapter 4

Acha, Omar. *Crónica sentimental de la argentina peronista: Sexo, inconsciente e ideología, 1945–1955*. Buenos Aires: Prometeo, 2013.

Acha, Omar, and Nicolás Quiroga. *El hecho maldito: Conversaciones para otra historia del peronismo*. Rosario: Prohistoria, 2012.

Adamovsky, Ezequiel. *Historia de la clase media argentina, apogeo y decadencia de una ilusión, 1919–2003*. 8th ed. Buenos Aires: Crítica, 2019.

Adamovsky, Ezequiel, and Esteban Buch. *La Marchita, el escudo y el bombo: Una historia cultural de los emblemas del peronismo, de Perón a Cristina Kirchner*. Buenos Aires: Planeta, 2016.

Amaral, Samuel. *Perón presidente: Las elecciones del 24 de febrero de 1946*. Sáenz Peña: Universidad Nacional de Tres de Febrero, 2018.

Ascolani, Adrián. *El sindicalismo rural en la Argentina*. Bernal: Universidad Nacional de Quilmes, 2009.

Balsa, Javier. *El desvanecimiento del mundo chacarero*. Bernal: Universidad Nacional de Quilmes, 2006.

Barry, Carolina. *Evita capitana: El Partido Peronista Femenino, 1949–1955*. Caseros: Universidad Nacional de Tres de Febrero, 2009.

Bayer, Osvaldo. *La Patagonia rebelde*. 2 vols. Buenos Aires: La Página, 2009.

Bisso, Andrés. *Acción Argentina: Un antifascismo nacional en tiempos de guerra mundial*. Buenos Aires: Prometeo, 2004.

Caimari, Lila. *Perón y la Iglesia Católica: Religión, Estado y sociedad en la Argentina (1943–1955)*. Buenos Aires: Ariel, 1995.

Camarero, Hernán. *A la conquista de la clase obrera*. Buenos Aires: Siglo Veintiuno, 2007.

Cantón, Darío, José L. Moreno, and Alberto Ciria. *La democracia constitucional y su crisis*. 2nd ed. Historia Argentina 6. Buenos Aires: Paidós, 2005.

Carrera, Nicolás Iñigo. *La estrategia de la clase obrera, 1936*. Buenos Aires: La Rosa Blindada, 2000.

Carrera, Nicolás Iñigo, and Jorge Podestá. *Movimiento social y alianza de obreros y campesinos: Chaco, 1934–1936*. Buenos Aires: Centro Editor de América Latina, 1991.

Cattaruzza, Alejandro. *Historia de la Argentina, 1916–1955*. Buenos Aires: Siglo Veintiuno, 2009.

Chamosa, Oscar. *The Argentine Folklore Movement: Sugar Elites, Criollo Workers, and the Politics of Cultural Nationalism, 1900–1955*. Tucson: University of Arizona Press, 2010.

Cortés Conde, Roberto. *The Political Economy of Argentina in the Twentieth Century*. Cambridge: Cambridge University Press, 2009.

del Campo, Hugo. *Sindicalismo y peronismo*. Buenos Aires: Consejo Latinoamericano de Ciencias Sociales, 1983.

Doyon, Louise M. *Perón y los trabajadores*. Buenos Aires: Siglo Veintiuno, 2006.

Elena, Eduardo. *Dignifying Argentina: Peronism, Citizenship, and Mass Consumption*. Pittsburgh: University of Pittsburgh Press, 2011.

Frydenberg, Julio. *Historia social del fútbol: Del amateurismo a la profesionalización*. Buenos Aires: Siglo Veintiuno, 2013.

Gené, Marcela. *Un mundo feliz: Imágenes de los trabajadores en el primer peronismo, 1946–1955*. Buenos Aires: Fondo de Cultura Económica, 2005.

Girbal de Blacha, Noemí. *Estado, chacareros y terratenientes (1916–1930)*. Buenos Aires: Centro Editor de América Latina, 1988.

Goebel, Michael. *Argentina's Partisan Past: Nationalism and the Politics of History*. Liverpool: Liverpool University Press, 2011.

Healey, Mark A. *The Ruins of the New Argentina: Peronism and the Remaking of San Juan after the 1944 Earthquake*. Durham, NC: Duke University Press, 2011.

Horowitz, Joel. *Argentina's Radical Party and Popular Mobilization, 1916–1930*. University Park: Pennsylvania State University Press, 2008.

Karush, Matthew. *Culture of Class: Radio and Cinema in the Making of a Divided Argentina, 1920–1946*. Durham, NC: Duke University Press, 2012.

Karush, Matthew, and Oscar Chamosa, eds. *The New Cultural History of Peronism: Power and Identity in Mid-Twentieth-Century Argentina*. Durham, NC: Duke University Press, 2010.

Kindgard, Adriana M. "Procesos sociopolíticos nacionales y conflictividad regional: Una mirada alternativa a las formas de acción colectiva en Jujuy en la transición al peronismo." *Entrepasados* 22 (2002): 67–87.

Korzeniewicz, Roberto P. "Las vísperas del peronismo: Los conflictos laborales entre 1930 y 1943." *Desarrollo Económico* 33, no. 131 (1993): 323–54.

Lobato, Mirta Z. *Historia de las trabajadoras en la Argentina (1869–1960)*. Buenos Aires: Edhasa, 2007.

Mackinnon, Moira. *Los años formativos del Partido Peronista (1946–1950)*. Buenos Aires: Siglo Veintiuno, 2002.

Macor, Darío, and César Tcach, eds. *La invención del peronismo en el interior del país*. Santa Fe: Universidad Nacional del Litoral, 2003.

Milanesio, Natalia. *Workers Go Shopping in Argentina: The Rise of Popular Consumer Culture*. Albuquerque: University of New Mexico Press, 2013.

Nállim, Jorge. *Transformations and Crisis of Liberalism in Argentina, 1930–1955*. Pittsburgh: University of Pittsburgh Press, 2012.

Palacio, Juan Manuel. *La justicia peronista: La construcción de un nuevo orden legal en la Argentina*. Buenos Aires: Siglo Veintiuno, 2018.

Plotkin, Mariano Ben. *Mañana es San Perón: A Cultural History of Perón's Argentina*. Translated by Keith Zahniser. Wilmington, DE: Scholarly Resources, 2003.

Rein, Raanan. *Peronismo, populismo y política: Argentina, 1943–1955*. Buenos Aires: Editorial de Belgrano, 1998.

Rock, David. *Authoritarian Argentina: The Nationalist Movement, Its History, and Its Impact*. Berkeley: University of California Press, 1993.

Rock, David. *Politics in Argentina, 1890–1930: The Rise and Fall of Radicalism*. Cambridge: Cambridge University Press, 1975.

Romero, Luis Alberto. *A History of Argentina in the Twentieth Century*. Translated by James P. Brennan. University Park: Pennsylvania State University Press, 2002.

Saítta, Sylvia. *Regueros de tinta: El diario "Crítica" en la década de 1920*. Buenos Aires: Sudamericana, 1998.

Torre, Juan Carlos. *La vieja guardia sindical y Perón*. Buenos Aires: Sudamericana, 1990.

Valko, Marcelo. *Los indios invisibles del Malón de la Paz*. Buenos Aires: Ediciones Madres de Plaza de Mayo, 2007.

Chapter 5

Belini, Claudio. *Historia de la industria en la Argentina: De la independencia a la crisis de 2001*. Buenos Aires: Sudamericana, 2017.

Brennan, James. *Argentina's Missing Bones: Revisiting the History of the Dirty War*. Oakland: University of California Press, 2018.

Brennan, James, and Mónica Gordillo. *Córdoba rebelde*. La Plata: De la Campana, 2008.

Carnovale, Vera. *Los combatientes*. Buenos Aires: Siglo Veintiuno, 2011.

Cavarozzi, Marcelo. *Autoritarismo y democracia (1955–2006)*. Buenos Aires: Ariel, 2006.

Cosse, Isabella. *Pareja, sexualidad y familia en los años sesenta*. Buenos Aires: Siglo Veintiuno, 2011.

De Riz, Liliana. *La política en suspenso, 1966–1976*. Historia Argentina 8. 2nd ed. Buenos Aires: Paidós, 2010.

Diamand, Marcelo. "El péndulo argentino: ¿Hasta cuándo?" *Cuadernos del Centro de Estudios de la Realidad Económica* 1 (1985): 1–39.

Ferrara, Francisco. *Los de la tierra: De las ligas agrarias a los movimientos campesinos*. Buenos Aires: Tinta Limón, 2007.

Franco, Marina. *Un enemigo para la Nación: Orden interno, violencia y "subversión," 1973–1976*. Buenos Aires: Fondo de Cultura Económica, 2012.

Gillespie, Richard. *Soldiers of Peron: Argentina's Montoneros*. New York: Oxford University Press, 1982.

Gordillo, Gastón, and Silvia Hirsch, eds. *Movilizaciones indígenas e identidades en disputa en la Argentina*. Buenos Aires: La Crujía, 2010.

James, Daniel. *Resistance and Integration: Peronism and the Argentine Working Class, 1946–1979*. Cambridge: Cambridge University Press, 1988.

Lorenz, Federico. *Las guerras por Malvinas*. Buenos Aires: Edhasa, 2006.

Luzzi, Mariana, and Ariel Wilkis. *El dólar: Historia de una moneda argentina (1930–2019)*. Buenos Aires: Crítica, 2019.

Manzano, Valeria. *The Age of Youth in Argentina: Culture, Politics, and Sexuality from Perón to Videla*. Chapel Hill: University of North Carolina Press, 2014.

Melon Pirro, Julio. *El peronismo después del peronismo*. Buenos Aires: Siglo Veintiuno, 2009.

Murmis, Miguel, and Juan Carlos Portantiero. *Estudios sobre los orígenes del peronismo*. Buenos Aires: Siglo Veintiuno, 2004.

Novaro, Marcos. *Historia de la Argentina, 1955–2010*. 4th ed. Buenos Aires: Siglo Veintiuno, 2016.

O'Donnell, Guillermo. *Bureaucratic Authoritarianism: Argentina, 1966–1973, in Comparative Perspective*. Berkeley: University of California Press, 1988.

Potash, Robert A. *The Army and Politics in Argentina*. 3 vols. Stanford, CA: Stanford University Press, 1969–96.

Pozzi, Pablo. *Oposición obrera a la dictadura, 1976–1982*. Buenos Aires: Contrapunto, 1988.

Rapoport, Mario. *Historia económica, política y social de la Argentina (1880–2000)*. Buenos Aires: Macchi, 2000.
Salas, Ernesto. *Uturuncos: El origen de la guerrilla peronista*. 2nd ed. Buenos Aires: Biblos, 2006.
Schneider, Alejandro. *Los compañeros: Trabajadores, izquierda y peronismo, 1955–1973*. Buenos Aires: Imago Mundi, 2005.
Schvarzer, Jorge. *La industria que supimos conseguir: Una historia político-social de la industria argentina*. Buenos Aires: Planeta, 1996.
Tarcus, Horacio. *El marxismo olvidado en la Argentina*. Buenos Aires: El Cielo por Asalto, 1996.
Torrado, Susana, ed. *Población y bienestar en la Argentina del primero al segundo centenario*. 2 vols. Buenos Aires: Edhasa, 2007.
Werner, Ruth, and Facundo Aguirre. *Insurgencia obrera en la Argentina, 1969–1976*. Buenos Aires: Ediciones IPS, 2007.
Ziccardi, Alicia. "El tercer gobierno peronista y las villas miseria de la ciudad de Buenos Aires (1973–1976)." *Revista Mexicana de Sociología* 46, no. 4 (1984): 145–72.

Chapter 6 and Epilogue

Adamovsky, Ezequiel. *El cambio y la impostura: La derrota del kirchnerismo, Macri y la ilusión PRO*. Buenos Aires: Planeta, 2017.
Alabarces, Pablo. *Fútbol y patria*. 4th ed. Buenos Aires: Prometeo, 2008.
Alabarces, Pablo, and María Graciela Rodríguez, eds. *Resistencias y mediaciones*. Buenos Aires: Paidós, 2008.
Alvaredo, Facundo. "The Rich in Argentina over the Twentieth Century, 1932–2004." In *Top Incomes: A Global Perspective*, edited by A. B. Atkinson and Thomas Piketty, 253–98. Oxford: Oxford University Press, 2010.
Arza, Valeria, and Wendy Brau. "El péndulo en números: Un análisis cuantitativo de los vaivenes de la política económica en Argentina entre 1955 y 2018." *Desarrollo Económico* 61, no. 233 (2021): 1–29.
Auyero, Javier. *Poor People's Politics: Peronist Survival Networks and the Legacy of Evita*. Durham, NC: Duke University Press, 2001.
Auyero, Javier. *Routine Politics and Violence in Argentina: The Gray Zone of State Power*. Cambridge: Cambridge University Press, 2007.
Basualdo, Eduardo, ed. *Endeudar y fugar: Un análisis de la historia económica Argentina de Martínez de Hoz a Macri*. Buenos Aires: Siglo Veintiuno, 2017.
Bellucci, Mabel. *Historia de una desobediencia: Aborto y feminismo*. Buenos Aires: Capital Intelectual, 2014.
Bohoslavsky, Ernesto, and Marina Franco. "Elementos para una historia de las violencias estatales en la Argentina en el siglo XX." *Boletín del Instituto de Historia Argentina y Americana "Dr. Emilio Ravignani"* 53 (2020): 205–27.

Bona, Leandro M. *La fuga de capitales en la Argentina: Sus transformaciones, alcances y protagonistas desde 1976*. Documento de trabajo 24 del Área de Economía y Tecnología. Buenos Aires: Facultad Latinoamericana de Ciencias Sociales, 2018.

Carnese, Francisco Raúl. *El mestizaje en la Argentina: Indígenas, europeos y africanos: Una mirada desde la antropología biológica*. Buenos Aires: Editorial de la Facultad de Filosofía y Letras, Universidad de Buenos Aires, 2019.

CORREPI. "Archivo de casos de gatillo fácil." Accessed May 3, 2023. http://www.correpi.org/archivo-de-casos/.

Crenzel, Emilio. *The Memory of the Argentina Disappearances: The Political History of Nunca Más*. Translated by Laura Pérez Carrara. New York: Routledge, 2012.

Gerchunoff, Pablo, and Lucas Llach. *El ciclo de la ilusión y el desencanto: Un siglo de políticas económicas argentinas*. Buenos Aires: Ariel, 1998.

Grimson, Alejandro. *¿Qué es el peronismo? De Perón a los Kirchner, el movimiento que no deja de conmover la política argentina*. Buenos Aires: Siglo Veintiuno, 2019.

Halperin Donghi, Tulio. *La larga agonía de la Argentina peronista*. 3rd ed. Buenos Aires: Ariel, 1998.

Horowicz, Alejandro. *Los cuatro peronismos*. Buenos Aires: Planeta, 1991.

Kessler, Gabriel. *El sentimiento de inseguridad*. Buenos Aires: Siglo Veintiuno, 2009.

Lapegna, Pablo. *Soybeans and Power: Genetically Modified Crops, Environmental Politics, and Social Movements in Argentina*. New York: Oxford University Press, 2016.

Levitsky, Steven. *Transforming Labor-Based Parties in Latin America: Argentine Peronism in Comparative Perspective*. Cambridge: Cambridge University Press, 2003.

López, Artemio, and Martín Romeo. *La declinación de la clase media argentina: Transformaciones en la estructura social, 1974–2004*. Buenos Aires: Libros de Equis, 2005.

Manzanal, Mabel, and Federico Villarreal, eds. *El desarrollo y sus lógicas en disputa en territorios del norte argentino*. Buenos Aires: Centro de Integración, Communicación, Cultura y Sociedad, 2010.

Míguez, Daniel, and Pablo Semán, eds. *Entre santos, cumbias y piquetes*. Buenos Aires: Biblos, 2006.

Morgenfeld, Leandro. *Vecinos en conflicto: Argentina y Estados Unidos en las Conferencias Panamericanas (1880–1955)*. Buenos Aires: Ediciones Continente, 2011.

Ostiguy, Pierre. "Peronism and Anti-Peronism: Class-Cultural Cleavages and Political Identity in Argentina." PhD diss., University of California, Berkeley, 1998.

Pucciarelli, Alfredo, and Ana Castellani, eds. *Los años del kirchnerismo*. Buenos Aires: Siglo Veintiuno, 2017.

Quirós, Julieta. *Cruzando la Sarmiento*. Buenos Aires: Antropofagia, 2006.

Ranis, Peter. *Argentine Workers: Peronism and Contemporary Class Consciousness*. Pittsburgh: University of Pittsburgh Press, 1992.

Rouquié, Alain. *El siglo de Perón: Ensayo sobre las democracias hegemónicas*. Buenos Aires: Edhasa, 2017.

Schuster, Federico, et al. *Transformaciones de la protesta social en Argentina, 1989–2003*. Documento de Trabajo 48. Buenos Aires: Instituto Gino Germani, 2006.

Segato, Rita. *La nación y sus otros*. Buenos Aires: Prometeo, 2007.

Semán, Pablo, and Pablo Vila, eds. *Youth Identities and Argentine Popular Music: Beyond Tango*. New York: Palgrave Macmillan, 2012.

Svampa, Maristella. *La sociedad excluyente*. Buenos Aires: Taurus, 2005.

Svampa, Maristella, and Sebastián Pereyra. *Entre la ruta y el barrio*. Buenos Aires: Biblos, 2003.

Vommaro, Gabriel. *La larga marcha de Cambiemos*. Buenos Aires: Siglo Veintiuno, 2017.

Zack, Guido, Daniel Schteingart, and Federico Favata. "Pobreza e indigencia en Argentina: Construcción de una serie completa y metodológicamente homogénea." *Sociedad y economía* 40 (2020): 69–98.

Zibechi, Raúl. *Genealogía de la revuelta*. La Plata: Letra Libre, 2003.

INDEX

abortion, 280–81, 293
Acción Argentina, 147, 155
Acción Católica, 149, 176
Administradoras de Fondos de Jubilaciones y Pensiones (AFJP), 240, 248, 275
Aerolíneas Argentinas, 275
Affirmation for an Egalitarian Republic (ARI), 266
Afirmación para una República Igualitaria (ARI), 266
Africa/Africans, 21–22, 26, 70, 78, 90, 101, 114, 126, 128, 196, 205, 301–3
Afro-Argentines, 59, 78–79, 99, 120, 125–26, 255, 276, 304, 308
Agrarian Leagues, 200
Agrarian Movement of Misiones, 259
agriculture, 3–5, 12, 18–20, 30, 103–7, 112, 115, 142–145, 177, 193, 213, 224, 235, 241, 258–59, 265, 267, 273–75, 282, 289, 292
A la Ciudad de Londres, 115
Alberdi, Juan Bautista, 73–74, 84, 86–89, 96, 130, 176
Aldao, José Félix, 64

Alem, Leandro N., 112, 130
Alemann, Roberto, 220, 236
Alfonsín, Raúl, 226–38, 242, 248–49, 251, 279, 311
Alianza (political coalition), 238, 245, 260–61
Alianza de la Juventud Nacionalista / Alianza Libertadora Nacionalista, 148
Aljaba, La (newspaper), 80
Allende, Salvador, 206
All for the Fatherland Movement, 233
Alsina, Adolfo, 96, 98, 101
Alsina, Valentín, 82
Alsogaray, Álvaro, 187, 189, 216, 236–37, 239
Álvarez, Agustín, 124
Álvarez, Carlos "Chacho," 260
Álvarez Jonte, Antonio, 49
Álvarez Thomas, Ignacio, 51
Alvear (family), 113
Alvear, Carlos de, 50–51, 55
Alvear, Marcelo Torcuato de, 138, 141–42
Álzaga, Martín de, 44, 57

anarchism, 122–23, 128, 135–37, 140, 146–47, 153–54, 173
Anchorena (family), 113
Angeloz, Eduardo, 236–37
antifascism, 147, 154–55
anti-imperialism, 147, 149, 185, 196, 203
anti-Peronism, 157, 160, 171, 173–77, 179–87, 190, 200–201, 207, 226, 239, 273, 284, 299, 317–20
Antilles, 34
Aramburu, Pedro Eugenio, 182, 184, 197
Araucanians, 30
Areco, 30
Argentina (name/identity), 60, 67, 103–8, 123–28, 149–50, 172, 175–77, 252–55, 276, 300–304, 317–22
Argentine Agrarian Federation, 134
Argentine Airlines, 275
Argentine Business Council, 220, 222
Argentine Feminist Union, 202
Argentine Homosexual Community (CHA), 279
Argentine Institute for the Promotion of Trade (IAPI), 164, 184
Argentine Jewish Mutual Aid Association (AMIA), 243, 285
Argentine Radical Youth Force (FORJA), 147, 170
Argentine Regional Workers' Federation (FORA), 121–22, 136, 153
Argentine Revolution, 192
Argentine Syndicates' Union (USA), 153
Argentine Workers Movement (MTA), 256
Arlt, Roberto, 146
armed forces, 45–47, 53–54, 57, 59, 68, 73, 90–92, 95–99, 102, 112, 137, 139–41, 148–49, 155, 166, 177, 179, 181–84, 187–90, 195, 217–33, 243–45, 270, 309, 311–12
Artigas, José, 45, 49–53, 58, 79
artisanal production, 19–20, 26–27, 63, 70, 75, 77, 108
Ascasubi, Hilario, 80
Asia, 70, 101, 196, 267, 316

Asociación de Trabajadores del Estado (ATE), 256–57
Asociación Mutual Israelita Argentina (AMIA), 243, 285
Assembly of the Year XIII, 49, 60
Association of Argentine Banks, 222
Association of Government Employees (ATE), 256–57
Asunción, 8, 12–13, 48
Australia, 281, 311
Austral Plan, 235, 239
Avás, 5, 13
Avellaneda (family), 113
Avellaneda, Nicolás, 91, 98–99, 101
Aymara, 54
Azules and Colorados, 190
Azurduy, Juana, 46, 59

Balbín, Ricardo, 186, 217, 226, 242
Banda Oriental. *See* Uruguay
bandeirantes, 18
banks, 221–22, 224, 260–61, 263, 265, 272
Baring Brothers, 65, 306
Barranca Yaco, 70
barter clubs, 260–61
Battle of Ayacucho, 47
Battle of Caseros, 81, 183, 186
Battle of Cepeda (1820), 53; (1859), 83
Battle of Pavón, 84, 90
Battle of Pozo de Vargas, 97
Battle of Vuelta de Obligado, 74
Beagle Channel, 224, 234
Belén, 259
Belgium, 105
Belgrano (town), 99
Belgrano, Manuel, 38, 43, 46, 53, 60, 124
Benítez, Francisco, 58
Berkeley, 201
Berlin, 238
Bernal, 260
Bignone, Reynaldo, 225–26, 270
Binner, Hermes, 277
bisexuality, 280
Boers, 114

Bogotá, 43
Bohorques, Pedro, 29
Bolívar, Simón, 47
Bolivia/Bolivians, 1–2, 7, 10, 22, 29, 33, 43, 45–46, 51, 54, 56, 59, 62, 72, 75, 193
Bolsonaro, Jair, 291
Bonaparte, Napoleon and Joseph, 40–41
Bordabehere, Enzo, 142
Borges, Jorge Luis, 146
Bourbons, 32, 35–36, 38, 60
Braden, Spruille, 161
Bramuglia, Juan Atilio, 190
Brazil, 1, 18, 21, 38, 42, 58, 67–69, 75, 81, 95, 103, 155–56, 267, 269, 272, 291
Bretton Woods, 215
British invasions, 39–40, 55
Buenos Aires, 8, 12, 16, 19, 22, 25–30, 32–36, 38–39, 42–48, 50–55, 57–59, 62–70, 73–84, 89–90, 92–94, 96–100, 108, 112–15, 121–24, 145–46, 150–51, 243–45, 262–64, 302–5
Buenos Aires Stock Exchange, 112, 222
Bulgheroni, 221
Bullrich (family), 113
Bullrich, Patricia, 295
Bunge, Carlos Octavio, 124
Bunge y Born, 221, 224, 239
businesspeople, 163, 185, 191, 207, 210, 212, 214, 216, 222, 224, 227, 234, 237, 265, 286–87
Bussi, Antonio, 251
Bustos, Juan Bautista, 64

Caballero, Ricardo, 133
cabildos, 15, 22, 28, 31, 35, 39–40, 42–44, 48, 50, 53, 55, 59, 64–65
cacerolazos, 263–64, 273
Cachul, 77
Cádiz, 41, 48–49
Cafiero, Antonio, 237
Calchaquí, Juan, 13
Calchaquí people, 3, 13–14, 29, 56
Calfucurá, 77, 100
Cambiemos, 286–88, 296, 299

Campesino Movement of Santiago del Estero (MOCASE), 259
Cámpora, Héctor, 205, 207–8, 274
Canada, 105, 107
candombe, 78, 172
Cané, Miguel, 124
Cañete, 13
Cantoni, Federico / Cantonism, 133
Cape Verde, 114
capitalism, 6–7, 21, 88, 109, 119–20, 143, 146, 196–97, 200, 214, 221, 238, 304–5, 317, 321
captives, 12, 30, 101
Caracas, 43
carapintadas, 232–33, 243
Carios, 13
Carlés, Manuel, 136
Carlota, Infanta de Borbón, 42
Carnival, 31, 36, 78, 117, 151, 219
Carrasco, Omar, 259
Carrillo, Ramón, 165
Carrió, Elisa, 266, 272, 277, 286–87
Casilda, 195
Castelli, Juan José, 43, 45–46, 56
caste system, 22–25, 27–28, 36, 40, 60, 301
Castillo, Alberto, 172
Castillo, Ramón, 142, 155
Catamarca, 24, 31, 34, 47, 69–70, 74, 97, 107, 109, 114, 153, 190, 235, 259
Catholic Church, 6, 10, 17–19, 79, 85, 93–94, 179–80, 197, 225, 254–55
Catriel, 77, 98
cattle ranching, 20, 31, 35–36, 62, 65, 70, 88, 105–6, 109, 132, 142
caudillos, 50, 53, 64, 67, 69–71, 79, 83, 90, 94, 97–98, 124, 128, 149, 157, 174, 176–77, 237, 318
Cavallo, Domingo, 239–40, 245, 260–62
Central Bank, 144, 164, 220, 239, 282, 290–91, 314
Central de Trabajadores de la Argentina (CTA), 257–58, 262
Central Federation of Argentine Workers (CTA), 257–58, 262

Index

Central Junta, 41–43
Cevallos, Pedro de, 33
Chaco, 1, 3, 5, 11, 13–14, 21, 31, 51, 57, 77, 101–3, 109, 115–16, 138–39, 178, 195, 200, 235, 259
Chalemín, 29
chamamé, 172, 205
Chamber of Commerce, 222
Chané, 5
Charles III, 33
Charles IV, 40–42
Chascomús, 30
Chávez, Hugo, 269
Chicago boys, 220, 239
Chichas, 13
Chiclana, Feliciano, 48
Chile/Chileans, 10, 15, 22, 30, 33, 43, 46–47, 53–54, 58, 75, 91, 103, 137, 193, 206–7, 220, 224, 234
China, 269, 291
Christian Democrats, 245
Chuquisaca, 38
cinema, 150–52, 169, 205, 233
Cipolletti, 195
circus, 127, 150
Cisneros, Baltasar Hidalgo de, 42–43
Civic Coalition, 272
Civic Union, 112
civilization, 22, 70, 87, 95, 101–2, 174, 176, 302
Clarín (newspaper) / Grupo Clarín, 172, 234, 275–76, 294
class, 2–3, 9, 11–12, 15, 24–29, 31, 34, 36, 38, 43, 45, 50, 54–55, 59–62, 64–69, 73–74, 76–80, 82, 84–85, 87–90, 97, 99–100, 112–13, 115, 117–20, 122–24, 126–28, 131, 133–34, 152–54, 158–62, 165, 168–70, 172–77, 181–82, 185–86, 190, 192–95, 199–201, 203–6, 229–31, 245–58, 261–63, 274, 301–4, 306–9, 317–18
Classist and Combative Current (CCC), 257–58
clientelism, 89, 133, 249–50, 258, 266

Coalición Cívica, 272
Cobos, Julio, 271, 274
Cold War, 189
Colombia, 205
Columbus, Christopher, 5, 9
Comechingones, 5
Comité de Unidad Sindical Clasista (CUSC), 153
Committee of Class and Union Unity (CUSC), 153
Communist Party / communists, 136, 143, 146–47, 153–54, 156, 160, 168, 174, 185, 255, 257–58, 318
Comodoro Rivadavia, 138
Comunidad Homosexual Argentina (CHA), 279
CONADEP, 231
Concordancia, 141–42, 155
Confederación de Trabajadores de la Educación de la República Argentina (CTERA), 256–57
Confederación General Económica (CGE), 178, 216
Confederación General del Trabajo (CGT), 153–54, 158–59, 161–62, 166, 169, 178, 182, 185, 190–91, 194, 207–9, 211, 213–14, 216–17, 222–23, 230, 233–34, 255–57, 262, 279; "de los Argentinos" (CGTA), 194
Confederación General de Profesionales, 178–79
Confederación Indígena Neuquina, 200
Confederation of Education Workers of the Argentine Republic (CTERA), 256–57
Congress (national), 64, 66–68, 82, 99, 122, 133, 135, 142, 183, 192, 208, 212–13, 232, 242, 244, 265, 270, 274–76, 278–80, 285, 290, 293–95
Congress of Productivity, 178
Congress of Tucumán, 51–53, 63
Conintes Plan, 189
Conquest of the Desert, 100–101, 220

Consejo Nacional de Investigaciones Científicas y Técnicas (CONICET), 183, 281
Conservative Party, 131, 249
conservatives. *See* Partido Demócrata Nacional and Conservative Party
constitution, 47, 50, 53, 58, 67–70, 82–83, 85, 87, 89, 94, 99, 132–33, 163, 183, 242, 244
Constitution of Cádiz, 41, 48–49
consulate, 33, 39
conventillos, 121
Cooke, John William, 184, 196, 198
Coordinating Commission of Indigenous Institutions, 200
Córdoba, 8, 10, 16, 18–19, 24, 27, 30–31, 33–36, 38–39, 48, 50–51, 57, 64, 66–67, 69–70, 92–94, 105–6, 112, 114–15, 121, 134, 153–54, 158, 161, 171, 180, 187, 197, 199, 205–6, 211, 213, 217, 219, 254, 256, 259, 262, 287
Córdoba del Calchaquí, 13
Cordobazo, 195–97, 205
Corpus Christi (dam), 259
corralito, 261–63, 265
Correntinazo, 195
Corriente Clasista y Combativa (CCC), 257–58
Corrientes, 19, 31, 34, 42, 47, 50, 57, 64, 66, 73, 75, 81, 95, 163, 195
corruption, 111–12, 140–42, 224, 243, 251, 253–54, 256, 264, 284–85, 287, 293–94, 296
Cortés, Hernán, 6
Council of Regency, 41, 45, 48
Council of the Magistrature, 283
criollos, 29, 50, 73, 80, 86–87, 114–17, 120, 122, 125, 127–28, 130, 146, 148–50, 161, 172, 308
Criterio (magazine), 148
Crítica (newspaper), 150, 152, 174
cuarteto, 205, 219, 254–55
Cuba, 34, 189, 196, 207
Cuban Revolution, 189
cumbia, 205, 254–55, 304

currency, 65, 85, 91–92, 111, 221, 235, 239–40, 260, 265, 267, 272, 277–78, 299. *See also* dollar / foreign currency
Cutral-Co, 257
Cuyo, 3, 5, 8, 10, 15, 19, 33, 46, 67, 70, 94, 97, 102, 107, 109, 115, 117, 293
Cuzco, 3, 46

Dagnino Pastore, José María, 220
da Silva, Luiz Inácio Lula, 269
de la Rúa, Fernando, 245, 260, 262–65, 267, 295, 311
de la Sota, José Manuel, 237
de la Torre, Lisandro, 131, 142
del Mazo, Gabriel, 147
del Valle, Aristóbulo, 130
del Valle, María Remedios, 59
democracy, 66, 129, 133, 138–40, 142, 153, 155, 161, 199, 228–33, 242, 251, 263, 308, 313, 316
Democratic Union, 154, 160–61, 173
Department of Labor (Buenos Aires province), 154
Derqui, Santiago, 83–84
devaluation, 111, 184, 188–89, 193, 206, 209, 221, 223, 236, 240, 265, 268, 272, 278, 287, 291, 299
Diaguitas, 3
Díaz de Solís, Juan, 13
Di Giovanni, Severino, 140
disappeared persons (*desaparecidos*), 218–19, 295
Di Tella Institute, 204
Diz, Adolfo, 220
dollar / foreign currency, 143–45, 177, 265, 277–78, 282, 305, 316
Dorrego, Manuel, 66–68, 70, 78
drugs, 213, 224, 250, 254, 285, 288
Duhalde, Eduardo, 237, 249, 265–66
Duhalde, Hilda, 271
Duhau, Luis, 142

Echeverría, Esteban, 73, 80
Ecuador, 1, 267

Index

education, 18, 38, 66, 84, 88–89, 93, 107, 118, 123, 165, 171, 201, 213, 233, 247–48, 256, 263, 269, 318, 320
Ejército Guerrillero del Pueblo, 197
Ejército Revolucionario del Pueblo (ERP), 197, 199, 204, 207, 212, 214, 231
El Chocón, 195
El Proletario (newspaper), 120
empresas recuperadas, 258, 264
encomienda, 9–14, 18, 21, 28, 31
England. *See* Great Britain
Entre Ríos, 30, 34, 47, 50, 53–55, 64, 72, 75, 81, 83–84, 90, 92, 97–98, 105, 114–15, 153, 262
environment, 109–10, 241, 244, 259, 282, 309
Espert, José Luis, 298
ethnicity, 9, 12–13, 19, 21–29, 55, 60, 76–77, 85, 87, 90, 114–16, 118, 120, 123, 125, 171–72, 176, 255, 274, 300–302, 305, 308, 317
Europe, 2, 5, 8, 11–12, 14–17, 21–25, 27–32, 34, 36–39, 70–71, 73–74, 76, 85, 87–89, 101, 103, 106, 112, 115, 119–20, 124–26, 128, 148, 155, 164, 176–77, 196
European Union, 291, 301–5, 318, 320–21
evangelical faithful, 254–55
Evita, 163, 165–66, 169, 171, 178, 182, 209, 250, 318
Ezcurra, Encarnación, 71
Ezeiza, 208

Famatinas, 29
Farrell, Edelmiro, 155
fascism, 140–41, 147–48, 154–55, 161
Federación Agraria Argentina, 134
Federación Indígena del Chaco, 200
Federación Obrera Regional Argentina (FORA), 121–22, 136, 153
federalists, 49, 53, 60, 64, 67, 69–71, 77–79, 83, 87–90, 94–95, 97–99, 126, 134, 149–50, 237
feminism, 135, 165, 202, 280–81, 293

Ferdinand VII, 40–43, 46, 49
Fernández, Alberto, 272, 298–99
Fernández, Roque, 239
Fernández de Kirchner, Cristina, 271–76, 278–79, 282–85, 288, 292–94, 298, 316
Ferrer, Aldo, 206
Figueroa Alcorta, José, 130
First International, 121
fleet and galleon system, 16
Flores, 92, 99
folklore, 98, 127, 148
folk music, 150, 172, 203, 205, 304
foreign debt, 65, 95, 111, 141, 144, 164, 212, 221, 223–24, 227, 234–35, 242–44, 260–61, 265, 268–69, 277–78, 289–92, 306–7
Formosa, 51, 109, 115, 168, 249, 259
Fortabat, 221
fracking, 282, 306
Framini, Andrés, 189
France/French, 32, 37–42, 60, 73–75, 105, 114, 122, 164
Franceschi, Gustavo, 148
Freedom Party, 82, 96
Free Trade Area of the Americas (FTAA), 269
French Revolution, 40, 49
Frente Amplio Progresista, 276–77
Frente de Liberación Homosexual (FLH), 203–4
Frente Nacional contra la Pobreza (FRENAPO), 257
Frente País Solidario (FREPASO), 245, 260, 264
Frente para la Victoria, 271
Frente Villero de Liberación Nacional, 199
Fresco, Manuel, 141, 149, 153
Fretes, Joaquín, 58
Friedman, Milton, 220
Frondizi, Arturo, 186–89, 191–93, 220
Front for a Country in Solidarity (FREPASO), 245, 260, 264
Front for Victory, 271

Fuerza de Orientación Radical de la Joven Argentina (FORJA), 147, 170
Fuerza Republicana, 251

Galtieri, Leopoldo, 224–25
Gálvez, Manuel, 149
Garay, Juan de, 8, 13
García, Juan Agustín, 124
Gardel, Carlos, 152
Gas del Estado, 244
Gath y Chaves, 115
Gauchito Gil, 255
gaucho poetry, 61–62, 79–80, 126–28, 148
gauchos, 21, 50, 55–56, 77, 90, 116, 125, 133, 148–50, 152, 170, 302. *See also* gaucho poetry
Gay, Luis, 160
Gelbard, José, 207–8, 210, 212
gender, 11–13, 85, 119–20, 120, 146, 165–66, 270, 276, 279–81, 293, 301, 308, 317
General Agreement on Tariffs and Trade (GATT), 215–16
General Confederation of Labor (CGT), 153–54, 158–59, 161–62, 166, 169, 178, 182, 185, 190–91, 194, 207–9, 211, 213–14, 216–17, 222–23, 230, 233–34, 255–57, 262, 279; "of Argentines" (CGTA), 194
General Confederation of Professionals, 178–79
General Economic Confederation (CGE), 178, 216
General Roca, 195
General Workers' Union, 122
Generation of 1837. *See* New Generation
Germani, Gino, 183
Germany/Germans, 114–15, 122, 137, 143, 155, 157
Ghioldi, Américo, 174, 176
GOU, 155
Grandmothers of Plaza de Mayo, 225
Great Britain / British, 32–33, 37, 39–40, 42, 55, 63, 65–66, 68, 71, 73–75, 79, 81, 92, 95, 105, 107, 109–10, 114–15, 130, 137, 141–43, 145, 149, 151, 155, 164, 224, 238, 305
Greater Buenos Aires, 146, 187, 193, 197, 199, 213, 240, 247, 250, 255, 259, 260
Grinspun, Bernardo, 235
Grito de Alcorta, 134
Grosso, Carlos, 237
Groussac, Paul, 124
Guacurarí, Andresito, 57
Guaraníes/Guaraní, 5, 9, 12–14, 17–18, 35, 54, 56–57, 77, 172
Guayaquil, 47
Guaycurúes, 13
Güemes, Macacha, 59
Güemes, Martín Miguel de, 46, 56–58, 77, 79
Guevara, Ernesto "Che," 197
Guido, José María, 189–91, 220
Gutiérrez, Eduardo, 127
Gutiérrez, Juan María, 73

Haiti, 37–38, 58
Haitian Revolution, 37
Halperin Donghi, Tulio, 321
Harguindeguy, Albano, 220
Harrods, 115
Hayek, Friedrich, 215–16
Heredia, Alejandro, 64, 70
Hernández, José, 126–27, 170
Hidalgo, Bartolomé, 61
hippie movement, 202, 204
Hitler, Adolf, 285
homosexuality, 17, 173, 203–4, 279
Homosexual Liberation Front (FLH), 203–4
Homosexual Liberation Movement, 279
Huarpes, 5, 255
human rights, 38, 218, 222–23, 225, 229, 231–33, 269–70, 281, 295, 297, 308

Ibarguren (family), 113
Ibarguren, Carlos, 149
Ibarra, Juan Felipe, 64
IDEA (business forum), 219

Index

Illia, Arturo, 186, 191–92, 235
immigration, 84, 87, 89, 107, 114, 117, 120, 125
imperialism, 39, 65, 71, 97, 142, 147, 149, 155, 161, 168–69, 185, 196, 201, 203, 265, 306
Incas, 3–7, 10, 29, 53, 56
Independent Socialist Party (PSI), 141
India, 9
Indigenous Federation of Chaco, 200
indigenous peoples, 7–8, 10–15, 17–26, 28–32, 45–46, 49, 51, 54, 56–57, 60, 68–69, 71, 73, 76–77, 85, 89–92, 100–104, 115–16, 118, 125, 133, 138–39, 167–68, 200, 244, 255, 259, 276, 280–81, 283, 301–4, 308
Industrial Revolution, 32, 103
Industrial Union, 112
industry, 107, 120, 144–45, 154, 164, 191, 193–94, 210, 216–17, 220, 291, 305, 316
inequality, 3, 9, 12–13, 25, 62, 114, 117–20, 216, 245–46, 292, 305, 309–310, 317
Infamous Decade, 142, 314
inflation, 139, 177, 191–92, 210–13, 223, 235–40, 242, 265, 267, 272, 277–78, 283, 290–91, 299, 311
Ingeniero Budge massacre, 259
Ingenieros, José, 124–25, 128, 147
Instituto Argentino para la Promoción del Intercambio (IAPI), 164, 184
Instituto Nacional de Estadística y Censos (INDEC), 242, 283, 293, 311
intellectuals, 89, 116, 146–48, 157, 170–71, 175, 186, 213, 215, 219, 233, 284–85, 295, 302, 318
International Eucharistic Congress, 149
International Monetary Fund (IMF), 188, 193, 216, 218, 220–21, 227, 235–36, 238, 242, 244, 260–61, 263, 265, 268, 290–91, 306, 309, 313
International Workers' Association, 121
Intransigent Party, 236, 245
Intransigent UCR. *See* Unión Cívica Radical

Iran, 243, 285
Irazusta, Rodolfo and Julio, 148
Israel, 169, 243
Italy/Italians, 114–16, 122, 125, 128, 140, 143

Japanese, 114
Jauretche, Arturo, 147, 186
Jesuits / Jesuit missions, 17–19, 29, 35, 57, 77
Jews / Jewish community, 114–15, 136, 169, 219, 243
Jockey Club, 179
Juárez Celman, Miguel, 111–12
judiciary, 83, 86, 91, 243, 250, 286, 295–96
Jujuy, 8, 10, 19, 21, 23–24, 27, 29, 45–46, 48, 56, 62, 74, 77, 102–3, 123, 133, 167, 256, 270, 296
Jujuy Exodus, 46
Junta Central, 41–43
Junta Grande, 48, 55
Junta Nacional de Granos, 144
Juríes, 13
Justicialist Party. *See* Peronism
Justo, Agustín Pedro, 141–42
Justo, Juan Bautista, 122
Juventud Trabajadora Peronista, 198

Kicillof, Axel, 278, 299
Kirchner, Cristina. *See* Fernández de Kirchner, Cristina
Kirchner, Néstor, 266–67, 269–274, 276
Kollas, 167–68, 172, 270
Kosteki, Maximiliano, 266
Krieger Vasena, Adalbert, 192–95

La Alumbrera mine, 259
La Boca, 122
Labor Party, 160–61
La Cámpora, 274
La Forestal, 109, 137
La Matanza, 258
Lanteri, Julieta, 135
Lanusse, Alejandro, 206–7, 220
La Pampa, 51, 114, 178, 249, 259

La Paz, 29, 43
La Plata, 99, 158, 171, 178
La Rioja, 8, 24, 31, 42, 64, 67, 69–70, 74, 90, 94, 97, 107, 109, 114, 235, 237
Las Lomitas, 168
La Tablada, 233
Latin America, 25, 37, 61–62, 65–66, 93, 108, 122, 124, 130, 135, 147, 151, 155, 185, 189, 196, 199, 203, 225, 237–38, 251, 272, 282, 291, 306, 321
Lautaro Lodge, 46, 49
Lavagna, Roberto, 268, 272
Lavalle, Juan, 68–69, 73
League of Free Peoples, 49–53
League of Governors, 99
League of the South, 131
Ledesma (sugar mills), 219
Legión Cívica, 148
Legión de Mayo, 148
Lencinas, Carlos W. / Lencinism, 133, 139
lesbianism, 279–80
lettered culture, 8, 61, 80, 88, 123–28, 146
Levingston, Roberto, 206, 220
liberals/liberalism, 38, 41, 64–65, 67, 73, 82–86, 88–90, 94–95, 97, 100, 110, 125, 128–33, 140–141, 143, 146–49, 154, 156, 160, 163, 173, 181–83, 192, 200, 206, 312, 314, 318, 321
Liberating Revolution, 182
Libres del Sur, 73
Liga de los Pueblos Libres, 50
Liga del Sur, 131
Lima, 16, 33, 43, 45–47, 54, 56
Liniers, Santiago de, 39–40, 42, 48
literature, 62, 80, 126–27, 186, 233
littoral region, 8, 12, 19–21, 23, 28, 33–34, 62, 64, 67, 69, 74–76, 121, 145, 172
livestock farming, 18–21, 30, 34, 62, 65, 69, 75–77, 101, 103, 105, 111, 113, 145, 193, 241, 273, 309
Loma Negra, 224
Lonardi, Eduardo, 182
London, 46, 65, 110
Londres (Argentina), 13

looting, 81, 140, 237, 239, 262
López, Estanislao, 53–54, 64, 69–70
López, Vicente Fidel, 73, 82
López Jordán, Ricardo, 97–98, 126
López Murphy, Ricardo, 266
López Rega, José, 209, 214
Luder, Ítalo, 226
Lugones, Leopoldo, 148
Lules, 9, 13
Luna, Buenaventura, 172
Luro (family), 113

Macri, Franco (and Macri Group), 221, 224, 237, 269
Macri, Mauricio, 220, 228, 270, 272, 281, 286–99, 306, 312, 314, 317
Madrid, 181
Mallea, Eduardo, 146
malocas, 11–12
malones, 30, 77, 100–101
Malvinas, 71, 224–25
Manchester, 76, 306
Mansilla, Lucio V., 124
Manso, Juana, 119
manzaneras, 249
Mapuches, 17, 20, 77, 200, 295
Mapudungun, 30
Mar del Plata, 165, 180, 262, 269
Marechal, Leopoldo, 146
Marquisate of Tojo, 10
Martínez, María Estela ("Isabel"), 208, 212, 217, 226
Martínez de Hoz, José Alfredo, 220–21, 227, 239
Martínez Estrada, Ezequiel, 146
Martínez Zuviría, Gustavo, 149
Martín Fierro (Hernández), 126–27, 148, 170
Martín García (island), 102, 140, 157–59
Marxists, 192, 195–97, 199, 204, 209, 230, 258
Masetti, Jorge, 197
Massa, Sergio, 286, 298
mass culture. *See* popular culture
May Revolution, 43–45, 54, 60, 69

Index

Mazorca, 71, 74, 82
meat-packing plants, 105, 108, 110, 138, 141–43, 188
Mendoza, 3, 8, 25, 30, 46–48, 51, 58, 64, 69, 75, 78, 94, 97, 112, 114, 133, 136, 139, 153, 172, 195, 247, 262, 271
Mendoza, Pedro de, 8
Menem, Carlos, 237–45, 247–49, 251, 255–56, 266–67, 270, 278, 286, 291, 295–96, 308, 311, 313–17, 320
Mercedes Benz, 219
Mercosur, 234, 269, 291
mestizaje/mestizos, 12–14, 23–26, 28–31, 43, 46, 59, 76, 88, 125, 172, 174–76, 276, 301–4, 321
Mexico, 6, 34, 43, 130, 201, 244, 280
middle class, 173–77, 186, 230, 274. *See also* class
Milei, Javier, 298
mining, 11, 20, 32, 34, 241, 259, 282, 289, 306, 308. *See also* Potosí
Misiones, 47, 50, 115, 249, 259
mita, 3, 10, 18, 49
Mitre, Bartolomé, 73, 82–84, 90–100, 112, 124, 127, 149, 169, 183, 242, 302
Mocovíes, 17, 77, 102
Moda, La (magazine), 74
Modin, 251
Monsanto, 283
Montevideo, 31, 40, 42–43, 45, 48, 50, 72–73, 81
montoneras, 55, 68, 87–88, 90–91, 97–98, 100, 128, 149, 177, 308
Montoneros, 197–99, 204, 207, 209, 212, 214, 231
Morales, María Soledad, 259
Moreau, Alicia, 135
Moreno, Mariano, 38, 43, 45, 48–49, 55, 60
Mosconi (town), 257
Mothers of Plaza de Mayo, 225
Movement for Socialism (MAS), 256
Movement of Agricultural Women in Struggle (MMAL), 259

Movement of Priests for the Third World, 197, 258
Movements of Unemployed Workers (MTD), 258
Movimiento Agrario Misionero, 259
Movimiento al Socialismo (MAS), 256
Movimiento Campesino de Santiago del Estero (MOCASE), 259
Movimiento de Inquilinos Peronistas, 198
Movimiento de Mujeres Agropecuarias en Lucha (MMAL), 259
Movimiento de Trabajadores Argentinos (MTA), 256
Movimiento Popular Neuquino, 190
Movimientos de Trabajadores Desocupados (MTD), 258
Movimiento Todos por la Patria, 233
Movimiento Villero Peronista, 198–99
Moyano, Hugo, 256
Mugica, Adolfo, 174

Nación, La (newspaper), 234
Namuncurá, Manuel, 101
Napalpí, 139
national army. *See* armed forces
National Autonomist Party (PAN), 99–100, 131
National Council for Scientific and Technical Research (CONICET), 183, 281
National Democratic Party (PDN), 141
National Department of Roads and Highways, 144
National Feminist Party, 135
National Feminist Union, 135
National Food Program, 248
National Front Against Poverty (FRENAPO), 257
National Grain Board, 144
National Indigenous Parliament, 200
National Institute of Statistics and Census of Argentina (INDEC), 242, 283, 293, 311
nationalism, 125, 147–49, 158, 161, 169–70, 173, 185, 196, 220, 318

National Labor Department, 136, 156
National Military College, 270
National Pedagogical Congress, 233
National Reorganization Process, 181, 218, 225, 227
national territories, 103–4, 131, 167, 178
National Women's Gatherings, 280
NATO, 243
Navarrazo, 211, 217
Navarro, Domingo, 211
Nazism, 143, 148, 155, 157, 161, 169, 174
neoliberalism, 220, 228, 238, 242, 245, 247, 251–52, 257, 269, 288, 316, 320
Netherlands, 281
Neuquén, 51, 101, 190, 200, 256–57, 259, 262
Neuquén Indigenous Confederation, 200
Neuquén Popular Movement, 190
New Generation, 73–74, 80, 82, 86
New Granada, 46
New York, 139, 277
New Zealand, 311
Night of the Long Batons, 192
Nisman, Alberto, 285
Ni una menos, 280–81
northeast (region), 5, 35, 77, 96, 200
Northern League, 74
northwest (region), 1, 3, 5, 7–8, 13, 19–20, 25, 29, 31, 33–34, 36, 62, 76, 102–3, 116–17, 138, 145, 199, 212, 217, 293
Nuestro Mundo (Our World), 202–3
Nueva República, La (newspaper), 148

Ocampo, Victoria, 146
Ocloyas, 13
oil, 138–39, 178, 184, 187, 191, 210, 224, 240, 257, 277
Olivos Pact, 242
Omaguacas, 3, 13
Onganía, Juan Carlos, 190, 192, 195, 206, 216, 220
Ongaro, Raymundo, 194
Operation Independence, 212
Organization of American States, 297

Oribe, Manuel, 74
Ortiz, Roberto M., 142

Padilla, Manuel, 46
Palacio, Ernesto, 149
Palacios, Alfredo, 122
Pampas (region), 1, 3–5, 14, 20, 30, 78, 93, 101, 103, 107–110, 113, 115, 117–18, 193, 224, 258, 302, 305
Panama, 16
Panama Papers, 294
Papel Prensa, 234
Paraguayan War, 94–97, 103
Paraguay/Paraguayans, 1–2, 8, 10, 12, 18–19, 21, 31, 33, 48, 51–54, 74, 81, 94–97, 103, 115, 180, 193, 234
Paraná, 5, 74, 83–84, 259, 262
Paris, 73, 151–52, 201
Parlamento Indígena Nacional, 200
Partido Autonomista Nacional (PAN), 99–100, 131
Partido Comunista Revolucionario (PCR), 257
Partido Conservador, 131, 249
Partido de la Libertad, 82, 96
Partido del Orden (Party of Order), 64–67
Partido Demócrata Nacional (PDN), 141
Partido Demócrata Progresista (PDP), 131, 134, 154, 160, 173
Partido Feminista Nacional, 135
Partido Intransigente, 236, 245
Partido Justicialista. *See* Peronism
Partido Laborista, 160–61
Partido Obrero, 237
Partido Peronista. *See* Peronism
Partido Revolucionario de los Trabajadores (PRT), 199, 204, 214
Partido Socialista, 122, 141, 146, 153–54, 173–74, 179, 245
Partido Socialista Independiente (PSI), 141
Partido Único de la Revolución Nacional, 161
Paso, Juan José, 48–49

Patagonia, 3, 5, 14, 30–31, 51, 77, 91, 101, 103, 115, 125, 137, 282
Patriotic League, 136–37, 148
Patrón Costas, Robustiano, 155
Paz (family), 113
Paz, José María, 69, 74
Pedraza, Manuela, 39
Pehuenches, 5, 57
Pellegrini, Carlos, 112, 129, 242
Peñaloza, Ángel Vicente, 90, 94, 128, 237, 242
Pentecostals, 254
People's Guerrilla Army, 197
People's Revolutionary Army (ERP), 197, 199, 204, 207, 212, 214, 231
Pérez, Luis, 79–80
Pérez Companc, 221, 224
Perón, Juan Domingo, 156–86, 190–92, 196, 198–99, 202, 204, 206–213, 217, 237, 242, 276, 284, 314, 316, 318–19, 321
Peronia, 320
Peronism, 129, 158–87, 189–91, 195–201, 206–9, 213–14, 216, 226–27, 230, 233, 236–37, 242–43, 249–51, 257–58, 260–61, 264–66, 271, 274–77, 286, 288, 297–99, 304, 308, 313, 316–21
Peronist Party. *See* Peronism
Peronist Shantytown Movement, 198–99
Peronist Tenants' Movement, 198
Peronist Youth, 196, 198, 208
Peru, 6–7, 15–16, 29, 33–34, 45–47, 65, 75
Peruvian–Bolivian Confederation, 72
Pichetto, Miguel, 299
Pierri, Alberto, 249
Pilagás, 168
Pinedo, Federico, 141, 144–45, 189, 216
Pinochet, Augusto, 220
piqueteros, 257–59, 261, 264, 266, 270, 280, 308
Pizarro, Francisco, 6
Plaza Huincul, 257
Poles / Polish people, 115
Ponferrada, Juan Oscar, 171
popular assemblies, 66, 263–64

popular culture, 61–62, 79, 123–24, 126, 150–52, 170–72, 200–201, 203, 205, 253
populism, 217, 221, 225, 284–85, 297, 302
Portugal/Portuguese, 7, 16, 32–33, 50, 53–54, 57
Potosí, 7, 10, 15, 19–20, 32–34, 45, 62, 304
poverty, 236, 241, 245–48, 250, 252–53, 257, 261, 268, 272, 283, 292, 299, 311–12
Prague, 201
Prensa, La (newspaper), 169
Primera Junta, 43, 47
Proceso de Reorganización Nacional, 181, 218, 225, 227
Progressive Democratic Party (PDP), 131, 134, 141, 154, 160, 173
Propuesta Republicana (PRO), 272, 286–89, 292–93, 297, 299
psychoanalysis, 202
Pulares, 29
Puna, 1–2, 56, 167

Quechua, 3, 54, 172
Querandíes, 5, 9
Quilmes (people), 29
Quintana, Manuel, 130
Quiroga, Facundo, 64, 67, 69, 72, 237
Quiroga, José, 29
Quito, 43

racism, 125, 186, 302, 308
Radical Civic Union (UCR). *See* Unión Cívica Radical
radio broadcasting, 150–51, 169, 275
Raid for Peace, 167–68
railroads, 84, 91–93, 105–6, 108–9, 111, 115, 121, 143, 164, 240
Ramírez, Francisco, 53–54
Ramírez, Pedro Pablo, 155
Ramos, Jorge Abelardo, 186
Ramos Mejía, José María, 124
Ranqueles, 30, 57, 77–78
Rawson, Arturo, 155
Raynal, Guillaume-Thomas, 38

Razón, La (newspaper), 234
Reagan, Ronald, 223–24, 238
Real Audiencia, 15, 33
Rearte, Gustavo, 197
Red Week, 121
Republican Proposal (PRO), 272, 286–89, 292–93, 297, 299
Resistencia (city), 102
Retirement and Pension Fund Administrators (AFJP), 240, 248, 275
retirement/retirees, 240, 256, 261, 268, 292
Reutemann, Carlos, 266
revisionism, 149, 170, 174, 186, 302
Revolución Libertadora, 182–83, 186–87, 192, 216, 274
Revolutionary Communist Party (PCR), 257
revolutionary syndicalism, 122–23
Revolutionary Workers' Party (PRT), 199, 204, 214
Revolution of 1890, 112
Revolution of the Colorados, 97
Reyes, Cipriano, 161
Rico, Aldo, 232–33, 251, 271
Río Gallegos Workers' Federation, 137
Rio Grande do Sul, 95
Río Negro, 101, 138, 256, 259
Río Santiago Shipyard, 269
Río Tercero, 243
Rivadavia, Bernardino, 65–67, 73, 75, 78–79, 82
Roca, Julio Argentino, 91, 93, 99–101, 112, 130
Roca, Julio Argentino, Jr., 141
rock music, 203–5, 213, 223, 253–54
Rodrigazo, 213, 220, 320
Rodrigo, Celestino, 213–14, 217
Rodríguez Peña, Nicolás, 49
Rodríguez Saá, Adolfo, 264, 266
Rojas (town), 30
Rojas, Diego de, 13
Rojas, Isaac, 242
Rojas, Ricardo, 147
Rosariazos, 195

Rosario, 113, 121, 133, 137, 151, 195, 205, 223, 247, 262, 279
Rosas, Juan Manuel de, 64, 68–79, 81–82, 90, 100, 103, 108, 134, 149, 157, 170, 183, 242
Rosende, Petrona, 80
Rousseau, Jean-Jacques, 38
Rousseff, Dilma, 291
Rucci, José Ignacio, 209
Rural Society, 112, 132, 137, 220, 222
Russian Revolution, 136, 143
Russia/Russians, 115, 136, 146, 269, 291

Saadi, Vicente, 190
Saavedra, Cornelio, 43, 48, 55
Sabattini, Amadeo, 154
Sáenz Peña, Luis, 130
Sáenz Peña, Roque, 129–30
Sala, Milagro, 270, 296
Salta, 8, 10, 19, 21, 24, 27, 29–30, 45–46, 48, 51, 55–58, 62, 74–75, 77, 102, 107, 140, 149, 155, 158, 167–68, 197, 235, 249, 257, 259
Salto, 30
Sánchez, Mariquita, 59
San Juan, 8, 34, 47, 69, 83, 94, 107, 133, 153, 156, 256
San Luis, 8, 25, 30, 47, 51, 94, 112, 249, 264
San Martín, José de, 46–47, 53–54, 57–58
San Miguel, 251
San Nicolás, 256
Santa Cruz, 114, 137, 249, 266
Santa Fe, 8, 10, 12, 19, 31, 34, 42, 47, 50–53, 57, 63–64, 69, 75, 77, 81, 83–84, 92, 105–6, 109, 112, 114–16, 131, 134, 149, 153–54, 161, 211, 213, 249, 259, 266, 272, 277
Santiago de Chile, 43
Santiago del Estero, 8, 10, 13–14, 20, 23–24, 47, 51, 64, 67, 109, 123, 147, 153, 196, 256, 262
Santiagueñazo, 256
Santillán, Darío, 266
Santo Domingo. *See* Haiti

Index

São Paulo, 18
Sapag, Felipe, 190
Sarmiento, Domingo Faustino, 73, 84, 86–89, 91, 93–94, 96–98, 102, 119, 124–26, 174, 176–77, 183, 242, 302
Sarratea, Manuel, 48
Saygüeque, Valentín, 101
Scalabrini Ortiz, Raúl, 146
Scarfó, Paulino, 140
Scioli, Daniel, 284, 287
Sebreli, Juan José, 186
Second Five-Year Plan, 177
Secretariat of Labor and Social Security, 156
Seineldín, Mohamed Alí, 233
Selk'nam, 5, 102, 255
Seven Years' War, 32
Seville, 41
sex/sexuality, 12, 17, 119–20, 173, 202–5, 219, 254, 276, 279–80, 301, 308
Shantytown Front for National Liberation, 199
shantytowns, 146, 165
sistema de castas, 22–25, 27–28, 36, 40, 60, 301
Sitram-Sitrac, 199
62 Organizations, 185, 188, 190
slavery / enslaved people, 10–11, 16, 18, 20–27, 30–31, 33–34, 37–39, 49, 57–58, 75–76, 85, 301
Smith, Adam, 84
Sobremonte, Rafael de, 39–40
soccer, 151, 184, 223, 253
Socialist Party / socialism, 122, 134–35, 141, 146–47, 153–54, 160, 173–74, 179, 182–83, 187, 194, 196–99, 206, 209, 215, 228, 245, 256, 258, 277, 318
Socialist Workers' Movement, 258
Socialist Workers' Party, 258
socialists. *See* Socialist Party
Solá, Felipe, 241
Solano López, Francisco, 95
Sole Party of the National Revolution, 161
Somisa, 256

Sourrouille, Juan, 235
South Africa, 114
Soviet Union, 136, 168, 193, 238
Spain/Spaniards, 1–3, 5–16, 18, 22–25, 27, 29, 31–49, 51, 55, 59, 63, 65, 103, 114, 116, 151, 206, 301
Spanish Civil War, 147
state, 25, 65, 76, 81, 83–85, 88–94, 96–103, 107–113, 115–16, 121–23, 125, 127–28, 132–36, 138–39, 144–45, 147–48, 153–54, 156–58, 162–64, 167–69, 172–73, 178, 184–85, 187–88, 190, 206–8, 213, 215–16, 223–25, 227, 234–36, 238–40, 243, 247–52, 254–58, 260, 265, 268–69, 275–78, 282–84, 289–90, 297, 301–2, 304–6, 308–9, 314, 318–19
state terrorism, 219–20, 308, 312
Sturzenegger, Federico, 260, 290
suffrage, 41, 73, 133, 135, 148, 165, 229, 308
Supreme Court, 86, 140, 158, 163, 183, 243, 263, 270, 285, 295–96
supreme director, 49–53, 55
Swiss (people), 112, 115
Syrian-Lebanese (people), 114

Tanco, Miguel, 133
Tandil, 116
tango, 128, 150, 152, 172, 203
Tarija, 48, 73
Tartagal, 257
Techint, 221
Tehuelches, 5, 77
Tejedor, Carlos, 99
Telégrafo Mercantil (newspaper), 38
television, 169, 205, 207, 219, 233, 266, 275–76, 279, 287, 294, 296
tenants' strike, 121
Thatcher, Margaret, 238
theatre, 127, 136, 150, 169, 207, 233, 279
Tiahuanaco, 45
Tierra del Fuego, 2, 5, 102–3
Tobas (Qom people), 138, 200
Tomaso, Antonio de, 141
Tormo, Antonio, 172

Torres, Elpidio, 195
Tosco, Agustín, 195
Tragic Week, 136, 175, 195
trans people, 280
Traslasierra, 31
Treaty of Pilar, 53
Trelew, 195, 206
Triple Alliance / Triple A (Argentine Anti-Communist Alliance), 209, 212–13
triumvirates, 48–49, 55, 63
Trotskyists, 199, 237, 255
Tucumán, 8, 10–11, 14–15, 19, 22, 24, 27, 33, 39, 44–48, 51, 54, 63–64, 66, 70, 74–75, 93, 98–99, 107, 153, 158, 184, 187, 192, 195–96, 199, 212, 219, 235, 251, 262
Tucumán Arde (exhibit), 205
Túpac Amaru, 270
Túpac Amaru II, 29
Túpac Katari, 29

Ubaldini, Saúl, 234
Ugarte, Manuel, 147
Umbanda, 255
Unión Cívica, 112
Unión Cívica Radical (UCR), 112, 128–34, 137–38, 140–41, 145, 147, 158, 160, 166, 173, 186, 195, 206–7, 217, 222, 226–29, 235, 237, 245, 264, 267, 271–72, 277, 286–88, 293, 299, 313; "antipersonalists," 134, 138–39, 141–42; del Pueblo (People's UCR), 186; Intransigente (UCRI), 186; Junta Renovadora, 160
Unión del Centro Democrático (UCEDE), 236, 239
Unión Democrática, 154, 160–61, 173
Unión Feminista Argentina, 202
Unión Feminista Nacional, 135
Unión General de Trabajadores, 122
Union of South American Nations (UNASUR), 291
Union of the Democratic Center (UCEDE), 236, 239
Unión Sindical Argentina (USA), 153

Unitarians, 67–74, 78–80, 82–83, 87, 89, 90
United Nations, 277
United States, 60, 85, 105, 107, 110, 143, 145, 147, 150, 152, 155, 164, 178, 189, 192, 196, 218, 220–21, 223, 225, 234, 238, 243, 254, 269, 278, 281, 285, 291, 305–6, 311
Universal Child Allowance, 275, 292, 320
University of Buenos Aires, 66, 134, 183, 192, 207, 213
University of Córdoba, 18, 134
University Reform, 134–35, 147
Upper Peru. *See* Bolivia
Uriburu, José Evaristo, 130
Uriburu, José Félix, 140, 148, 153
Urquiza, Justo José de, 81–84, 90, 92, 94–95, 97
Uruguay, 1–2, 18, 33–34, 39, 44–45, 50–51, 54–55, 57, 67–68, 73–75, 81, 93–95, 97, 130, 234, 269, 320
Uturuncos, 196

Valcheta, 102
Valle, Juan José, 184
Vallese, Felipe, 190
valleys of the Calchaquí people, 3, 13–14, 29, 56
Vandor, Augusto / Vandorism, 188, 190–91, 194, 198
vaquerías, 19
Varela, Felipe, 97
Vatican, 94, 179
Vázquez, Tabaré, 269
Venezuela, 46, 234, 269, 291
Viborazo, 206
Viceroyalty of the Río de la Plata, 33–34, 38–39, 44, 54, 63
Vidal, María Eugenia, 287, 294, 299
Videla, Jorge Rafael, 218, 220–21, 223, 270
Vietnam, 196
Villa Constitución, 211
Villagra, Francisco de, 10
Villar, Alberto, 209, 212

Index

villas miseria, 146, 165
Villazo, 211
Viltipoco, 13–14
Viola, Roberto E., 223–24
violence, 1–2, 22, 60, 70, 82, 88–89, 94, 100, 137–38, 140, 181, 185, 198, 217–18, 220, 226, 229, 247, 251, 253–54, 271, 280–81, 283, 295, 300–302, 309, 312, 319–20
Voz de la mujer, La (newspaper), 135
vulture funds, 268, 277–78, 289, 306

Washington, DC, 243
Washington Consensus, 238, 242
Wichis, 29, 102, 200
Wilde (family), 113
women, 2, 5, 11–14, 17, 19–21, 23, 26–29, 38–39, 58–59, 76, 80, 85–86, 88, 95, 102, 119–21, 123, 131, 133, 135, 165–68, 170, 173, 192, 199, 201–4, 213, 218, 244, 247, 253, 258–59, 270, 279–81, 293, 308
worker-run enterprises, 258, 264
Workers' Confederation, 153

workers' movement, 120–23, 128–29, 134–40, 153–54, 156, 159–60, 162, 178, 182, 185, 189–91, 194, 198–99, 211–14, 216, 256–58, 308
Workers' Party, 237
World Bank, 215–16, 236, 238, 313
World Trade Organization, 215
world wars, 142, 144–45, 147, 155, 164

xenophobia, 116–17, 147, 169, 255, 299

yanaconas, 10–11
Yanquetruz, 78
yellow fever, 93
Young Peronist Workers, 198
YPF, 138, 140, 257, 278
Yrigoyen, Hipólito, 112, 130–41, 147, 163, 169, 182, 242, 276, 302
Yupanqui, Atahualpa, 172

Zalazar, Aureliano, 97
Zapala, 259
Zárate, 158
Zinn, Ricardo, 220

Printed and bound by CPI Group (UK) Ltd, Croydon, CR0 4YY
27/03/2024
14476730-0003